THE OXFORD HISTORY OF PHILOSOPHY

Jewish Philosophy in the Middle Ages

THE OXFORD HISTORY OF PHILOSOPHY

Jewish Philosophy in the Middle Ages

Science, Rationalism, and Religion

T. M. Rudavsky

OXFORD
UNIVERSITY PRESS

OXFORD
UNIVERSITY PRESS

Great Clarendon Street, Oxford, OX2 6DP,
United Kingdom

Oxford University Press is a department of the University of Oxford.
It furthers the University's objective of excellence in research, scholarship,
and education by publishing worldwide. Oxford is a registered trade mark of
Oxford University Press in the UK and in certain other countries

First Edition published in 2018

Impression: 1

Published in the United States of America by Oxford University Press
198 Madison Avenue, New York, NY 10016, United States of America

British Library Cataloguing in Publication Data
Data available

Library of Congress Control Number: 2018937598

ISBN 978-0-19-958090-3

Printed in Great Britain by
Clays Ltd, Elcograf S.p.A

Contents

Contents

Preface

Medieval Jewish philosophy, like Islamic and Christian philosophy, is fundamentally focused on the relationship between "faith and reason." The Islamic philosophers Avicenna and Averroës, the Jewish philosophers Ibn Daud, Maimonides, and Gersonides, and the Christian scholastics Albertus Magnus and Aquinas, all attempted to reconstruct a unified system that accommodated both theological and natural-philosophical considerations in the wake of Platonism, Neoplatonism, as well as Aristotelian natural philosophy and metaphysics. Arising as an effort toward harmonizing the tenets of Judaism with philosophic teachings, medieval Jewish philosophers dealt with conflicts between philosophical speculation and acceptance of Judaic beliefs. The Jewish philosopher is constrained to reconcile two distinct bodies of knowledge—the secular and religious domains—where "secular" itself incorporates both Christian and Islamic thought. In this work, we will examine the extent to which this reconstruction in the Jewish domain is successful.

The purpose of this volume is to provide an account of how Jewish philosophy, from the tenth century to Spinoza, forms part of an ongoing dialogue with medieval Christian and Islamic thought. It is intended to supplement available histories of medieval philosophy, many of which have devoted little space to Jewish philosophy. Our focus is on the tensions between Judaism and rational thought, as reflected in particular philosophical controversies arising in the context of issues in metaphysics, language, cosmology, and philosophical theology. Much new research has occurred in these latter areas, and so it is important to introduce readers to the rich discussions found in medieval Jewish philosophical texts in light of this new research. This volume will thus achieve two aims: to provide a broad historical survey of major figures and schools within the medieval Jewish tradition, and to focus more narrowly on the importance and challenge of rationalist discourse within this tradition.

For a long time, standard histories of medieval philosophy, when they devoted any attention to Jewish philosophy, did so almost solely for the purpose of illuminating the Christian intellectual world. Both the Islamic and Jewish philosophical traditions were regarded as "background" and "context," recognized primarily for their influence on Latin philosophy. Over the last decade or so, this neglect has begun to be overcome and the richness and importance of Jewish philosophy addressed in its own right by volumes devoted explicitly to it. Most of these volumes address a more specialized scholarly audience, one familiar with the broad strokes within Jewish philosophy.[1] My hope is that this work will function as a resource for scholars in a wide variety of disciplines: intellectual historians, scholars of religion, theologians, historians, and literary scholars (especially of the medieval period). It should also be useful for undergraduate and graduate students in those disciplines, but especially in the history of philosophy. Further, it should be accessible to philosophers who want

---

[1] See for example Sirat 1990; Frank and Leaman 2003; Jospe 2009; Nadler and Rudavsky 2009.

to learn more about the role played by science in the field of medieval Jewish philosophy.

In contradistinction to most recent histories of Jewish philosophy, I have organized the major topics and chapters of this study thematically, ranging from Jewish philosophy's earliest awakening in the Hellenistic era with the Greek writings of Philo of Alexandria, through its flourishing in the medieval period, to its culmination in the seventeenth century with the radical thought of Baruch Spinoza. The first two chapters provide an historical overview of the sources (e.g., Platonic, Neoplatonic, and Aristotelian) and contexts (e.g., Islamic, Scholastic) of Jewish philosophizing in the medieval and early modern periods, as well as the textual traditions of Jewish philosophy. Emphasis in this section will be upon the ways in which medieval Jewish philosophers viewed the many philosophical sources available to them.

While Chapters 1 and 2 present a preliminary chronological overview of the major figures discussed in the work, the remaining chapters focus upon recognizable philosophical issues, each of which reflects a particular set of tensions originating between secularism, science, and Jewish belief. It will be taken for granted by the volume that Jewish philosophy represents an important and identifiable strand within medieval and early modern philosophy as a whole, one worth investigating in its own right. By concentrating on topics such as medieval Jewish science, cosmology, and theory of knowledge, this volume will underscore the important contributions made by Jewish philosophy to the general field of philosophy.

Chapter 3 focuses upon the nature of science, and what it is we are looking for when exploring the tension between science and Judaism. What is science? How does it differ from philosophy? How do philosophers describe their methodological and epistemological assumptions? How do they characterize reason and faith, in light of their commitments to both scientific and theological commitments? Chapters 4 and 5 are devoted to divine science, broadly construed. In Chapter 4, we examine attempts on the part of Jewish philosophers to delineate the essential nature of God. And as we shall see in Chapter 5, God's nature carries tremendous implications when we turn to the origin of human choice, free will, and the existence of evil. Chapter 6 is devoted to the attempted reconciliation of the biblical view of creation with Greek and Islamic philosophy.

In Chapter 7, we turn to a more careful examination of the natural order, focusing upon both the natural world that comprises the "sublunar" sphere (viz., the space between the earth and the moon) and the heavenly bodies that comprise the "superlunar" (above the moon). Even in the context of moral and political philosophy, Jewish philosophers discussed issues within the wider context of a rational perspective. Chapter 8 deals broadly with philosophical anthropology—the psycho-physical composition of the human being and the implications of these theories upon moral theory and reward and punishment. Chapter 9 is concerned with social and political behavior, leading us to content with both moral and political theory.

Let me end with several acknowledgements. First, to my editor Peter Momtchiloff, who proposed this project to me a number of years ago, I owe a debt of gratitude. His remarkable patience in light of a much delayed manuscript I greatly appreciate. To the entire production team who have worked so hard to catch many infelicities, my gracious thanks. To the OSU Philosophy department, and the Melton Center for

Jewish Studies, which provided me with much needed research support, I would like to express my gratitude. To Judaica research librarian Joseph Galron, who tirelessly provided me with elusive texts and reference materials, thank you. To my anonymous readers, who caught many infelicities in the manuscript, my thanks and relief. To my many students, both at The Ohio State University, and in the community, who have forced me to clarify my thoughts while teaching the material contained in this volume, I cannot offer sufficient thanks. For Nathaniel, who continues to encourage me to write clearly and with passion, I hope I have succeeded. And to Miriam and Brandon, both of whom have read the manuscript with infinite care and attentiveness, I am deeply indebted; their careful reading has prevented many more errors from creeping into the final work. And finally to Richard, to whom this book is dedicated.

Commonly used Abbreviations

Beliefs   Saadiah Gaon, *Book of Beliefs and Opinions*; note, there are two editions, which will be specified in the notes.

BK   Maimonides, *Mishneh Torah: Book of Knowledge* (1962), Moses Hyamson (trans.) (Jerusalem: Boys Town Publishers).

CM   Maimonides, Moses (1972a), *Commentary on the Mishnah. Introduction to Helek: Sanhedrin, Chapter Ten*, in Isadore Twersky (ed.), *A Maimonides Reader* (New York: Behrman House), 387–400.

CT   Maimonides, Moses (1975b), *Laws Concerning Character Traits*, in *Ethical Writings of Maimonides* (New York: Dover), 27–58.

Duties   Baḥya Ibn Paquda (1970; 1986), *Duties of the Heart*, Moses Hyamson (ed. and trans.), 2 vols. (Jerusalem: Feldheim).

EC   Maimonides, *Eight Chapters* [introduction to commentary on *Mishnah Avot*] (1975a), in Raymond L. Weiss with Charles Butterworth (eds. and trans.), *Ethical Writings of Maimonides* (New York: New York University Press), 60–104.

ER   Maimonides, *Essay on Resurrection* (1985b), in Abraham Halkin and David Hartmann (eds. and trans.), *Epistles of Maimonides: Crisis and Leadership* (Philadelphia: Jewish Publication Society), 209–33.

Fusûl   Al-Fârâbî, *Fusûl al-Madanî: Aphorisms of the Statesman* (1961), D. M. Dunlop (ed. and trans.) (Cambridge: Cambridge University Press).

Guide   Maimonides, *Guide of the Perplexed* [Arabic *Dalâlat al-hâirîn*; Hebrew *Moreh Nevukhim*] (1963), 2 vols., Shlomo Pines (trans.) (Chicago: University of Chicago Press); (2002) Hebrew trans., Michael Schwartz, 2 vols. (Ramat Aviv: Tel Aviv University Press).
Unless otherwise noted, references will be given by listing part, chapter, and page number of the Pines edition.

HYT   Maimonides, *Hilkhot Yesodei ha-Torah* (1962), in Moses Hyamson (trans.), *Mishneh Torah: The Book of Knowledge by Maimonides* (Jerusalem: Boys Town Publishers).

Kuzari   Judah Halevi, *Book of Kuzari* (1964), Hartwig Hirschfeld (ed.) (New York: Pardes Publishing House).

Light   Crescas, *Light of the Lord*; several editions, will be specified in the notes.

MA   Maimonides, *Medical Aphorisms of Moses Maimonides* (1970–1), Fred Rosner and Suessman Muntner (ed. and trans.) (New York: Yeshiva University Press).

MT   Maimonides, *Mishneh Torah: Book of Knowledge* (1962), Moses Hyamson (trans.) (Jerusalem: Boys Town Publishers).

NE   Aristotle, *Nicomachean Ethics*, in Aristotle (1984), *The Complete Works of Aristotle*, Jonathan Barnes (ed.) (Princeton: Princeton University Press).

PH   Maimonides, *Commentary on the Mishnah. Introduction to Perek Helek: Sanhedrin, Chapter Ten* (1972a), in Isadore Twersky (ed.), *A Maimonides Reader* (New York: Behrman House), 387–400.

TL   Maimonides, *Treatise on the Art of Logic* (1938), Israel Efros (ed. and trans.), *Proceedings of the American Academy of Jewish Research*, 8:1–65 [English sect.]; 8:1–136 [Hebrew sect.]; (1966). "Maimonides' Arabic Treatise on Logic," *Proceedings of the American Academy of Jewish Research*, 34: 155–60 [English]; 34: 1–42 [Arabic].

Tractatus Spinoza, Benedict (2001), *Theological-Political Treatise*, 2nd ed., Samuel Shirley (trans.) (Indianapolis: Hackett Press).

Wars   Gersonides (1984–99), *The Wars of the Lord*, Seymour Feldman (trans.), 3 vols. (Philadelphia: Jewish Publication Society). Unless otherwise noted, reference will be to volume number, book, chapter, and page. Note that Book V.1 does not appear in this edition, and will be referenced separately.

1
What Is Jewish Philosophy?

I Judaism and Science: Tension or Accommodation

Medieval Jewish philosophy, like Islamic and Christian philosophy, is fundamentally focused on the relationship between "faith and reason." Arising as an effort toward harmonizing the tenets of Judaism with philosophic teachings, medieval Jewish philosophy deals with conflicts between philosophical speculation and acceptance of Judaic beliefs. The Jewish philosopher is constrained to reconcile two distinct bodies of knowledge—the secular and religious domains—where "secular" itself incorporates both Christian and Islamic thought.

Let me be more specific regarding the tension between Judaism and secular thought. For the People of the Book, as Jews are known, the word of God is as revealed in Scripture and in the Oral Torah. But Jewish devotion to these sacred Jewish texts, which has been essential to the survival of Judaism over the centuries, is double edged. For if it is the content of Jewish texts that is prized above all, where do secular studies in general, and the study of science in particular, fit into the Jewish paradigm of Torah Study? And what do we do when the contents of secular study contravene those texts of traditional learning?

This question, introduced already by the Greco-Jewish philosopher Philo in the first century CE, reappears throughout the history of Jewish thought. As described by Lamm in his work *Torah u-Madda*, this struggle between rational speculation, represented by Athens, and Torah-based study, represented by Jerusalem, has been replayed in every generation.[1] As a minority religion within the larger context of a majority culture, be it the Hellenistic world, the Islamic world, the world of Enlightened Europe, or most recent examples of modernity (and post-modernity), Jews have both rejected and adopted various aspects of these majority civilizations. And so for generations of Jews the issue has thus been twofold: first, how to justify taking time from Torah study for any other type of study (including the most mundane level of career-learning); and second, how to reconcile the content of the secular learning with that of religious knowledge.

Consider the recent contention made by Aviezer Ravitzky, namely that to approach Jewish philosophical texts with the presumption that their authors were completely isolated from their non-Jewish intellectual environment is to misunderstand the underlying tension inherent in these very texts.[2] Medieval philosophers—Islamic,

---

[1] Lamm 1990.
[2] See Ravitzky 1996 for a penetrating discussion of the status of Jewish philosophers vis à vis their intellectual environment.

Christian, and Jewish—have had to wrestle with the project of reconciling "outside" sources and influences with their understanding of Scripture. Especially in the late medieval and early modern period, religious belief was often threatened by the adoption of a scientific cosmology antithetical to religious thought, be it the cosmology of Plato, Aristotle, Ptolemy, or Copernicus. Sometimes, as in the case of Maimonides, we shall see that this wrestling results in a mode of discourse that obfuscates the full force of the compromise. Other times, as in the case of Spinoza, the wrestling results in expulsion from the Jewish community altogether.

I shall argue in this volume that for Jewish philosophers the tension between Athens and Jerusalem, or faith and secular thought, acquires an additional urgency. Clearly, Jewish thinkers worked hard to accommodate the findings of secular learning, which included science, with Judaic texts. But it is important to remember that Jewish examinations of the religion/science debate are (for the most part) elaborated in counter-position to a not unrelated issue, namely the impact of secular Christian and Islamic culture upon Judaism. Hence whereas for the Christian theologian (St. Augustine, St. Thomas Aquinas, Galileo) the problem is uni-dimensional, namely, how to accommodate Christianity and modern scientific outlooks, for the Jew the question becomes more complex: how to accommodate Judaism to a more broadly construed secularism, which itself has been infiltrated first by Greek, and then by Christian, influences.[3] Is it the case, then, that the very scientific world view, one that the Christian sees as "godless" and void of religious content, is for the Jew already tinged (and contaminated, as it were) with classical "Christian" elements? And if so, does not the enterprise of accommodating secular thought to religious belief become even more complex for the Jew than for the Christian? The real issue in Jewish thought can thus be stated succinctly: at what point does the introduction of secular knowledge dilute the basic teachings found in Jewish sources?

By the ninth century CE, most Jews were living under Islamic rule. Under the reign of the Abbasid Caliph al-Ma'mun (813–33), we find the first phase of a major translation project of Greek philosophical and scientific texts into Arabic, followed by a second phase in the tenth century. The importance of this project to Jewish philosophy should not be underestimated. Both Jewish and Islamic philosophers were confronted with a similar set of challenges posed by these texts. As put by Guttmann, Jewish philosophers "received philosophy from the outside, and the history of Jewish philosophy is the history of the successive absorptions of foreign ideas which were then transformed and analysed according to specific Jewish points of view."[4] What we have is a clash between two opposing world views—the Jewish world view, and those of external philosophical systems—reflective of two sources of truth.

Is it truly possible, however, to harmonize the domains of science and religion?[5] By suggesting that medieval Jewish philosophical texts represent the tensions inherent between religion and science, I am not simply adverting to the adversarial model of

---

[3] For a classic discussion of the relationship between religion and science, see Brooke 1991; see also Cantor and Kenny 2001, for a discussion of the relevance of Barbour's taxonomy to Jewish thought.

[4] Guttmann 1964, 3.

[5] In Chapter 3, we shall demarcate the term "science" more carefully; suffice it for the moment to note that in the medieval period, "science" refers primarily to Aristotelian natural philosophy.

the science–religion wars as they were portrayed by late nineteenth-century historians of science. These historians would have us believe that science has been
persecuted by religion: more specifically, that western science has been persecuted
by the Catholic Church. For example, in his enormously influential work *History of
the Conflict between Religion and Science*, John William Draper argued that the
Church became a stumbling block in the intellectual advancement of Europe for
more than a thousand years.[6] On this model, the history of scientific development
was presented as a war against a narrow-minded establishment that feared science;
the conflicts between science and religion were seen as a one-sided affair in which the
Church sought to suppress truth-seeking scientists. Jewish and Islamic institutions
were not castigated nearly as maliciously on this view (perhaps, the cynic may argue,
because by this point in history they possessed so little power). Perhaps as a
throwback to this attitude, theologians often harbor a lingering suspicion that
scientists view their own scientific method as infallible, and have paid them little
attention. Scientists, on the other hand, often seem reluctant to "forgive" the church
for what they see as a long-standing antagonism.

But, as recent historians of science have reminded us, the Draper-White model of
conflict between science and religion is overly simplistic.[7] We must keep in mind two
points. First, it is important to recognize that, especially in the early modern period,
religious doctrine, western philosophy, and science influenced one another. Amos
Funkenstein has, for example, articulated many examples in which theological
concepts influenced scientific and philosophical modes of discourse in the seventeenth century.[8] Second, it must be recognized that many of the struggles that do
occur between religion and science are not merely ideological wars, but have a human
dimension as well; ultimately, it is people who interact, not theories—personalities
loom large and can affect the outcome of a debate.[9]

Is there any hope, then for fruitful exchange between the scientific domain and the
religious domain as exemplified by Judaism? Following the work of Ian Barbour,[10] let
me suggest that throughout the history of medieval Jewish philosophy, at least three
strands have manifested themselves:

Conflict: that there are serious conflicts between contemporary science and
classical Judaic beliefs, and so one must choose between them;

Independence: that the two enterprises are totally independent and autonomous,
each with its own distinctive domain and method, which can be justified on their
own; that Judaism is based on divine revelation, and science is based on human
observation and reason; and that these spheres must be kept totally separate.

---

[6] For the statement of this description, see Draper 1874.
[7] For different ways of characterizing the relationship, see Barbour 1997; Brooke 1991; Funkenstein
1986; Feldhay 1995; Feldhay 1998.
[8] Funkenstein 1986.
[9] For further examples of the ways in which personality can affect philosophical positions, see for
example the discussion found in Rudavsky 2001.
[10] Barbour 1997. In his ground-breaking work surveying the ways of approaching religion and science,
Barbour actually described four such positions, but I have combined two into my "integration" strand.

Integration: that the boundaries between religion and science are not so clear-cut; that in fact the two disciplines share certain presuppositions and methods, which can lead to fruitful dialogue, and possibly even integration. This position is summarized by McMullin's statement that "The Christian cannot separate his science from his theology as though they were in principle incapable of interrela-tion. On the other hand, he has learned to distrust the simpler pathways from one to the other. He has to aim at some sort of coherence of world-view... he must strive to make his theology and cosmology consonant..."[11]

As we delve in subsequent chapters into the works of major medieval Jewish figures, we shall see all three of these attitudes developed as responses to secularism, rational inquiry, and science from the perspective of Jewish belief. Each chapter will develop more fully one or more of these attitudes in an attempt to come to terms with the challenges posed to Jewish belief by a scientific view of the world.

II What is Jewish *Philosophy*?

We have been talking generally about "Jewish philosophy" and its interaction with secular thought. But any history of Jewish philosophy must deal with two essential questions—what is Jewish *philosophy*, and what is *Jewish* philosophy. The first question involves distinguishing Jewish philosophy from the variety of other kinds of Jewish literature—Torah and Bible commentaries, halakhic (legal) and aggadic (homiletic) midrashim or exegeses, rabbinic responsa, and so on. Does the Bible contain philosophy? Ze'ev Levy suggests that, "there are no philosophical elements in biblical thought that might be characterized as being uniquely Jewish, and that can therefore be regarded as Jewish philosophy."[12] There are philosophical notions—such as moral precepts—but they are of a "general nature" and not specifically Jewish. There is no "Jewish" morality as such, but just general, universally applicable moral codes. The Bible, Levy says, is "not a book on philosophy, nor a book on ethics."[13]

But surely, one might be tempted to argue, the rabbis of the Talmud were profoundly good philosophers. Their recorded discussions range over a host of metaphysical, ethical, and epistemological issues, and they apparently excelled as logicians. And yet here too, despite the wealth of philosophic interest to be found in many rabbinic works, the primary *intention* of these texts is not philosophical but religious. The authors and the figures appearing in these texts were concerned not with addressing philosophical questions per se but with putting their analytical skills to use in resolving legal, social, theological, exegetical, and liturgical issues of Judaism. With respect to the rabbinic literature, Levy suggests that the sages helped develop some of the "major concepts," such as God's incorporeality and creation ex nihilo, that had a "great proximity to philosophical thought."[14] "One might perhaps say that the common denominator for ancient Jewish thought and Greek philosophy was the struggle against the mythological picture of the world."[15] He further suggests

---

[11] See Mcmullin 2005.   [12] Levy 1987, 142.   [13] Levy 1987, 143.
[14] Levy 1987, 145.   [15] Levy 1987, 145.

that possibly this common denominator gave rise later to the reciprocal ties between Jewish and general thought.

Nonetheless, it is important to note that many of our Jewish philosophers were also "rabbis" or "rabbinical leaders." Consider, for example, Saadiah Gaon, a major religious and philosophical figure in the tenth century CE. And of course, no philosopher holds a more august position in the rabbinical world than Maimonides, whose *Mishneh Torah* is to this day held to be a canonical work in rabbinic thought. And so the very attempt to distinguish between rabbinical thinkers and philosophers is itself fraught with contention. One possible distinction is that Jewish philosophers are engaged by and in the same sorts of issues that consumed their non-Jewish philosophical peers, and use the tools and forms of argumentation common to other traditions, sometimes even for the same purposes. Based on this distinction, let me suggest that Jewish philosophy is based on a kind of logical reasoning, rooted in claims drawn from experience, that purports to make the authority for its claims more than mere opinions.[16]

But this raises yet a further question: what is *Jewish* about Jewish philosophy? Is there anything particularly "Jewish" about the writings of these thinkers? Some skeptics have famously suggested that there is and can be no such thing as *Jewish* philosophy. For example, Isaac Husik famously insisted in his *History of Mediaeval Jewish Philosophy* that, "there are Jews now and there are philosophers, but there are no Jewish philosophers and no Jewish philosophy."[17] And the noted historian of philosophy Julius Guttmann argued that rather than Jewish philosophy we should speak of the philosophies of Judaism: philosophy in which Judaism—its beliefs, ceremonies, and history—is the object of philosophizing, perhaps making it a sub-field of the philosophy of religion.[18]

On this view, philosophy represents a non-denominational enterprise, a rational approach to universal questions, and it makes no more sense to speak of Jewish philosophy than it does to speak of, say, Jewish physics. Philosophy is a discipline that searches for objective, universal truths that are available in principle to all rational enquirers. Philosophers are looking for objective truths about the universe that are independent of personal opinion.[19] Think for example of Descartes' search for indubitable certainty, or Husserl's life-long search for a phenomenological method that eschews particularity. And yet Judaism is a particular religion shaped by a particular normative system set out in the Torah and intended for a specific nation. How then do we reconcile the universalism of philosophy vs. the particularism of religious Judaism? It would appear that the very notion of Jewish content must either contradict or be incidental to the philosophical nature of the enterprise.

More pointedly, Levy points out that in case of other disciplines, take for example mathematics, we do not speak of "Jewish mathematics" or "Jewish physics," nor do we speak of "Jewish empiricism" or "Jewish nominalism," and yet we feel comfortable speaking of "Jewish philosophy." So how does one go about characterizing Jewish philosophy? Does it stand in a class of its own? Surely we have no problem

---

[16] See Samuelson 2003, 3, for a careful analysis of what constitutes Jewish philosophy.
[17] Husik 1946, 432.   [18] Guttmann 1964.   [19] Rynhold 2009, 2.

understanding such disciplines as Greek philosophy, Eastern philosophy, or British empiricism. Further, as Levy points out, one cannot complete one's philosophical education without studying Greek philosophers such as Plato and Aristotle, French philosophers such as Descartes, or German philosophers such as Kant, Hegel, and Husserl; and yet students of general philosophy can complete their studies without studying the works of Saadiah Gaon, Maimonides, Rosenzweig, and Gersonides. And so Levy asks, "how can a certain concept be truly philosophical, and simultaneously Jewish in its essence?"[20]

Clearly "being Jewish or of Jewish origin" is not a sufficient criterion. Take for example Ibn Gabirol, the eleventh-century philosopher whose work *Fountain of Life* (*Mekor Hayyim*) was assumed to have been written by an Islamic or Christian scholar by the name of Avicebron. As we shall see in Chapter 2, the work itself contains no reference to Judaism, to Jews, or to Jewish sources, and yet now we include it in the panoply of Jewish philosophical works. Nor is writing in Hebrew sufficient. We need only consider the many works in analytic philosophy written in Hebrew in modern Israel, or the fact that many Jewish philosophers wrote in languages other than Hebrew, including Greek, Arabic, and German. Nor can we consider biographical criteria in isolation: what do we do with Spinoza for example, who was born a Jew, was excommunicated, and wrote most of his work in Latin? We shall return to the anomalous case of Spinoza in Chapter 3.

But it is not just Jews who have grappled with issues of definition and categorization. Compare, for example, Gilson's famous definition of Christian philosophy as the union of philosophical study with obedience to the Christian faith. In a similar vein, Adamson and Taylor point to the significance of their edited volume entitled *Companion to Arabic Philosophy*, denoting that it is a companion to "Arabic" and not "Islamic" philosophy. Why Arabic? "It is *Arabic* philosophy because it is philosophy that begins with the rendering of Greek thought, in all its complexity, into the Arabic language."[21] Many of the figures discussed in their volume, they point out, were not ethnically Arabs but were actually Christians or Jews. Second, these figures were not particularly interested in "putting forward a properly 'Islamic' philosophy";[22] they were more focused upon coming to grips with the Greek philosophical texts made available in the translation movement in the eighth to tenth centuries. Adamson notes that both Jewish and Christian philosophers contributed to "Islamic" philosophy. Arabic language was not restricted to Muslims— both Christian and Jewish philosophers wrote in Arabic. He notes that, "Islamic Philosophy" and "Arabic Philosophy" tend to ignore these "Christians and Jews who will be such an important part of our story."[23] Hence, the title is meant to indicate the broad scope of this work, which covers "philosophers from three religions, who wrote in several languages, and lived across a swath of land from modern-day Spain to modern-day Afghanistan."[24] As we shall see in subsequent chapters, much of early Jewish philosophy was influenced by these very Arabic texts and translations.

---

[20] Levy 1987, 101.

[21] For a sustained discussion of what constitutes and delimits Arabic philosophy, see Adamson and Taylor 2005, 3.

[22] Adamson and Taylor 2005.   [23] Adamson 2016, 5.   [24] Adamson 2016, 5.

In response, one might insist that Jewish philosophy is philosophy that addresses specific questions pertaining to central claims of Judaism—for example, the meaning of the "election" of Israel or the validity of the Torah of Moses in the contemporary world—or that attempts rationally to articulate and justify Jewish doctrine or practice. On this essentialist view, what distinguishes Jewish philosophy as *Jewish* must include a religious component: Jewish philosophers engaging philosophically with Judaic notions and beliefs. Analogically, Jewish philosophy would be the union of philosophical study with obedience to the Jewish faith, and a similar case can be made with respect to Islamic philosophy. A more moderate version of the essentialist approach is suggested by historian of Jewish philosophy Colette Sirat, who claims that the essence of Jewish philosophy consists in the harmonization of philosophy with the Jewish sources: "The history of Jewish philosophy in the Middle Ages is the history of efforts of Jews to reconcile philosophy (or a system of rational thought) and Scripture."[25] But as Israeli scholar Raphael Jospe points out in his extensive survey of Jewish philosophy, the actual *essence* of Judaism is itself a contested question, and without a clear conception of the essence of Judaism, the essentialist versions fall short.[26]

One of the assumptions behind this volume is that there is indeed a particular intellectual tradition that can meaningfully be called "Jewish philosophy." In our recent volume on Jewish philosophy, my co-editor and I struggled with the various approaches to this set of questions, and suggested that

being a Jewish philosopher need mean only that an individual—perhaps necessarily of Jewish descent, perhaps not—is in his/her philosophical thinking engaged in an honest dialogue with a particular philosophical and religious tradition and wrestling with a certain set of questions and responding to a certain coterie of thinkers. Even if one's answers to those questions differ radically from those provided by other, perhaps more orthodox thinkers, still, s/he is addressing the same questions. S/he is also referencing (for the most part) the same religious and philosophical textual canon, and engaged in an extensive conversation across time with the same figures (e.g., Saadiah ben Joseph, Ibn Gabirol, Maimonides).[27]

On this view, Jewish philosophy consists in philosophizing with and about the Jewish tradition, asking questions about Judaism as well as using Jewish texts and doctrines to engage in general philosophical speculation about classic problems such as freedom of the will, happiness, the nature of time, epistemological problems about prophecy, and so on. We turn now to say a bit more about the philosophical relevance of these questions.

---

[25] Sirat 1990, 4–5.

[26] The very task of articulating the "essential" nature or properties of Judaism is itself hotly contested. See Jospe 2009 for sustained discussion of this issue.

[27] See Nadler and Rudavsky 2009. See also the discussion in Morgan and Gordon 2007: Jewish philosophy is "whatever is the outcome of a multi-faceted engagement between, on the one hand, thinking about issues relevant to understanding the Jewish condition or the meaning of Judaism and Jewish life, and, on the other hand,... thinking that is indebted to and responds to the tradition of... philosophy." Other historians of philosophy have continued to grapple with this issue. For further attempts to demarcate Jewish philosophy, see Guttmann 1964; Husik 1946; Jospe 2009; and for modern Jewish thought, see Katz 2014, who struggles with similar issues.

III   Overview of Major Topics and Chapters

In contradistinction to most recent histories of Jewish philosophy, I have organized the major topics and chapters of this study thematically, ranging from Jewish philosophy's earliest awakening in the Hellenistic era with the Greek writings of Philo of Alexandria, through its flourishing in the medieval period, to its culmination in the seventeenth century with the radical thought of Baruch Spinoza. Chapter 2 presents a preliminary chronological overview of the major figures discussed in the work, while subsequent chapters focus upon recognizable philosophical issues, each of which reflects a particular set of tensions originating between secularism, science, and Jewish belief.

Chapter 3 focuses upon the nature of science, and what it is we are looking for when discussing the tension between science and Judaism. What is science, how does it differ from philosophy? How do philosophers describe their methodological and epistemological assumptions? How do they characterize reason and faith, in light of their commitments to both scientific and theological commitments? In fact, many of these issues are addressed in the introductions to their major works, and so reading these introductions carefully will provide us with a means of viewing the faith and reason tension.

Chapters 4 and 5 are devoted to divine science, broadly construed. In Chapter 4, we examine attempts on the part of Jewish philosophers to delineate the essential nature of God. Do the different attributes of God constitute many distinct aspects or persons in the Divine essence? Jewish philosophers were divided on this question, as were medieval thinkers in general. Saadiah Gaon, a tenth-century Jewish philosopher whose works reflected the influence of the Islamic theologians, followed the tradition of both Philo and the Islamic Kalâm thinkers in denying multiplicity to God. It is due to the deficiency of human language that the various attributes of God cannot be expressed in one single term. Maimonides' theory of divine predication followed the Neoplatonic tradition and was built primarily upon Al-Fârâbî's and Avicenna's distinction between essence and existence: this distinction implied that in the case of contingent beings existence was accidental to essence, whereas in God essence and existence were one. Hence, God's nature is totally unlike ours, and terms used to describe God must be used either in a homonymous way or as negative predicates. In the fourteenth century, Gersonides, on the other hand, disagreed with Maimonides' celebrated theory of negative theology and sided with Averroës, who, rejecting the Avicennan distinction between essence and existence, argued that existence is not an accident of Being. In following Averroës, Gersonides paves the way for a positive theology that permits of positive attributive ascription to God.

The topic of divine predication leads more broadly to issues in philosophical theology, in particular the issues surrounding divine omniscience, freedom, and evil. Medieval philosophers in all three Abrahamic traditions (Jewish, Christian, and Islamic) were committed to maintaining the freedom of human action; in an attempt to safeguard both moral responsibility and autonomy, they worried whether God's foreknowledge of future contingent events entailed the necessary occurrence of these events. That the force of God's knowledge need not be causal was already claimed by Saadiah Gaon. What concerned medieval philosophers in general, and Jewish philosophers in particular, was the fact that if God is infallible, then the objects of his knowledge *cannot fail to be* what God already knows them to be. How to account for the ability of humans to contravene the prior infallible knowledge that God has of their actions became of paramount importance to Maimonides, Gersonides, and later Jewish philosophers. And as we shall see in Chapter 5, the scope of God's knowledge carries tremendous implications when we turn to the origin of human choice, free will, and the existence of evil.

Chapter 6 is devoted to attempts of our thinkers to reconcile the biblical view of creation with Greek and Islamic philosophy. No medieval philosopher—Jewish, Christian, or Islamic—denied the centrality of the doctrine of creation; that God is the creator of the universe represents one of the foundational beliefs of the Abrahamic tradition. Jews were enormously affected by Scripture and in particular by the creation account found in *Genesis* I–II. But medieval Jewish philosophers thinking about creation were influenced as well by Aristotle's model of an eternally existing world. Like their Christian and Islamic counterparts, Jewish thinkers did not always agree upon what qualifies as an acceptable model of creation. When trying to prove that the world was created by God at a first instant of time, philosophers who wanted to support a biblical theory of creation had to reject Aristotle's position that time is infinite. Working within a framework that upheld the infinity of time, Aristotle posited an eternal universe that had no temporal beginning. Creation theory is thus embedded in the larger context of the ontology of time. So when they turn to consider whether the world was created by God in time, Jewish philosophers must deal critically with Greek and Islamic philosophical notions of time, infinity, and cosmology. By understanding the notion of creation, and how an eternal, timeless creator created a temporal universe, we may begin to understand how the notions of eternity and time function within the context of Jewish philosophical theories of creation.

In Chapter 7 we turn to a more careful examination of the natural order, focusing upon both the natural world that comprises the "sublunar" sphere (viz., the space between the earth and the moon) and the heavenly bodies that comprise the "superlunar" (above the moon). In this geocentric cosmology, the heavenly bodies occupied an important role in ancient and medieval cosmology, natural philosophy, metaphysics, medicine, and theology. Two rival cosmologies, those of Aristotle and of Ptolemy, competed for acceptance in the medieval world, and they affected related issues in natural philosophy. Works of Aristotle and Ptolemy influenced medieval views on astrology as well, as philosophers considered the causal efficacy of the heavenly bodies in the sublunar world. In this chapter, we shall focus upon the ingredients that comprise the universe, both superlunar and sublunary. The superlunar cosmology includes the heavenly bodies, and any effects they may have upon the sublunary world. In the sublunary world, we must focus upon those features of the natural order, including in particular time, place, and void. We finally must take seriously those events that, contravening the natural order, fall into the general category of miraculous events. How, in a cosmology ruled by law and order, can we account for miracles?

Chapters 8 and 9 deal broadly with philosophical anthropology—the psycho-physical composition of the human being and the implications of these theories upon moral theory and reward and punishment. In Chapter 8, we address the following issues: what is the soul, and how is it related to the body?; if the soul is part of the body, does it perish along with the destruction of the body, or does a part of the soul survive?; if part of the soul is immortal, can it acquire new knowledge after death?; is the body resurrected in the world to come, or is salvation purely spiritual?; if salvation is spiritual, are rewards and punishments in the world to come spiritual as well, or are they material? Concomitant with the issue of immortality is the connection obtaining between human intellect and the Active Intellect, as characterized by Avicenna and Averroës.[28] Medieval philosophers took seriously the question of whether the soul retains its individuality upon separation from the body: in other words, whether immortality is personal or general. The very doctrine of reward and punishment, and ultimate human felicity, is all predicated upon individual immortality of the soul. In Chapter 9, we return to the ramifications of soul, in the context of the whole question of human perfection. Our philosophers' responses to these interrelated issues reinforce themes we have seen discussed in Chapter 3, and reflect the attempt once again to reconcile Jewish beliefs with the views set forth by the ancient Greek philosophers.

Chapter 9 is concerned with social and political behavior. Have we now moved to a topic that veers away from these tensions? Not at all. Even in the context of moral and political philosophy, Jewish philosophers discussed issues within the wider context of a rational perspective. Hava Tirosh-Samuelson articulates clearly the point that the science of ethics concerns "many assumptions about the structure of the world, the nature of human beings, the purpose of human life...Therefore the discourse on virtue and happiness was inseparable from a host of metaphysical, cosmological, psychological, epistemological, political and theological theories."[29] Many of the themes and issues we have visited in previous chapters reappear in the context of how to live the good life. Jewish philosophers incorporated material from Greek philosophy, from the rabbis, and from their intellectual peers. In this con-cluding chapter, I position the moral conversation against the backdrop of scientific perspectives. We turn first to specific moral codes developed by Jewish thinkers, focusing in particular upon the works of Ibn Gabirol, Baḥya ibn Paquda, Maimoni-des, and Crescas. Each of these thinkers manifests the tension described above, trying to accommodate biblical and rabbinic views of moral behavior with that of their philosophical peers. We must then determine whether or not we can locate a moral or ethical theory in medieval Jewish philosophy independent of *halakhah* (Jewish law, both written and oral).[30] While I focus primarily upon the status of law and

---

[28] The "Active" (or "Agent") Intellect is a term that refers back to Aristotle's actual intellect as described in *De Anima* 3.5. The term was transmitted to Jewish and scholastic writers through Islamic philosophers, and it came to represent not only a part of the human soul but the domain of Divine intellectual cognition as well. We will discuss this term more extensively in Chapter 8.

[29] Tirosh-Samuelson 2009, 707. See also Tirosh-Samuelson 2003 for an extended study of the nature of happiness in Jewish philosophy.

[30] See Lichtenstein 1975 for a contemporary version of this discussion.

ethical theory in the works of Moses Maimonides, brief discussions of ethical works composed by Maimonides' predecessors Saadiah Gaon, Baḥya ibn Paquda, and Solomon ibn Gabirol enable us to situate Maimonides' discussions more fully. We then end with a look at whether human felicity can be achieved in this life, and whether the prophet best represents the ideal model for such achievement. The answer to this set of questions, not surprisingly, is fraught, and brings us back full circle to the ultimate purpose of existence.

2

Athens, Jerusalem, and Beyond
The Formative Schools and Personalities within Medieval Jewish Philosophy

I Introduction

My purpose in this chapter is twofold: first, to trace some of the most important influences—of both individuals and schools—upon the development of medieval Jewish philosophy; and second to introduce the major Jewish philosophers within the context of these influences. I shall briefly examine biblical, rabbinic, and ancient Greek philosophy precursors. I will then turn to influential developments within late antique philosophy and Islamic philosophy, keeping in mind our main argument in the first chapter that Jewish philosophy reflects a conversation with many other schools of philosophy.

My concern is not so much to present a comprehensive study of medieval Jewish philosophy, but rather to introduce and trace those important themes that reappear in medieval Jewish writings. Clearly, we cannot deal with all the thinkers and issues in the medieval period, and so I have chosen to focus upon those writers that most clearly exemplify our main theme, the tension between science, rationalism, and Judaism. This presentation should not be viewed as exhaustive, nor is the information presented here meant to replace the more substantive accounts to be found in the *Encyclopaedia Judaica*, the *Encyclopedia of Religion*, and the *Stanford Online Encyclopedia of Philosophy*. Additional information can be found in works by noted historians of Jewish philosophy: Colette Sirat, Raphael Jospe, Daniel Frank, and Oliver Leaman; and Steven Nadler and T. M. Rudavsky.[1] Secondary material is provided in the footnotes and the comprehensive bibliography.

II The Formative Traditions

II.1 The Greek philosophical schools

Without pretending to present a complete account of the development of Greek philosophy and science, I should like to emphasize several motifs and arguments in classical Greek thought that reappear in subsequent medieval Jewish discussions.

---

[1] For a more comprehensive history of medieval Jewish philosophy, see Guttmann 1964; Jospe 2009; Sirat 1990; Frank and Leaman 2003; Nadler and Rudavsky 2009. Studies of individual authors will be mentioned in subsequent pages.

The very term "science" should be used advisedly; in Chapter 3 we shall examine the meaning and use of this term more fully: suffice it to say that the term is being used here in the broadest sense of "natural philosophy."[2] The earliest sustained philosophical discussions that we might associate with "natural philosophy" or "science" occur in the fragments of the Presocratic philosophers. Both Heraclitus (*fl. c.* 500 BCE) and Parmenides (*c.* 515 BCE) engaged in the context of trying to account for change in reality. Heraclitus attempts to support his contention that flux and becoming are alone real, and that permanence and constancy are merely apparent. Every physical object is subject to temporal change, hence Heraclitus' emphasis upon the eternal flux of reality, and his insistence that all is in flux.[3] Parmenides, however, disagrees with Heraclitus and argues that only the permanent and enduring are real, and all time, flux, motion, and change are unreal. In contradistinction to Heraclitus who emphasized the ontological priority of change, Parmenides denies that change can occur.[4] By introducing the problem of change in the natural order, Parmenides and Heraclitus set the stage for thinking about natural science among the two "greats" of ancient Greek thought: Plato and Aristotle.

II.1.1 PLATO (427–347 BCE)

It is Plato who, against the backdrop of his Presocratic predecessors, tries to resolve the paradoxes of change and permanence. Plato's Academy was founded in 387/8 BCE in Athens and lasted close to nine centuries. Of the many doctrines found in Platonism, the most important for our study is Plato's Theory of Forms, which provides the underpinning for both his cosmology and metaphysics. Plato wrote primarily in dialogue form, but we can extract from his major dialogues what has come to be known as Plato's Theory of Forms. Forms, according to Plato, constitute what is really real, as opposed to the "appearances" or phenomena of empirical reality. The material world, he argues, is but a poor shadow, or imitation of what is "really real." Forms can never be known empirically, only conceptually. Thus, for example, an abstract concept of a triangle turns out to contain "more reality" or be "more perfect" than any particular, sensible triangle. So too, in the case of human beings: the human body is an imperfect, material, corporeal carrier for the soul, which represents the "more real," perfect representation of the individual. When the sensible human body dies, the soul continues to exist, and participates in the quest for truth and knowledge unencumbered by physicality. So for Plato the abstract, conceptual world of forms or ideas turns out to be more real than the physical world around us; and one of the purposes of philosophy is to lead us to this realization.

The influence of Parmenides can be felt most fully when we turn to Plato's most explicitly cosmological dialogue, the *Timaeus,* which influenced Jewish cosmogonic

---

[2] For a sustained discussion of the history of Greek science, and the various uses of the term science in this context, see Lloyd 1970; Lloyd 1973.

[3] Heraclitus, Fragm 10.77 (30) in McKirahan 1994, 124. Heraclitus insists that the world was not created: "The cosmos, the same for all, none of the gods nor of humans has made, but it was always is and shall be: an ever-living fire being kindled in measures and being extinguished in measures."

[4] For a discussion of the import of Parmenides' language, and different understandings of his expression *esti,* see McKirahan 1994, 160.

and cosmological writing. Drawing upon his Theory of Forms, Plato distinguishes in the *Timaeus* between eternity (*aionios*) and everlastingness (*aidios*): everlastingness is "the nearest approach to eternity of which sensible things are capable."[5] On Plato's account, the Demiurge [which plays a role not unsimilar to God's role as creator in Genesis] created the cosmos out of his goodness, not jealousy.[6] Desiring all things to be like him, the Demiurge instills order into inherent chaos. More specifically, the Demiurge creates the cosmos according to an eternal model that is independent of him. There can be only one cosmos since uniqueness is itself a perfection.[7] The Demiurge is not omnipotent, however: he works with eternal forms that he did not create and he inherits the domain of chaos that is independent of his creative powers. The Demiurge is ultimately only concerned with the world of becoming. That the Demiurge is not identical with the Form of the Good is evidenced by the fact that the Demiurge uses the idea of good in order to impose order, but the Demiurge is not good in itself.

II.1.2 ARISTOTLE (384–322 BCE)

Notwithstanding the importance of Plato's cosmology for the Neoplatonic world (about which more below), the most influential scientific strands in the medieval world were those of Aristotle, Plato's student and most famous critic. Born in Stagira, Chalcidice (Macedonia) in 384 BCE, Aristotle studied in Plato's Academy; after tutoring Alexander the Great, he eventually returned to Athens in 335 BCE and founded the Lykeion (Lyceum) as his own school. Aristotle rejected his teacher Plato's Theory of Forms, replacing it with a metaphysical system rooted in sense perception. According to Aristotle, we can only discover the definitions or essences of entities by investigating their causes, which are rooted in empirical reality. Thus, our senses provide us with genuine knowledge of the world around us. Unlike Plato, who claimed that the senses are deceptive and sensory knowledge is ephemeral and rooted in appearances, Aristotle established a scientific method of demonstration that started with sense perception. This method was rooted in a system of logic, developed in six works collected in his so-called *Organon*; this collection had enormous influence in the Middle Ages. Aristotle wrote on practically every scientific topic known in the ancient world.

In the Aristotelian cosmology, the universe is a finite sphere whose center is at the earth and bounded by the sphere of the fixed stars. The sphere of the moon separated the universe into the sublunar, or terrestrial, region, and the superlunar or celestial region. The superlunar heavens differed in composition from the sublunar bodies in that the former were composed of a single incorruptible element, *aether*, while the earth was comprised of the four elements.[8] The ultimate source of motion in this Aristotelian system is god, or the unmoved first mover.[9] But did god move the first moving sphere as an active, efficient cause, or as a passive, final cause? Aristotle had attributed to all the celestial spheres a mover, the ultimate source of motion being

---

[5] Lloyd 1976, 138.   [6] Plato *Timaeus* 29d.   [7] Plato *Timaeus* 31a-b.
[8] Aristotle *De Caelo* I.2–4; II.4. For a discussion of this doctrine of *aether*, see Lloyd 1970, 109–11. See also details in Chapter 7.
[9] See Aristotle *Metaphysics* 7.7; *Physics* 8.6.

god. Medieval thinkers, however, introduced immobile created intelligences to explain celestial motion. These separate intelligences move the orbs with both intellect and will.[10] Each sphere has a soul or internal moving source; as we shall see in Chapter 7, Maimonides, along with other medieval philosophers, identifies these spheres with angels.[11]

Although cosmology and astronomy represented separate disciplines, as it were, nevertheless they intersected in the area of theory formation. As Pederson has argued, tensions centered on the metaphysical status of mathematical theories in science.[12] For on the one hand, the universe, as described by Aristotle in *De Caelo*, was a material entity based on the laws of physics. On the other hand, mathematical astronomy made use of geometrical devices that violated these very physical laws. More specifically, Aristotle argued that there must be a plurality of spheres to account for the motion of each planet. These spheres, as we have seen, were nested contiguously. On Aristotle's model there was a series of concentric orbs, each moving in a natural, uniform, circular motion, all sharing the earth as a common center. The astronomer Ptolemy, however, recognized that Aristotle could not account for variations in the observed distances of the planets. This recognition led to the postulating of an alternative cosmological scheme, to which we now turn.

II.1.3 PTOLEMY (C. 100–170 CE)

Ptolemy was a Greco-Egyptian astronomer, best known for his work in mathematics, astronomy, astrology, and geography. He is best known for his astronomical treatise the *Almagest*, and his astrological treatise the *Tetrabiblos*; his geocentric cosmology was almost universally accepted until the Copernican Revolution. In his two astronomical works *Almagest* and *Hypothesis of the Planets*, Ptolemy argued that the planets were carried about by a system of eccentric and epicyclical spheres.[13] In the *Almagest*, Ptolemy had proposed that his astronomical theory was merely a method the purpose of which was to "save the appearances," or account for the observed phenomena.[14] On Ptolemy's model, each concentric planetary orb contained at least three partial eccentric and epicyclical spheres. As we shall see in Chapter 7, most medieval astronomers found that Ptolemy's system did a better job of "saving the appearances" of astronomical data. As Grant has argued, "the medieval conflict between the Aristotelian and Ptolemaic systems centered on efforts to demonstrate that eccentric and epicyclical orbs did not imply consequences that were subversive and destructive of Aristotelian cosmology and physics."[15] In other words, medieval philosophers were faced with a dilemma: they could either reject the earth's centrality and abandon a vital part of Aristotelian physics in the name of astronomical and mathematical purity, or accept a cosmology that was untenable from

---

[10] See Grant 1997, 285.   [11] See Maimonides *Guide* 2.6.   [12] Pederson 1978, 321.
[13] For a brief introduction to these works, cf. Lloyd 1973, 53–74; Duhem 1913–59; 1985; and Clagett 1955, 83–99.
[14] See Ptolemy *Almagest* 13.2. For a discussion of the importance of Ptolemy's description of theory, see the classic work of Duhem 1913–59.
[15] Ibid.

the perspective of the astronomers.[16] Influenced by Aristotle's physical and natural works, many cosmologists followed Aristotle rather than the astronomer Ptolemy in their quest to provide a comprehensive theory of the universe.[17] The formative classical texts included Aristotle's *De Caelo*, supplemented by relevant passages from the *Metaphysics*, *Physics*, and *De Generatione et Corruptione*. Ptolemy's *Almagest*, Plato's *Timaeus* and commentaries upon *Genesis* presented an additional dimension to this corpus.

II.1.4 PLOTINUS (204–270) AND THE NEOPLATONIST TRADITION

The last important Greek philosophical school we must discuss is Neoplatonism, a tradition largely based on the writings of Plato, Aristotle, Plotinus, and Proclus. It provided the philosophical context for the thought of many cultivated Jews of the eleventh and twelfth centuries, and during the Arabic period, it was complemented by elements stemming from Islamic religious traditions. Founded by Plotinus in the third century CE, Neoplatonism became the dominant philosophical school from the third to the sixth centuries and provided a unique cosmological and ontological theory. To define Neoplatonism thematically would require a chapter in itself. Recent articles, for example, have questioned even whether Plotinus himself is a Neoplatonist.[18] Following Sweeney, I suggest that Neoplatonism incorporates minimally these three traits:

1. It posits as the primal reality an Existent who is the One/Good; who transcends all becoming, being, knowledge, and description; and who actually exists.
2. It grants that there are existents other than the One, but that inasmuch as any reality they have is congruent with the One, they are at bottom identical with the One.
3. It finds operative two sorts of causality: first, the emanation of effects from the perfection of the One to the imperfection of existents (termed hypostases); second, a return of imperfect effects to the perfection of the One which commences with contemplation and culminates in full identification with the One.[19]

In short, Neoplatonist philosophers embrace a monistic ontology that incorporates a theory of causal emanation. Positing the existence of the One as the basic reality that transcends all existing things, Neoplatonists, following Plotinus, claimed that the world emanated from the Deity [God or the One] in a manner similar to the emanation of the rays of the sun. They emphasized the qualitative difference between the emanating cause [the One] of existence, and the effects of emanation, which included both spiritual and material substances. Neoplatonists also introduced the

---

[16] See Grant 1997. Grant goes on to describe a third alternative as well, namely one in which additional orbs are introduced according to which the variation in planetary distances was incorporated into a system of concentric planetary spheres. In this way, both Aristotelian and Ptolemaic systems are salvaged.

[17] Grant 1997, 266.

[18] See for example Blumenthal 1981, 212–22 where he outlines four major areas of disagreement between Plotinus and other Neoplatonists; see also Sweeney 1983, 177–202.

[19] For a fuller exposition of these three traits, see Sweeney 1983, 191.

important motif of "union" or "return," namely that human beings could achieve perfection or salvation through an upward journey back toward a union with God/the One.

At the top of the Neoplatonic cosmology is the One, from which everything else emanates in successive stages—universal intellect, universal soul, nature, and the material world. The process of emanation does not derive from will, but rather it is a necessary impersonal outpouring from the One. Plotinus's radical monism thus posits three stages or hypostases from which lower stages emanate: The One; the universal intellect; and the universal soul. The universal intellect is the only hypostasis that emanates directly from the One; the universal soul, which emanates from the universal intellect, is the bridge between it and the natural order, both superlunary and sublunary. As Jospe notes, one of the challenges faced by Jewish philosophers was to attempt to bridge this "impersonal, emanationist scheme of Neoplatonist philosophy with the biblical doctrine of creation by a personal God who knows and relates to his creatures in love."[20]

The One in Plotinus's ontology is "beyond being": in its pure simplicity, it lacks nothing, or as Plotinus says, the One is "no-thing" and yet the source of everything.[21] The One transcends all attributes. As we noted earlier, it is impersonal and wills the process of emanation out of necessity—there is no choice, or deliberation, involved in the process of emanation. Unlike the One, the universal intellect does not reflect a perfect unity—it knows both what is above it (the One) and what is below it (universal soul and nature). The universal soul forms a link as well, between what is upper (the One and universal intellect) and lower (nature): it comes into existence out of a desire of the universal intellect to cause something else to exist.[22] From this desire, the universal soul, and by extension the human soul, come into existence. Plotinus agrees with Plato that the human soul is enslaved, or trapped, within the human body. As it purifies itself and separates itself from bodily desires, the more can the soul ultimately reunite with the One. Plotinus even envisions the quasi-mystical possibility of a soul's union with the One while still alive (in fact, Plotinus supposedly achieved such a union while still alive). The ultimate purpose of human existence lies in freeing one's soul from the constraints of a physical, material, degrading existence, and ultimately uniting with the universal intellect, or even with the One.

Not surprisingly, Plotinus's system found a receptive audience in the medieval period: that these traits are all, to some extent, reflected in Jewish Neoplatonist writings will become evident in subsequent chapters. But one other trait must be mentioned as well, namely the problem inherent in the very process of philosophical analysis. As pointed out by Steven Katz,[23] Neoplatonism generally, and especially Jewish Neoplatonism, presents a familiar yet profound problem. According to its declared premises, verbal descriptions of the ultimate realities are not possible: language operates upon and within a given categorical structure and is of limited applicability to those entities that lie outside its domain. Plotinus, for example, suggests that inasmuch as the One must be without form and is thereby not a

---

[20] Jospe 2009, 79.   [21] Plotinus *Enneads* V:5.
[22] Plotinus *Enneads* IV:7.   [23] Katz 1992.

substance, it transcends being and language. By the Middle Ages, the ineffability of the One was taken as an indisputable axiom by both mystics and Neoplatonic philosophers.[24] One way, Katz notes, that medieval Neoplatonists used to interpret this axiom was to emphasize the utter ineffability of God's true nature. Strictly speaking, when we deny the possibility of linguistic expression, nothing more should be said. On this line of argument, it becomes impossible to say which linguistic forms are appropriate to the One, because all language is equally inappropriate. One problem with this approach, however, is that negative predicates become more appropriate for describing God than positive ones. Metaphysical attributes are no more attributable than their opposites. Katz is right to note that the Neoplatonists never really overcome this difficulty. For as we shall see in our ensuing discussion, Jewish Neoplatonists speak of the One in ways that carry content, even if only implicitly and connotatively, by reference to the larger conceptual context that informs everything they say. And when we turn in Chapter 5 to Maimonides' theory of negative predication, we will appreciate more keenly the problems associated with ineffability.

Plotinus's major work the *Enneads* was transmitted to Jewish thinkers through an Arabic paraphrase called the *Theology of Aristotle* (more about this transmission below). For serious Jewish thinkers, the speculations of certain Neoplatonist philosophies provided epistemological and metaphysical notions that were quite compatible with their own attempts to characterize the nature of God and his nature and relation to humans. Although not all Jewish thinkers supported Neoplatonism, it was extremely influential on the formation of Jewish thought during the late Hellenistic, Roman, and medieval periods.[25] We will turn below to the most influential and important Jewish Neoplatonists.

II.2 The world of the rabbis

II.2.1 BIBLICAL WORKS

Having provided a brief summary of the major figures in ancient Greek philosophy, let us turn even more briefly to canonical works in Jewish thought. These works include not only Scripture itself but the entire rabbinic tradition contained in the Talmud. Of the books contained in the Mosaic Bible, the ones most influential to medieval Jewish philosophy included the *Book of Genesis*, with its account of creation, as well as Abraham's trial [known as the *Akedah*]; the *Book of Deuteronomy*, which recounts the giving of the Law; and the *Book of Job*, which introduces the problem of evil. Other biblical books contain passing discussion of what we might consider philosophical topics, but in general, the Bible does not represent a systematic philosophy.[26] Other more philosophical works of the Bible, including *Proverbs*, *Book of Job*, *Song of Songs*, and *Ecclesiastes*, gave rise to a robust commentary literature. But even the *Book of Job* does not provide a complete theodicy: at most, we can point to a theology that influenced later philosophers.

---

[24] Among Jewish Neoplatonists, it was a premise in Zoharic and post-Zoharic Kabbalah as well as in the philosophy of Ibn Gabirol and Ibn Paquda, and even Moses Maimonides, who says that we cannot grasp God's essence as it truly is. See Katz 1992, 281.

[25] Harris 1992, xi.   [26] See Carmy and Shatz 1997.

The situation is somewhat different when we consider what is known as the "wisdom tradition," which represents the initial influence of Greek philosophy upon biblical works. Works such as the text of *Ecclesiastes*, the *Wisdom of ben Sira*, and the *Wisdom of Solomon* all reflect more marked interest in philosophical themes. As David Winston has noted, the work *Wisdom of Solomon* "so palpably verges on the philosophical that we can readily identify this book's Middle Platonist affinities and its considerable use of Greek philosophical terminology."[27] Written in Greek by a Hellenized Jew of Alexandria, the work emphasizes immortality of the soul, as well as the search for Wisdom.

Ecclesiastes provides an interesting example of an author grappling with philosophical themes. *Ecclesiastes* is a work devoted, among other things, to expressing the futility of temporal flow. Chapter 3 of *Ecclesiastes* can be read in several ways. Most obvious is the prevalence of God's predetermination of all human events: that "everything has its appointed time and there is a season for every event under the sky,"[28] points to the futility of human striving in light of God's predetermining of all events in their appointed time. This predetermination is reinforced in *Ecclesiastes* 3:11: "Everything He has made proper in its due time." And yet the predetermination of temporal events brings with it the comfort of cyclicity as well as the recognition that a providential deity controls human affairs. In recognizing that "there is a time to be born, a time to die, a time to plant and a time to uproot,"[29] our sage underscores the comforting reality that events do not happen randomly, out of sequence. Rather do events have both an inner and outer sequence that is repeated on a cyclic basis. Planting and uprooting, living and dying, mourning and dancing, all occur and recur with constant regularity, reinforcing the motif of time as recurrence. Death too is a constant motif, underscoring the futility of human endeavors. "Again, I saw that beneath the sun the race is not to the swift, nor the battle to the brave, nor is bread won by the wise, nor wealth by the clever, nor favor by the learned, for time (*'et*) and accident overtake them all,"[30] and human beings are "trapped in a time of misfortune, when it befalls upon them suddenly."[31] Time, then, comes to represent not only the predetermined order into which human beings are thrust, but the cruel means by which they are yanked out of this order into nonexistence, notwithstanding all efforts to the contrary. *Ecclesiastes* emphasizes the futility of marking time in light of its repetitiveness: "What has been, already exists, and what is still to be, has already been, and God always seeks to repeat the past."[32]

II.2.2 THE JEWISH MYSTICAL TRADITION

The *Sefer Yezirah* (*Book of Creation*) is the earliest extant book in Jewish mystical esotericism. When it was written is unclear, nor is its author known. Scholem suggests that the main part of the work was written between the third and sixth centuries in Palestine "by a devout Jew with leanings toward mysticism, whose aim was speculative and magical rather than ecstatic...who endeavored to "Judaize" non-Jewish speculations which suited his spirit."[33] The work exists in a short and a

---

[27] Winston 1997, 43.   [28] *Ecclesiastes* 3:1.   [29] *Ecclesiastes* 3:2.
[30] *Ecclesiastes* 9:11.   [31] *Ecclesiastes* 9:12.   [32] *Ecclesiastes* 3:15.
[33] For an introduction to the mystical literature, see Scholem 2007.

longer version and has given rise to an enormous commentary tradition, culminating in the publication of *The Zohar* in the thirteenth century.

The work is devoted to a description of the act of God's creation of the world through different combinations of the "32 wondrous ways of wisdom": "With 32 mystical paths of Wisdom engraved Yah, the Lord of Hosts / the God of Israel."[34] These ways include the ten numbers (or *sefirot*) and the twenty-two letters of the Hebrew alphabet. Of the letters, it is said, "Twenty-two Foundation letters: He engraved them, He carved them, He permuted them, He weighted them, He transformed them, and with them, He depicted all that was formed and all that would be formed."[35] Chapter 1 deals with the ten *sefirot* and the subsequent five chapters with the function of the twenty-two letters. These 32 paths, introduced in the first chapter as *sefirot* of nothingness, "ten *sefirot beli mah*,"[36] represent the foundations of all creation.

What follows is an intricate, convoluted elaboration of the letters. The author emphasizes, though ambiguously, the mystical character of the *sefirot*, describing each one in detail and discussing their hierarchical ordering. At least the first four *sefirot* emanate from each other. In chapters 3–5 the twenty-two basic letters are divided into three groups, according to the author's special phonetic system. The first group contains the three "mother letters"—*alef, mem, shin*—from which the other letters come into being. They in turn represent the source of the three elements mentioned in a different context in the first chapter—air, fire, water—as well as the three seasons of the year (according to a system found among Greek and Hellenistic writers) and the three parts of the body: the head, torso, and the stomach. The ten *sefirot* constitute a closed unit, for as we see in 1:7, "their end is embedded in their beginning and their beginning in their end like a flame in a burning coal."[37] Everything else in reality came into existence through the interconnection of the twenty-two letters, and especially by way of the "231 gates"; i.e., the combinations of the letters into groups of two representing the possible roots of the Hebrew language.

The *Sefer Yeẓirah* had an enormous impact upon subsequent Jewish thought. Saadiah Gaon (see below) wrote an extended commentary on the work that reappeared throughout the early medieval period. Drawing upon some of the ideas in the *Sefer Yeẓirah*, the *Sefer ha-Bahir* appeared in Provence between 1150 and 1200, and presented an even more mystical vision than the former. In this mystical work, the hidden God (*En-Sof*), who is unknowable and infinite, reveals part of his Being in creation through the ten *sefirot*. These *sefirot* are no longer, as they were in *Sefer Yeẓirah*, separate emanations, but rather now in *Sefer ha-Bahir* they exemplify dynamic aspects of the godhead. The names of the ten *sefirot* are: *Keter Elyon* (crown); *Ḥokhmah* (wisdom); *Binah* (intelligence); *Ḥesed* (love/mercy); *Gevurah/ Din* (power/judgment); *Raḥamim* (compassion); *Neẓaḥ* (lasting endurance); *Hod* (majesty); *Yesod* (basis or foundation); and *Malkhut* (kingdom, or the *Shekhinah*).[38] All the sefirot are linked to one another, and God expresses his relation to creation through these sefirot. As Sirat notes, "the *sefirot* provide the key to a mystic 'topography' of the divine world and each of them is revealed in the multiple metamorphoses

---

[34] *Sefer Yetzirah* 1:1 in Kaplan 1997, 5.   [35] *Sefer Yetzirah* 2:2 in Kaplan 1997, 100.
[36] *Sefer Yetzirah* 1:2 in Kaplan 1997, 22.   [37] *Sefer Yetzirah* 1:7 in Kaplan 1997, 57.
[38] See Scholem 1995, 212.

of the biblical and traditional texts."[39] This mystical tradition culminated in the 1270s with the arrival of *The Zohar* (*The Book of Splendor*): once the *Zohar* absorbed many of the motifs found in the *Sefer ha-Bahir*, Kabbalah soon became associated with the *Zohar*.[40] We will not in this text pursue the kabbalistic works formally, since that would take us far afield from our primary focus.[41] However, we will have several occasions to highlight kabbalistic themes that permeate philosophical discussions.

II.2.3 THE WORLD OF THE TALMUD

Turning finally to the world of the rabbis of the Tannaitic period between the first century BCE and second century CE, and the Amoraic period between the second and sixth centuries CE, we are faced once again with the quandary of whether the rabbis were technically philosophers. The major works of this period, all of which constitute commentary upon Scripture, include the *Mishnah*, the *Midrash*, as well as both the Palestinian and Babylonian Talmuds. The *Mishnah* represents rabbinic conversations and texts from the second century BCE through the first two centuries CE; these conversations are organized into "orders" (*sedarim*) under a variety of topics and represent a variety of legal positions. The *Midrash* is a collection of books that represent rabbinic interpretations of the Bible. Both the Palestinian and Babylonian Talmud were edited in the sixth century CE by the *amoraim* as commentaries on the *Mishnah*: these commentaries included elaborate conversations on a wide variety of texts, words, and chapters.[42] In all these works, we see little if any evidence that the rabbis had any intellectual contact with Greek philosophy, nor can we posit an overarching philosophical unity to the many books of the Talmud. Even if we agree that philosophical questions and concerns occasionally appear in rabbinic texts, nonetheless, the rabbis do not develop a coherent philosophical theory or system as we find in the Greek philosophical tradition.[43] As noted by David Novak, "not only is the Talmud, like the Bible, not a philosophical work, but, unlike the Bible, it does not even seem to lend itself to ever becoming the object of philosophical meditation."[44]

In order to exemplify the absence of analytic philosophical thinking among the rabbis, let us use as an example the notion of time, a concept that very much occupied the minds of subsequent medieval thinkers. For reasons having to do as much with contemporary theological concerns as with pedagogical research, modern Biblical scholars have devoted much time trying to uncover a "theory of time" in the Hebrew

---

[39] Sirat 1990, 249.

[40] For a detailed study of the *Zohar* and Kabbalah, see Scholem 1995; Wolfson, E. 1994.

[41] Wolfson, E. 1994 has studied extensively the philosophical dimensions of Jewish mystical texts.

[42] For extensive discussion of the history of the Talmud and the entire commentary tradition, see Neusner 1991; Steinsaltz 1976.

[43] See for example Samuelson's comment in Samuelson 2003, 109: "all of the kinds of questions we recognize as philosophical are discussed in the early rabbinic literature, even though the format of its discussion is not one that we of the modern West commonly recognize as philosophical."

[44] Novak 1997, 64. See also the famous statement by the Talmud scholar Saul Lieberman who stated "Greek philosophic terms are absent from the entire ancient rabbinic literature" (Lieberman 1963, 130). We should note, however, the view of Jacob Neusner, developed in many of his works, that the Greek sciences were known to the rabbis, and that a sizeable portion of the Mishnah is philosophical in method and overall program. See also Neusner 1991.

Scriptures. But inasmuch as the earliest Jewish authors were not philosophers, they were not interested in elucidating a philosophical theory of time per se. The enterprise has thus been fraught with frustration and has not reached a scholarly consensus. In Chapter 6 we shall examine the notion of time more fully; suffice it to note that both biblical and rabbinic texts present a model of time that transcends a simple binary distinction between linear and cyclic time. Both the linearity of historical events and the cyclicity of natural cycles must be recognized in this model.[45] Given the pre-eminence of ritualized events in Judaism, the marking of time assumes overwhelming importance in the rabbinic period. Inasmuch as the rabbis are equally concerned with the daily rituals and events that are performed at specific times, so the exact determination of temporal demarcations, e.g., "day," "twilight," "cycle," becomes of paramount importance in rabbinic literature.

The architectonic of time is captured by what Higgins characterizes as the liturgical cycle of time; this cycle is most applicable to religious ritual and practice. In medieval Christian practice, for example, liturgical time refers to the specific times for reciting prayer, the ringing of the ecclesiastical bells at appropriate times, the setting of the ecclesiastical calendar, etc.[46] A similar point can be made with respect to Jewish attitudes toward liturgical time. Yerushalmi has suggested that while in the Bible there is a sense of chronology, a genuine sense of the flow of historical time, the rabbis in contrast "seem to play with Time as though with an accordion, expanding and collapsing it at will."[47] Even a casual glance at rabbinic texts supports Yerushalmi's claim, for in rabbinic texts the ordinary chronological barriers of time have truly been ignored, and all ages interact with one another. Witness, for example, the importance of ritualized, recursive, readings of Scripture, during which temporality becomes atemporal.[48]

Each reading of the weekly Torah portion hearkens back not only to other weekly portions read sequentially during the year, but to previous years' readings as well, thus elevating the event to an atemporal plane. The cyclicity of temporally individuated events is emphasized in their yearly, monthly, or weekly repetition.

We have seen, then, that the demarcation of a "beginning" to philosophical thinking in Jewish texts is problematic. While some rabbinic texts evince an interest in philosophical concerns, others are markedly devoid of philosophical speculation. In Chapter 8 we return to the concept of time, which plays a crucial role in theories of creation. The medieval concern over whether there is a "first" instant to creation, or

---

[45] Steensgaard as well wants to argue that in the Old Testament we find both historical, linear time as well as mythical time that has a cyclical character. For example, he points to early cultic, cyclical conception and then asks "when did the consciousness of historical time become so strong that it repressed the idea of a cultic-cyclical repetition?" In the prophets, for example, time is understood in a "linear" fashion. See Steensgaard 1993, 65. See also Rubenstein 1997, 157–83; Kaye 2018.

[46] Higgins 1989, 232ff. See also the excellent discussions in LeGoff 1982.

[47] Yerushalmi 1982, 17.

[48] As stated so eloquently by Neusner: "What it seems to me Mishnah's system expresses is a totally ahistorical, possibly even anti-historical, conception of sanctification. In this conception, curiously, historical time plays no role, beginning, middle or end. Before us is a theory of sanctification focused upon timeless ontology, and set wholly apart from, conceived as entirely other than, sanctification provoked by the advent of an event, whether in history, supernature or nature." See Neusner 1991, xv.

whether the universe is eternal, will incorporate both biblical and rabbinic conceptions of time and temporality.

II.3   The Hellenization of Jewish thought

II.3.1   PHILO OF ALEXANDRIA (PHILO JUDAEUS, C. 20 BCE–50 CE)

So far, we have introduced two strands of influences, Judaic and philosophical. These two strands reached fruition in the Hellenistic world during the first century CE, and gave rise to attempts among Jews to provide a philosophical underpinning to their beliefs. Philo is renowned as one of the first Jewish thinkers to attempt a reconciliation of Jewish and Greek influences. It is important to note that although Philo's works were not directly influential upon subsequent Jewish texts, they did permeate and influence Christian writers, and thus entered the medieval world indirectly.[49] Born in Alexandria, Egypt, little is known of Philo's travels and life. We do know that Philo was selected by the Alexandrian Jewish community as the primary representative of the embassy sent in 39/40 CE to meet with the Roman emperor, Caligula (Gaius). During this time, there was much civil tension between the Alexandrian Jews and the Hellenized Alexandrian community, and at least one of the purposes of the embassy was to confront the emperor about these problems. Philo is reported to have led his community in refusal to recognize the emperor as a god, erect statues in his honor, and build religious venues such as temples or alters to him.

We know a great deal more about Philo's philosophical life. In Wolfson's view, Philo is the most important western philosopher after Plato and Aristotle. A Hellenized Jewish thinker, Philo was the first philosopher to attempt a synthesis of religious and rational truth, harmonizing Greek thought with Torah. Philo saw himself as the "great reconciler" who would bridge the traditions of Judaism and Greek philosophy. In this attempt, Philo pioneered what Wolfson has called the "double-belief" theory, according to which both revelation and reason yielded truth. We must be careful to distinguish "double-belief" from the "double-truth" theory of the Latin Averroists (thirteenth century) for whom something can be true in one system while not being true in the other system—the point being that reason and revelation are two entirely autonomous and separate realms of truth.[50] In Chapter 3 we will return to the implications of both these theories of truth. Nonetheless, although they are both sources of truth, Philo argues that philosophy is the "handmaiden" of Judaism—it is ultimately subservient to revelation and fallible.

Philo used the method of allegory to express his harmonization of Judaism and Greek philosophy. While in some of his treatises he presented what he considered to be universal Judaic truths to the pagans, in others he tried to argue to Jews that the Greek truths were akin to those found in Judaic sources. Philo's religious works were later embraced by prominent Christian scholars, some of whom insisted that Philo was, in fact, Christian. In addition to his interpretation of the Bible, Philo extracted from it a theory of number, cosmology, anthropology, and ethics. Philo distinguishes

---

[49] For extensive discussion of Philo's influence, see Wolfson 1947.
[50] Wolfson 1947 discusses this extensively; see also Jospe 2009, 37.

the principle of *Logos* as God's "blueprint" of the world, according to which God created the sublunar spheres. In addition to his numerology and cosmology, Philo determined an anthropology and from it, an ethics. His major works, written in Greek and translated into Latin, include his *Treatise on the Eternity of the World*; *De Somniis*; *De Vita Contemplativa*; *De Abrahamo*; *Quæstiones in Genesin*; *Legum Allegoriæ*; *De Specialibus Legibus*; and *De Decalogo*. We will examine Philo's views on creation in Chapter 7.

III   The Transmission of Greek Philosophy

As noted above, medieval Neoplatonism provided the philosophical context for the thought of many cultivated Jews of the eleventh and twelfth centuries, and during the Arabic period, it was more or less complemented by elements stemming from Islamic religious traditions and some Aristotelian ideas. Serious Jewish thinkers had to deal with Neoplatonism (tinged with Aristotelian ingredients) if only because they saw in the speculations of certain Neoplatonist philosophies the epistemological and metaphysical notions that were quite compatible with their own attempts to characterize the nature of God and his nature and relation to humans. Although not all Jewish thinkers adopted Neoplatonism, it was extremely influential on the formation of Jewish thought during the late Hellenistic, Roman, and medieval periods.[51]

The Arabic Neoplatonist philosophers most clearly influenced medieval Jewish writers. The work of Plotinus was transmitted in a variety of ways, most notably through the *Theology of Aristotle* (a paraphrase of books 4, 5, and 6 of the *Enneads*), and through doxographies, collections of sayings of Plotinus which were circulated among religious communities. The *Theology of Aristotle* exists in two versions. The shorter (vulgate) version, belonging to a later period and found in many manuscripts, was the version first published by F. Dieterici. The second, longer version exists in three fragmentary manuscripts in Hebrew script, discovered by A. Borisov in Leningrad.[52] Underlying the longer version of the *Theology of Aristotle* is an additional pseudographical work discovered by S. M. Stern called *Ibn Ḥasday's Neoplatonist*. In an important article, Stern has argued that the independent treatise *Ibn Ḥasday's Neoplatonist* was incorporated into the long version of the *Theology of Aristotle*; that it strongly influenced Isaac Israeli's philosophy; and that it was preserved almost in its entirety in a Hebrew translation incorporated into Ibn Ḥasday's work *Ben ha-Melech ve-ha-Nazir* (*The Prince and the Ascetic*).[53]

---

[51]   Harris 1992, xi.

[52]   For further discussion of the relation between these two versions, see the discussions by Pines 1954. Altmann and Stern argue, along with Pines, that the shorter version is the original and the longer is the result of editorial refashioning of the text, cf. Altmann and Stern 1958, 80. Detailed discussion of recent editions and translations of the *Theology of Aristotle* can be found in Taylor 1992, 26, note 5. P. Fenton has recently discovered that Shem Tov Ibn Falaquera translated quotations directly from the original "vulgate" Arabic version of the *Theology*, into his own work *Sefer ha-ma'alot*, making Ibn Falaquera the only medieval Jewish author to have done so. See Fenton, 1986, 27–39.

[53]   S. M. Stern traces the history and influence of this treatise, offering a reconstruction of the text (Stern 1961, 58–120). Ibn Ḥasday's treatise *Ben ha-Melech ve-ha-Nazir* is a Hebrew adaptation of the Arabic book *Bilawhar wa-Yudasaf*, which goes back to the legend of the Buddha. A complete translation of Ibn Ḥasday's work can be found in Stern 1961, 102ff.

Two other influential works are worthy of note. Proclus' *Elements of Theology* was transmitted to Jewish thinkers in the period between the early ninth and late tenth centuries through an Arabic translation *Kalâm fi mahd al-khaîr*. Known to Latin thinkers as the *Liber de causis*, it was translated in the twelfth century from Arabic into Latin most likely by Gerard of Cremona and was generally attributed by medieval philosophers to Aristotle.[54] And finally, the *Book of Five Substances* attributed to Empedocles was originally written in the ninth century in Arabic and translated into Hebrew in the fourteenth to fifteenth centuries. Published by David Kaufman in 1899, this pseudo-Empedoclean work represents a variant of Ibn Ḥasday's Neoplatonism and was highly influential upon the work of Ibn Gabirol.[55]

The works and thought of Aristotle underwent a transmission process as well. Greek philosophy declined after the closure of the Academy in Athens in 529 CE. But during this period, Syrian Christians began translating Greek works into Syriac, and then into Arabic. These Arabic translations were supported even further by the Abbasid Caliph Al-Ma'mun in Baghdad, who established "The House of Wisdom" (*Bayt al-Ḥikmah*) in 830 CE as a center for scientific learning and research. Al-Ma'mun's support thus made possible the rapid spread of philosophy in the Islamic, and ultimately the Jewish, world. By the twelfth century, most of the Aristotelian corpus had been translated. By the thirteenth century, when Hebrew translations were made, many of the translations actually incorporated the influence, if not the actual theories, of the Islamic philosophers al-Fârâbî, Ibn-Sina (Avicenna), and Ibn Rushd (Averroës).

As we examine in subsequent chapters the works of the major players in Jewish philosophy, it will become clear that while many of them wrote within the context of a particular philosophical school, often doctrines from various schools were mixed. But before turning to the details, let us introduce the major thinkers. We will therefore look first at Jewish Kalâm philosophers writing against the backdrop of the Islamic Kalâm theologians; then Jewish Neoplatonists Isaac Israeli, Solomon ibn Gabirol, and Abraham ibn Ezra; Jewish Aristotelianism as represented by Abraham ibn Daud and Maimonides; and post-Maimonidean critique of Aristotelianism in the works of Gersonides, Crescas, and Albo. In addition, we must introduce several eclectic thinkers who do not fit into any particular school: Judah Halevi and Baḥya ibn Pakuda are notable examples of those who weave elements from Neoplatonism, Kalâm, Aristotelianism and even Islamic Sufism into a unique, eclectic theory.

IV Major Figures and Schools in Medieval Jewish Philosophy

IV.1 The Kalâm theologians

The individual who enabled medieval Jewish philosophers to transform Aristotle's cosmology and adapt it to a theological context was John Philoponus, whose works

---

[54] For the extensive history of this work, see Taylor 1992, 11ff. Fenton also traces influences upon Jewish philosophers (see Fenton 1986; 1992).

[55] For a critical examination of this work, see Kaufman 1962.

contain a refutation of Aristotle's theory of the eternity of the world from the perspective of theories of the infinite. His major work *Contra Aristotelem* has been lost and survives only in quotations from Simplicius' commentaries on Aristotle's *De Caelo* and *Physics*.[56] In this work, Philoponus hopes to demonstrate the creation of the world by arguing that Aristotle's assumption of eternal motion leads to untenable conclusions. Philoponus' works were known to Arabic philosophers, and were transmitted by the Islamic school of Kalâm, through Saadiah Gaon, to eleventh- and twelfth-century Jewish and Christian philosophers.[57]

The major figure in this transmission was Abu Hâmid Muhammed ibn Muhammad al-Ghazâlî (1058–1111), a Persian theologian and philosopher whose work was known to Jews through translations, and whose presentation of Kalâm atomism in his *Maqāsid al-falasifah* (*Aims of the Philosophers*) may have been quite influential. The Kalâm theologians were a school of Islamic thinkers who presented a strict and rigorous interpretation of the Qur'an. Followers of Kalâm were called Mutakallimûn, and were divided into two main schools of thought: the Mu'tazilites, a moderate branch of Kalâm that emphasized human freedom, and became known as "the partisans of justice and unity," and the Ash'arites, who emphasized God's unknowability, and God's power over human action. The Mu'tazilite school was founded in 748 CE by Wasil bin 'Ata in Abbasid Baghdad. His followers referred to themselves as "the partisans of justice and unity" [*ashab al-'adl w'al-tawhid*].

The Mu'tazilite school remained the official theology of the Abbasid Empire until it was replaced by the Ash'arite Kalâm, a school founded by Abu Al-Hasan 'Ali Al-Ash'ari. The Ash'ariyya rejected the rationalist tenets of the Mu'tazilah in favor of a more orthodox view. They disagreed about a number of doctrinal points, including the eternity of God and eternal status of the Qur'an; God's attributes; and human free will. Both schools, however, agreed on a basic occasionalist ontology rooted in God's absolute omnipotence. We shall discuss the implications of this occasionalist ontology in Chapters 6 and 7.

By the time of Isaac Israeli, in the ninth century, Kalâm atomism was as influential as the atomism of Democritus. Ben Shammai speaks of a "Jewish Mu'tazilism," the roots of which we can trace to Judah Halevi and Abraham ibn Daud.[58] Judah Halevi (1075–1141) was clearly influenced by Kalâm atomism, and in particular by al-Ghazâlî.[59] Notably, al-Ghazâlî's attitude toward the philosophical tradition is one of harsh criticism, and yet he integrates into his thought various aspects of the same philosophical tradition that he outwardly rejects. This dialectical approach to philosophy can be found in Judah Halevi's major work *The Kuzari* as well: like al-Ghazâlî, Halevi excoriates the philosophers (and in particular the atomists) while at the same adopting their rationalist methodology. Ibn Daud, living in Toledo between 1110 and 1180, is not only the first Jewish Aristotelian, as evidenced in his

---

[56] For a detailed discussion of the history and transmission of these texts, see Davidson 1987, 86ff. and Sorabji 1983, 197ff. Some of Philoponus' relevant texts can be found in Philoponus 1987.

[57] For a history of this transmission, see Davidson 1987, 86–116. Davidson notes at least thirteen medieval discussions that draw upon Philoponus' position that the infinite cannot be traversed.

[58] See the recent synthesis discussed by Ben-Shammai 1997, 115–48.

[59] Krinis notes several lines of influence between the two. See Krinis 2013, 1–56.

philosophical work *The Exalted Faith* (*al-'Aqida al-rafi'a; Ha-Emunah ha-Ramah*), but he made extensive use of both Avicenna and al-Ghazâlî. Zonta suggests that Ibn Daud's main source for Avicenna may in fact have been al-Ghazâlî.[60] As we shall see in Chapter 6, while both the Aristotelian and atomist positions were available to Jewish thinkers, the majority sided with Aristotle against atomism.

IV.1.1 SAADIAH BEN JOSEPH GAON (882–942)

Saadiah Gaon is known as the founder of scientific activity in Judaism, and was one of the first Jewish thinkers to engage critically with Kalâm ontology. One of the pioneering creators of rabbinic literature, he was born in Pithom, in the Fayyum district of Egypt. Little is known about his life from 905 to 921. In 921, Saadiah was a leading opponent of Rabbi Aaron Ben Meir, who argued that the Jewish calendar was inaccurate and proposed to have holidays and new moons reestablished in light of his findings. The dispute resulted in a schism, wherein the Jews living in Israel and those in Babylonia celebrated Rosh Hashanah on different days. Once the schism was resolved, Saadiah composed a detailed account of the events by request. In 928, he was given the appointment of head of the Sura Academy, where he made it his personal mission to increase student enrollment and acquire funds to maintain the academy.

Saadiah was a strong opponent of Karaism, an anti-rabbinic movement within Judaism. Rabbinic law relies on circuitous arguments that often diverge from a straightforward (*peshat*) reading of Scripture. The eighth-century Babylonian sage Anan ben David rejected the rabbinic tradition and advocated a return to the text of the Bible itself. Many Babylonian Jews, surrounded by Muslims who referred to the Qur'an as the central authoritative Scripture of Islam, were compelled by Anan ben David's arguments to reject the rabbinic tradition and to seek truth in the text of the Bible itself, not in external interpretations. This anti-rabbinic movement came to be called Karaism.[61] In an ongoing effort to invalidate polemical Karaite claims, Saadiah and other rabbis of his time were devoted to validating the legitimacy of rabbinical Judaism.

Saadiah composed one of the first complete prayer books, a Hebrew dictionary for poetry (*Sefer Ha-Agron*), and a comprehensive dictionary of terms that appear only once in the Bible. In 931 CE, Saadiah wrote an Arabic commentary to the mystical work *Sefer Yeẓirah* (*The Book of Creation*). After a stormy period, Saadiah turned to philosophical writings. His major work *Kitâb al-Amânât wa-al-I'tiqâdât* (*The Book of Beliefs and Opinions*) was written in Arabic in 933 CE, and was translated into Hebrew by Judah ibn Tibbon in 1186 under the title *Sefer ha-Emunot ve-ha-De'ot*. In this work, he attempted, along Mu'tazilite lines, to establish a rational basis for the dogmas of the Law. Influenced by Islamic Kalâm epistemology and cosmology, Saadiah distinguished between the rational commandments, which in theory are discoverable by means of reason, and the traditional laws, which comprise rituals and ceremonial laws (such as the dietary laws) that are not rooted in reason. Saadiah is

---

[60] See Zonta 2000, 127–40. See also Eran 2007.   [61] Ibid.

the first Jewish philosopher to frame his discussion of ethical precepts in the context of rational apprehension. Two modern English translations of the work exist: an abridged translation by Alexander Altmann in 1945, and a complete translation by Samuel Rosenblatt in 1948.

IV.2 Jewish Neoplatonism

IV.2.1 ISAAC BEN SOLOMON ISRAELI (C. 855–C. 955)

Isaac Israeli was born in Egypt and is known as the father of Jewish Neoplatonism. He was the first writer after Philo to attempt an integration of Greek thought into Jewish tradition. He was born in Egypt and began his career as an oculist.[62] At about age fifty, he emigrated to Tunisia to study medicine. Later, he was appointed court physician and became known as one of the great physicians of the early medieval period. His works were widely circulated and translated into Arabic, Latin, and Hebrew.[63] Israeli wrote many works on medical topics, including urine, fevers, the pulse, and drugs. Israeli also appears to have been influenced by al-Kindī, a ninth-century Arab philosopher, as well as by Plotinus, since he discusses the series of emanations from the intellect as the various stages of being. Of his many surviving works, the *Book of Definitions* and the *Book of Substances* are the main sources of Israeli's philosophical ideas. His best-known work, the *Book of Definitions*, deals with definitions of philosophical, logical, and other terms.[64] In this work, he offers fifty-six definitions that invoke Aristotle's four types of inquiry: whether, what, which, and why. This work was translated into both Latin and Hebrew and became quite influential. The *Book of Substances* has survived only in incomplete fragments of the original Arabic.[65] Finally, the *Chapter on the Elements* (the *Mantua Text*) exists only in manuscript, at Mantua.[66] From this text, we learn that Israeli based his view of creation and the series of emanations on an earlier text known as *Ibn Ḥasdai's Neoplatonist*. In an important study, Altmann and Stern showed that Israeli, Ibn Ḥasdai and the long version of the *Theology of Aristotle* all shared a common but unidentified Neoplatonic source.[67] Along with Solomon Ibn Gabirol, Israeli is the major exponent of medieval Jewish Neoplatonism.

As noted above, Israeli made use of two groups of texts: the works of al-Kindī, and the vanished treatise of an unknown Neoplatonic philosopher whose work has been partially reconstructed by S. Stern. As we shall see in Chapters 6 and 8, his cosmology reflects a Neoplatonic universe in which First Matter and First Form arise from

---

[62] Altmann and Lasker 2007 dates this from 875 to 904 CE.

[63] Ibid. For the impact of Isaac and the Kairouan School upon medieval science, see Singer 1978.

[64] The entire treatise exists in Hebrew and Latin translations; only a portion survives in the original Arabic. It opens with an account of Aristotle's four types of inquiry ("whether," "which," "what," "why") and an elaboration of al-Kindi's definitions of philosophy.

[65] Discovered by A. Borisov and edited by S. M. Stern, this work seems to have been written in Arabic characters, though the extant manuscripts are in Hebrew script. See Altmann and Stern 1958, 80.

[66] Attributed to Israeli by Altmann and Stern, this text is a commentary on a work by Aristotle. The *explicit* says that the aim of the text is to explain the words of the philosopher by way of arguments and proofs. See Altmann and Stern 1958, 118.

[67] Ibid., 119.

God and give rise to Intellect; from Intellect emanates the world of souls, spheres, and finally the sublunary world with the four elements and their compounds.[68]

IV.2.2 SOLOMON IBN GABIROL (C. 1021–C. 1057/8)

Living during the height of Arabic rule in southern Spain, Solomon ibn Gabirol is a product of the rich Judaeo-Arabic interaction that colored Spanish intellectual life during the eleventh century. Gabirol represents the flourishing of Jewish intellectual life in Andalusia under the enlightened rule of the Umayyad caliphate. Much of his work was written in Arabic, and many of his ideas and poetic styles reflect Arab intellectual and stylistic components.

Of Ibn Gabirol's life we know very little. He was likely born in Malaga, Spain, in 1021/22, and spent the majority of his life in Saragossa. From his poetry, we can infer that he was orphaned at a young age and relied upon the patronage of others for his support. In his poems he describes himself as "small, ugly, and sickly, and of a disagreeable disposition"; in one poem he describes the terrors of his recurrent skin diseases. At the age of sixteen, Gabirol came under the protection of Yekutiel ben Ishâq ibn Hasân, a Jewish dignitary at the court of the king of Saragossa. But Gabirol was known for his arrogant, sometimes virulent temper, and upon the death of his patron Yekutiel he was soon forced out of Saragossa to Granada, and finally to Valencia. It is not clear exactly when Gabirol died: his near contemporaries place his death anywhere from 1054 to 1070. It is most likely, however, that he died in 1057/8 in Valencia at the age of between thirty-five and thirty-eight.

Although Gabirol himself boasted of having written over twenty books, only two such works are extant: Mekor Ḥayyim (Fountain of Life) and Tikkun Middot ha-Nefesh (On the Improvement of the Moral Qualities). At age nineteen, he wrote his great didactic poem Anak, a 400-verse compendium of Hebrew grammar. Several other works have been attributed to him over the years, but with little evidence. For example, the treatise Mibḥar Peninim (Choice of Pearls) is a collection of practical morality composed of 610 proverbs, maxims, and parables, but there is not sufficient evidence to determine whether Gabirol actually composed the work. Two other philosophical treatises mentioned by Gabirol in Mekor Ḥayyim are not extant, and it is not clear whether these works ever really existed. Many of Gabirol's hundreds of poems have been scattered throughout the Jewish liturgical and literary corpus and have not yet been fully collected. A relatively recent edition contains several volumes of Gabirol's poetry.[69]

Gabirol's poetry falls into two camps, what we might term the secular and philosophical genres. His secular output represents one of the first attempts in Hebrew literature to write a purely nonreligious poetry, unconnected to scriptural or liturgical themes. Gabirol's knowledge of the Hebrew language is remarkable, as is reflected in the poem Anak. In addition, he wrote numerous elegies, love poems, and panegyrics. However, Gabirol's major literary contribution comprises what we may

---

[68] As Jospe points out, we have a combination in this cosmology of a theory of creation ex nihilo along with emanation. See Jospe 2009, 102.

[69] Gabirol's poems are available in Yarden 1973. A new translation of selected poems appeared in Scheindlin 2016.

term his "wisdom poetry." Here his work most clearly spans the interface between poetry and philosophy. In these poems, Gabirol is obsessed with the search for knowledge, the ascent, and rediscovery of wisdom. The underlying motif of these poems, reflected in his philosophical works as well, is that our sojourn on this earth is but temporary, the purpose of which is to acquire knowledge and ultimate felicity. The mystical undercurrents are much akin to Sufi poetry, as well as to themes in earlier Kabbalistic literature.

The best-known and most elegant example of this philosophical poetry is Gabirol's masterpiece *Keter Malkhut* (*Royal Crown*), an elaborate poem that to this day forms the text for the Jewish Day of Atonement service in some communities. It comprises forty songs of unequal length, and is divided into three parts. Song nine in the first part is particularly noteworthy in that it reflects several motifs found in *Mekor Hayyim*. Part Two of the poem is cosmological in nature, and describes the sublunar elements, the throne of glory, angels, and human corporeal existence. For this cosmology, Gabirol turned to the works of the *Epistles of the Brethren of Purity* (*Rasāil ikhwān al-safā'*), and to the astronomical works of Al-Farghāni. Gabirol incorporates as well the basic elements of Ptolemy's *Planetary Hypotheses*: a series of concentric spheres around the earth, with the five planets, moon and sun, the Zodiac, and a ninth diurnal sphere that imparts motion to all the other spheres. In *Cento X*, the earth is described as an orb, with the moon and four elements encircling it. The moon excites new events in our world every month, but Gabirol cautions that "Always her own Creator's will (*razon ha-Bore'*) she heeds," noting that astrological influences are subject to divine will. After describing Jupiter, Mars, and Saturn, Gabirol turns to the Zodiac, whose signs have a power to affect sublunar events. In all these passages, Gabirol emphasizes that the influences that flow through the planets to the sublunar sphere do so at the will of their Creator, a motif that will reappear in *Mekor Hayyim*.

Gabirol's major contribution to ethical literature is his work *Tikkun Middot ha-Nefesh*. This work was written in 1045 in Saragossa, and is available in the original Arabic, as well as in a Hebrew translation of Judah ibn Tibbon dated 1167. In *Tikkun Middot ha-Nefesh*, which is primarily a treatise on practical morality, the qualities and defects of the soul are described, with particular emphasis upon the doctrine of the Aristotelian mean. This mean is supported by biblical references, as well as by quotations from Greek philosophers and Arab poets. One original element in this work is Gabirol's connection between the moral and physiological makeup of the human. That is, each of twenty personal traits is correlated to one of the five senses. Hence, the body as well as the soul must participate in the person's aspirations toward felicity. In effect, Gabirol delineates a complete parallel between the microcosm as represented by the human being and the macrocosm that is the universe. We will discuss Gabirol's ethical views in greater detail in Chapter 9.

The contrast between the microcosm and the macrocosm finds its fullest expression in Gabirol's most comprehensive philosophical work, *Mekor Hayyim* (*Fountain of Life*). This text has had a checkered history. The original work was written in Arabic, and has come down to us in a Latin translation of the twelfth century made by John of Spain, in collaboration with Dominicus Gundissalinus. Hebrew extracts were compiled in the thirteenth century by the philosopher Shem Tov ben Josef ibn

Falaquera, and then subsequently translated into Latin under the name of "Avicebrol" or "Avicebron." Latin Scholastics (including Thomas Aquinas) reading the *Fons Vitae*, as it had become known by the thirteenth century, assumed that the author of the work was a Muslim or Christian; they did not connect the work to the Spanish Jewish author. In 1857, a French scholar named S. Munk edited and translated the Hebrew extracts once again. It was while comparing the editions in Falaquera and Albert the Great that Munk noted that the appellations "Avicebron," "Avencebrol," and "Avicebrol" in fact referred to the great Jewish poet Solomon ibn Gabirol. Munk thus reintroduced Ibn Gabirol to a nineteenth-century audience.[70]

Many scholars have mentioned the lack of Jewish content in *Mekor Ḥayyim*: unlike his poetry, this work contains virtually no references to other Jewish texts, ideas, or sources. As noted above, Gabirol's primary influences appear to reside in several Neoplatonist texts that represent a variation upon standard Plotinian cosmology. The form of *Mekor Ḥayyim*, a dialogue between a teacher and his disciple, reflects a style popular in Arabic philosophical literature of the period. However, unlike Platonic dialogues in which the student contributes to the philosophical integrity of the argument, Gabirol's players function primarily as literary interlocutors without much philosophical bite. The work comprises five books of unequal length, of which the third is the most comprehensive (over 300 pages in the Latin edition).

Ibn Gabirol introduces several innovations into his Neoplatonic ontology. Like Isaac Israeli, Ibn Gabirol posits universal matter and universal form as preceding universal intellect; thus all beings are characterized by both matter and form. What this means is that Ibn Gabirol introduces both spiritual and material form, as well as spiritual and material matter. But in a sharp contrast to classical Neoplatonism, he also introduces divine will at the top of the hierarchy, and Nature near the bottom of the hierarchy.[71] A succinct summary of the work is given by Gabirol himself in his introduction:

Inasmuch as we propose to study universal matter and universal form, we must explain that whatsoever is composed of matter and form comprises two elements: composed corporeal substance and simple spiritual substance. The former further subdivides into two: corporeal matter that underlies the form of qualities; and spiritual matter which underlies corporeal form.... And so in the first treatise we shall treat universal matter & universal form; in the second we shall treat spiritual matter. This will necessitate subsequent treatises as well. In the third we shall treat the reality of simple substances; in the fourth, the search for knowledge of matter and form of simple substances; and in the fifth universal matter and form in and of themselves.[72]

Gabirol's most creative and influential contribution in *Mekor Ḥayyim* comprises his rigorous hylomorphism, according to which all substances, both physical and spiritual,

---

[70] See Rudavsky 1997; Pessin 2013; Scheindlin 2016. For earlier editions, see Ibn Gabirol 1857–9; Ibn Gabirol 1892–5; a modern Hebrew translation can be found in Ibn Gabirol 1926. "The Kingly Crown" can be found in Ibn Gabirol 1961.

[71] For an example of these many hierarchical ontologies, see Pessin 2013. Pessin describes and analyzes several different versions of Ibn Gabirol's ontological hierarchies.

[72] Ibn Gabirol 1926, *Mekor Ḥayyim* I.1. Unless otherwise noted, translations are mine.

are composed of prime matter. Gabirol's purpose is to show that all substances in the world, both spiritual and corporeal, are composed of matter and form. Unlike Aristotle, he postulates the existence of spiritual matter, which underlies incorporeal substances. Even intellects, souls, and angels are composed of matter and form. Types of matter are ordered in a hierarchy that corresponds to a criterion of simplicity: general spiritual matter; general corporeal matter; general celestial matter; general natural matter; and particular natural matter. Individual matter is associated with prime matter, which lies at the periphery of the hierarchy, thus epitomizing the very limits of being.[73] Each level of matter is coarser ontologically than its predecessor.

Gabirol's philosophical masterpiece had a mixed reception among subsequent thinkers. Unfortunately, *Mekor Ḥayyim* was not translated into Hebrew during Gabirol's lifetime, and the original Arabic text was soon lost. Possibly because Gabirol does not discuss issues close to the heart of the thirteenth century Jewish world, such as faith and reason, Jewish philosophers steeped in Aristotelianism had little interest in his work. Abraham ibn Daud attacked *Mekor Ḥayyim* on several levels: that it was aimed toward all religious faiths, and not for Jews alone; that it developed one single subject to excessive length; that it lacked scientific method; and finally, that it seduced Jews into error. However, *Mekor Ḥayyim* did influence several important Jewish Neoplatonists such as Ibn Tzaddik and Moses ibn Ezra, as well as important Kabbalistic figures such as Ibn Latif.

In contrast, Gabirol's work influenced several generations of Christian philosophers. Upon the translation of *Mekor Ḥayyim* into Latin in the twelfth century, many scholastics read and were affected by Gabirol's voluntarism, his theory of plurality of forms, and the doctrine of universal hylomorphism. Importantly, the *Fons Vitae*, as it became known to the Latin schoolmen, contained elements compatible with significant themes in Augustine and Boethius; it also complemented certain aspects of the twelfth-century Parisian "School of Chartres."[74] Franciscans such as Bonaventure and Scotus accepted a number of Gabirol's views. Most importantly, his hylomorphic ontology provided a way of explaining the difference between creatures and God by introducing the ontological distinction of spiritual matter. The doctrine of universal hylomorphism allowed scholastics to posit to angels a "spiritual matter" in order to distinguish them from God.

Gabirol's influence resonated throughout the late medieval and renaissance period. A number of important sixteenth-century Jewish and Christian Kabbalists were influenced by the more esoteric conceptions of Gabirol's cosmology. We should also mention the influence of Ibn Gabirol upon the sixteenth-century revival of Neoplatonism, in which philosophers primarily in Italy "rediscovered" the beauty of Neoplatonist metaphysics and ethics. In short, the works of Solomon ibn Gabirol, the most original medieval Jewish Neoplatonist, came to influence scholasticism under the pseudonym Avicebron, his true identity concealed as a result of his efforts to systematize the basic principles of Jewish thought without any recourse to religious dogma or belief.

---

[73] Ibn Gabirol 1926, *Mekor Ḥayyim* 5.4.   [74] McGinn 1992, 93.

IV.2.3 ABRAHAM IBN EZRA (C. 1089–1164)

Born in Tudela in c. 1089, Abraham ibn Ezra was a poet, grammarian, biblical exegete, philosopher, astronomer, astrologer, and physician. His life falls into two periods: until 1140 he lived in Cordoba and Seville in Spain where he was a friend of Ibn Tzaddik, Ibn Daud, Ibn Ezra, and Judah Halevi. The second period dates from 1140 when he left Spain for a period of extensive wandering in Lucca, Mantua, Verona, Provence, London, Narbonne, and finally Rome. It was during this period that most of his works were composed. His wanderings forced him to write in Hebrew as well as Latin, a fact that perhaps saved his works from oblivion. He died in c. 1164 in either Rome or possibly Palestine.

Ibn Ezra's ill fortune is registered in a short poem in which he claims that inasmuch as the moment of his birth coincided with a deviation of the celestial bodies from their fixed paths, he can never succeed in life—were he to be a shroud dealer, he declaims, nobody would ever die! As a result of his extreme poverty, Ibn Ezra was dependent upon sponsors for his economic support. Many of his works were commissioned by patrons, thus explaining in part the existence of so many versions of his treatises.

Ibn Ezra is best known for his Biblical commentaries, which are written in an elegant Hebrew, replete with puns and word plays. These commentaries were commenced in Rome when Ibn Ezra was already sixty-four. Ibn Ezra was the first Jewish author to interpret a significant number of biblical events in an astrological way, and to explain certain commandments as defenses against the pernicious influence of the stars. It is the science of astrology that permits knowledge of impending disaster, and thus enables humans to take appropriate precautionary measures. Recognizing that one who is born in a defective stellar configuration cannot "become like the one who was born in a perfect configuration," Ibn Ezra nevertheless avers that "man can by means of his mind mitigate his misfortune somewhat."[75] Because of his constantly alluding to "secrets" in these commentaries based on astrological doctrines, Ibn Ezra's works inspired numerous super-commentaries. Ibn Ezra himself claimed that only the individual schooled in astrology, astronomy, or mathematics will understand these commentaries properly.[76]

Although Ibn Ezra did not write any specifically philosophical works, he was strongly influenced by Ibn Gabirol, and his works contain much Neoplatonic material. For example, he accepts Ibn Gabirol's doctrine that intelligible substances are composed of matter and form, and he uses Ibn Gabirol's descriptions of God as the source from which everything flows. Ibn Ezra's theory of soul reflects Neoplatonic motifs as well. The source of the rational soul is the universal soul and immortality is understood as reunification of the rational soul with the world soul.

Whereas Ibn Ezra was one of the foremost transmitters of Arabic scientific knowledge to the West, most of his scientific works are extant in manuscript only.

---

[75] Langermann 1993, 51.

[76] See Sela 2000, 166. Perhaps the most famous commentator upon Ibn Ezra was Spinoza, who adduced "Aben Ezra, a man of enlightened intelligence and no small learning" in support of his own contention that Moses could not have written the Pentateuch. See Spinoza 2001, ch. 8.

Interestingly, almost all of his works appear in two or more versions; most scholars agree that inasmuch as Ibn Ezra was an itinerant scholar wandering from city to city, he would write new versions for each group of patrons he encountered. Sela has managed to ascertain the existence of twenty-six different treatises, representing fourteen distinct treatises in all, written mostly in Hebrew and partly in Latin.[77] The first group is devoted to teaching skills related primarily to astronomy and mathematics, as well as the use of scientific tools and instruments. The major works in this group are: *Sefer ha-Mispar* (*The Book of the Number*) designed to be a basic textbook in mathematics; *Sefer Ta'amei ha-Luḥot* (*The Book of the Reasons behind the Astronomic Tables*), a treatise written in four different versions (two in Hebrew and two in Latin) to provide astronomical and astrological knowledge to persons interested in using the astronomical tables; *Keli ha-Neḥoshet* (*The Instrument of Brass, or The Astrolabe*), a technical manual, written in three different Hebrew versions as well as a Latin version, designed to teach the astronomical and astrological uses of the astrolabe; *Sefer ha-Ibbur* (*Book of Intercalation*), written in two versions, designed to establish the Jewish calendar and explain its fundamentals; and finally, *Sefer ha-'Eḥad* (*Book on the Unit*), a short mathematical treatise devoted to the attributes of the numbers.

The second group of treatises comprises astrological works exclusively, and includes both astrological textbooks as well as a series of astrological works that deals with the various branches of astrology. Of these, the most important works include *Reshit Ḥokhma* (*Beginning of Wisdom*), a textbook written in 1148 explaining the main tenets of astrology; *Sefer ha-Te'amim* (*Book of Reasons*), a treatise also finished in 1148 devoted to the reasons for astrological concepts; and *Sefer ha-Moladot* (*Book of Nativities*), a treatise devoted to genethlialogical astrology, that is, to the problems associated with determining the criteria to choose an ascendant for the nativity, according to which the astrological houses may be calculated. In addition to these treatises, Ibn Ezra translated into Hebrew a no longer extant Arabic scientific treatise, *Ibn al-Muthannâ's Commentary on the Astronomical Tables of al-Khwârizmî*. This work includes Ibn Ezra's introductory assessment of the transmission of Hindu and Greek astronomy to the Arabic sciences.

Because Ibn Ezra was one of the first Hebrew scholars to write on scientific subjects in Hebrew, he had to invent many Hebrew terms to represent the technical terminology of Arabic. For example, he introduced terms for the center of a circle; for sine; and the diagonal of a rectangle. His own research he describes as *ḥokhmat ha-mazzalot* (science of the zodiacal signs), a term he uses often to refer to a number of branches of science: astrology, mathematics, astronomy, and regulation of the calendar. Sela has argued that Ibn Ezra's scientific treatises are all cross-referenced, suggesting that they represent a single body of texts designed to deal with the different branches of *ḥokhmat ha-mazzalot*.[78] Inasmuch as the purpose of these works was primarily to educate and introduce scientific findings to a lay audience, they serve as an excellent source for learning about scientific texts available in twelfth-century Spain.

---

[77] See Sela 2001 for extensive discussion and details regarding these treatises.   [78] Sela 2000, 163.

As noted by Sela, one of Ibn Ezra's main aims was to "convey the basic features of Ptolemaic science, astronomical as well as astrological, as it was transformed by the Arabic sciences, especially in al-Andalus."[79] Thus, for example, his best-known work *Beginning of Wisdom* functions as an introductory astrological text book and deals with the zodiac constellations and planets, their astrological characteristics, and more technical aspects of astrology. Ibn Ezra's starlist appears as a section of his work *The Astrolabe*. The list is given in the form of a paragraph, in which the coordinates are given in Hebrew alphabetic numerals, and the Arabic names are transliterated into Hebrew characters. As Goldstein has pointed out, many of the discrepancies between Ibn Ezra's star positions and those in the Greek text of the *Almagest* can be traced to the Arabic versions of the *Almagest*. In his translation of *Ibn al-Muthannâ's Commentary*, Ibn Ezra describes the early stages of astronomy among the Arabs, listing a number of prominent astronomers whose works he consulted. The Hebrew versions of Ibn al-Muthannâ's commentary have been useful for interpreting a set of canons for tables with Toledo as the meridian preserved in a Latin manuscript.[80]

According to North, Abraham ibn Ezra was the earliest scholar to record one of the seven methods for the setting up of the astrological houses.[81] This method was used, for example, by Gersonides who made use of Ibn Ezra's *Book of the World* in his prognostication of 1345. Goldstein suggests that Gersonides may have had access to this work through the paraphrase of the Provençal philosopher Levi ben Abraham ben Ḥayyim (see below) in the latter's encyclopedic work *Livyat Ḥen*.

Inasmuch as Ibn Ezra's works were widely copied in Hebrew and translated into European languages, he was responsible for the availability of much Arabic science in Hebrew and Latin. His astrological treatise *Beginning of Wisdom*, for example, was translated into French by Hagin le Juif (1273) and then into Latin (1281) by Henry Bate of Mechelen. And his work *Book of Nativities*, also translated into Latin by Bate, was published in Venice in 1484 under the title *Liber Abraham Iude de nativitatibus*. Based on these translations, Ibn Ezra was not only considered a major authority on astrology, but he helped to spread the new Hebrew astronomical literature throughout Europe.

IV.3 Two eclectic thinkers: Baḥya ibn Paquda and Judah Halevi

IV.3.1 BAḤYA IBN PAQUDA (MID-ELEVENTH CENTURY)

Baḥya ibn Paquda was an eleventh-century Jewish philosopher and rabbi who lived in Saragossa, Spain. Extremely learned, Baḥya's texts show evidence of knowledge of Arabic, Greek, and Roman science and philosophy as well as a clear grasp of traditional Jewish texts. Baḥya aligned with Neoplatonic mysticism, and may have gravitated toward asceticism. Baḥya seems to have been influenced by both Sufism and the "Pure Brethren" (*Ikhwân al-Safâ*). Sufism is the mystical movement in Islam: in order to achieve union with God, they eschewed material consumption, and developed steps by which an individual could become purified and achieve a more spiritual stage. Techniques such as incessant repetition of the name of Allah, often

---

[79] Sela 2000, 168.   [80] Goldstein 1996, 12.
[81] Ibn Ezra's elaborate astrology is described in Sela 2000; see also North 1987; 1989.

accompanied by beating of drums, music, and dance, bring the Sufi to a state of ecstasy that allows for closeness with God.[82] Jospe, however, following Vajda, Guttmann and others, claims that Baḥya, although reflecting some of these Sufi notions, is not himself a mystic. Baḥya himself is a much more eclectic thinker, drawing upon a variety of sources, including Sufism, Kalâm, Neoplatonism and the Pure Brethren as well as classical Jewish sources.

Baḥya is best known for his system of Jewish ethics, which appeared in 1040 in Arabic and was later translated into Hebrew by Judah ibn Tibbon. His major work *Sefer Torat Ḥovot ha-Levvavot* (*Guide to the Duties of the Heart*) is one of the first attempts to present ethical laws and duties espoused by Judaism in a coherent philosophical system. Baḥya describes his motivation for compiling his ethical system in the introduction of the work. It was his impression that many Jews either paid little attention to the duties of Jewish law, or paid exclusive attention to duties to be performed by the body. He was underwhelmed by the evidence that people were obeying and cultivating duties of the heart, from which his book gets its title. His primary focus is upon the tension between "the formal practices of institutional religion on the one hand, and on the other hand, inner spiritual life and pure intention."[83]

The purpose of *Duties of the Heart* is to provide a sort of instruction manual away from "duties of the limbs" [material existence] toward a more spiritual existence [duties of the heart]. The focus is upon the *intention* with which material actions, religious rituals, are performed. Baḥya hopes to wake readers from their slumber, as it were, and reinfuse ordinary, mechanical actions with spiritual meaning.

IV.3.2 JUDAH HALEVI (BEFORE 1075 TO 1141)

Judah Halevi was born at Tudela, moved to Córdoba, Lucena, Granada, Christian Toledo, and finally the Land of Israel, and along with Ibn Gabirol is considered one of the most important Hebrew poets of the middle ages. He participated in poetry contests and won at least one of them for a poem he wrote in imitation of one of Moses ibn Ezra's more complicated poems. He subsequently befriended Moses ibn Ezra, and the two remained close throughout his life. Halevi was also close friends with Abraham ibn Ezra. While in Granada, Halevi wrote close to 800 poems, including eulogies, poetical letters, wine poems, and love poems. Halevi had to leave Granada shortly after 1090 due to the arrival of the Almoravides of Africa, who conquered Muslim Spain and persecuted the Jews of Andalusia. Eventually, Halevi became overwhelmed with an urge to see the land of Israel, for in his (philosophical) view it was the "Gate of Heaven" and the only place where prophecy occurred. He thus embarked on a long and arduous journey (by way of Alexandria and Cairo) for the land of Israel in his old age. He died shortly thereafter; it is not clear whether he actually reached Israel.

Philosophically, Halevi's interests lay in defending the truth of Judaism and the essential superiority of the Jewish people. Although he is often included among the Neoplatonist thinkers, Halevi is an interestingly eclectic thinker in that he was

---

[82] See Jospe 2009, 133.   [83] Jospe 2009, 136.

influenced not only by Neoplatonism, but by Kalâm thought and Aristotelianism as well. His major philosophical work *The Kuzari* [*Kitâb al-Radd wa'l-Dalîl fi'l-Dîn al-dhalîl*], written originally in Arabic, is presented in the form of a fictional reconstruction of an actual historical event that took place between 786 and 809, during the reign of King Bulan of the Khazars [a Turkish people].[84] The king of the Khazars was on a quest for the most authentic monotheistic religion, and called together Muslim, Christian, and Jewish scholars, along with a philosopher. After asking each about their beliefs, the king was so impressed by the description of the Ḥaver (who represents the official friend or spokesperson for the Jews), that he converted his entire tribe to Judaism.

Like his predecessor Baḥya, Halevi drew upon many sources, including the Kalâm, Neoplatonism, and Aristotelianism, as well as the Islamic philosopher al-Ghazâlî. In the context of presenting the views of the other interlocutors, *The Kuzari* thus represents a trenchant critique of the various philosophical schools of his time. Although the work clearly contains Neoplatonic elements, Jospe is careful to point to the many contexts in which Halevi takes the Neoplatonic emanationist ontology to task. As Jospe notes, Halevi "rejected in principle emanation as such," and argued that it ultimately is nonsense: "these rudiments are as unacceptable to reason as they are extravagant in the face of logic. Neither do two philosophers agree on this point, unless they be disciples of the same teacher."[85] The King is not convinced by either the Christian or the Muslim; nor does he accept the views of the philosopher. Through the mouth of the king, Halevi rejects Neoplatonic views of emanation, and he denies Aristotelianism even though, like Aristotle, he thinks that truth (of Jewish doctrine) can and ought to be defended by rational means. Halevi criticizes Aristotelian science on the grounds that they failed to demonstrate their philosophical claims conclusively, arguing that "their philosophy was based on conventional assumptions which they accepted without scientific justification, and is, therefore, a 'closed system'."[86] Aristotelianism in Halevi's view does not qualify as a true scientific method, for as Halevi points out to the king, no two philosophers ever agree: "They are full of doubts, and there is no consensus of opinion between one philosopher and another."[87] Inasmuch as Halevi's work represents an interesting and instructive foil against which to gauge Maimonides' rationalism, we shall revisit his views below.

How to reconcile science and revelation? Halevi is adamant that universal scientific truth (not the error-prone science of Aristotelianism) does not, indeed cannot, contradict revelation. In fact, following a trope we have seen already in Philo, he claims that scientific truth derives from Jewish sources: philosophy was once native to Jewish-Semitic culture, from which it passed to the Greeks. Greek science and philosophy, according to the Ḥaver, belong "to the descendants of Japheth... The Greeks only received it when they became powerful, from Persia. The Persians had it from the Chaldeans. It was only then that the famous [Greek] philosophers arose."[88] Aristotle's philosophy, he claims, is "not deserving of credence," since "he had no

---

[84] Stampfer has recently argued that "while a splendid story," there is little evidence to support the claim that the Khazars converted to Judaism. See Stampfer 2013.

[85] Jospe 2009, 248; see Halevi *Kuzari* IV:25, 238–9.   [86] Jospe 2009, 238.

[87] Halevi *Kuzari* V:14, 273.   [88] Halevi *Kuzari* I:63, 53.

tradition from any reliable source at his disposal."[89] And yet, despite Halevi's dismissal of Aristotle, Jewish philosophers found much to admire in Aristotelianism, as we shall now see.

IV.4 The Aristotelian tradition

As noted above, the works of Aristotle slowly permeated both Islamic and Jewish thought. The systematic transition to Aristotelianism commenced in Andalusia with Abraham ibn Daud and Maimonides, and culminated in Southern Spain and Provence with the works of Gersonides and Crescas. Of these figures, Maimonides is clearly the most influential medieval Jewish philosopher, and we shall spend considerable time on his works. What was so attractive about this new Islamic-tinged Aristotelianism? Most important was the claim that scientific knowledge arose from empirical observation. The speculative sciences resulting from observation included physics, mathematics, and metaphysics; the practical sciences included ethics, economics, and politics. The underlying methodology of these sciences was logic, a method of demonstration developed in Aristotle's logical works. Aristotelianism also included a rejection of a system of emanation, the hylomorphism of matter of form, and a new conceptualized view of God as "thought thinking itself."[90] Aristotle designated metaphysics as the "queen of the sciences," inasmuch as it represented the study of "being qua being."

The importance of the Aristotelian influence upon Islamic and then Jewish philosophy should not be underestimated; as Samuelson notes, "Jewish Aristotelianism functions for Jewish belief as the Babylonian Talmud functions for Jewish praxis, that is, as the foundation and most critical body of literature for any contemporary discussion of the nature or character of Judaism."[91] As we turn now to the major figures writing within the shadow of Aristotelian science, we shall appreciate both the allure and threat provided by Aristotle.

IV.4.1 ABRAHAM IBN DAUD (C. 1110–80)

Abraham ibn Daud, the first Jewish Aristotelian, was a Spanish astronomer, historian, and philosopher who published works in all three areas. Born in Cordova, Spain and moving eventually to Toledo, he is best known for his *Sefer ha-Kabbalah*, a history of the Jewish people, and his philosophical work *Sefer ha-Emunah ha-Ramah* (*The Exalted Faith*). In his work on the history of the Jews, he speaks against the Karaites, Muslims, and Christians who challenge or doubt that rabbinic tradition records the revelation given to Israel at Sinai. The purpose of the work is to justify rabbinic tradition rather than simply record historical events.

Ibn Daud's philosophical work was written in Arabic in 1160 and translated twice into Hebrew, first by Samuel Motot, and then in 1391 by Solomon ibn Lavi; eleven copies of Ibn Lavi's translation survive in manuscript. Fontaine notes that Ibn Daud represents the entry of Aristotelianism into Jewish philosophy, "since he makes much more use of Aristotelian arguments and principles than his predecessors."[92]

---

[89] Halevi *Kuzari* I:65, 53.   [90] See Jospe 2009, 322; Samuelson 1997, 230.
[91] Samuelson 1997, 232.   [92] For a sustained study of Ibn Daud's work, see Fontaine 1990.

Although he is the first Jewish philosopher to apply the works of Aristotle to a religious philosophy of Judaism, his rigorous arguments have been overshadowed by those of his immediate successor Maimonides, whose work *Guide of the Perplexed* was published thirty years after Ibn Daud's own work. Further, since *The Exalted Faith* was translated quite late in the fourteenth century, it presumably had little influence on medieval philosophers who did not read Arabic.

The *Exalted Faith* is divided into two parts: the first deals with physics, and includes proofs for the existence of a prime mover, and the second deals with revealed religion. Both topics, however, turn out in Ibn Daud's mind to be one and the same, since scientific truths can be found already in sacred texts. We shall return in Chapter 3 to the details of his introduction to this work.

IV.4.2 MOSES MAIMONIDES (1138–1204)

We turn now to Maimonides, perhaps the most famous and influential Jewish philosopher of all time. Unlike most medieval Jewish philosophers, about whom very little is known, Maimonides provided future generations with ample information about himself in letters and documents; many of these documents have been preserved in part in the Cairo Geniza, a repository of discarded documents discovered over a century ago in the Ben Ezra synagogue of Fustât (Old Cairo) where Maimonides lived. From these snippets of texts, scholars have been able to reconstruct at least some details surrounding Maimonides' life. He was known by several names: his original Hebrew name Moses ben Maimon; his Latinized name Maimonides; the Hebrew acronym RaMBaM, standing for Rabbi Moses ben Maimon; his Arabic name al-Ra'is Abu 'Imran Musa ibn Maymun ibn 'Abdallah ('Ubaydallah) al-Qurtubi al-Andalusi al-Isra'ili; the honorific title "the teacher (*ha-Moreh*)"; and of course "the great eagle." Recent biographies by Kraemer and Davidson have provided us with a detailed reconstruction of Maimonides' life, drawn from Geniza fragments, letters, observations by his intellectual peers, and comments by Maimonides himself.[93]

Moses ben Maimon was born in Cordova, Spain in 1138 and died in Fustât (Old Cairo) in 1204. Cordova was at this time the capital of Andalusia (Muslim Spain) and the most affluent city in Europe. Under the Spanish Umayyads (756–1031), and in particular under the reign of enlightened Caliph 'Abd ar-Rahman III, Jews and others experienced a cultural flourishing. During this period he wrote several early books, including his *Treatise on the Art of Logic* and a primer on the calendar (*Ma'amar ha-'ibbur*).

Maimonides wrote during the height of twelfth-century Andalusian Aristotelianism. The most important names in this school were Abû Bakr ibn Bâjja (Avempace, d. 1139), Ibn Tufayl (d. 1185), and Ibn Rushd (Averroës, d. 1198). Although both Maimonides and Averroës were born in Cordova and wrote during the same time period, they never met in person. Nevertheless, Maimonides knew of Averroës' works and recommended them to his own pupil Joseph ben Judah, as well as to his translator Samuel ibn Tibbon. Scholars have noted the many similarities between

---

[93] I am very much indebted to recent biographies by Kraemer (2008b) and Davidson (2005) for details of Maimonides' life and writings. Kraemer has also included an extensive (online) bibliography in conjunction with his biography. See also Halbertal 2015; Ivry 2016; Stern 2013; Rudavsky 2010.

Maimonides and Averroës. Kraemer points out that both were descendants of venerable Andalusian families of scholars. Both were outstanding jurists and physicians, both mastered the sciences and philosophy, both embraced a naturalistic Aristotelianism, both emphasized that the law summons us to study philosophy. The writings of both Averroës and Maimonides were soon translated into Latin, and introduced Aristotelianism to the Latin scholastics.

When the Almohads invaded Andalusia and occupied Cordova in 1148, the Maimon family left Cordova, wandering from place to place in Andalusia. Maimonides and his family arrived in Fustât in 1166, after a brief stay in Morocco and then Alexandria. They settled in the Mamsûsa quarter of Fustât, a neighborhood that had both Christian and Muslim residents as well as Jews. During this period, Maimonides wrote his celebrated *Mishneh Torah*. Shortly after Maimonides' arrival in Egypt (1171–2), Saladin became sultan over Egypt and founded the Ayyûbid dynasty. Maimonides had in Fustât a patron, Al-Qâdî al-Fâdil al-Baysani (1135–1200), who was a scholar in his own right. He collected many books on Arabic thought, some of which presumably Maimonides read and studied. Maimonides' major work *The Guide of the Perplexed* was written between 1185 and 1190, followed by many of his medical works. Maimonides continued to devote himself to both the community and his intellectual needs. In a letter of 1199 written to Samuel ibn Tibbon, translator of the *Guide* from Judaeo-Arabic into Hebrew, Maimonides attests to his harried schedule:

God knows that in order to write this to you, I have escaped to a secluded spot, where people would not think to find me, sometimes leaning for support against the wall, sometimes lying down on account of my excessive weakness, for I have grown old and feeble... I attend to my patients, write prescriptions... I converse and prescribe for them while lying down from sheer fatigue, and when night falls, I am so exhausted that I can scarcely speak.[94]

Maimonides seems to have devoted himself seriously to medicine in the later years of his life, after the composition of his theological and philosophical works. Some of these medical works were translated into Hebrew and Latin, and contributed to his fame as a physician. According to his grandson David, Maimonides died on December 13, 1204 and is supposedly buried in Tiberias.

Maimonides' works fall into three broad categories: rabbinic thought (*halakha*), philosophy, and medicine. Little is known about Maimonides' educational situation or teachers. He did not consider philosophy prior to Aristotle worthy of the title of "genuine philosophy," although it is not clear what his sources of Arab Aristotelianism were. Davidson concludes that "by the age of forty [Maimonides] was thus familiar with the contours of medieval Arabic Aristotelian philosophy, he had studied other sciences, and he was well-versed in mathematics and astronomy."[95] A different story emerges when we turn to Islamic philosophers.[96] Maimonides had clear regard for the works of al-Fârâbî, Ibn Bâjja, Avicenna, and Averroës. Abu Nasr al-Fârâbî (c. 870–c. 950) was considered the "second Aristotle," because of his

---

[94] In Twersky 1972, 7.   [95] Davidson 2005, 98.

[96] For a detailed discussion of the impact of Islamic philosophy upon Maimonides, see Pines 1963; Pessin 2007; and Zonta 2007; see also Schwarz 1991.

numerous treatises and commentaries upon Aristotle's works, and he evinced a great influence in many fields of medieval Jewish philosophy, including logic, epistemology, metaphysics, ethics, politics, and jurisprudence. Al-Fârâbî is the Arabic philosopher most cited in the *Guide*, and clearly a thinker whom Maimonides read carefully and held in high esteem. We shall see that Maimonides is very much influenced by al-Fârâbî's conception of philosophy,[97] as well as by Ibn Bâjja, Ibn Sînâ, al-Ghazâlî, and Ibn Rushd. Ibn Bâjja is referred to five times in the *Guide*. Although an important philosopher in his own right, Ibn Sînâ (Avicenna) played a less obvious role in Maimonides' thought. Ibn Rushd (Averroës) represents a tantalizing case study. Maimonides held Averroës in high regard, telling Ibn Tibbon not to read Aristotle's works without the commentaries of Alexander of Aphrodisias, Themistius, and Averroës.[98] As noted above, both Averroës and Maimonides embraced a naturalistic Aristotelianism, and both emphasized the importance of philosophy. Yet scholars have yet to determine explicit evidence of Averroës' influence, if any.

How extensive was Maimonides' knowledge of Islamic Kalâm? In the *Commentary on the Mishnah*, composed when he was thirty years old, Maimonides mentions several Kalâm positions briefly and rejects them. By the time he wrote the *Guide*, in his fifties, Maimonides refers to Kalâm arguments much more extensively. Four chapters in the *Guide* are devoted to Kalâm arguments for the creation of the world and the existence of God. Maimonides distinguishes between different Kalâm schools of thought, and provides extensive details of their positions. And yet, as recent scholars have demonstrated, the accuracy of his accounts is questionable at best. This raises a tantalizing but unanswerable question, namely what sources provided Maimonides with his acquaintance of Kalâm thought? Davidson has suggested that possibly Maimonides was extrapolating what he inferred to be Kalâm principles from their proofs, rather than having actual knowledge of their texts.[99]

Maimonides began work on the *Commentary on the Mishnah* in Fez around 1161, and published it in Egypt in 1168. The Mishnah is a compendium of Jewish law compiled by Rabbi Judah the Prince (*ha-Nasi*) around 200 CE. It contains six "orders," divided into sixty-three tractates, each of which is further divided into chapters and subdivisions. This work became the basis for legal discussions in both the Babylonian and Jerusalem Talmud. Maimonides' commentary reproduced the entire text of the Mishnah with a commentary written in Judaeo-Arabic, and later translated into Hebrew. In this work, he proclaimed his aim, namely to simplify and

---

[97] Maimonides wrote to Samuel Ibn Tibbon that there was no need to study any logical texts other than those of al-Fârâbî, since "all that he wrote" was "full of wisdom" (Marx 1934–5, 379). In his *Book of Letters* and other works, al-Fârâbî, argued that religion is subordinate to philosophy, seeing the former as a tool or "handmaiden" for the latter: this theory has important repercussions for the relation between religion and philosophy. Berman has argued that Maimonides was more influenced by al-Fârâbî than was anybody else in the medieval world: that while others read al-Fârâbî, "no one else in a major work attempted to apply this theory in detail to a particular religious tradition" (Berman 1974, 155). In al-Fârâbî's view, philosophy represents the highest of the disciplines, flanked on one side by dialectic and on the other side by religion, jurisprudence, and theology. See al-Fârâbî's description of philosophy in Lerner and Mahdi (1963).

[98] Marx 1934–5, 378.

[99] For the influence of Islamic thinkers upon Maimonides, see Davidson 2005; see also Pines 1963, and Pessin 2007.

synthesize the content of the Mishnah. Three major introductions were incorporated into his commentary: a long introduction to the entire Mishnah; an introduction to the tenth chapter of tractate *Sanhedrin*, known as *Perek Ḥelek*, in which he set out the thirteen articles of faith; and a prelude to the tractate *Avot* (*Pirke Avot* or *Ethics of the Fathers*) known as *Eight Chapters* (*Shemona Perakim*) in which he set out his views on ethics.

Maimonides' major works are undoubtedly the *Mishneh Torah* and *Guide of the Perplexed*. In the years 1168–78/80, Maimonides compiled his monumental compendium of Jewish Law, known as the *Mishneh Torah* (*Repetition of the Torah*). Maimonides chose to write in the Hebrew of the Mishnah, rather than the Hebrew of the Bible, in order to reach as wide an audience as possible. To this end, he reworked many of the Talmudic passages (written in Aramaic) into an intelligible, eloquent Hebrew. His organization of the laws in this work was designed to make it easy for the student to learn the laws by memory.[100] One important philosophical section of this work is the first book *The Book of Knowledge* (*Sefer ha-Madda*), which sets forth the foundations of Jewish belief. This first book of the *Mishneh Torah* is divided into five treatises: Foundations of the Law, Ethical Qualities, Torah Study, Idolatry, and Repentance.[101] Maimonides clarifies at the start of the work that his main concern is science and the study of nature, the foundation of his restoring Judaism as a "religion of reason and enlightenment."[102]

Maimonides composed his major philosophical work *The Guide of the Perplexed* between the years of 1185 and 1190. The work is written in Judaeo-Arabic, that is, in Arabic using Hebrew letters, which was a common mode of writing for Maimonides' contemporaries. The dedicatory epistle describes the circumstances surrounding the composition of the work. Maimonides tells us that an individual named Joseph ben Judah ibn Shimon had traveled from Morocco to Egypt, hoping to study philosophy with him. Maimonides accepted Joseph as a student and the two studied together for several years (1182–84/5), focusing on astronomy, logic and philosophy. When Joseph departed (not having accomplished his full course of study), Maimonides wrote the *Guide* for him and other similar students. The *Guide* is divided into three parts. The first part deals primarily with issues associated with a philosophical conception of God: in the first fifty chapters, Maimonides offers philosophical interpretations of terms found in Scripture that attribute to God corporeality. Part Two starts with Maimonides' own arguments for the existence of God (1). He then turns to issues of philosophical cosmology (2–12), creation (13–31), and prophecy (32–48). In the final part of the *Guide*, Maimonides addresses the cluster of problems connected with theodicy and providence (8–24), moral theory and reasons for the commandments (25–50), and ultimate perfection and happiness (51–4). Many of these topics will be discussed in subsequent chapters.

---

[100]   See Kraemer 2005, 5ff. for extensive discussion of the importance of this work.

[101]   Note that al-Ghazâlî began his theological work *Revivification of the Religious Sciences* with a *Book of Knowledge* as well. Franz Rosenthal suggests that Maimonides' *Book of Knowledge* owes "its title, its being, and its place to the attitude of Muslim civilization toward knowledge." See Rosenthal 1970, 96.

[102]   Kraemer 2008, 326.

Less than ten years after the publication of the *Guide*, Maimonides' admirers asked the scholar and translator Samuel ibn Tibbon, who lived in Lunel, France, to make a translation of the work from Judaeo-Arabic into Hebrew. Ibn Tibbon studied the original work carefully, providing clear annotations, and consulting the author whenever he encountered translation difficulties. On November 30, 1204 (fourteen days before Maimonides' death in Fustât), the translation was completed and immediately disseminated throughout Provence, northern Spain, and Italy. Almost immediately, however, opposition to the work sprung up. Ibn Tibbon himself was denounced, and the work was burnt in Paris and elsewhere by Jewish legal authorities, who feared the views contained in the work. But within a century, the *Guide* emerged from the opposition even more influential than before. Numerous commentaries were written in an attempt to penetrate the depths of the work. A Latin translation was undertaken during the thirteenth century, and was read by Alexander of Hales (*d.* 1245), William of Auvergne (*d.* March 30, 1248), Albertus Magnus (*d.* 1280), and Thomas Aquinas (*d.* 1274), among others. Aquinas studied the *Guide* carefully and quoted it regularly in his discussions of creation and divine attributes.[103]

In addition to these works, Maimonides wrote a number of letters and essays. These include his famous *Epistle to Yemen*, written in 1172; the *Letter on Astrology* addressed to the rabbis of southern France; and the *Essay on Resurrection*. The *Essay on Resurrection* is the most personal of Maimonides' works, and contains a response to attacks upon his views on the afterlife and the world to come.[104] After the composition of his theological and philosophical works, Maimonides devoted himself more seriously to medicine and composed ten medical treatises between 1190 and 1204. Maimonides' most important and popular medical work was his *Medical Aphorisms* (*Fusûl Mûsâ*), a work whose purpose was to transmit Galen's ideas in

---

[103] See Rubio 2006.

[104] The attacks were precipitated by comments he had made in his *Commentary on the Mishnah* and the *Mishneh Torah* suggesting that Maimonides did not include the resurrection of bodies in his conception of the "world to come." Maimonides' opponents identified the world to come with the resurrection of the dead, whereas it appeared that Maimonides himself considered resurrection as only an ancillary step in the final process of immortality. In fact, statements in Maimonides' works give credence to this latter interpretation: in the *Commentary on the Mishnah*, his position appears to be that while resurrection of bodies of the righteous will occur at some future time, they will not live forever, but will give way to ultimate intellectual perfection in the guise of immortality of soul. A similar point is made in the *Mishneh Torah* (Tractate Hiklhot Teshubah 3.5–6). In response to this position, R. Samuel ben Eli, principal leader of the Baghadi rabbinic academy, wrote a twenty-page treatise in Arabic, in which he laid out a veiled criticism of Maimonides. Maimonides' own student Joseph ben Judah entered the controversy and clashed several times with Samuel ben Eli, ultimately sending to his teacher Maimonides a copy of Eli's attack. Maimonides' rejoinder, the *Treatise on Resurrection*, was published in 1191 in response to Rabbi Samuel ben Eli's attacks. Maimonides' tone throughout the work is acerbic, sarcastic, and bitter; the reader cannot help but note the deep anger and resentment at having to respond publicly to what he regards as a ridiculous accusation. Hartmann suggests that in a way, this treatise represents an acknowledgement of failure: the very fact that the Jewish community was determined to hold on to a notion of bodily resurrection, despite all of Maimonides' attempts to instill in them an ideal of personal immortality, was "a sign that all that he had tried to accomplish as a Jewish leader and educator might have failed." Does this essay represent, then, as Hartmann suggests, the painful acknowledgement of the ultimate futility of the philosopher's "return to the cave"? See Halkin and Hartmann 1985 for further discussion. If so, then it serves in part at least as a commentary on Maimonides' assessment of his own life and achievements. We shall have ample opportunity to explore these issues in Chapters 8 and 9.

summary form. This work was repeatedly reprinted in Hebrew, as well as in Latin translations. It consists of twenty-five chapters, each consisting of brief paragraphs, devoted to specific medical topics. It has been characterized as a medical equivalent of the *Mishneh Torah* in that it offers a summary and compendium of over ninety of Galen's works. Galen (129–?200 CE) was a prominent Greek physician and philosopher who influenced subsequent theories of general anatomy, medicine, and science.[105] The first chapter is concerned with physiognomy, the second with the four humors, etc. In the long final chapter, Maimonides presents his "doubts" regarding various of Galen's comments. In this chapter, he deals with about fifty inconsistencies found in Galen's works, and concludes with a polemic against one of Galen's religious interpolations having to do with the doctrine of creation.

IV.5 Post Maimonidean philosophy: the thirteenth century

IV.5.1 RECEPTION OF MAIMONIDES' WORKS

The complex story of the reception of Maimonides' works has been traced by many scholars.[106] Let me mention just some of the highlights of what have come to be known as the Maimonidean controversies. Not surprisingly, rabbinic leaders even before Maimonides' death were threatened by what they saw as an attack on Jewish belief. One issue had to do with anthropomorphic descriptions of God found in Scripture. We shall discuss below Maimonides' attempt to move Jews away from a literal reading of these descriptions to a more philosophically nuanced reading. A second issue had to do with resurrection of the dead, which, as we have noted above, holds tremendous theological implications for theories of retribution. Yet another issue centered on Maimonides' contention that all the commandments had rational explanations. Controversy swirled around the naturalistic doctrine of prophecy and miracles as well. These controversies mirrored similar controversies in the fourteenth-century scholastic world, during which period the Christian Church had to accommodate Church teachings with the new and somewhat threatening philosophies of Aristotle and Averroës.

The controversy over Maimonides' works commenced in the East, with an argument over the legitimacy of traditional Jewish institutions.[107] The publication of the *Mishneh Torah* enabled Jews to consult a systematic compendium of Jewish law themselves, and so, not surprisingly, the rabbinic academies were opposed to Maimonides' encroachment upon their authority, which they saw as undermining the institutional foundations of Judaism. This controversy resulted in the Gaon of Baghdad's challenge that Maimonides did not believe in the resurrection of the dead. After Maimonides wrote his *Treatise on Resurrection*, in which he pointed out that the doctrine of resurrection was already included in his thirteen articles of faith, the controversy died down.

But other controversies arose in its wake. The second stage of controversy arose in Provence and spread to northern France and Spain. Provence had an influx of both

---

[105] For details of Galen's influence, see Langermann 2008; see also Galen 1996.
[106] See recent discussions by Drews 2004; Harris 2007; Hasselhoff 2002; Twersky 1980.
[107] Drews 2004, 119.

Sephardi Jews from Andalusia who brought with them from Spain the rich traditions of Arabic philosophy, and Ashkenazi Jews from Northern France who were more interested in traditional rabbinic learning. The Ashkenazi Jews worried that the essence of Judaism was in danger of being overrun by secular learning, as epitomized by philosophy. This second stage was set off by Rabbi Solomon ben Abraham of Montpellier's ban on the study of Maimonides' philosophical works (both the *Guide* and the *Book of Knowledge*, the first book of the *Mishneh Torah*). A counter-ban was then proposed by the scholars of Lunel, which was a center of Maimonidean scholarship. We see then two opposing camps: that of Rabbi Solomon, which opposed philosophical study and in particular the allegorical interpretation of Scripture, and the scholars of Lunel who were in favor of pursuing philosophy. The thirteenth-century Jewish philosopher, Rabbi Moses ben Naḥman (Naḥmanides or Ramban, 1194–1270), tried to reconcile the two camps, but failed in his attempts. Scholars have traced these two stages of the controversy to social and political upheaval within organized Jewish society, as well as to interactions with the Christian Church during this period. The second stage of the controversy ended violently, with the anti-Maimunists bringing the Christian inquisition into the picture, resulting in the subsequent burning of Maimonides' works by the Church.[108] It is worth noting that during this same period, a similar controversy raged among scholars at the University of Paris, leading to the famous 1277 condemnations of the works of Aristotle and Averroës by Bishop Tempier. The third ban occurred around 1288/9, leading to another round of bans and counterbans. In this third stage, only the works of Greek philosophy were banned, not those of Maimonides. In fact, the study of scientific and philosophical works continued throughout this period.

Yet another area of study has centered on Maimonides' impact upon Latin scholastics, including Thomas Aquinas and Henry of Ghent. In a recent study, Hasselhoff has argued that Maimonides' influence upon thirteenth-century scholastic thought was quite extensive, encompassing "philosophy, astronomy, questions of Christian hermeneutics of the Hebrew Bible and medicine."[109] This story of Maimonides' incorporation into scholastic thought has yet to be fully documented. The most famous Jewish philosophers writing within the shadow of Maimonides include Gersonides, Crescas, and Albo, to whom we return below.

IV.5.2 LATE THIRTEENTH AND FOURTEENTH CENTURY: TRANSLATIONS
AND ENCYCLOPEDIAS

As noted by Colette Sirat, "the thirteenth century is a century of translations and of encyclopedias."[110] During the twelfth century, both Christian and Provençal Jews discovered the science that was transmitted from Spain. Provençal Jews did not read Arabic, and so relied on translators of Spanish origin, particularly the Tibbonid family, to transmit the new science. Several generations of Tibbonid translators transmitted almost the entire body of Greek science that had reached the Arabs

---

[108] Drews 2004, 127.   [109] Hasselhoff 2002, 20.   [110] Sirat 1990, 231.

during the great translation project of the ninth to eleventh centuries.[111] The authors cited included Aristotle and Plato, and their commentators, including Alexander of Aphrodisias, Themistius, al-Fârâbî, Avicenna, Ibn Bâjja, and of course Averroës. The works of Averroës, rooted in a thorough-going Aristotelian naturalism, became increasingly important during this period; Averroës' emphasis upon the eternity of the world and the lack of individual immortality after death became more prominent in Jewish works as well.

Concomitant with the translation efforts from Arabic to Hebrew, the medieval Hebrew encyclopedias of science and philosophy made their appearance in the twelfth and thirteenth centuries. The main purpose of these encyclopedias, in both the Christian and Jewish traditions, was to provide a "well-ordered, easy-to-use, comprehensive account of already existing information."[112] Hebrew encyclopedists, in particular, offered a general introduction to the sciences as well as translations and summaries of the most advanced scientific texts available. Unlike the Latin encyclopedias that served primarily as a didactic function, the Hebrew encyclopedias "were intended for a much more intellectually sophisticated readership."[113]

Early encyclopedias were written by Abraham bar Ḥiyya in the early 1200s, by Abraham Ibn Ezra, and by Levi ben Abraham of Villefranche. Levi ben Abraham of Villefranche de Conflent lived in Provence at the end of the thirteenth century (c. 1245–c. 1315). His major work Livyat Ḥen (Ornament of Grace) was a major encyclopedia, although only portions of it still survive. It was divided into six books, the first five of which discuss science and philosophy, and the sixth, faith. Sirat notes that for Levi ben Abraham, "science" is the Maimonidean-Averroist philosophy that was current at the period, "and his erudition is truly remarkable."[114] He cites almost all the authors whose texts were available in Hebrew. In part as a result of this encyclopedia, Levi ben Abraham became a target in the Second Maimonidean Controversy (1303–5); he was singled out by the Catalonian Talmudist Rabbi Solomon ben Abraham ibn Adret (known as Rashba) and other anti-Maimonidean fundamentalists for espousing anti-religious, philosophical views that threatened to undermine the fabric of Judaism.[115] Why was Levi hounded, and a ban placed against reading his work? Harvey suggests that given his professed purpose of educating the ignorant multitude, and exposing uneducated non-philosophers to philosophy, "those who were worried about the danger of philosophy had reason to be worried about Levi."[116]

Another "little work of scientific popularization" was the Ruaḥ Ḥen (Spirit of Grace) by an unknown author. This work was probably composed around 1240 in an attempt to provide useful background knowledge to readers of the Guide. Sirat notes that this short text provides us with "the level of the average man. It most probably represents the minimum scientific knowledge that everybody should possess to be

[111] Sirat 1990, 213–14.
[112] S. Harvey 2000b, 5. Much of the material in this section is drawn from the detailed studies found in S. Harvey's recent work.
[113] S. Harvey 2000b, 10.   [114] Sirat 1990, 245.   [115] See S. Harvey 2000b.
[116] S. Harvey 2000b, 211–47.

considered well-informed... even today it remains one of the best introductions to Jewish medieval philosophy."[117] Other thirteenth-century encyclopedias include Judah ben Solomon ha-Cohen's *Midrash ha-Ḥokhmah*, Shem-Tov Falaquera's *De'ot ha-Filosofim* (*The Opinions of the Philosophers*), and Gershom ben Solomon's *Sha'ar ha-Shamayim*. This latter work proved quite popular and was reproduced several times.

The thinker Isaac Albalag, a Spanish Jewish Averroist and rabbi, lived in northern Spain at the end of the thirteenth century/beginning of the fourteenth century. He translated and annotated al-Ghazâlî's *Aims of the Philosophers* (*Maqâsid al-Falâsifah*) in 1292; these annotations were collected into a separate book entitled *Sefer Tiqqun ha-De'ot* (*Book of Correction of Opinions*). In this work, Albalag presents fairly straightforward exposition with little original thought.

The two major encyclopedias were those of Falaquera and Judah ha-Cohen. Judah ha-Cohen (*c.* 1215) was born in Toledo; he moved eventually to the Holy Roman Emperor Frederick II's court in Lombardy, and it was there that he translated his encyclopedia *Midrash ha-Ḥokhmah* (*Exposition of Science*), written originally in Arabic, into Hebrew. This work is often considered to be the oldest extant Hebrew encyclopedia of science.[118] The work is divided into three parts: physical science; mathematical and astronomical sciences; and divine science. The first part begins with logic, and then physics and metaphysics; the second part is based on Euclid's *Geometry*, as well Ptolemy's *Almagest* and *Tetrabiblos* and al-Bitrûji's *Physics*. The third section, on divine science, does not quote philosophers but only traditional Jewish texts by Rashi and Ibn Ezra.[119]

Shem Tov ben Joseph Falaquera (1223/8–after 1290) was born in northern Spain or Provence. Known as one of the most prolific of the philosophical translators, his most important work is *The Opinions of the Philosophers*, one of the first Hebrew encyclopedias of science in the Middle Ages. As noted by Harvey, Falaquera "strives to teach the reader true science and instruct him in the opinions of the true philosophers about beings."[120] In the introduction, Falaquera spells out his purpose in writing the work: to bring together philosophical ideas, and to give a good Hebrew translation of philosophical doctrines. He confines himself to reporting the words of the philosophers, and does not strive for originality: "there is not a thing in this entire composition that I say of my own: rather all that I write are the words of Aristotle as explained in the commentaries of the scholar Averroës."[121] The encyclopedia is divided into two books, one on natural beings and the other on divine beings. The book on natural beings comprises discussion of Aristotle's *Physics, On the Heavens, On Generation and Corruption, Meteorology, Book of Animals, On the Soul,* and *Parva Naturalia*: in other words, what we have is a complete summary of Aristotelian science, following the overall structure of Averroës' commentaries.[122]

---

[117] Sirat 1990, 232.   [118] Fontaine 2000, 191.

[119] See Sirat 1990, 254–5 for details; see also Fontaine 2000.   [120] S. Harvey 2000b, 213.

[121] Falaquera *De'ot*, quoted in S. Harvey 2000b, 215; quoted also in Jospe 1988, 50–1.

[122] For a detailed discussion of Falaquera's use of these sources, see S. Harvey 2000b, 221–47.

IV.6 Fourteenth- and fifteenth-century reactions to Maimonideanism

IV.6.1 GERSONIDES (1288–1344)

Levi ben Gershom (Gersonides) has emerged in recent years as one of the most significant and comprehensive medieval Jewish philosophers. He has been quoted by his successors (even if only to be criticized), and, through the works of Ḥasdai Crescas, Gersonides' ideas have influenced such thinkers as Leibniz and Spinoza. Emphasizing Gersonides' "religious rationalism in Judaism," Feldman describes Gersonides as one who "has taken seriously the fact that he has reason, who believes that this faculty is God-given, and who attempts to understand God with this instrument."[123] Attempting to show that philosophy and Torah or reason and revelation are co-extensive, Gersonides is a philosophical optimist who believes that reason is fully competent to attain all the important and essential truths in religion. And yet, at the same time, perhaps no other medieval Jewish philosopher has been so maligned over the centuries as Gersonides. Indeed, his major philosophical work *Milḥamot Adonai* (*Wars of the Lord*) was called "Wars against the Lord" by one of his opponents Isaac Arama, and was depicted as a radical rejection of traditional Jewish tenets.

Gersonides left few letters and does not talk about himself in his writings, nor is his life discussed at great length by his contemporaries. Hence, what is known of his biography is sketchy at best. Gersonides was born in 1288 possibly in Bagnols, Provence, and lived for a time in Orange and Avignon. Gersonides spoke Provençal; his works, however, are all written in Hebrew, and all of his quotations from Averroës, Aristotle, and Moses Maimonides are in Hebrew as well. One of the most prolific medieval Jewish philosophers, his output covers a variety of fields, including mathematics, astronomy, philosophy, logic, biblical commentaries, and philosophical commentaries on Averroës. His *Sefer Ma'aseh Ḥoshev* (*The Work of a Counter*, 1321) is concerned with arithmetical operations and uses of a symbolic notation for numerical variables. Gersonides' major scientific contributions in astronomy are contained primarily in book 5, part 1 of *Milḥamot Adonai*, in which he reviewed and criticized astronomical theories of the day, compiled astronomical tables, and described one of his astronomical inventions. This instrument, which he named *Megalle 'amuqqot* (*Revealer of Profundities*) and which was called *Baculus Jacob* (Jacob's staff) by his Christian contemporaries, was used to measure angular distances of the heavenly bodies.[124] Although there exists no explicit evidence that Gersonides read Latin, he may have learned of the views of Ockham, Nicholas Oresme, and other scholastic thinkers in oral conversations with his Christian contemporaries.[125] There is some evidence that Gersonides had connections with high-ranking Christians during his lifetime. In 1342, Gersonides dedicated to Pope Clement VI the Latin version of a trigonometric treatise drawn from his astronomy. The astronomical parts of *Milḥamot Adonai* were translated into Latin during

---

[123] Feldman's comment is found in Gersonides *Wars* vol. 2, 54.   [124] See Feldman 1984, 21.
[125] For more discussion of Gersonides' possible interactions with other contemporary scholastics, see Sirat 1990; Klein-Braslavy 1989; and Sirat, Klein-Braslavy, and Weigers 2003.

Gersonides' lifetime, possibly at the request of the Papal court.[126] Also in 1342, Philippe de Vitry (future Bishop of Meaux) asked his advice about a mathematical theorem in connection with his own *ars nova* in musical theory.[127] One of the craters of the moon, Rabbi Levi, is named after him. Gersonides also wrote philosophical commentaries on Averroës' commentaries on Aristotle. His innovative work in logic, *Sefer ha-Heqesh ha-Yashar* (*Book of the Correct Syllogism*) (1319), examines the problems associated with Aristotle's modal logic as developed in the *Prior Analytics*, and was translated into Latin at an early date, although Gersonides' name was not attached to it.

Finally, Gersonides contributed to the corpus of philosophical biblical commentaries, including commentaries on the *Book of Job* (1325), *Song of Songs* (1326), *Ecclesiastes* (1328), *Esther* (1329), *Ruth* (1329), *Genesis* (1329), *Exodus* (1330), most of *Leviticus* (1332), and finally the remaining books of the Torah (completed in 1338). Many of them draw from the philosophical material in the *Wars*, and incorporate a "mix of philosophical material and more purely exegetical exposition."[128] Gersonides incorporates "*to'alot*" or lessons in most of his commentaries, in which he reviews and summarizes the major philosophical lessons gleaned from the particular portion of Scripture. These lessons represent practical maxims that enable one to achieve perfection, and they offer philosophical insights into three main areas: the commandments, moral and political philosophy [*hokhmah medinit*], and theoretical philosophy [*hokhmat ha-mitzvoth*], that include metaphysics and natural science. The third category is the only one in which Gersonides envisions an interaction between the biblical text and pure philosophical speculation.[129]

In 1317, Gersonides began an essay on the problem of creation. This problem, which has vexed Jewish philosophers since Philo Judaeus, had recently received elaborate treatment by Maimonides. But Gersonides was dissatisfied with Maimonides' discussion and proposed to reopen the issue. This project was soon laid aside, however, for Gersonides felt that it could not be adequately discussed without proper grounding in the issues of time, motion, and the infinite. By 1325, his manuscript had developed to include discussion not only of creation but also of immortality, divination, and prophecy. By 1328, it included a chapter on providence as well. Books 5

---

[126] Freudenthal 1996, 741; see also Feldman 2010.

[127] For discussion of Gersonides' interactions with medieval Christian scholastics, see Feldman 2010.

[128] See Eisen 1995, 4; Gersonides 1992; Eisen provides an extensive summary and analysis of several of these commentaries.

[129] Feldman suggests that the latter are the most philosophical, and that one "could collect all the [*to'alot*] dealing with the *de'ot* (beliefs) and systematize them into a coherent Jewish theology." See Feldman's discussion in Gersonides *Wars* vol. 1, 11–16. Given the wealth of philosophical material in these commentaries, and their popularity among subsequent biblical exegetes, it is surprising, Eisen notes, that they have received so little attention from scholars of Jewish philosophy. (See Eisen 1995, 4.) Touati was the first to highlight the significance of these works, but recent scholars (Green 2016; Horwitz 2006) have begun ground-breaking work in the area. Further, it is important to note that Gersonides' *Commentary on the Torah* (Gersonides 1992) has finally begun to appear in a critical edition. Why have these commentaries been neglected for so many centuries by scholars of philosophy? Eisen suggests one reason may be that the ease of reading them might have scared away scholars more used to Gersonides' terse, technical style in the *Wars*: there is the temptation to view these exegetical works as "simplistic compositions that are at best an adjunct to the more complex philosophical discussions in the Wars" (Eisen 1995). For a recent study of the reception of these commentaries, see Kellner 2013; Green 2016.

and 6 were completed, by Gersonides' own dating, by 1329, and the final work was entitled *Milḥamot Adonai*. In this work, Gersonides' aim is to integrate the teachings of Aristotle, as mediated through Averroës and Maimonides, with those of Judaism. Gersonides specifies six questions to be examined in rigorous, scholastic fashion: Is the rational soul immortal? What is the nature of prophecy? Does God know particulars? Does divine providence extend to individuals? What is the nature of astronomical bodies? Is the universe eternal or created? With each issue, Gersonides attempts to reconcile traditional Jewish beliefs with what he feels are the strongest points in Aristotle's philosophy. Although a synthesis of these systems is his ultimate goal, it turns out that philosophy often wins out at the expense of theology.

As we shall see in subsequent chapters, Gersonides' philosophical ideas went against the grain of traditional Jewish thought. Whereas his commentaries occupied a central place in Jewish theology, his philosophical work was rejected, or roundly criticized. Jewish philosophers such as Ḥasdai Crescas and Isaac Abravanel, for example, felt obliged to subject his works to lengthy criticism. Only in recent years has Gersonides received his rightful place in the history of philosophy, recognized and appreciated as an insightful, ruthlessly consistent philosopher, committed to logical argument even when it forces a reconceptualization of Jewish belief.[130]

IV.6.2 ḤASDAI CRESCAS (C. 1340–1410)

Ḥasdai Crescas was a Catalonian philosopher, rabbi, statesman, and amateur poet. As we shall see in Chapters 6 and 7, although Ḥasdai Crescas had no interest in science per se, he is embroiled in precisely the same set of scientific issues that occupied scholastic philosophers after the condemnation of 1277. Crescas was born in Barcelona and studied with the famed philosopher Nissim ben Reuben Girondi. He served as secretary of the Jewish community in Barcelona and because he soon became the local authority on Talmudic law, he was asked by King Peter IV of Aragon to adjudicate cases concerning Jews. When King John I and Queen Violante took the throne, he befriended them and enjoyed a strong social connection with the royal court. Crescas served as a Rabbi of the main royal court at Saragossa in 1389, and by 1390 he was considered the "judge of all the Jews of the Kingdom of Aragon." In 1391, responding to riots against the Jews, Crescas wrote a polemic *Sefer bittul Iqqarei ha-Noẓrim* (*The Book of the Refutation of the Principles of the Christians*) (1397–8), in which he argues that major Christian principles such as Original Sin, the Trinity, and Transubstantiation are all self-contradictory and philosophically absurd. After the turmoil, he was given the king and queen's blessing to organize the reconstruction of the destroyed communities.

Philosophically, Crescas' interests lay in distinguishing the fundamental beliefs, or religious concepts that follow analytically from his view of the nature of the Torah. His major work *Sefer 'Or Adonai* (*The Book of the Light of the Lord*), finished several months before his death in 1410, is a polemic against his two Aristotelian predecessors Maimonides and Gersonides. In this work, Crescas sought to undermine the

---

[130] Feldman (2010) makes a forceful case in his intellectual biography of Gersonides. See also Glasner 2015. See Gersonides 1329 for the original manuscript. For major editions and translation of *Wars of the Lord*, see Gersonides 1984; Gersonides 1987; Gersonides 1999.

Aristotelian cosmology and physics that pervaded the works of his predecessors. He argues that the Torah is a product of voluntary action from the Commander (Lord), and certain concepts follow from this fact undeniably. For example, a human being's power to choose must follow; for if humans were not free, there would be no sense in producing commandments for humans to obey or disobey. The non-fundamental obligations are those that must be learned empirically, according to Crescas. For example, that the soul should survive death does not follow from the understanding of the bare essential nature of the Torah.

In an attempt to weaken Aristotle's hold upon Jewish philosophy, and to uphold the basic dogmas of Judaism, Crescas subjects Aristotle's physics and metaphysics to a trenchant critique. Crescas rejects Aristotle's theory of place and argues that place is prior to bodies: in contradistinction to Aristotle's conception of place, space for Crescas is not a mere relationship of bodies but is the "interval between the limits of that which it surrounds."[131] Space is seen by Crescas as an infinite continuum ready to receive matter. Because this place or extension of bodies is identified with space, there is no contradiction in postulating the existence of space not filled with body, i.e., the vacuum.[132] Crescas, in fact, assumes that place is identical with the void, on the grounds that "place must be equal to the whole of its occupant as well as to [the sum of] its parts."[133]

Further, as we shall see in greater detail in Chapter 8, Crescas rejects Aristotle's theory of time, arguing that "the correct definition of time is that it is the measure of the continuity of motion or of rest between two instants." By *hitdabequt* Crescas means to emphasize that time is not to be identified with physical motion or bodies, but with the duration of the life of the thinking soul. Time is "indeed measured by both motion and rest, because it is our conception (*ziyurenu*) of the measure of their continuity that is time." On this basis, Crescas concludes that "the existence of time is only in the soul."[134] It is because humans have a mental conception of this measure that time even exists. The continuity of time depends only upon a thinking mind, and is indefinite, becoming definite only by being measured by motion. Were we not to conceive of it, there would be no time. It is in this context that Crescas comes closest to reflecting his near scholastic contemporaries Peter Aureol and William Ockham, both of whom develop a subjective theory of time.

The *Light* contains as well a theory of physical determinism. Crescas lists six fundamental doctrines: God's knowledge of particulars, Providence, God's power, prophecy, human choice, and the purposefulness of the Torah. Against Gersonides, he affirms God's knowledge of future contingents, even those determined by human choice. He then argues that human freedom is only apparent and not genuine: humans think they are free because they are ignorant of the causes of their choices. Human responsibility for action lies not in the actual performance of the action, but rather in the agent's acceptance of an action as its own. The feeling of joy an agent

---

[131] Crescas *Light* I.2, in Wolfson, H. A. 1929, 195.
[132] See Wolfson's discussion in 1929, 38–69.
[133] Crescas *Light* I.2, in Wolfson, H. A. 1929, 199.
[134] Crescas *Light*, prop. 15, in Wolfson, H. A. 1929, 289.

feels at acquiescing to certain actions, e.g., fulfilling the commandments, provides its own reward. So too, God experiences joy in giving of himself to the world.

Many scholars have tried to trace the formative influences upon Crescas' doctrine of will. In his study of Crescas' *Sermon on the Passover*, Ravitsky has argued that Crescas' discussion of will appears to reflect a connection to Latin scholasticism in its acceptance of Scotist ideas regarding the moral and religious primacy of the will. After noting important similarities and differences between Aquinas' and Crescas' conceptions of belief, Ravitsky turns to a comparison of Scotus and Crescas, arguing that both philosophers reject their predecessors' insistence upon an intellectualist conception belief which leads to ultimate felicity, and replace it with a conception of belief based on the primacy of will.[135]

Harvey suggests that Crescas' work was "perhaps connected in some way with the pioneering work in natural science being conducted at the University of Paris."[136] More specifically, Harvey has compared the works of the two contemporaries Nicholas Oresme and Crescas, arguing that they are the two most important philosophers representing the new physics. Working in Pamplona in the 1330s, both argue for the existence of many worlds; both claim that many worlds do not imply existence of more than one God; both argue that generation and corruption in the sublunary world is evidence for successive worlds. Crescas himself describes his analysis and critique of Aristotelian science as having "no small benefit for this science."[137] In fact, it can be argued that Crescas' critique of Aristotle helped lay the groundwork for the abandonment of Aristotelian science in subsequent centuries.

IV.6.3 JOSEPH ALBO (FL. FIFTEENTH CENTURY)

Born in the Crown of Aragon, Albo studied as a youth with Ḥasdai Crescas of Saragossa.[138] He moved to Soria around the time that Daroca was destroyed. He was famed as the representative for Daroca in the famous Jewish–Christian debates at Tortosa and San-Mateo from 1413 to 1414. In his major philosophical treatise *Sefer ha-Ikkarim* (*Book of Principles*), Albo addresses the following religious dogmas: God's existence, divine revelation, and punishment and reward. He discusses God's unity, incorporeality, atemporality, and perfection. In addition to arguing for the divine attributes, Albo takes a critical look at Maimonides' proofs for God's existence.

IV.7 Prelude to the early modern period

IV.7.1 ISAAC ABRAVANEL (1437–1508) AND JUDAH ABRAVANEL (C. 1460 TO AFTER 1523)

Two final sixteenth-century figures, to whom we return in Chapter 9, are Isaac Abravanel (also Abarbanel, Abarvanel, or Abrabanel), and his son Judah Abravanel. Isaac Abravanel is best known for his philosophical work *Mifalot Elohim* (*Wonders of God*). As Manekin points out, Isaac Abravanel's attacks upon the Jewish Aristotelians display a fierce "impatience with the naturalism and hyper-rationalism of these

---

[135] Ravitzky 1981–2, 54–60.   [136] Harvey 1998. See also Harvey, W. 2007; 2010.
[137] Crescas *Light* I, prop. I.2, in Wolfson, H. A. 1929, 180.   [138] For details, see Ehrlich 2016.

Jewish philosophers that one finds in Christian attacks on the Latin Averroists."[139] Despite his participation in the world of Renaissance humanism, Isaac Abravanel's conservative philosophical thought "remains medieval in conception."[140]

Writing at the height of the Renaissance in Italy, Judah Abravanel (better known as Leone Ebreo) is best known for his work the *Dialoghi di Amore* (*Dialogues of Love*), which was written possibly in roughly 1511–12. Judah was born in Lisbon and spent much of his youth studying under his father. He was friendly with scholars of the Platonic Academy in Florence, and served as the physician to the Spanish viceroy, Don Gonsalvo de Córdoba. The work was written in Italian as an extended dialogue between two courtiers Philo and Sophia who cover practically every philosophical topic of the era, but most notably the nature of love. In the work, Abravanel constructs an allegory between the two Jewish courtiers, Philo and Sophia, in order to illustrate the importance of the philosophical love of God.[141] *Dialoghi di Amore* represents an excellent example of the fusion of Hebraic thought with Ficino's revival of Greek philosophy.

IV.7.2 JOSEPH SOLOMON DELMEDIGO (1591–1655)

By the early seventeenth century, Jewish thinkers were interacting even more fully with their intellectual peers, and were fully absorbing the scientific advances in astronomy, mechanics, optics, and mathematics. Jewish astronomers such as David Gans (1541–1613) and Joseph Solomon Delmedigo were thoroughly conversant with developments in the scholastic world, and sought to introduce Jews to these exciting advances. Delmedigo, known also as "Yashar of Candia," is a case in point. Having studied under Galileo, he, like his mentor, recognized the challenge of the new Copernican astronomy and tried to understand the natural world outside the framework of Aristotelian physics.[142] His major work *Elim* was published in 1629 in Amsterdam, just four years before Galileo's trial. The very style of *Elim* is reminiscent of Galileo's dialogues.[143] Delmedigo places in the mouth of Moshe Metz a thorough critique of the philosophical foundations of the old astronomy.[144] As Barzilay puts it, "in no other part of Yashar's writings does one come across such an unprecedented, all-out assault on the basic concepts of ancient and medieval metaphysics, in general, and astronomy, in particular, as in this relatively short tract."[145]

In *Elim*, Delmedigo discusses in great detail the scientific theories of Kepler, Tycho Brahe, Copernicus as well as Galileo, and he describes the "strange astronomy," as well as the dangers inherent in this new astronomy, which challenged the reigning metaphysics. Galileo introduced Delmedigo to the Copernican system, which Delmedigo

---

[139] See Manekin in Frank, Leaman, and Manekin 2000, 265. See Isaac Abravanel 1988.

[140] Manekin in Frank, Leaman, and Manekin 2000, 265.

[141] Judah Abravanel 2009. See Tirosh-Rothschild 1997, 522ff. for details of the dialogue.

[142] See Ruderman 1995, 134. Ruderman himself does not offer a study of *Sefer Elim*, choosing to concentrate instead upon the *Matzref la-Hokhman*, a defense of Kabbalah, and *Mikhtav Ahuz*, a condemnation of Kabbalistic thought.

[143] With respect to the style of *Sefer Elim*, Ruderman notes the similarity to Galileo's dialogues. Like Galileo, Delmedigo's works propose a new direction, a questioning of authority, as well as an enthusiastic confidence in the new sciences. See Ruderman 1995.

[144] Delmedigo *Sefer Elim* 48–62, esp. 54ff.   [145] Barzilay 1974, 153.

praises, although he is careful never to abandon Ptolemy totally.[146] Both Galileo and his Jewish disciple sought to understand the natural world outside the framework of Aristotelian physics, notwithstanding their strong indebtedness to it in shaping their conceptual discourse.[147]

IV.7.3 BARUCH SPINOZA (1632–77)

We end this whirlwind tour of major figures in medieval Jewish philosophy with Spinoza who, contending with Maimonides for the title of most influential Jewish philosopher of all time, is also one of the most celebrated early modern philosophers. Baruch (Benedict) Spinoza was born in Amsterdam in a Marrano family from Portugal.[148] Spinoza attended the Talmud Torah school in Amsterdam up through at least the fourth grade (roughly age fourteen) and presumably excelled in his studies in Jewish law (halakha) and Hebrew. That Spinoza read works in Jewish philosophy, including medieval Jewish commentaries, is undeniable. From the list of books in Spinoza's estate, we know that he owned a number of Jewish philosophical texts, including works of Maimonides, Abravanel, and Delmedigo.[149] From this listing, we can assume that Spinoza was at least aware, if not already reading, such works as Maimonides' Guide for the Perplexed, Crescas' Light of the Lord, Abravanel's Dialoghi di Amore, and works by Delmedigo. Crescas' influence upon Spinoza is undeniable, and he is one of the few Jewish philosophers mentioned by name by Spinoza. In one of his famous letters (Letter 12), Spinoza refers to Crescas as "a certain Jew, called Rab Ghasdaj," referring to Crescas' argument for God's existence. Crescas' main work adumbrates many of the themes found in Spinoza's work. For example, Crescas and Spinoza both reject the view of infinite extension being made

---

[146] Delmedigo Sefer Elim, 301; See Levine 1983, 208–9. Delmedigo most admired Tycho Brahe and Kepler; he praises the precision of his instruments in Elim, 317–19; 432; he calls Kepler the "greatest mathematician of our time" in Elim 300; and draws attention to his studies. See also Delmedigo Sefer Elim 1864, 300, 304, 315.

[147] Ruderman 1995, 134 Perhaps nowhere else do we find more disagreement over how to read Delmedigo. Consider, for example, Barzilay (1974) who argued that while Delmedigo embraced the new views, his major efforts nevertheless centered on Ptolemy. "We should however stress the new ideas and the new method he so amply and strongly displays. Though in details and specifics he still leans on the Ancients, notably Aristotle and Ptolemy, he is completely modern in his general view of the heavens and the universe at large. He assimilated not only Copernicus' heliocentric view, but the more advanced astronomical notions of the post-Copernican era as well. He is acquainted with the researches of Bruno … the planetary laws of Kepler, and finally, the new celestial discoveries by Galileo." And so, while Delmedigo is portrayed as being unoriginal in scope, Barzilay concludes that his studies are impressive "by their scope and versatility. He mastered not only ancient and modern astronomy, but also adopted, for his own independent studies, the new methods of scientific observation and experimentation that were coming into use with such astounding results" (Barzilay 1974, 166). Barzilay claims that Delmedigo often embraces "multiple and often contradictory points of view." He is attracted both by Aristotle's logic and naturalism, but at the same time by Platonism and mysticism. "This eclecticism runs through almost every subject of his speculations, leaving the reader perplexed as to which views he is ultimately committed."

[148] Spinoza's family, along with other Marranos in the Portuguese community in Amsterdam, fled from the Portuguese Inquisition and resettled in the Netherlands, which was much more hospitable toward Jews. The term Marrano refers to these religious refugees many of whom continued to practice their Judaism secretly.

[149] See Freudenthal 1899 for details of Spinoza's life and library. See also Freudenthal 1904; Adler 2008.

up of measurable parts; both hold matter to be eternal, the act of creation consisting in the ordering of matter; the material world participates in the Divine nature. One of the most striking aspects of Spinoza's ontology is the doctrine of infinite extension. Wolfson has already noted that Spinoza's discussion in *Letter 12* of the indivisibility of infinite extension involves many details that reflect Crescas' own discussion in *Light*. Both Crescas and Spinoza establish the existence of an infinite by positing an incorporeal quantity. What Crescas calls incorporeal extension or vacuum logically corresponds to what Spinoza calls extended substance or the attribute extension; what Crescas calls corporeal extension corresponds to Spinoza's particular modes of extension.[150]

Scholars have argued over whether any of these works might have contributed to Spinoza's ultimate apostasy. Gebhart, for example has argued that it was Abravanel's book that inspired Spinoza to leave the synagogue.[151] Nadler maintains that it was Spinoza's denial of personal immortality, a doctrine discussed extensively in Jewish thought, that played the key role in his excommunication. Jonathan Israel, on the other hand, has argued that it was Spinoza's public repudiation of the fundamentals of Rabbinic Judaism that led to the excommunication.[152] According to Israel, the individual most likely to have guided the young Spinoza in a heretical and radical direction was his Latin master Franciscus van den Ende.

In any event, by 1656, Spinoza was excommunicated via the writ of *ḥerem* by Amsterdam's Sephardic community; this excommunication was never rescinded. While this event took place prior to the publication of Spinoza's works, Nadler has suggested that the excommunication was a result of Spinoza's radical views.[153] For instance, Spinoza rejects central religious notions such as the immortality of the soul, a providential God, and human free will (as it is typically construed as standing outside of nature). He held that adequate understanding of God's nature was possible for humans. One of the most distinctive aspects of his philosopy was Spinoza's pantheism: the universe contains only one substance, which is infinite, uncaused, and necessarily exists. All that exists is in God and God is the underlying substance that sustains all that exists. All particular, individual things are "affections of God's attributes, or modes by which God's attributes are expressed in a certain and determinate way."[154] As an ethical egoist, he thought it was right for each of us to pursue the path that was in our best interest; it just so happens that the best path for each of us is this rational understanding of God. While he was still quite spiritual, Spinoza's views diverged from Judaism, and he left Amsterdam a few years after being excommunicated. He later lived in Rijnsburg, Voorburg, and finally, The Hague, carrying on correspondences with major Western philosophers of the day. His major works include the *Ethics; Treatise on the Emendation of the Intellect; Short Treatise on God, Man and His Well-Being; On Descartes' Principles of Philosophy;* and *Theological-Political Treatise, Political Treatise.* As we shall see in greater detail in subsequent chapters, Spinoza thus represents the bridge between late medieval and early modern philosophy.

---

[150] See Wolfson 1934, I, 265; Rudavsky 2001.   [151] See Nadler 2001.
[152] See Israel 1985, 162–74.   [153] See Nadler 2001.   [154] Spinoza *Ethics* I. 25 corollary.

3

On Achieving Truth
Science, Philosophy, and Faith

I Introduction

Throughout the history of Jewish thought, Jewish philosophers have addressed theoretical issues against the backdrop of their intellectual neighbors: the works of Maimonides incorporate the theories of his Islamic peers; Crescas and Albo reflect influences of Christian scholasticism; and sixteenth-century thinkers evince the effects of the rise of the "new science." This cultural interaction affected interpretations of Scripture as well. Already in the first century CE, the philosopher Philo Judaeus incorporated Neopythagorean and Neoplatonic elements into his reading of Scripture, attempting to show, for example, that the account of creation in *Genesis* was compatible with the scientific views of late Greek cosmologists. So too, Maimonides presents a view of both creation and time that attempts to harmonize a biblical account of creation with the theories propounded by Plato and Aristotle. Both Crescas and Albo reject Aristotelian metaphysics and physics; their interpretations of *Genesis* reflect an alternative theory of temporality that does not depend upon Aristotelian constraints.

Many of the philosophical works in this book give eloquent testimony to the tensions apparent in trying to reconcile traditional Jewish beliefs with the methods and content of philosophical speculation. Often these philosophical ideas and methods conflict with the views found in Scripture. Take for example the doctrine of creation: while *Genesis* portrays God as having created the world at an initial instant in time, Aristotle and Plato both postulate an eternal world in which matter has always existed. Or consider the underpinnings of morality—do our notions of good and evil depend upon God's command, or is there a rational basis for morality independent of revelation? Finally, consider the process by which Judaeo-Christian faiths have made their peace with heliocentric cosmology, a doctrine originally regarded as a heretical claim. For many religious thinkers, heliocentrism is diametrically opposed to the literal meaning of the Scriptures. Take for example Joshua's commanding the sun to stand still at Gibeon (*Joshua* 10:11–12); the very picture of the sun's normally moving around a stationary Earth contravenes the heliocentric picture. If the Bible describes the sun as revolving around the earth, that description, according to Jewish thinkers, must accord with reality. How Jewish thinkers in the post-Copernican universe grappled with a heliocentric cosmology is a separate question, but it clearly exemplifies the challenges wrought by a scientific theory upon maintaining a literal reading of Scripture.[1]

It is worth pointing out that these challenges have certainly not disappeared in our own era. Jeremy Brown, for example, has described the contemporary ultra-Orthodox world as one that subscribes to a rejection of knowledge that stands at odds with Judaic texts; in this community, study is limited to the Talmud and its commentaries, and university attendance is forbidden. For the ultra-Orthodox, Brown argues, "there can be no conflict between science and Jewish teachings, because traditional Torah teachings always trump other sources of knowledge."[2] And so the challenges of reconciling Judaism with the constraints of a scientific world view continue to our own day.

As we shall see in subsequent chapters, many of our thinkers regularly incorporate ideas from Greek and Islamic philosophy, science, and logic, and present an eclectic synthesis of Judaic and philosophical materials. But what is "science" and to what does the term refer? Recent scholars have noted the ambiguity of the term "science," that did not commonly refer to what we now consider to be science until the middle of the nineteenth century.[3] In earlier centuries, what we now call a *scientist* would have been thought of as a *natural philosopher*, and science broadly construed, following the Aristotelian model, was considered *natural philosophy*. Ancient and medieval philosophers up until Newton, Kepler, and Galileo thought of themselves as doing "natural philosophy," as articulated in Aristotle's scientific works and developed throughout the medieval period. The very notion of doing "science" has thus changed over the centuries: the methods, subject matters, and goals of science in the twentieth century have changed drastically from those of the fourteenth, and certainly the third century BCE. Consider for example that astrology and alchemy were regarded as legitimate scientific studies in the fourteenth century, but certainly not in modern times.

Natural philosophy designates a group of disciplines that includes, among other things, physics, chemistry/alchemy, biology, and physiology. Aristotle defined its domain as covering those entities that are independent of us and undergo change.[4] Thirteenth-century natural philosophy was rooted in Aristotle's conception of science, expressed in the *Prior* and *Posterior Analytics* as well as the *Physics*. For Aristotle, science or *episteme* is based upon demonstrative reasoning and takes the form of a syllogism. Aristotle distinguished further between metaphysics and physics, the latter being associated with natural philosophy. During the medieval period, Aristotelianism was constitutive of natural philosophy: it provided the problems that natural philosophy dealt with, the means of solving them, and the criteria for what counted as a satisfactory explanation.[5] By the twelfth century, the works of Aristotle

---

[1] For many examples of such attempts to reconcile Copernican thought with Scripture, see Brown 2013, 3–5. The Joshua example is discussed in Rudavsky 2001. We will return to the import of this example in Chapter 8, in the context of miracles.

[2] See Brown 2013, 256; Gaukroger 2006.

[3] See Tirosh-Samuelson 2011; Levy 1987; Gaukroger 2006.

[4] See Gaukroger's detailed description (2006) of the development of science in the ancient and early modern period.

[5] See Gaukroger 2006, 48.

were being translated into Latin for the first time; commentaries began to be produced at the University of Salerno, and Aristotle's works became available to theologians and philosophers at Paris by the beginning of the thirteenth century. Hava Tirosh-Samuelson notes that, "Judaism's absorption of Aristotelian science, which was quite different from the original Aristotle, began in earnest only in the twelfth century."[6] By the time of Ibn Daud and Maimonides, Aristotelian natural philosophy was fast becoming the ruling system and largely replaced Platonic and Pythagorean strands.[7]

But what were the theological benefits of Aristotelianism? Why did Albertus Magnus, Aquinas, Averroës, Maimonides, and their followers gravitate toward a philosophy that was clearly at odds with theological beliefs? Steven Gaukroger suggests that with the introduction of Aristotle's texts in the West, there came the realization that, "there may be more than one legitimate way of dealing with certain basic questions...and that different ways of arriving at a conclusion on a question might generate different conclusions."[8] Averroës' double-truth theory, namely that theology and Aristotelian natural philosophy were each autonomous disciplines that could generate conflicting and irreconcilable doctrines, gave rise to the notion that there could be in fact "different truth statements" about such topics as immortality of the soul, eternity of the world, miracles, etc. It is this conception of philosophy and its role vis à vis faith that was condemned in 1277 by Bishop Tempier in Paris. What was at issue was the doctrine of "two truths," namely the notion of two completely different kinds of enterprise, which engage some of the same questions, but in completely different ways. As Gaukroger puts it, the real threat lies not so much in conflicting discourses, but rather in "the emergence of parallel discourses with different aims and concerns."[9] The Islamic philosophers Avicenna and Averroës, the Jewish philosophers Ibn Daud, Maimonides, and Gersonides, and the Christian scholastics Albertus Magnus and Aquinas, all attempted to reconstruct a unified system that accommodated both theological and natural-philosophical considerations in the wake of the introduction of Aristotelian natural philosophy and metaphysics.[10] Our major quest in this work is to determine the extent to which this reconstruction in the Jewish domain is successful.

In this chapter, we focus on the epistemological methods introduced by our major figures in grappling with these tensions between Athens and Jerusalem, between the domains of faith and reason, between Judaism and science broadly conceived. Not surprisingly, these methods are often stated explicitly in the introductions and prefaces to their major works. And so in a way, this chapter provides an "Introduction

---

[6] Tirosh-Samuelson 2011, 478.

[7] But this does not mean that Platonism disappears totally. Tirosh-Samuelson traces the enduring influence of Platonism in medieval Jewish kabbalistic texts. As she notes, the difference between the two is: for Jewish Aristotelians, science meant a causal explanation of the physical world on the basis of sensory perception and observation; while for Jewish Platonists (primarily kabbalists) the physical world was only a metaphor of physical reality and so not representative of true scientific research. See Tirosh-Samuelson 2011, 498.

[8] Gaukroger 2006, 68.   [9] Gaukroger 2006, 70.

[10] Gaukroger's work focuses on the Christian philosophers primarily, but his analysis applies as well to both Islamic and Jewish thinkers.

to Introductions." We start with the influence of Aristotle's logic and natural philosophy upon Jewish thought, and then turn to the difficulties of incorporating a largely Aristotelian method and ontology into a world view shaped by rabbinic texts.

II The Methodological Influence of Aristotle: Demonstration and Natural Philosophy

One way of getting a handle on these issues is to examine Aristotle's paradigm of scientific knowledge, which is developed in three of his works: *The Posterior Analytics*, devoted to demonstration; the *Topics* to dialectic; and the *On Sophistical Refutations* to sophistic argument. In the *Posterior Analytics*, Aristotle specifies the kind of "showing" that would qualify as "science," or knowledge in the fullest sense of *episteme*. He weaves together the three meanings of "showing" (*apodeixis*), which include proving, explaining, and teaching, into an account of demonstration. According to Aristotle, in order for knowledge to qualify as fully scientific, it must satisfy all three goals.[11] Aristotle distinguishes further between demonstration and dialectic, arguing that only demonstration leads to scientific knowledge. "By demonstration (*apodeixis*) I mean a syllogism productive of scientific knowledge (*syllogismos epistemonikos*), a syllogism, that is, the grasp of which is *eo ipso* such knowledge."[12] According to Aristotle, demonstration differs from other forms of knowledge on the basis of its premises, which must be true, primary and indemonstrable, immediate, better known than the conclusions following them, and causes of the conclusions.[13] The premises in demonstration answer the question "why" and represent the highest sort of scientific knowledge. Dialectic is related to demonstration, but is less certain. It is important in establishing the basic premises of demonstration, in refuting false claims to knowledge, and for establishing correct opinions for questions for which no demonstrative knowledge exists.

This emphasis upon both demonstration and rational argument appears in early Jewish texts. Take for example, Saadiah Gaon's attempts to grapple with the roots of knowledge. In his introduction to *The Book of Beliefs and Opinions*, Saadiah distinguishes four sources of reliable knowledge: sensation, reason or *nous*, logical inference, and reliable tradition. Sense knowledge is based on empirical contingents and is posited as the basis for all other knowledge forms, which are rooted in this indubitable epistemic foundation. Reason represents the faculty of immediate, intuitive knowledge by means of which we apprehend self-evident axioms of reason. Reason, Saadiah tells us, emanates ultimately from God, resulting in an innatist theory according to which ideas are "implanted" in the mind—the word "implanted" connotes a source for knowledge that lies outside the realm of human consciousness. In chapter II.13, for example, Saadiah asks how it is possible to establish the concept of God in our minds if we have never seen God, and responds that, "it is done in the same manner in which such notions arise in them as the approbation of the truth and the disapproval of lying, although these matters are not subject to the perception of

---

[11] See McMullin 1978, 213.   [12] Aristotle *Posterior Analytics* 1.2.71b 17–19.
[13] Aristotle *Topics* 1.1.100a 27–9.

any of our senses."[14] In a similar manner, we are able to "recognize" a violation of the law of non-contradiction, even though it is not based on the senses.

In contradistinction to reason, reliable tradition is not universal, but is common to "the community of monotheists." If however, reason, with the help of this outside source, enables humans to determine both the self-evident axioms and necessary principles of thought, why do we even need tradition? Saadiah relegates to tradition two roles: first, tradition enables us to determine the particulars necessary for observing the more general rational precepts; and second, tradition also speeds up the rather tedious process of discovering these rational principles. Thus while reason allows one a limited amount of epistemic authority, tradition with the aid of revelation enables us to achieve salvation. As Jospe points out, what is known in revelation is rational, and in principle is identical to the truth arrived at by rational investigation. Revelation permits us to access truth we could arrive at rationally after a long process.[15] As we shall see in Chapter 9, Saadiah applies these epistemological distinctions to his discussion of moral obligation.

In a similar vein, Aristotelian demonstration reappears throughout Maimonides' corpus as a way of distinguishing between true scientific knowledge and lesser forms of knowing. As Joel Kraemer notes, "demonstrative reasoning was Maimonides' ultimate touchstone of truth."[16] In chapter 8 of his Treatise on the Art of Logic, Maimonides enumerates the four kinds of premises upon which arguments are based: sense percepts; first intelligibles or axioms; generally agreed upon opinions; and opinions received through tradition. He then goes on to argue that, in contradistinction to sense perceptions, conventions, and traditions, only demonstrative arguments or syllogisms based on "first intelligibles" are productive of scientific knowledge; these must rest on premises that are true and available to everybody. Maimonides here defines a demonstrative syllogism as one whose premises are certain.[17]

This notion of demonstration plays a prominent role in a number of contexts in the Guide. There are numerous examples in the Guide of what can be demonstrated, e.g., the existence, unity, and incorporeality of God.[18] Maimonides agrees with

---

[14] Saadiah Gaon 1972, Beliefs II.13, 131. Unless otherwise noted, references will be to this text; do see Saadiah 1948 as well though.

[15] Jospe 2009, 59.   [16] Kraemer 2008, 12.

[17] We have seen that demonstrative arguments differ from other types of syllogistic arguments by their premises, which function as the "causes" of their conclusions. What does Aristotle mean by saying that premises are "causes" of their conclusions? In Posterior Analytics 1.2 70b 30–1, Aristotle maintains that in order to have demonstrative scientific knowledge of something, one must first know its causes: we "only understand when we know the explanation" and knowledge is based on this understanding. Hence, demonstrations furnish an explanation of the demonstrated proposition: they are "demonstrations of the reason why" (propter quid), as opposed to syllogistic deductions of the second kind, which explain only that the conclusion is true and not why it is true (demonstration quia). Maimonides himself did not draw this distinction, and he uses the term demonstration (burhan) in a number of ways; but as Kraemer notes, Maimonides specifically states in his Treatise on the Art of Logic that he was omitting scientific demonstration from his discussion. The difference between demonstrative and non-demonstrative (dialectical) premises in Maimonides' work reflects Aristotle's distinction between scientific and nonscientific thought. In fact, however, recent scholars have noted that in actual practice, dialectical arguments hold for Aristotle at least as (if not more) prominent a role in scientific discourse. So too, argue Maimonides' scholars, it should be noted that Maimonides in fact accords great weight to dialectical arguments.

[18] See Maimonides Guide 1.1; 1.18; 11.1.

Aristotle that demonstrative arguments are not subject to disagreement: "For in all things whose true reality is known through demonstration there is no tug of war [disagreement] and no refusal to accept a thing proven."[19] Anticipating Galileo's claim that truth cannot contradict truth, Maimonides characterizes demonstrative argument as the ultimate criterion for scientific and philosophical truth. In cases where demonstration is not possible, Maimonides is careful to maintain that, "the two contrary opinions with regard to the matter in question should be posited as hypothesis and it should be seen what doubts attach to each of them: the one to which fewer doubts attach should be believed."[20]

Turning now to the parameters of scholastic logic and science in post-Maimonidean Jewish philosophy, we must note several historiographical issues. First, we must be careful to distinguish by area as well as by period. Aristotelian logic became most prominent in the thirteenth and fourteenth centuries, and as Charles Manekin has noted, the influence of scholastic logic upon Jewish thought was extensive.[21] By the mid-thirteenth century, many works of Arab logicians had been translated into Hebrew and became part of the curriculum of Jewish students. Maimonides himself, in a letter to his translator Samuel ibn Tibbon, recommended the commentaries of Alexander of Aphrodisias, Themistius, and Averroës over the works of Aristotle; in the case of logic, he stated that the only philosopher worth reading was Al-Fârâbî. In fourteenth-century Provence we find treatises that demonstrate the influence of Aristotelian logic. Manekin surveys translations and commentaries on logic by a number of important Provençal Jewish philosophers, including among others Joseph ibn Caspi, Moses of Narbonne, Todros Todrosi, and Judah Cohen.[22] Gersonides himself wrote three works in logic: *The Book of the Correct Syllogism*; *The Commentary on Logic*; and *The Commentary on Averroës' First and Second Treatises Concerning Some Points in the Prior Analytics*.[23]

While Manekin has argued that the major fourteenth-century Jewish philosophers of northern Spain and Provence (e.g., Gersonides, Isaac Pollegar, Ibn Caspi, and Narboni) show little signs, if any, of scholastic influence, not all scholars agree on this assessment.[24] We do know, however, that the Spanish Jewish philosophers of the late fourteenth and fifteenth centuries (Profiat Duran, Crescas, Albo, Bibago, Arama, and Abravanel) were involved in Christian polemics; this involvement necessitates an engagement with scholasticism in order to address the challenges posed by Christianity.[25] But how was this engagement effected? Did Jewish philosophers, for example, know Latin? Daniel Lasker argues that although the anti-Christian polemicists certainly were familiar with Christian sources, not all had a reading knowledge of Latin. It is not unreasonable to postulate, however, that Jews and Christians communicated with one another in the vernacular. A good example is the apparent interaction between Gersonides and the Christian clerics who commissioned from him works in astronomy, music (*De Numeris Harmonicis*), and

---

[19] Maimonides *Guide* 1.31.   [20] Maimonides *Guide* 2.22:230.
[21] See Manekin 1991; see also Freudenthal 2005; 2005a; 2009.
[22] See Manekin 1991, 4ff. for details.   [23] Manekin 1991, 12.
[24] Manekin 1997b, 352. For slightly different assessments, see Glasner 2015.
[25] See Tirosh-Rothschild 1997, 504.

astrology.[26] Furthermore, inasmuch as Jewish philosophers during this period rarely mention Christian writers by name, it is often difficult to trace individual scholastic influences. Hillel of Verona, for example, used unattributed passages (a not uncommon practice) from the Latin Avicenna and Averroës, interwoven with passages from Thomas Aquinas' *Tractatus de Unitate Intellectus contra Averroistas* and Dominico Gundisalvo, in his own work *Tagmulei ha-Nefesh* (*Retributions of the Soul*), written in 1291.[27]

By the time we reach the works of Gersonides in the early fourteenth century, Aristotelian method has thus been firmly concretized in all three Abrahamic traditions, Islamic, Jewish, and Christian. Gersonides however is one of the first, along with several scholastic peers, to begin to subject Aristotelian method to stringent critique. As a scientist, Gersonides stands out as "one of the more creative and daring figures in the medieval west."[28] While we shall examine Gersonides' astronomy and cosmology in subsequent chapters, let us for the moment emphasize his importance in the history of science. Gersonides develops a new scientific method based on empirical principles.[29] This method was one of Gersonides' most impressive accomplishments; his success in developing it and in applying the method illustrates Gad Freudenthal's observation that Gersonides' double role as a philosopher and a mathematical astronomer is "the key to the understanding of his originality."[30] Gersonides states his empiricist principle often and emphatically: as described by Ruth Glasner, "what is verified by experience cannot be denied by any theoretical argument."[31] Glasner notes that Gersonides "was notable in his unequivocal empiricist interpretation" in contradistinction to a strictly rationalistic interpretation based on Aristotle's *Posterior Analytics*.[32] And Bernard Goldstein notes that Gersonides was "almost unique" in his basing a new system of astronomy on his own observations rather than on those of the ancients.[33]

This is not to say that Gersonides was a total anti-Aristotelian. Glasner suggests that unlike his Christian peers who studied and taught at a university, Gersonides' academic profile as rooted in applied mathematics and astronomy allowed him to leave metaphysics behind. We might say that his "outsider" status, combined with his rigorous empiricism, left him freer from the constraints of Aristotelian philosophy.

Gersonides describes his methods in a variety of contexts. In his commentary to *Song of Songs*, Gersonides provides a brief blueprint of the methods and hierarchy of knowledge acquisition, ranging from mathematics, to physics, and ultimately metaphysics. Mathematics provides the underpinning for the other sciences: it "trains our intellect, actualizes, and causes it to acquire the proper mode of speculation,

---

[26] For further discussion of Gersonides' interaction with Christian clergy, possibly even the Avignonese pope, Clement VI, see Feldman's introductory comments in Levi ben Gershom, *The Wars of the Lord*.
[27] Hillel of Verona *Sefer Tagmulei ha-Nefesh*.   [28] Glasner 2015, 13.
[29] Gersonides calls this method "the examination of the parts of the contradictory." For details, see Glasner 2015, 63.
[30] Glasner 2015, 51; see also Freudenthal 1987, 360; 1992, 176–7.
[31] See Glasner 2015, 54. Glasner provides at least five or six texts in which Gersonides states a version of this principle, including *Wars* 5.1.45; 5.22.193; 5.1.43; 5.1.42. See Glasner *op. cit.*, for detailed discussion of Gersonides' adherence to empiricist methodology.
[32] Glasner 2015, 55.   [33] See Goldstein 1974, 247; Glasner 2015, 59.

thus guarding it from error in other sciences due to the strength of the demonstrations based on this science."[34] Astronomy reflects mathematical certitude.

Unlike mathematics, whose premises are a priori, physics relies on *a posteriori* demonstrations, and for this reason does not afford the certitude offered by mathematics: of those who demand of physics *a priori* certitude, "many fall by the way and do not achieve perfection in this science."[35] Gersonides is also well aware of the limits to empirical observation: one of the causes of our ignorance is "the difficulty in acquiring from the senses what is needed for the apprehension of many of the existent things."[36] Menachem Kellner suggests that in this regard, Gersonides might have been the first to suggest the need for something like a microscope in order to conduct empirical investigations properly.[37] Nonetheless, Gersonides offered a serious critique of Aristotle's theory of motion, for example, thus freeing himself from "the grip of Aristotelian physics, and even laid down a basis for an alternative understanding of motion."[38] Many aspects of his overall world picture were not Aristotelian, even to the point of moving in the general direction of mechanistic thinking. We shall return to the implications of this emphasis in Chapter 7.

By the middle of the fourteenth century, we see scholastic method firmly trenched among the Christian scholastic philosophers. The most prominent method used by the scholastics is the *quaestio* method adopted by Aquinas, Scotus, and the later scholastics.[39] This method followed a strict order: formulation of the question; citation of supporting arguments; citation of antithetical argument; and resolution of the original question, generally in support of the antithetical arguments. By mid-century, the *quaestio* method appears in Jewish texts as well. Marc Saperstein has documented the use of syllogistic forms of argument, as well as the incorporation of the scholastic method of *disputatio*, into medieval Jewish sermons; Crescas' celebrated *Sermon* for the Sabbath preceding Pesach represents an excellent case study.[40] That scholastic method influenced Jewish philosophical writings can be seen as well in the works of Gersonides, Crescas, and Isaac Abravanel, all of whom organized their discourse thematically as a set of disputed questions with the same order of exposition as found in scholastic texts.

One such work is an extensive gloss commentary upon Peter of Spain's *Tractatus*, written in 1320 by Hezekiah bar Halafta.[41] By the end of the fourteenth and beginning of the fifteenth centuries, we find Peter of Spain's *Tractatus* being translated into Hebrew and enjoying increased popularity. One reason for the popularity of scholastic logic undoubtedly rested in the perception among Jews that logical training would prepare them for the rigors of disputation with Christians; without such

---

[34] Gersonides *Song of Songs*, 9.   [35] Gersonides *Song of Songs*, 10.
[36] Gersonides *Song of Songs*, 7.
[37] See Kellner's note in Gersonides *Song of Songs*, 105.   [38] Glasner 2015, 106.
[39] For a brief discussion of the history and development of the *quaestio* method, see Marenbon 1987.
[40] For more detailed discussions of the influence of scholastic method upon Jewish sermons, see Saperstein 1996, 17, 83ff.
[41] The original manuscript (called *Be'ur la-Mabo* by Steinschneider) is found in Oxford, Bodley Ms. Mich. 314 [Neubauer 2187]. For more information on these logical works, see Manekin 1992; Manekin 2011.

training, the Jews saw themselves at a distinct theological disadvantage. Another reason may have had to do with the perceived importance of logic for a sound medical education; inasmuch as Jewish physicians were certified before a mixed tribunal of Jews and Christians, knowledge of scholastic logic was presumed to be helpful in their preparation.[42]

Scholastic thought is extremely influential upon Hebrew logic in Italy as well. Sermoneta has documented the Thomistic trend among Italian Jews, who translated Aquinas into Hebrew and used his logical analysis for their own purposes.[43] For example, Judah ben Moses Romano in the fourteenth century translated selected works of Aquinas and Giles of Rome into Hebrew. Once Jews were admitted to the faculties of medicine and philosophy in Italian universities, they were in a position to incorporate Christian teachings and specifically logic.[44] A good example of this university status for Jews is Judah ben Yeḥiel Messer Leon who studied at the universities of Bologna and Padua in the latter part of the fifteenth century, was awarded a doctorate in philosophy and medicine, and incorporated the scholastic logic as reflected in the works of the scholastic philosophers Walter Burley and Paul of Venice into his writings. Messer Leon wrote a treatise on Hebrew rhetoric, a history of Hebrew grammar, an introductory textbook on logic entitled *The Book of the Perfection of Beauty* (*Sefer Mikhlal Yofi*), and commentaries on Averroës' Middle Commentaries on the first five books of the *Organon*.[45]

By the early seventeenth century, Jewish thinkers were interacting even more fully with their intellectual peers, and fully absorbing the scientific advances in astronomy, mechanics, optics, and mathematics. Astronomers such as David Gans and Joseph Delmedigo were thoroughly conversant with developments in the scholastic world, and sought to introduce Jews to these exciting advances. We noted in Chapter 2 the curious parallelism between Delmedigo and Spinoza. If d'Ancona and Adler are right, then Delmedigo's *Elim* could very well have been one of Spinoza's first encounters with Renaissance mathematics, mechanics, and astronomy. Through Delmedigo, Spinoza could have become acquainted with the cosmology of Copernicus and Galileo, and embarked upon a journey that was to take him far from his roots in Jewish learning and texts; this interaction might have led in part to his leaving the Jewish community altogether.[46] Spinoza's adherence to the importance of using scientific method in approaching Scripture forced him to reject divine authorship of the Torah. But Spinoza's more radical move was to deny that Scripture had any philosophical or scientific veracity. Unlike Maimonides and Ibn Ezra, both of whom tried to read the Torah in light of modern philosophical and scientific teachings, Spinoza denied the tenability of this entire enterprise.

While sharing with Galileo the notion that God has written two books—the book of the Law, and the book of Nature—Spinoza insists that scientific method should be used exclusively for both books. According to Spinoza, the Bible must be read and

---

[42] For further discussion of this point, see Manekin 1997b.
[43] See Sermoneta's comments in Hillel ben Samuel of Verona 1981.
[44] For extensive discussion of the development of medicine among Jews, see Ruderman 1995.
[45] For further discussion of Messer Leon, see Manekin 2011; Tirosh-Rothschild 1991; and Sirat 1990.
[46] See Levy 1989, 27.

understood naturalistically, that is, in terms of the laws of physical causation: inasmuch as everything in Scripture must accord with the laws of nature, it follows that whatever in Scripture contravenes nature must be rejected.[47] According to Spinoza, Scripture cannot be accommodated to the new sciences; because it is neither a philosophical nor a scientific work, the rational methods used by these latter disciplines simply cannot be applied to Scripture. Scripture provides only moral guidance and piety, not even moral truth, and certainly not scientific or mathematical truth. By pushing the views of Maimonides and Ibn Ezra to their logical extreme, Spinoza thus destroyed the carefully constructed hermeneutic methodology introduced by his Jewish predecessors.

Spinoza insists upon what Amos Funkenstein has called the secularization of theology. This insistence is characterized by applying the paradigm of mathematical certitude to nature as a whole, as well as to theology: this mathematical paradigm forms the basis for his respective models of demonstrative science. The theological implications of this appropriation are reflected in his respective biblical hermeneutics, a hermeneutic method that is construed as antithetical to the inerrancy of Scripture. Although Spinoza had not yet formulated this method in a published form, nevertheless there is reason to believe that he was already very much involved with thinking about (and possibly promulgating orally) such matters at a young age.[48] Spinoza upheld the ideal of the mathematization of nature as a whole, preferring the guidance of mathematical reason above the suggestions of experience. According to Spinoza, for example, mathematics "which is concerned not with ends but only with the essence and properties of figures, had not shown men another standard of truth."[49] By eliminating the quest for final causes, mathematics reintroduces a model of proper order against which other objects can be studied. For example, in his preface to *Ethics* III, Spinoza says that he will "consider human actions and appetites just as if I were considering lines, planes, or bodies."[50] Here the proper method of study of human action, including human emotions, is geometry: not, for sure, the Archimedean geometry of Galileo, but a Euclidean geometry nonetheless.

But what do we do in situations that appear to be impervious not only to the mathematical certitude exemplified by geometry, but also to the entire domain of natural science? In particular, how do we approach the truths of theology, which utilize their own measure of certitude independent of scientific method? According to Spinoza, herein lies the source of the conflict between science and theology. Spinoza recognizes the difficulties inherent in understanding theological statements and dogmas. The certainty reflected in prophecy itself is based on the imaginative and not the rational faculty, he argues, and so does not carry the sort of certainty reflected by metaphysics and ontology: "the certainty afforded by prophecy was not a mathematical certainty, but only a moral certainty."[51] And so it is the method of science, that is, a method that aspires toward the certitude represented by mathematical

---

[47] Spinoza *Tractatus* 15:169. See also Galileo 1989.
[48] For an exploration of the relationships Spinoza was already having in early years with individuals outside the community, see Popkin 1986; Popkin 1987; and Popkin 1996.
[49] Spinoza *Ethics* 441.   [50] Spinoza *Ethics* Intro III.492.   [51] Spinoza *Tractatus* 2:22.

geometry, which is pitted against the constraints of biblical interpretation, and which gives rise to the antagonism of Spinoza's audience. The techniques used by Spinoza to analyze Scripture are a direct result of the challenges of the new science.

III The Ultimate Desideratum: Removing Perplexity

Imagine the medieval Jewish intellectual (or the modern one, for that matter) torn between two worlds: that of religious belief and that of secular learning. The enlightened Jew, seduced by the scientific systems of his/her day, would like to retain as much as possible of the latter, without relinquishing the former. But how best to accomplish this most delicate balance of accommodation? To this question we now turn.

The twelfth-century Jewish philosopher Abraham ibn Daud writes in the intro-duction to *Sefer ha-Emunah ha-Ramah* that his entire work was written to solve the problem of necessity and human choice, a problem to which he returns only briefly at the very end of the work. This problem he sees as part of a larger issue, namely the "agreement between philosophy and religious law."[52] He thus begins his treatise with a description of the sort of conundrum that introduces "confusion and disorder" in the minds of his contemporaries. "Confusion has happened to matters of speculation in our time because speculation forsook them in [their examination of] the basic principles of their Israelite faith and [in their] search for instances of evidence and the agreement that [obtains] between [their Israelite faith] and the true philosophy upon which falls the agreement of the philosophers."[53] It often happens, he says, that people who concern themselves with philosophical issues become confused, in part because they have neglected the philosophical roots of Jewish belief. That rejection of the sciences "was not the way of our nation in past times," and Ibn Daud tells us in the introduction that the early rabbis were all familiar with philosophy.[54] Ibn Daud sees himself as returning to this earlier tradition in which philosophy and science were respected as equal ways to truth: his work is thus addressed to the reader who is confused by traditional belief, but has not learned enough philosophy to dispel the perplexities.

Ibn Daud directs his work to those readers who are perplexed or confused by the apparent conflict between Judaism and science: "When someone is just beginning his study of the sciences, he is perplexed about what he knows from the point of view of the traditional knowledge because he has not attained in science the degree where he could state the truth in the questions which are not clear."[55] Take, for example, somebody trying to reconcile a rational conception of the deity with images given in Scripture: such a reader is "in the situation of a man with two masters, one great and the other not small; he cannot please the first without opposing the opinion of the second."[56] In this regard, Ibn Daud's work adumbrates Maimonides' *Guide*, which evinces a similar purpose.

---

[52] Ibn Daud *Emunah Ramah* 39.　　[53] Ibn Daud *Emunah Ramah* 39–40; Abstract.
[54] Ibn Daud *Emunah Ramah* 40.　　[55] Ibn Daud *Emunah Ramah* 2–4.
[56] Ibn Daud *Emunah Ramah* 82.

As Sirat notes, Aristotelian science was spreading rapidly, and Ibn Daud believed it was necessary to justify Jewish belief in the face of this new science, which had been rapidly adopted without being sufficiently studied.[57] But in order to open the eyes of his readers, who are perplexed with respect to the relation between science and religion, Ibn Daud must first introduce them to "the first principles of the science of nature and what follows from it."[58] Only then, after a thorough grounding in Aristotelian logic, natural philosophy, including both the sublunary and superlunary spheres, and finally practical philosophy, does Ibn Daud feel he can return to the original query, namely the tension between necessity and choice. Ibn Daud believes that it is incumbent upon us to "grasp with both his hands two lights, in his right hand the light of his religious law, and in his left hand the light of his science."[59] While he was not totally successful in achieving this balance, it remained for Maimonides to articulate how in fact both lamps could remain lit simultaneously.

Ibn Daud's attempts to defuse perplexity and confusion are reflected famously in Maimonides' own work, the magisterial *Guide of the Perplexed*, which soon over-shadowed Ibn Daud's treatise. Was Maimonides familiar with Ibn Daud's work? Evidence demonstrating a direct influence is unavailable, but the similarities between the two are undeniable: both writers are concerned to alleviate perplexity on the part of their readers, and both are wrestling with the problem of reconciling science and religion, a concern for many thinkers during the thirteenth century. Maimonides tells us in the introduction to the *Guide* that the work was addressed to Maimonides' student Joseph son of Judah, who had traveled to study with him. The introduction clearly spells out two major purposes of the work. The first purpose of the *Guide* is to "explain the meanings of certain terms occurring in books of prophecy," while the second purpose is to explain "very obscure parables occurring in the books of the prophets."[60] Maimonides delineates these two purposes in a passage worth quoting in full:

For the purpose of this Treatise and of all those like it is the science of Law in its true sense. Or rather its purpose is to give indications to a religious man for whom the validity of our Law has become established in his soul and has become actual in his belief – such a man being perfect in his religion and character, and having studied the sciences of the philosophers and come to know what they signify. The human intellect having drawn him on and led him to dwell within its province, he must have felt distressed by the externals of the Law and by the meanings of the above-mentioned equivocal, derivative, or amphibolous terms, as he continued to understand them by himself or was made to understand them by others. Hence he would remain in a state of perplexity and confusion as to whether he should follow his intellect, renounce what he knew concerning the terms in question, and consequently consider that he has renounced the foundations of Law. Or he should hold fast to his understanding of these terms and not let himself be drawn on together with his intellect, rather turning his back on it and moving away from it, while at the same time perceiving that he had brought loss to himself and harm to his religion. He would be left with those imaginary beliefs to which he owes his fear and difficulty and would not cease to suffer from heartache and great perplexity.[61]

---

[57] Sirat 1990, 143.   [58] Ibn Daud *Emunah Ramah* 41.
[59] Ibn Daud *Emunah Ramah* 40.   [60] Maimonides *Guide* Intro: 5–6.
[61] Maimonides *Guide* Intro: 5–6.

More generally, Maimonides hopes to remove perplexity on the part of intellectually sophisticated readers who have been reading Scripture against the backdrop of philosophical and scientific ideas. His work is written to enable such a reader to understand the often hidden meanings to be found in scriptural texts. Note the following points contained in the above passage. The *Guide* is presented as an exercise in the "science of the Law," that is, as a rigorous, analytic study of Judaism. Maimonides is clear that the *Guide* is directed not to the "vulgar or to beginners," but to an individual like his own student Joseph who "has philosophized and has knowledge of the true sciences."[62] Presumably, his reader is the very sort of individual described: one who has studied both Scripture and philosophy and is caught between the two disciplines, embroiled in a state of perplexity and confusion. In fact, we might suspect that Maimonides sees himself as having been caught between Aristotelian science and Judaism.[63] Is there any cure for the individual caught in this state of perplexity? Maimonides introduces the second purpose of the *Guide*, namely biblical hermeneutics, as a way to neutralize the sort of perplexities exacerbated by ambiguous passages in Scripture. Once we understand the true meaning of difficult biblical parables, or understand at least that they are parables and not to be taken literally, Maimonides assures the reader that, "he will take the road and be delivered from this perplexity."[64]

This classic tension between faith and reason, between what Maimonides terms "intellect" and "imaginary beliefs," was described by many of his Islamic and Jewish philosophical contemporaries. Such an individual, standing at the crossroads, as it were, between Torah and philosophy, between faith and reason, might feel compelled to choose between the two paths. Torah offers a way of life, while philosophy offers a critical way of thinking. Maimonides is clear that each choice carries its own price: choosing reason (philosophy) carries with it the possibility of losing one's belief in Judaism, while choosing faith over reason undermines the epistemological integrity of Jewish belief. Once Pandora's box has been opened, there is no returning to a pre-reflexive, naïve standpoint. The very rejection of philosophy carries its own "heartache and great perplexity," which ultimately is harmful to Judaism. As Kraemer has aptly stated, the *Guide* thus addresses "a chronic existential condition of numbing perplexity."[65] One who is fully steeped in both Torah and philosophy can never be fully rid of perplexity. Perhaps we hear echoes of Maimonides the physician speaking: often the most we can hope for are degrees of cure, not a full instantaneous cure.

Maimonides complicates matters even further by distinguishing two levels of interpretation—exoteric and esoteric—suggesting that it is sometimes incumbent upon a philosopher to conceal his own esoteric position behind the veil of exoteric doctrine.[66] He enjoins his own student not to divulge his secret teachings to others.

---

[62] Maimonides *Guide* Intro: 10.

[63] Ivry suggests that Maimonides himself was "one of the perplexed for whom the Guide was written." See Ivry 2016, 4. See also Rudavsky 2010.

[64] Maimonides *Guide* Intro: 6.   [65] Kraemer 2008, 8.

[66] Alfred Ivry suggests that Maimonides could easily have picked up the method of concealment from the Islamic Ismā'īlī, an Islamic sect for whom dissembling had become a virtue. The Ismā'īlī distinguished between the exoteric (*zahir*) and esoteric (*batin*) aspects of sacred texts and became known as the Esotericist sect (*Batiniyya*). Ivry has argued in a series of articles that Maimonides may have been influenced by the

Maimonides thus introduces an ambiguity into the very reading and understanding of his texts, an ambiguity that has persisted to this day.[67] Partly as a result of Maimonides' portrayal of this deliberately obfuscating methodology in the *Guide*, readers of this work have disagreed over how much emphasis to place upon Maimonides' ostensible doctrine of concealment. The process of reading Maimonides, and how to approach the texts, turns out to represent a deconstructive exercise in its own right: one's attitude toward contradictions will determine to a large extent whether to see in Maimonides' words an esoteric subtext that conflicts with Jewish belief, an esoteric subtext that can ultimately be harmonized with belief, or simply a straightforward literal meaning that eschews esotericism altogether.

The hermeneutics of radical esotericism gained a rebirth with Leo Strauss' enormously influential work *Persecution and the Art of Writing*, in which Strauss reintroduced a modern audience to the importance of recognizing esoteric subtexts in philosophical works.[68] On Strauss' radical reading, the *Guide* contains two teachings: a public teaching addressed to the "vulgar" and a secret teaching addressed to the "elite." The "real truth," according to Strauss, is rooted in philosophical (often Aristotelian) doctrine, and often contravenes Jewish belief. Much like the philosopher-king in Plato's *Republic* who must occasionally lie for the sake of the common good, Maimonides on Strauss' reading must resort to hiding the truth for the health of his readers.[69]

Maimonides' immediate successor Gersonides rejects the policy of obfuscation. In contradistinction to Maimonides, who introduced allegory, metaphor, and imprecise language into his work to convey the ambiguity of the subject-matter, Gersonides saw his goal to elucidate philosophical issues as clearly as possible. He contrasts his method with that of Maimonides, whose *Guide* he saw as unnecessarily obscure and esoteric: "Opacity of language or faulty arrangement should not hide the defect and weakness of our intention. For this reason we have not employed rhetorical flourishes or obscure language...there is no need to add obscurity of language and bad organization."[70] Clearly, Gersonides has Maimonides' introduction to the *Guide* in mind as an example of what not to do!

Adhering to the ability of human beings to attain to an overarching truth comprising all of reality, Gersonides presents a unified cosmology rooted in a thoroughgoing

---

Ismāʿīlī, and that this encouragement of a skeptical reading is *prima facie* evidence for the non-orthodox nature of Maimonides' beliefs. See Ivry 1986a.

[67] In order to conceal his real intentions from the novice, or unschooled reader, Maimonides makes use of various strategies and warns us that any contradictions found in the *Guide* itself are intentional: "Divergences that are to be found in this Treatise are due to the fifth cause and the seventh." The fifth cause of contradictory statements results from having to teach obscure matters in a way that oversimplifies them, thus introducing apparent contradictions into the explanation. The seventh mode of contradiction results from having "to conceal some parts and to disclose others," in a way that precludes the "vulgar" from noticing the contradiction. Maimonides is thus quite open about his alleged secrecy, encouraging his more philosophically sophisticated readers not to accept the text of the *Guide* at face value. See Maimonides *Guide* Intro: 20.

[68] Strauss 1952.

[69] See Halbertal 2015; Rudavsky 2010; Ivry 2016 for readings that recognize the underlying esotericism of Maimonides' doctrines. Ivry summarizes succinctly the different interpretative schools.

[70] Gersonides *Wars* vol. 1.1. Intro: 101.

epistemological realism based on reason. Gersonides laid down the general rule that, "the Law cannot prevent us from considering to be true that which our reason urges us to believe."[71] His adherence to this principle is reflected throughout his works, both philosophical and biblical. Robert Eisen describes the relationship between philosophical inquiry and Scripture in Gersonides' works as one of mutual interdependence. The biblical text "must be interpreted to conform to demonstrative truth" while, on the other hand, Scripture itself provides "crucial hints and clues" to philosophical inquiry by specifying a "series of irrefutable principles" that are then incorporated into the philosophical discussion.[72] As we shall see in Chapter 6, Gersonides includes a lengthy exegesis of *Genesis* in the course of articulating his own theory of pre-existent matter out of which the universe is created. In this case, *Genesis* provides justification for a somewhat radical cosmology.

Are there cases (such as the problem of creation) that are incapable of rational proof and demonstration? Gersonides replies that, "unless a proof is forthcoming that shows the impossibility of such a philosophical demonstration, this is not a valid objection against us."[73] Again, Gersonides' method of investigation very much reflects the empiricist tradition that would come to dominate European philosophy in the eighteenth century. Furthermore, in *Wars* V.1, Gersonides contends that, "no argument can nullify the reality that is perceived by the senses, for true opinion must follow reality but reality need not conform to opinion."[74] That Gersonides clearly considered his own observations to be the ultimate test of his system is explicit from his attitude towards Ptolemy. He values his own observations over those of others, and when his observations do not agree with those of Ptolemy, he tells us explicitly that he prefers his own.

In his introductory remarks to *Wars*, Gersonides upholds the primacy of reason, attributing to Maimonides the position that, "we must believe what reason has determined to be true. If the literal sense of the Torah differs from reason, it is necessary to interpret those passages in accordance with the demands of reason."[75] Gersonides believes that reason and Torah cannot be in opposition: "if reason causes to affirm doctrines that are incompatible with the literal sense of Scripture, we are not prohibited by the Torah to pronounce the truth on these matters, for reason is not incompatible with the true understanding of the Torah."[76] In summary, Feldman notes that Torah and philosophy are mutually complementary, each expressing its own truth in its own way and each reinforcing the other: "To Levi there is no distinction to be made between *veritas fidei* and *veritas rationis*: faith and reason are one."[77] Thus, reason is upheld as a criterion for achieving truth both in Scripture and in philosophy.

We turn finally to Spinoza, whose stated aims are juxtaposed against those of his predecessors and in particular those of Gersonides. Spinoza is quite explicit about his intentions in the *Tractatus Theologico-Politicus*. In a letter to Oldenberg, written in 1665, he states two explicit aims of his work: to enable ordinary humans to engage in

---

[71] Gersonides *Wars* vol. 1.1. Intro: 98.   [72] See Eisen 1995, 93.
[73] Gersonides *Wars* vol. 1.1. Intro: 96.   [74] Goldstein 1985a, 24.
[75] Gersonides *Wars* vol. 1.1. Intro: 98.   [76] Gersonides *Wars* vol. 1.1. Intro: 98.
[77] See Feldman's comment in Gersonides *Wars* 247.

philosophical thinking by freeing them from the errors and prejudices of the theologians; and to free philosophy itself from the shackles and authority of religious authorities.[78]

I am now writing a Treatise about my interpretation of Scripture. This I am driven to do by the following reasons: 1. The Prejudices of the Theologians; for I know that these are among the chief obstacles which prevent men from directing their mind to philosophy; and therefore I do all I can to expose them, and to remove them from the minds of the more prudent. 2. The opinion which the common people have of me, who do not cease to accuse me falsely of atheism; I am also obliged to avert this accusation as far as it is possible to do so. 3. The freedom of philosophizing, and of saying what we think; this I desire to vindicate in every way, for here it is always suppressed through the excessive authority and impudence of the preachers.[79]

In order to achieve his aims, Spinoza sees as his task the development of a biblical hermeneutic that can allow for a new understanding of Scripture that does not enslave philosophy or would-be philosophers. In the preface to his theological–political treatise (*Tractatus*), Spinoza rails against those who "do not even glimpse the divine nature of Scripture, and the more enthusiastic their admiration of these mysteries, the more clearly they reveal that their attitude to Scripture is one of abject servility rather than belief."[80] Because of their anti-intellectual attitude toward Scripture, nothing is left of the old religion but the outward form. Therefore Spinoza resolves to "examine Scripture afresh, conscientiously and freely, and to admit nothing as its teaching which I did not most clearly derive from it."[81]

Concerned to free philosophy and the study of nature from what he sees as the shackles of theology, Spinoza holds controversial views on how to read and evaluate statements in Scripture. In the *Tractatus*, Spinoza postulates the incommensurability of religion and science: the authority of the prophets carries weight only in matters concerning morality and true virtue. In other matters, their beliefs are irrelevant.

Now I found nothing expressly taught in Scripture that was not in agreement with the intellect or that contradicted it, and I also came to see that the prophets taught only very simple doctrines easily comprehensible by all... So I was completely convinced that Scripture does not in any way inhibit reason and has nothing to do with philosophy, each standing on its own footing... I show in what way Scripture must be interpreted, and how all our understanding of Scripture and of matters spiritual must be sought from Scripture alone, and not from the sort of knowledge that derives from the natural light of reason.[82]

As Edward Curley has duly noted, Spinoza's rallying cry echoes that of the Protestant Revolution: "Scripture is its own Interpreter,"[83] but with a twist. Here Spinoza argues for a model according to which faith (theology) and reason (philosophy) occupy different realms: "we may maintain as incontrovertible that neither is theology required to be subordinated to reason nor reason to theology, and that each has its

---

[78] Spinoza Letter to Oldenberg, in Spinoza Correspondence, 185.   [79] Ibid.
[80] Spinoza *Tractatus* Preface: 52.   [81] Spinoza *Tractatus* Preface: 55.
[82] Spinoza *Tractatus* Preface: 6.
[83] See Curley 1994, 79. Curley quotes Luther's "Scriptura sui ipsius interpres."

own domain. The domain of reason, we have said, is truth and wisdom, the domain of theology is piety and obedience."[84] Gersonides had already maintained that reason is compatible with Torah when the latter is correctly interpreted; Spinoza takes a further step by removing theology from the domain of truth functionality. Note that this move paves the way to denying "truth" in the religious sphere altogether. Truth is associated with reason, with philosophical reflection, and does not pertain to what we find in Scripture, which as noted above, is associated with the imaginative sphere.[85]

According to Spinoza, Scripture was written in a certain way for the common people:

Therefore, since the whole of Scripture was revealed in the first place for an entire nation, and eventually for all mankind, its contents had to be adapted particularly to the understanding of the common people, and it had to appeal only to experience.[86]

We have already seen that the idea that the accommodation of Scripture to the capacities of the intended audience is a mainstay of medieval Jewish philosophy and hermeneutics. That "Scripture speaks the language of man" (*Scriptura humane loquitur*) comes from the Hebrew *dibra tora kileshon bne'adam*, which first appeared in Jewish legal contexts.[87] Spinoza is thus drawing upon a rich literary and hermeneutic tradition, one that already recognized the intellectual limits of readers of Scripture, and was ready to acknowledge that the Bible is written in a way to accommodate these limits. As we noted above, Maimonides' entire work *The Guide of the Perplexed* reflects this leitmotif.

In short, truth for Spinoza is defined as residing in the domain of reason alone, and Spinoza concludes that Scripture cannot speak the truth. Scripture can give us moral claims, but we should be careful not to confuse moral claims, however salutary, with epistemic truths.[88] It is not just that Scripture does not, to paraphrase Galileo, tell us "how the heavens go," but that Scripture does not tell us how "anything at all goes." The purpose of Scripture is to teach obedience, not truth; because there are no epistemic claims to be found in Scripture, there can be no conflict between what Scripture exhorts and what we find to be the case in nature. Spinoza thus paves the way for the independence of philosophical (and scientific) truth on the one hand, and religious doctrine on the other.

IV Heresy and the Limits of Faith

Now clearly Spinoza is an outlier with respect to his assessment of scripture. But Spinoza's position provides us with an interesting case study. Although Spinoza's views were not actually published before his excommunication (or *herem*), they were

---

[84] Spinoza *Tractatus* 15:169.
[85] In the *Ethics*, Spinoza returns to the notion of truth in more detail, and elaborates three distinct epistemic levels of truth, which he articulates in terms of imagination, reason, and intuitive science. According to to Spinoza, the knowledge of the first kind (imagination) is the cause of falsity, whereas knowledge of the second and third orders is necessarily true. Spinoza goes on to argue in the demonstration to *Ethics* 2:41 that the first kind of knowledge concerns all those ideas that are inadequate and confused.
[86] Spinoza *Tractatus* 5:67.   [87] Funkenstein 1986, 213.   [88] See Smith 1997, 66.

freely circulated among intellectual circles in Amsterdam. The rabbinical court in Amsterdam objected to the perceived "objectionable views and heresies" reflected in Spinoza's conduct. As a result of these "objectionable" views Spinoza was accused of heresy in 1656, refused to recant, was excommunicated from the Jewish community, changed his name from Baruch to Benedict, and lived the remainder of his short life on the margins of the Jewish world. I shall not enter into the details of Spinoza's drama. The details of the excommunication have been documented in Steven Nadler's admirable biography of Spinoza.[89]

Compare Spinoza's situation to the medieval Jewish world in which we are ensconced. In order to appreciate the content of scholastic discussions during this period, we must say more about the importance of the Condemnation of 1277. The Condemnation of 1277 represents the culmination of a series of earlier condemnations in the Christian universities, and raised the thorny issue of heresy. In the thirteenth century, academic censure involved university-trained scholars who were accused of heresy. The word heresy was used among thirteenth- and fourteenth-century scholastics to refer to false teachings and erroneous views, as well as to clear-cut heresies. Many scholastics used the criterion of willful adherence to distinguish a heretical from an erroneous doctrine: errors become heresies when they are "defended with pertinacity."[90]

On December 10, 1270, Bishop Steven Tempier condemned a series of thirteen propositions, among them being the eternity of the world. As is often the case with policies of repression, this condemnation appears to have been largely ignored, as evidenced, for example, by the fact that at least four separate treatises on the eternity of the world were written shortly after 1270.[91] This was followed with a condemnation of 219 propositions in philosophy and theology by Bishop Steven Tempier on March 7, 1277; this condemnation is one of the most studied events in the history of the University of Paris.[92] Many historians have presented the condemnations as a reaction to the radical Aristotelian teachings being disseminated at the University of Paris. Doctrines such as the eternity of the universe were seen to be in conflict with Christian belief, and it was forbidden to hold or defend them on pain of excommunication.[93]

In contradistinction to the scholastic world, in fact, we find relative absence of schisms, sects, and charges of heresy in the medieval Jewish theological arena.[94] Despite the many differing accounts concerning the basic principles of Judaism in Maimonides, Duran, Crescas, Albo, Arama, Bibago, and Abarbanel, we find few accusations of heresy or sectarianism. Kellner suggests that in part this phenomenon can be traced to the traditional Jewish notion of faith as associated with a non-cognitivist "trust in God" rather than as a propositional affirmation or denial. Until the late fourteenth century, the term 'emunah, a translation of the Arabic term i'tiqâd, was used to convey the sense of belief or conviction.

---

[89] Nadler 1999.
[90] For a discussion of the different attitudes toward heresy in the scholastic world, see Thijssen 1998, 2.
[91] See Dales 1990, 129.
[92] For a careful study of the condemnation, see Thijssen 1998, ch. 2.
[93] See Thijssen 1998, 40–1.   [94] See Kellner 1986, 207.

In fact, it is Maimonides who introduced into Judaism a propositional or cognitivist notion of belief by defining heresy as the questioning of any of the thirteen principles of faith articulated in his introduction to the tenth chapter of *Tractate Sanhedrin* (*Perek Ḥelek*). Maimonides recognizes that not everybody is able to grasp and understand philosophically complex truths, and that there exist real differences in individual abilities. Maimonides is adamant, however, that certain beliefs must be taught to everybody regardless of their abilities, and presents these basic beliefs in many of his works. This work provides a commentary upon the rabbinic passage in the Mishnaic tractate *Sanhedrin* 10.1, which states that having a share in the world to come is dependent upon accepting certain theological beliefs. In the introduction to tractate *Sanhedrin* (chapter 10 of the Babylonian Talmud) called *Perek Ḥelek*, Maimonides outlined the fundamental principles of Judaism.

The section in *Sanhedrin* starts with the words "All Israelites have a share in the world to come..." Maimonides used this text as an opportunity to articulate the necessary and sufficient criteria for somebody's being included among the "Israelites." Maimonides expounds upon this statement by providing a list of thirteen articles of faith incumbent upon all Jews, without which they cannot achieve immortality. These thirteen principles include (1–4) the existence, unity, incorporeality, and primordiality of God; (5) denial of idolatry; (6–7) prophecy and uniqueness of Moses' prophecy; (8–9) the divine origin and non-abrogation of the Torah; (10–11) God's omniscience and providence; (12) the coming of the Messiah; and (13) resurrection of the dead. Acceptance of these fundamental principles, argues Maimonides, is a necessary condition for achieving a place in the world to come. Maimonides emphasizes God's unity and incorporeality repeatedly. Thus, for example, in his introduction to the *Mishneh Torah*, Maimonides states that the "basic principle of all basic principles and the pillar of all sciences" is the realization that there is a First Being; this is followed with God's unity and incorporeality.[95] This first attempt to articulate a creed in Judaism came under attack by subsequent Jewish thinkers, and as we shall see in later chapters, it is not always clear how many of these principles Maimonides himself accepted.

Maimonides returns to these principles in the *Guide*. In *Guide* 1.34 Maimonides explains that the multitude cannot be taught divine science but warns that everybody, regardless of their mental limitations, must be taught both the unity and incorporeality of God.[96] Realizing that not all humans have the same intellectual capacities, Maimonides recognizes that one individual may understand a matter that another finds obtuse and he warns his reader not to overstrain the intellectual faculties with respect to these topics.

Although Maimonides does not intend the *Guide* to be a work on language *per se*, nonetheless the first sixty chapters are framed within the context of logical and linguistic analysis. Language is reflective of our beliefs, and Maimonides is concerned to rectify what we *say* as well as what we *believe* about God. Maimonides' major principle is articulated as follows: "Belief is not the notion that is uttered, but the notion that is represented in the soul when it has been averred of it that it is in fact

⁹⁵ Maimonides *BK* 1.1:34a.   ⁹⁶ Maimonides *Guide* 1.35:80–1.

just as it has been represented."[97] His point here is that beliefs are not just linguistic utterances but internal mental states. Having a belief in one's mind, and uttering a belief, are independent activities: one may entertain a belief without uttering or articulating it, and one may profess a belief without actually believing it.[98]

Maimonides' conception of belief defined post-Maimonidean philosophy, as Jews tried to respond to a cognitivist theory that tied immortality to intellectual attainment. Influenced by Averroës, many Jewish philosophers replaced Maimonides' cognitivist conception with an even more stringent Aristotelian distinction between knowledge and true opinion. Arguing that only knowledge can be truly certain, philosophers such as Gersonides maintained that non-philosophers who do not attain to rational knowledge (in the robust Aristotelian sense of demonstrated science) cannot achieve immortality; thus rational speculation is a sufficient condition for attaining immortality.[99]

The subject of dogma and belief is revisited with even greater urgency in the fifteenth century. In large part, this revisitation is due to the intense persecutions experienced by Iberian Jews between the years 1391 and 1418 brought on by Christian attacks. Jewish intellectual leaders were drawn into the attempt not only to define who is a Jew, and who merits immortality, but also to articulate the doctrinal content of Judaism in contradistinction to Christianity. In this way, Jews were forced to respond to a Christian challenge that was rooted in credal concerns, thus raising serious questions concerning the nature of belief.[100]

When scholasticism infiltrates Jewish circles, the term 'emunah takes on the additional meaning of "faith" (fides).[101] We find both Jewish and Christian philosophers vacillating between a volitional and a non-volitional understanding of belief (fides, 'emunah), which becomes superimposed upon the rationality of belief. Some philosophers collapsed the distinction between true and certain beliefs altogether, arguing that rational knowledge is inferior to the state achieved through 'emunah. Other theories emphasized the primacy of will over that of intellect in the acquisition of beliefs. Many examples of the volitional or nonrational status of belief abound in fourteenth- and fifteenth-century Jewish literature. In his work Derech Emunah (The Way of Belief), Abraham Bibago (d. c. 1489), for example, acknowledges that knowledge can be achieved through rational inquiry, but argues that accepting propositions on faith (the way of 'emunah) is often superior to the first mode. Reflecting Aquinas' characterization of fides, Bibago claims that the superiority of 'emunah lies in its volitional character.[102]

---

[97] Maimonides Guide 1.50:111.
[98] The importance of this point is reflected in Maimonides' Epistle on Forced Conversion. In this work, Maimonides is asked whether forced (Jewish) converts to Islam should recite the Islamic creed (Shahada) to avoid being killed. Maimonides responds that mere verbal utterance of a credal statement, without inner assent, is not sufficient to constitute belief to that statement. Echoing his definition of belief as an inner state, Maimonides claims that the outward linguistic professing of the creed matters less than the inner mental state. See Kraemer 2008, 106–7. See also Stern 2013.
[99] See Gersonides Wars 1:11–12:218ff.
[100] Kellner 1986, 80–2.   [101] See Manekin's discussion of 'emunah in Manekin 1997b.
[102] See Abraham Bibago, Derech Emunah 2.5:227–8. The comparison to Aquinas' De Veritate is made by the editor of Bibago's work.

Ḥasdai Crescas, however, rejected the volitional view of belief. In *Light of the Lord*, Crescas argued, in direct contradistinction to Maimonides, that Jews are not commanded to believe anything, since assent or denial is not subject to choice or will.[103] Arguing that the will has no power over extra-mental existents, Crescas rejects the notion that the will moves the intellect in the realm of cognitive activity. In *Light* II.5 Crescas argues that the human act is motivated by the agent's own will, but the will is determined by prior causes, both internal and external. Beliefs, however, are imposed upon our minds, leaving no room for will.[104] In this determinist scheme (which we shall discuss in greater detail in Chapter 6), the will affects the emotional response taken to beliefs, that is the "joy and pleasure" we experience, and thus our divine reward and punishment. And as we shall see in Chapter 9, Crescas' emphasis upon the emotional content of belief brings us back full circle to the emphasis upon faith in contradistinction to that of reason.

---

[103] Hasdai Crescas *'Or Adonai* II.5.5.   [104] See Ravitzky 1988, vii.

4

Divine Science
The Existence and Nature of God

I Introduction

In clear opposition to an anthropocentric conception of God found in popular and religious texts, medieval Jewish philosophers spent much energy providing Jews with a picture of God that more accurately accorded with science and rational speculation. They were writing in light of Islamic and Jewish traditions that promulgated an anthropomorphic conception of the Deity. Not only was it believed that God had a body, but many Jewish works were quite willing to describe in great detail the particulars of this divine body. The quasi-mystical work *The Measure of the Divine Stature* (*Shi'ur Qoma*), for example, gave explicit descriptions of God's bodily features. Mystical traditions based on Ezekiel's vision of God ("*Merkabah* Mysticism") also described God's physical body in detail. Scripture itself reinforced a physical view of God, with its many references to God's actions, speech, location, and emotional life.

Medieval Jewish philosophers were determined to counteract these false beliefs, and their works tackled the implications of God's incorporeal nature directly. Carlos Fraenkel finds it useful to distinguish between the technical-philosophical and the religious aspects of the questions surrounding the existence and nature of God.[1] Whereas the latter was shaped by both philosophical and Jewish commitments, Jewish philosophers had to make a case that their God did not lack features associated with the God of the Jewish tradition.[2] As we shall see below, Jewish philosophers emphasized both the unity and incorporeality of God as basic features of the Deity.

In this chapter, we shall concentrate upon philosophical attempts to deconstruct corporeal descriptions and predicates of God in a way that avoids attributing to God physical or material features; we focus as well upon the implications of this conception with respect to divine predication. One of the most important of God's predicates is of course existence, and so we shall have to consider the classic attempts to prove the existence of God. These arguments follow an established tradition of proving, from certain facts in the created world, the existence of a creator, providing both cosmological and teleological arguments for God that are based on Aristotelian premises.

---

[1] Fraenkel 2009, 561. [2] Fraenkel 2009, 562.

II   Establishing the Unity and Incorporeality of God

Anthropomorphic descriptions of God abound in the Bible—God is described as king, judge, father, shepherd to mention only a few—and philosophers committed to the incorporeality of the Deity must grapple with these descriptions. Nowhere however does the Bible offer proofs for the existence of God; presumably, this is because biblical authors simply took the existence of God for granted, and felt no need to provide rational or speculative grounding for this belief.[3] The Bible does however emphasize God's uniqueness and unity in such noted passages as *Deuteronomy* 6:4; *Isaiah* 45:21; 46:9; 40:18; *Exodus* 20:4 (no likeness can be made of him). Other passages emphasize God's omnipotence—*Exodus* 19:18; 20:15; *Job* 42:2; *Psalms* 24:8—and omniscience *Job* 28:32; *Isaiah* 43:9.

The uniqueness and exalted nature of God is reinforced in rabbinic works, so much so that euphemisms were often used in order not to impute any imperfections to the deity. These include *Ha-Gevurah* (might), *Ha-Kadosh Barukh Hu* (The Holy One Blessed be He), *Ha-Maqom* (the Omnipresent), *Avinu she-ba-Shamayim* (Our Father who is in Heaven). Special significance was given by the rabbis to the name of God ("YHWH") expressed in the Tetragrammaton. But once again, actual proofs for the existence of God are not present in these Talmudic sources, and God is simply assumed to exist.[4]

The uniqueness of God is reiterated by Jewish philosophers as one of the key divine attributes. We have seen in Chapter 2 that Kalâm theologians were obsessed with how to correctly conceive God: the very designation "people of justice and unity" points to their efforts to demonstrate God's justice and unity in light of apparent inconsistencies within the Qur'an. Saadiah Gaon presents his work as an attempt to rescue his readers from confusion, particularly in light of Trinitarian and dualist views of the Christians and Persians respectively.[5] Saadiah states his twofold goals in his *Book of Beliefs and Opinions*: to establish the existence of God the creator, and to reinforce the incorporeality and unity of God in light of passages in Scripture that suggest God's corporeality. Saadiah provides an explanation of the attributes existence, omniscience, and omnipotence, claiming that since they are not distinct from God's essence, they do not imply plurality in God.[6] These arguments, he tells us, are couched in the context of what he terms "scientific research" and speculative reasoning.[7]

Like Saadiah, Maimonides emphasizes the unity and incorporeality of the Deity as givens. Already in his early halakhic works, Maimonides introduces to his readers a philosophical conception of the deity that is developed against a rigorous metaphysical and logical program. We noted in Chapter 3 that Maimonides had little regard for the intellectual acumen of the average person, and did not expect that the majority of individuals would be able to engage in sophisticated intellectual pursuits. Nevertheless, he does emphasize that everybody must be taught to accept two basic metaphysical truths about the Deity—incorporeality and unity. These two form the basis of subsequent discussion in both the *Mishneh Torah* and the *Guide*.

---

[3] See the article by Fox and Grintz 2007, 653; 657.   [4] Fox and Grintz 2007, 660.
[5] Fraenkel 2009, 573.   [6] Saadiah *Beliefs* I:2ff.   [7] Saadiah *Beliefs* II. exordium.

The first book of the *Mishneh Torah*, the *Book of Knowledge*, begins with an explicit statement of God's existence. The basic principle of all basic principles, and the pillar of all the sciences, is that "there is a First Being who brought every existing thing into being."[8] If there were no God, nothing else would exist. But even if nothing else were to exist, according to Maimonides, God still exists: "their non-existence would not involve His non-existence."[9] In the *Guide*, Maimonides reiterates the point that the following characteristics must be taught to all: that God is unique (one), and there is none like God; that God is not a body; that being incorporeal, God has no likeness to God's creatures in any way; that the difference between God and creatures is not one of degree, but rather "one concerning the species of existence"; and that even the term existence "can only be applied equivocally to His existence and to that of things other than He."[10] Everything else, Maimonides tells us, belongs to the domain of esoteric "obscure matters," but God's incorporeality must be taught to everybody. Included in God's incorporeality is the important teaching that God does not suffer affections; that is, God is not subject to emotions. Maimonides clearly traces theological confusion to the false belief that God is corporeal. When people mistakenly believe that God is a body or has a body, and is composed of matter and form, they become perplexed over passages in Scripture; these beliefs must therefore be exorcised from their minds.

But how can Maimonides convince his readers, used to reciting passages that uphold anthropomorphic descriptions of God, of the cogency of his position? Realizing that his task is difficult, Maimonides devotes the first part of the *Guide* to softening the opposition, as it were, using a method of biblical allegorical interpretation introduced by Philo Judaeus in the first century CE, and borrowed from the Stoics. The purpose of these preliminary chapters is to eliminate the anthropomorphisms associated with a literal reading of Biblical passages. Maimonides wants to wean his readers away from construing these passages literally, and to replace their exoteric meaning with a metaphorical understanding (a concept familiar to us, but less so to twelfth-century readers). But metaphorical readings include both "physical descriptions" of God, as well as descriptions of emotions/actions. And so Maimonides' purpose in these introductory chapters is to retrain the careful reader to think about, and parse, biblical passages in a way that does not attribute to God physical or human characteristics. In *Guide* 1.3, for example, Maimonides warns his reader that the term "shape" (*tabnith*) cannot be applied to God, since it implies the physicality of the object in question (e.g., its being a square, circle, etc.). *Guide* 1.8 warns us that the term "place" (*Maqom*) when used of God must be understood only in terms of rank of existence, and not in terms of material placement. By this process of hermeneutic deconstruction, Maimonides hopes that his readers will be able to construct a more sophisticated understanding of God.

III Proofs for the Existence of God

Turning now to the actual proofs for God's existence, let us recall the two types of proof employed by medieval (and many contemporary) philosophers: *propter quid*

---

[8] Maimonides *HYT* 1.1:34a.   [9] Ibid.   [10] Maimonides *Guide* 1.35:80.

and *propter quia* arguments. Demonstrations *propter quid* define God into existence. These arguments are based on reason alone, not sense experience—they are deductive and contain no empirical premises. Although found in scholastic philosophy (consider St. Anselm's celebrated ontological argument, for example), these arguments did not make their way into Islamic and Jewish philosophy. With the exception of a version of Avicenna's metaphysical argument, about which more below, the ontological argument seems to have been unknown to Jewish philosophers, who relied primarily upon two related versions of *propter quia* arguments.[11]

Propter quia arguments are those based on experience, on our sense perception, and they come in many flavors. We find in medieval literature both cosmological arguments (arguments from the existence of effects to the existence of an ultimate cause) and teleological arguments or arguments from design (arguments inferring from the existence of design in the world to the existence of a designer). Most Jewish thinkers adopt variations or combinations of these arguments. The teleological argument was used primarily by Saadiah Gaon, Bahya, and Gersonides, while different versions of the cosmological argument were presented by Saadiah, Bahya, Ibn Daud, and Maimonides.

But before turning to details of these arguments, we should mention yet another way of proving God's existence, namely fideism. Fideism was used by Saadiah and popularized by Halevi.[12] Fideists eschew rational arguments altogether, claiming that direct experience of God or tradition is a more reliable guide. Following the Kalâm position reflected in al-Ghazâlî, Judah Halevi argued that the philosophical conception of God was incompatible with the God of tradition for two reasons. First, he argued, the God of the philosophers was not an agent endowed with will, but rather was a necessary first cause; and second, the God of the philosophers was unable to know particulars and hence was not able to interact with individual human beings. As noted by Fraenkel, Judah Halevi's rejection of rational arguments for God's existence posed a challenge to subsequent philosophers.[13]

In response to philosophical attempts to prove the existence of God by means of rational demonstration, Halevi's main character in the *Kuzari*, the *Haver* (the term means "friend," one who is sympathetic to Jewish beliefs), articulates a classic fideistic position in describing to the king of the Khazars the unwavering belief of the Jewish people in God: "I believe in the God of Abraham, Isaac, and Israel, who led the children of Israel out of Egypt with signs and miracles."[14] The *Haver* has no need of rational proofs, either teleological, cosmological, or ontological, to prove God's existence: he regards the proof of God's existence as implicit in the words themselves, "and so evident that it requires no other argument."[15] In response to the

---

[11] In his detailed exploration of medieval proofs for God's existence, Davidson has argued that even Avicenna's argument, which is reproduced by Maimonides in *Guide* 1.57, namely that God's essence necessarily entails existence, is not an authentic ontological argument. Not only does Avicenna incorporate cosmological elements into the argument, but its author is unaware of ontological arguments and does not intend to present such an argument. Davidson concludes that medieval Jewish philosophy may as a whole be judged free of ontological arguments. See Davidson 1987, 215.

[12] See Altmann 2007, 662.

[13] Fraenkel traces the fideist challenge back to al-Ghazâlî. See Fraenkel 2009, 581.

[14] Halevi *Kuzari* I:11, 44.   [15] Halevi *Kuzari* I:11, 45.

king's query as to why he does not espouse belief in the god of the philosophers, the Ḥaver replies that philosophers rarely agree on doctrines. His own position, however, is grounded both on personal experience and "uninterrupted tradition, which is equal to the former."[16]

Halevi's point in this exchange between the king of the Khazars and the Ḥaver is that religious experience is a better guarantor of the veracity of divine revelation than is any form of philosophical speculation. But Halevi is careful to provide caveats necessary to guarantee the veracity of such experiences, including both the power and public nature of the testimony. How, for example, do we know that the story of manna really happened? "This [the manna] is also irrefutable, viz. a thing which occurred to six hundred thousand people for forty years."[17] Halevi thus validates sense experience alongside of demonstration, as a valid source of knowledge. Most philosophers, however, were determined to buttress faith with reason, and developed *a posteriori* arguments to demonstrate the existence of God.

III.1 Weak versions of the cosmological argument: Saadiah Gaon and Baḥya ibn Paquda

We mentioned above that Kalâm theologians were obsessed with how to correctly conceive God: the very designation "people of justice and unity" points to their efforts to demonstrate God's justice and unity in light of apparent inconsistencies found within the sources. They provided numerous arguments proving the necessary existence of a creator who sustains the universe; these arguments for God's existence were intertwined with the necessity of creation, and the impossibility of an eternal universe. Maimonides is much more negative with respect to the possibility of proving God's existence from the reality of creation. He is dismissive of Kalâm methods for demonstrating the existence of God, stating that he prefers the methods of philosophy over those of Kalâm on the grounds that while the philosophical arguments are grounded in our sense perception, Kalâm thinkers deny the senses altogether. Maimonides claims that the Kalâm theologians present a circular argument by <u>presupposing</u> the creation of the world, and using that supposition to posit the existence of God. In *Guide* 2.1, Maimonides offers the following dichotomy to portray their circularity:

2.1.1. Either the world is eternal, or it is created in time.
2.1.2. If it is created, it must have a creator, since
    2.1.2.i. what is created has not created itself, or
    2.1.2.ii. its creator is other than it.
2.1.3. If it is eternal, it must have a creator, since there must be a being other than the bodies of the world.
2.1.4. In either case, God's existence can be proved from philosophical premises.
2.1.5. And so God must exist.

(2.1.2), which was espoused by the Kalâm theologians, is circular in that it already, according to Maimonides, contains the conclusion (God's existence) in its premises.

---

[16] Halevi *Kuzari* I:11, 47.   [17] Halevi *Kuzari* I:86, 60.

Expressing a "strong aversion" to the Kalâm method, Maimonides claims that the burden of proof lies on the eternity theorist to prove the existence of the deity from the supposition that the universe is eternal, and not created.

Saadiah Gaon and Baḥya ibn Paquda regard the Kalâm arguments in a much more favorable light however, and they present arguments against the backdrop of these Kalâm discussions. Both use the existence of order and design in the universe to postulate the existence of a designer or creator, arguing for the extreme unlikeliness that the universe would have arisen by chance or accident.

Saadiah followed the Kalâm procedure, deriving the existence of God from his arguments for creation. His arguments that the world is not eternal but must have been *created* are developed against the backdrop of Kalâm proofs, and are problematic; we shall return to the details of these arguments in Chapter 6. Let us now focus upon his teleological argument for the existence of God.[18] As Jospe notes, it demonstrates at best that the order of the cosmos is evidence of some kind of design and plan, but does not prove that the elements were themselves created.

Having in *Book of Beliefs and Opinions* I.1 provided four arguments in support of the creation of the world (we shall return in Chapter 6 to these arguments), Saadiah turns to three arguments positing God's existence on the grounds that the world could not have created itself: "it seemed impossible to me, however, that they [all things] should have created themselves."[19] The third of these arguments can be summarized as follows:

2.1.a.   We have seen that the world is created (from Chapter 1).

2.1.b.   If the world is capable of creating itself, it must have been capable of desisting from creating itself.

2.1.c.   Therefore the world has the capacity both to exist or not exist.

2.1.d.   Because we assume the world to be nonexistent when we predicate that it is capable of not creating itself, it follows that we attribute to it both existence and nonexistence at "one and the same time."[20]

2.1.e.   But it is impossible that the world be both existent and non-existent at the same time.

2.1.f.   And so necessarily "someone outside of itself must have created it."[21]

Fraenkel notes that while Saadiah's notion of God preserves most of the features of the traditional Jewish conception of God, nonetheless that true knowledge of God "does not seem to be the outcome of a comprehensive scientific project culminating in the apprehension of the first principle of nature's rational order."[22] And in fact, it is worth noting that Maimonides criticizes the argument on the grounds that at best it demonstrates that the order of the cosmos is evidence of some kind of design and plan, but it does not prove that the elements were themselves created.

Baḥya ibn Paquda offers a similar argument in *Duties of the Heart* 1:5, claiming that since the world is composite, it must have been put together at some point in time; since nothing can make itself, it must have been created, its creator being God.

---

[18] This argument is similar to the third Kalâm proof of creation outlined by Maimonides in *Guide* 1:74.
[19] Saadiah *Beliefs* I.2:46.   [20] Saadiah *Beliefs* I.2:46.   [21] Saadiah *Beliefs* I.2:47.
[22] Fraenkel 2009, 575. Fraenkel provides extensive analysis of several proofs for God's existence.

In I:4, he claims, following Isaac Israeli, that we can only ask *whether* God is, not what he is, how he is, or why he is, since God's essence cannot be defined: "About the Creator, however, one may only ask whether He exists."[23] Baḥya posits three premises that underlie his argument: that a thing does not make itself, that causes are limited in number and so must have a first cause, and that everything that is a compound must have been brought into existence.[24] On the basis of these premises (the validity of which he attempts to demonstrate), Baḥya then employs in *Duties* 1.6 a standard version of teleological argument, based on the claim that the parts of the universe exhibit design and that the universe manifests order, intention and purpose. That the design manifest in the universe arose from chance is rejected outright: "There are men who say that the world came into existence by chance... How could any rational human being, in his right mind, entertain such a notion?"[25] Surely we would not expect that if some ink spills accidentally upon a page, that "it would take the shape of orderly writing and legible lines"; so too must we postulate "the existence of an intelligent Designer who intentionally created the order apparent in the universe."[26]

We noted above that Maimonides avoids this version of the cosmological argument, on the grounds of its circularity. Claiming that the burden of proof lies on the eternity theorist to prove the existence of the deity from the supposition that the universe is eternal, and not created, the only correct way, he tells us, "is to establish the existence and the oneness of the deity and the negation of corporeality through the methods of the philosophers, which methods are founded upon the doctrine of the eternity of the world."[27] Based on these considerations, Maimonides thus adopts (2.1.3), which he feels provides a more rigorous grounding to arguments for God's existence. This dialectical move should not, Maimonides warns us, be understood as a tacit acceptance of the eternity thesis (we shall return to this thorny issue in Chapter 6), but rather as an attempt to bolster the acceptability of his arguments. Maimonides' arguments, which are based on assumption that the world is eternal and not created, will reinforce what is given in sense experience, and will not disagree with Aristotle.[28] Maimonides feels that (2.1.3) provides for a stronger argument than one based on the assumption that the world must be created.[29]

III.2 Maimonides and Crescas on the cosmological argument for God's existence

Maimonides' own arguments in *Guide* 2.1 provide us a classic example of cosmological arguments. In order to lay out proofs for God's existence, Maimonides first summarizes (in *Guide* 2: Introduction) what he takes to be twenty-five Aristotelian

---

[23] Baḥya *Duties* I.4:79.   [24] Baḥya *Duties* I.5:81.   [25] Baḥya *Duties* I.6:91.
[26] Baḥya *Duties* I.6:93.   [27] Maimonides *Guide* 1.71:181.   [28] Maimonides *Guide* 1.71:182.
[29] But, as we shall see, Maimonides is not thoroughly convinced in the certainty of his own arguments. In speaking of the superlunar spheres, Maimonides tells us that "even the general conclusion that may be drawn from them [the motion of the spheres], namely, that they prove the existence of their Mover, is a matter the knowledge of which cannot be reached by human intellect" Maimonides *Guide* 2.24:326–7. We should keep in mind that in fact, neither the eternity thesis nor the creation thesis is demonstrable (a point we will discuss in greater detail), and so we shall have to return to the question of the ultimate demonstrability of God's existence.

premises that form the basis of metaphysics and physics. Several of these premises lie at the heart of Maimonides' arguments and can be restated as follows:

[P3]   Denial of the possibility of infinite regress: "the existence of causes and effects of which the number is infinite is impossible."[30]

[P5]   Definition of change: "every motion is a change and transition from potentiality to actuality."[31]

[P17]   The existence of movers: "everything that is in motion has of necessity a mover"; this mover can be outside the moved object, or in the body in motion.[32]

[P19]   Definition of possible existence: "everything that has a cause for its existence is only possible with regard to existence in respect of its own essence."[33]

[P20]   Definition of necessary existence: "everything that is necessarily existent in respect to its own essence has no cause for its existence in any way whatever or under any condition."[34]

[P25]   Definition of a proximate mover: everything is composed of matter and form. But inasmuch as matter does not move itself, there must be an agent, "a mover that moves the substratum so as to predispose it to receive the form." This mover is the proximate mover, which "predisposes the matter of a certain individual."[35]

[P26]   Eternity *a parte ante* of the world: "I shall add to the premises mentioned before, one further premise that affirms as necessary the eternity of the world. This premise . . . [consists in Aristotle's statement] that time and movement are eternal, perpetual, existing *in actu*."[36]

Maimonides notes in his explication of this last premise that Aristotle's arguments in favor of eternity *a parte ante* do not constitute a demonstration.[37]

In light of these principles, Maimonides offers four proofs for the existence of God, all of which presuppose the eternity of the world. The first and fourth arguments are based on the eternal movement of the celestial spheres.[38] Maimonides' first argument is based on P26 (above), which affirms the eternity and perpetuity of time and motion, thus relying upon the controversial Aristotelian thesis of eternity

---

[30]   Maimonides *Guide* 2 Intro: 235.   [31]   Maimonides *Guide* 2 Intro: 236.
[32]   Maimonides *Guide* 2 Intro: 237.   [33]   Maimonides *Guide* 2 Intro: 238.
[34]   Ibid.   [35]   Maimonides *Guide* 2 Intro: 239.   [36]   Maimonides *Guide* 2 Intro: 239–40.
[37]   Maimonides *Guide* 1.69:168. These premises must be understood against the backdrop of Maimonides' discussion in *Guide* 1.69 having to do with the nature of causes. In this chapter, Maimonides defines what he (and the philosophers) mean by cause. He follows the standard Aristotelian distinction of four causes (material, formal, efficient, and final) and claims that God is the "efficient cause," by which he means "the form, and . . . the end." Maimonides further maintains that for any series of causes and effects, it is only the first cause in a series that "is the efficient cause of all intermediaries." All the intermediate causes in a series of causes function as mediators for the causal power that resides in the ultimate cause. If there is no first cause, there cannot be any other cause, and hence no existence. Maimonides is clear that God as first cause endows the series with existence: were God not to exist, then "all that exists would likewise be nonexistent." Maimonides claims that in order for his arguments to prove the existence of God, and not just a first mover, we must establish not only the existence of a first cause, but also the incorporeality and unity of this cause. His arguments are therefore meant to demonstrate all three attributes.
[38]   The proof was already expounded by Aristotle in *Physics* 8.5–6 256a–2601 and in *Metaphysics* 12.6–7 1071b–1073a.

a parte ante of the universe.[39] The argument proceeds as follows: Assume that a state of affairs (subject to generation and corruption) is moved. By P25, there must be a proximate mover responsible for the movement of this matter. But if we ask, "what moves this mover," we recognize that the mover of the proximate mover must exist as well. But, as stated in premise three, motion does not go on to infinity. All motion ultimately stops with the sphere of the fifth body (*aether*), which too is in motion. But this outermost sphere must have a mover as well. This mover must be either inside or outside the outermost sphere. If it is outside the sphere, it is either a body or not, whereas if it is inside the sphere, it is either a force and divisible, or it is a force and not divisible. Maimonides then argues that the mover in question is not a body outside the sphere; nor, however, is that mover a divisible force in the sphere; nor is it indivisible. All of these are shown to be impossibly "absurd" states of affairs. Maimonides affirms that every motion and change in the sublunar world is thus traceable to the continual circular movement of the heavens; the cause of the motion of the heavens is thus the ultimate cause of all motion. This first cause of motion is shown, based on Aristotelian premises (16, 17, 18), to be indivisible and exempt from change, timeless and incorporeal. Maimonides then demonstrates on the basis of premise 19 that the first mover must be a unity.[40]

The fourth argument, which is based on the impossibility of an infinite regress of causes, differs from the first argument in a number of respects: first, unlike the first argument which brings in specific points from the science of physics, this fourth argument considers efficient causation in the abstract, with no mention of any particular type of causation. The argument is based on Aristotle's presentation in *Metaphysics* 2.2 994a 1–19 that an infinite regress of causes is impossible on the grounds that without a first cause, there would be no intermediary causes, and hence no cause whatever. Although Aristotle never uses this argument to prove the existence of God, it was appropriated by medieval philosophers, and is presented by Maimonides as follows:

2.2.1. We see things that pass from potency to act
2.2.2. Everything that is actualized must have a cause
2.2.3. This cause was originally in a state of potentiality
2.2.4. This cause therefore requires a prior cause to actualize it
2.2.5. This series of causes cannot continue to infinity
2.2.6. There must exist something that causes the move from potency to act in which there is no potentiality [from P23]
2.2.7. This entity is totally separate from matter [from P24]
2.2.8. This entity is God.

Maimonides notes the importance of supplementing the basic argument with additional premises having to do with the incorporeality and unity of God. He thus calls upon Aristotle's dictum that the ultimate cause of motion must exist in an eternal state of actuality; such a being (P24) must be immaterial and incorporeal, since it is

---

[39] I am much indebted to Harvey's discussion of this argument. See Harvey, W. 1998, 48ff.
[40] See Davidson 1987, 240–9 for discussion of this argument.

free of potentiality and hence of materiality. Furthermore, since it is incorporeal, it contains no ground of individuation, and hence is the sole instance of its kind.

Hasdai Crescas offers, in *Light of the Lord,* a trenchant critique of Maimonides' proofs. Crescas opens with a discussion of whether the existence of God "rests upon tradition alone" or "whether we may also attain to it by way of reason and speculation."[41] Summarizing the attempts of his predecessors, including among others Aristotle, Ibn Daud, and Maimonides, Crescas focuses upon those of Maimonides. In particular, his concern is twofold: whether the twenty-six propositions used by Maimonides in his proofs are established by demonstrative reasoning; and second, whether the Maimonidean principles can be shown to follow from those propositions.[42] The first propositions center on whether an actual infinite exists. Maimonides rejected the notion of an actual infinite while, as we shall see in Chapter 6, Crescas will accept the existence of an actual infinite. As a result, he rejects Maimonides' arguments for God's existence, which rested on the claim that an actual infinite is impossible.

In *Light* I.2. ch. 12, Crescas attacks Maimonides' two cosmological, or physical, proofs from two standpoints: first, on the grounds that they rely on premises 1, 2, 3, 8, 12, and 16, none of which has been validly proved, and second, that even if it could be shown that the *premises* were true, Maimonides' *proofs* would still be false.[43] Take, for example, premise 16, which ensures that the Prime Mover is One. Anticipating the criticisms of David Hume in the eighteenth century, Crescas points out that this premise does not rule out the possibility of a multitude of Prime Movers, each of which is a unity, and each of which is the cause of a different world order. As Warren Zev Harvey notes, Crescas' refutation of Maimonides' favored physical proof of the existence of God, is thus thoroughgoing and devastating.[44] Crescas himself does not offer a proof for the existence of God based on the study of the physical universe, but rather relies upon a metaphysical argument. His position on the efforts of "scientific speculation" to prove God's existence is explicit: "This shows that what removes perplexity and gives the truth in these questions has never yet been perfectly attained by philosophy, and that the lamp that shines light on all these profound subjects is the Law alone."[45]

III.3 Metaphysical argument for the existence of God: Ibn Daud, Maimonides, and Crescas

We turn now to the metaphysical argument for God's existence, derived from Avicenna's distinction between necessary and contingent existents. This popular and influential argument was appropriated by a number of Jewish philosophers, including Ibn Daud, Maimonides, and Crescas. The Islamic philosopher Avicenna (Ibn Sina) insisted both in his *Najât* and the *Ishârât* on the legitimacy and desirability of a metaphysical, as opposed to a physical, proof for God's existence. Avicenna

[41] Crescas *Light* Intro, Book 1, in Wolfson 1929, 131.
[42] Crescas *Light* Intro, Book 1, in Wolfson 1929, 133.
[43] Crescas *Light* I.2, ch. 15, in Harvey, W. 1998, 69.   [44] Harvey, W. 1998, 59.
[45] Crescas *Light* I.2, ch. 20, in Harvey, W. 1998, 72.

offered several versions of this argument.[46] Avicenna's argument appeals to his modal metaphysics and attempts to postulate the existence of something necessary through itself, which turns out to be both the efficient and final cause of the universe of possible things.[47]

Avicenna distinguishes two types of being. A "necessarily existent being" is one whose nonexistence involves a contradiction; a "possibly existent being" is one that contains no necessity for its existence or nonexistence. Necessarily existent is of two types: the necessarily existent by virtue of itself, and the necessarily existent by virtue of another but possibly existent by virtue of itself. And so Avicenna envisions three categories of existence in all: possibly existent beings; necessarily existent by virtue of itself; and necessarily existent by virtue of another. As Davidson notes, everything actually existent in the physical world is necessary in one sense or the other.[48]

But is existence identical with the necessary being's essence? Avicenna himself, unlike Averroës and his followers, is ambiguous on this point: on the one hand, he wants to maintain the total difference between essence and existence, but on the other hand, he is tempted to tie the Necessary Existent's *essence* with its necessary *existence*. In order to establish the latter point, Avicenna distinguishes between a thing's being/essence/thingness (*mâhiyya*) and that through which it is existent (*mawjûd; wujûd*). According to Avicenna, God is the only entity in which its essence (*mâhiyya*) does not require an external cause for its existence (*wujûd*). Thus in Avicenna's mind, the argument for God's existence is causal to the extent that contingent beings require an external cause that supplies their *wujûd*.[49]

As noted by Davidson, Avicenna's proof from the concepts of possibly existent and necessarily existent provided a new method of establishing the existence of God, without relying upon the question of an infinite regress.[50] Pieces of his argument reappear in Ibn Daud, Maimonides, and Crescas, as well as scholastic thinkers such as Thomas Aquinas and Duns Scotus. Avicenna's argumentation, whether accepted or not, whether even properly understood or not, "predominated in efforts by Avicenna's medieval Islamic and Jewish successors to prove the existence of God."[51] Let us turn then to several of these efforts.

---

[46] Scholars have disagreed over whether his argument constitutes an ontological argument or not. McGinnis himself, in contrast to other scholars, sees "nothing like an Anselmian ontological-style argument for the existence of God in Avicenna." See McGinnis 2010, 164 (and notes) for discussion of the various interpretations of Avicenna.

[47] See McGinnis 2010, 166–8 and 257 for details of the argument. See also Davidson 1987.

[48] Davidson 1987, 291.

[49] Avicenna further distinguishes between two sets of dichotomies: the dichotomy of possibly existent by virtue of itself and necessarily existent by virtue of another; and the dichotomy of necessarily existent by virtue of itself on the other. In his *al-Najât*, Avicenna argued that the category of entities described by the former is dependent upon entities described by the latter: that is, they depend for their existence upon a being necessarily existent by virtue of itself. Now the very notion "necessarily existent by virtue of itself" is itself problematic. What Avicenna means to say here is that such an entity cannot exist even, as Davidson argues, by reason of its parts or "internal factors making it what it is" (Davidson 1987, 304). It must thus be free of composition; furthermore, it turns out that there can only be one such being. Thus, a multiplicity of possible beings cannot add up to, or comprise, a necessary being by virtue of itself.

[50] Davidson 1987, 385.   [51] Davidson 1987, 388.

Ibn Daud is one of the first Jewish philosophers to appropriate Avicenna's distinctions. Having devoted the first treatise of *Sefer ha-Emunah ha-Ramah* to the sublunar world, Ibn Daud turns in the second treatise to the superlunar domain, starting with two proofs for the existence of God. The first proof, presented in the first treatise, is a modified version of Aristotle's first mover argument in the *Physics*, while the second argument (in the second treatise) leads to the existence of a necessary existent as distinct from all possible existents. It thus appears that Ibn Daud utilizes the Avicennian distinction between necessary and possible existence: according to Ibn Daud, what is necessary owes its existence to nothing else, whereas what is contingent does depend upon something else for its existence. In the context of explaining different senses of unity, Ibn Daud distinguishes in II.1 between two notions: possibility of existence and necessity of existence. The former is described as "anything whose existence depends on something other than itself."[52] He then in the second chapter uses this distinction to present two sets of arguments: first a set of arguments proving that there exists at least one necessary of existent being that is "necessary of existence in itself," and then that there exists at most one such necessary of existence.

Fontaine suggests that Ibn Daud does not follow any of Avicenna's texts to the letter, but "that he gives a free adaptation of Ibn Sina's proof."[53] In his second set of arguments, Ibn Daud follows the lead of Avicenna in establishing the existence of God as "the necessary being" in the sense that God's essence necessarily implies His existence, unlike all other beings whose existence is "possible" and extrinsic to their essence. As Fontaine has noted, Ibn Daud's arguments thus constitute a clear break from his predecessors, in that he does not refer to God as "creator," but rather uses words like "first mover" and "necessary existent": "he is too much of a philosopher to advance the creation of the world as a proof of the existence of God."[54] Following in the footsteps of Avicenna, who did not think it justified to simply identify the first, unmoved cause of motion with God, so too Ibn Daud felt that the physical proof based on motion was insufficient, and hence provided a "metaphysical" proof.[55]

Like Avicenna, Ibn Daud claims that the existence of a thing is separate from its essence; in the case of the necessary being, its essence is sufficient for its existence, whereas for possible beings their essence is insufficient to bring about their existence: "To Ibn Daud, the fact that the existence of a possible existent is not inherent in its essence means, as it does to Ibn Sina, nothing other than that such an existent requires a cause for its existence, and to that extent can never itself become a necessary existent."[56] While the actual arguments are somewhat garbled, Ibn Daud concludes that "it is proven that it is not possible for there to be in existence two gods; rather [there is] one."[57]

Avicenna's influence is felt in Maimonides' *Guide* as well. Maimonides' third proof, or the argument from possibility, has commonly been called a metaphysical

---

[52] Ibn Daud 1986, *Exalted Faith* II.1 128b.15, 141.   [53] Fontaine 1990, 93.
[54] Fontaine 1990, 89.
[55] See McGinnis 2010, 151 for further discussion of Avicenna's arguments for God. See also Davidson 1987.
[56] Fontaine 1990, 94.   [57] Ibn Daud 1986, *Exalted Faith* II.1 130a.15, 143.

proof for God's existence, and is based on Avicenna's distinction between necessary and contingent existents. Maimonides says of this argument that it is "a demonstration concerning which there can be no doubt, no refutation, and no dispute, except on the part of one who is ignorant of the method of demonstration."[58] On this point, Maimonides finds himself caught between two poles: that of Averroës, who argues that metaphysics alone is not sufficient to prove the existence of God, and that of Avicenna, who feels he has in fact offered such a metaphysical proof.

Whether Maimonides made use of Avicenna's formulation directly, or availed himself of secondary versions, has been hotly contested by recent scholars.[59] Remnants of Avicenna's distinctions are nevertheless apparent in Maimonides' third argument, which can be schematized as follows:

2.3.1. There exist many things we perceive with the senses

2.3.2. All these things must fall into one of three classes:

2.3.2a. no things are subject to generation and corruption

2.3.2b. all things are subject to generation and corruption

2.3.2c. or some things are subject to generation and corruption, while others are not

2.3.3. By experience we know that 2.3.3 is false; so either 2.3.2b or 2.3.2c must obtain

2.3.4. Assume 2.3.2b is true, then

2.3.4.a. let it be the case that everything undergoes corruption

2.3.4.b. then it is possible that all entities will cease to exist

2.3.4.c. but from premise 23, what is possible will necessarily be actualized

2.3.4.d. it follows therefore that there was a time at which nothing existed

2.3.4.e. but there could exist nothing now, from the principle "out of nothing comes nothing" (ex nihilo nihil fit)

2.3.4.f. given that we perceive things that are existent (we ourselves in fact), it follows that 2.3.4.b must not be the case

2.3.5. So 2.3.2c is the only option

2.3.6. So not everything that exists can be subject to generation and corruption

2.3.7. So there exists at least one object not subject to generation and corruption

Having shown that there exists at least one being not subject to change, Maimonides must demonstrate, once again, that this being specified in (2.3.7) is not only necessarily existent, but is itself incorporeal and a unity. At this point, Maimonides reverts to Avicenna's distinction between possible and necessary beings, and maintains that, based on premise twenty, this being must be "necessary in respect to its cause."[60] While Avicenna's distinctions are somewhat garbled in Maimonides' presentation, the philosophical point is clear: "there is an existent that is necessary of existence in respect to its own essence" (ibid.). This entity can contain no internal

---

[58] Maimonides Guide 2.1:248.

[59] See Davidson 1987; Pines 1963; Stern 2001. See Ivry's comment that Maimonides was "very taken with Avicenna's proof of God's existence, based on the non-Aristotelian distinction between essence and existence" Ivry 2016, 45.

[60] Maimonides Guide 2.1:248.

multiplicity, for if it did, the multiplicity (by P21) would be a cause of the existence of the being that is necessary of existence in respect of its own essence. For this reason, this being cannot (P22) be corporeal, and is identified with God. And so there exists as least and at most one such being that is necessary of existence in respect to its own essence.[61] Harvey offers a succinct summary of this argument as follows: "all observed existents are contingent; but everything cannot be contingent; ergo, something must be Necessary, and that is God."[62]

In his critique of the argument, Crescas notes that Maimonides makes two crucial steps: first, that something must be eternal, and second, that this entity is eternal in virtue of its own essence. Nevertheless, Maimonides' argument is subject to a number of questionable moves, most of which are rejected by Crescas. Once again, Crescas rejects both Maimonides' use of questionable premises (in this case P3 and P26), and the overall invalidity of the argument. First, between steps 2.3.4.c and 2.3.4.d, from the hypothesis that every individual thing has the possibility of being destroyed, it does not follow that the totality of things will at some moment cease to exist. Crescas' critique in *Light* 1.2.17 is straightforward: although each individual thing might eventually be destroyed, there is no reason to assume that all things will cease to exist simultaneously: "For if all existing things were subject to generation and corruption, and each had the possibility of corruption, it would not necessarily follow that they all be corrupted simultaneously, but one might come into existence after the passing away of the other . . . the proof then is false."[63]

Crescas does however accept Maimonides' statement of the metaphysical argument for the existence of a necessary being, calling it obviously the case: "since that which has a cause for its existence is not necessary of existence, it must inevitably follow that that which is necessary of existence has no cause for its existence."[64] But although the existence of a first cause is demonstrable, the intermediate links in the series of causes and effects can nonetheless be infinite; in other words, the existence of a first cause does not preclude an infinite series. In any event, however, Crescas claims that something is needed to tip the scale in favor of existence: "there is no escaping that there must be some cause of the entirety of them . . . that which gives preponderance to their existence, and this is God."[65] We might imagine Maimonides responding as follows: given that each entity is destructible, it is at least possible that all entities will cease to exist at the same moment. Since every possibility must be actualized (premise 23) it follows that at some instant of time in the infinite past, this possible state of affairs will have been actualized, and the totality of actual things will have ceased to exist.

Furthermore, the argument presupposes the acceptance of premise 26, the eternity of the world. But, as Maimonides' medieval (and modern) commentators have pointed out, the argument requires a version of eternity *a parte ante*: only if an

---

[61] Numerous scholars have suggested that Maimonides did not follow Avicenna slavishly, but that in fact both he and Averroes had incomplete information about the details of Avicenna's argument. See for example Stern 2001, 67; Davidson 1987, 383 n. 24; Harvey, W. 1998; Ivry 2016.

[62] Harvey, W. 1998, 73.   [63] Crescas *'Or Adonai* I.2, ch. 17, in Harvey, W. 1998, 95.

[64] Crescas *'Or Adonai* Proposition XX, in Wolfson 1929, 305.

[65] Crescas *'Or Adonai* I.3, ch. 2, in Harvey, W. 1998, 97.

infinite amount of time has already passed, can we say that there must be something incorruptible now. The weakness of this argument notwithstanding, it continued to reappear throughout the history of philosophy: it entered Scholastic thought through the works of Thomas Aquinas, Henry of Ghent, Duns Scotus, and Suarez, and reappeared in modern philosophy in the writings of Descartes, Spinoza, and Leibniz.

III.4 The teleological argument: Maimonides and Gersonides

The final *propter quia* argument incorporates versions of the teleological argument. Maimonides offers a variant on this argument in the context of his attempt to explain the presence of discrete particulars in the world. In *Guide* 2.19, Maimonides tells us that his purpose is to present arguments that "come close to being a demonstration," for the existence of a "purposer."[66] By "purposer" Maimonides means one who is accountable or responsible for all the contingent (particular) facts of the matter in the world. Given that all things in the world are composed of one common substance, how can we account for the multiplicity of individuals within each species, let alone the many varieties of species in the world? Maimonides first summarizes the Aristotelian response according to which prime matter is transformed into the four elements each with different qualities; these in turn form the basis for the myriad compounds found in the sublunar spheres. Since matter has great latitude with respect to its specific forms, individuals within each species differ corresponding to this latitude.[67] Midway through the chapter, however, Maimonides' tone changes, as he warns us to pay attention to what he has to say. Aristotle has told us that from the difference of acts, difference of forms can be inferred. In one case, however, the inference does not hold. While the motions of the four elements are rectilinear, that of the sphere is circular, and so "the matter of these elements is not the matter of the sphere."[68] They differ as well with respect to their forms, which is what distinguishes each element from the other. From this, it follows that the matter of the celestial spheres is one, and yet the form of every sphere differs.

But who is responsible for particularizing these substrata and predisposing them to receive these various forms?[69] In other words, how do we account for the particularization (or individuation) of the spheres' individual matter, so as to account for the entry of the forms? Kalâm philosophers had developed their own response to this issue, claiming that the very fact that a thing has been determined in terms of one particular size, place, location, and so forth is proof that there exists a Being that freely chooses these determinations. Inasmuch as objects in the atomist ontology do not have specific natures, the fact that they exhibit one set of characteristics rather than another must be explained. Hence, the Mutakallimûn concluded that a Being must be responsible for the characterization of each entity in the universe: the world as a whole requires someone to "particularize it as a whole and each of its parts by means of one of the various admissible possibilities."[70] Although

---

[66] Maimonides *Guide* 2.19:303.   [67] Maimonides *Guide* 2.19:304.
[68] Maimonides *Guide* 2.19:305.   [69] Maimonides *Guide* 2.19:306.
[70] Maimonides *Guide* 1.74:218–19.

Maimonides rejects atomist occasionalism as a metaphysical doctrine, he agrees with the Kalâm conclusion, namely that the fact that particularization exists is evidence of a particularizer.

Maimonides recognizes that Aristotle was unable to account for the how and why of particularization, and emphatically enunciates the limitation inherent in Aristotle's words: of all that Aristotle had to say about the sphere, he "has assigned no clear cause with regard to this, and that the matter, as he sets it out, does not follow an order for which necessity can be claimed."[71] In other words, Aristotle was unable to account for the necessary ordering inherent in the sublunar universe, and was forced to recognize that his arguments were tentative at best. Maimonides excuses Aristotle on the grounds that the science of mathematics "had not been perfected in his time," and that knowledge of astronomy was not as advanced as it is now. Had Aristotle been able to specify the cause for the differences of the motions of the spheres, we would have had no need for a particularizer. But in fact, Aristotle could not provide such an explanation. On the assumption of a created universe, there must exist "a being that has particularized . . . every sphere in regard to its motion and rapidity."[72]

Furthermore, how do we account for the contingent positioning of the stars in the outermost heavens? Maimonides attributes these and other apparently contingent cases to a "purposer" who brought about these celestial anomalies. Just as objects in the sublunar universe do not exist by chance, and did not happen by chance, so too in the superlunar universe. All these examples are "necessary according to the purpose of one who purposes."[73] The particularizer thus accounts for what "has been produced for an object that we do not know and is not an aimless and fortuitous act."[74] Although we have no knowledge of this final cause, we do know that the final causes are not aimless or fortuitous. "Who is the one who particularized the differences that are found in the spheres and the stars unless it be God, may He be exalted?"[75] The underscoring of a demonstrative argument with Scripture is repeated in the Guide, when Maimonides again attributes this argument to Abraham, telling us that, "all the prophets used the stars and the spheres as proofs for the deity's existing necessarily."[76] This demonstration quia he tells us is "the correct proof, which is not exposed to doubt."[77]

Gersonides provides a more nuanced and sophisticated version of the teleological argument: from the teleological nature of all existing things, he concluded that all things move together toward their common ultimate end. This ultimate end is the final cause of the world, namely God. Feldman notes that "Gersonides' cosmology is an excellent example of how biblical notions were interpreted in light of philosophical-scientific theories and conversely."[78] In Gersonides' case of course the science in

---

[71] Maimonides Guide 2.19:307.

[72] Maimonides Guide 2.19:308. See Ivry's comment: Maimonides is convinced of the "teleological aspect of nature" and describes the harmony to be found in nature as a whole, as reflected in bodies and souls. The whole of being is "one individual," in Ivry 2016, 77.

[73] Maimonides Guide 2.19:310.   [74] Maimonides Guide 2.19:310.

[75] Maimonides Guide 2.19:310.   [76] Maimonides Guide 2.19:310.

[77] Maimonides Guide 2.19:311.   [78] Feldman in Gersonides vol. 3, 25.

question was astrology. In contradistinction to Brian Leftow's worry about Gersonides' drawing upon astrology,[79] it should be kept in mind that during this period, astrology was considered a science alongside of astronomy; we shall discuss the implications of astrology in Chapter 7. Gersonides claims that what occurs in the sublunar world is "ordered by the heavenly bodies." He then claims that the cause of this order must be contained in the heavenly spheres, and will proceed to show that there is "one cause prior to the heavenly bodies that makes them partners in one concerted action."[80] This cause is the Agent Intellect.

For Gersonides, the Agent Intellect is directly responsible for the emergence of the soul in animate creatures; biological processes provide direct proof for the existence of this Agent Intellect, and indirect proof for the existence of God, who is the ultimate Agent responsible for all natural processes. Gersonides will argue not only that the Agent Intellect derives from God, but that the entire order exhibited in nature is grounded in God, who is the First Intellect.[81] As Feldman puts it, "the regularity inherent in earthly phenomena is just part of a more comprehensive plan governing the universe... God is or embodies the whole plan and order of the universe."[82] As Gersonides says, having postulated a separate existent that is the agent of sublunar generation and exhibits the order of the sublunar world, "it is evident that the First Intellect is the law, order, and rightness of existent things in the absolute sense."[83] His argument is fairly straightforward:

2.4.1. The domain of the spheres provides for the order of the sublunar world
2.4.2. The entire process [of order] is ordered by something that has total comprehension of his order
2.4.3. This First Intellect is not identical to the Agent Intellect, for if it were, it would only have an inadequate knowledge of the entire system
2.4.4. But if the First Intellect does not have complete knowledge of the order within the entire system, "it would not be possible to achieve a unitary system between the heavenly bodies and the sub-lunar domain."
2.4.5. Hence the First Intellect is the law, order, and rightness of the entire universe insofar as [this plan] is a unified system.[84]

Interestingly, Gersonides, along with Duns Scotus and William of Ockham, rejects the proof for the existence of an unmoved mover from motion, popularized by generations of philosophers, including Thomas Aquinas, Aristotle, and Maimonides. Gersonides envisions a situation in which a moving body can continue to move indefinitely by its own power.[85] In *Wars* III.5, ch. 11, he points out that God, or the First Cause, should not be identified with the mover of the sphere of the fixed stars.

---

[79] Leftow suggests that, "the most elaborate [teleological proof] scientifically was Levi ben Gershom's (Gersonides). Unfortunately, he notes the 'science' he drew on was astrology." In fact, as I shall argue in Chapter 7, astrology was considered to be a robust science during this period. See Leftow 2010, 735.
[80] Gersonides *Wars* vol. 3, 5.2.1: 35.   [81] Feldman's comment is in Gersonides *Wars* vol. 3, 18.
[82] Feldman's comment is in Gersonides *Wars* vol. 3, 21.   [83] Gersonides *Wars* vol. 3, ch. 5.2, 137.
[84] Gersonides *Wars* vol. 3, ch. 5.2, 137.   [85] Gersonides *Wars* vol. 3, ch. 6.

IV   Divine Predication: What Can we Say about God?

We turn now to what in fact we are justified to say about this existent deity. The problem of divine attributes is summarized succinctly by H. A. Wolfson: Given that the starting point of the problem is "the rationalistic attempt to invest the Scriptural predications of God with the validity of logical judgments," Wolfson then asks how can we form a logical judgment about God without at the same time "creating the anomaly of having the unrelatable Necessarily Existent brought into some logical relation with some predicate distinct from Himself?"[86] In other words, if we agree with Avicenna that God is the only Necessarily Existent, and qualitatively different from all other entities, how can we begin to describe this Existent?

Once again, several traditions prevailed in medieval Jewish texts. We have alluded already to the rich literature in which human-like characteristics are applied to God; Jewish liturgical works, poetry, mystical texts, and even philosophical texts are replete with ornate descriptions of God's actions, emotions, and nature. At the other end of the spectrum, the doctrine of skeptical theism rejects the ability of humans to know or say anything about the Deity. At its most extreme, skeptical theism raises what Michael Sells has called the paradox of transcendence: "The transcendent must be beyond names, ineffable. In order to claim that the transcendent is beyond names, however, I must give it a name, 'the transcendent.' Any statement of ineffability, 'X is beyond names,' generates the *aporia* that the subject of the statement must be named (as X) in order for us to affirm that it is beyond names."[87] Sells delineates at least three responses to this *aporia*. The first response is silence, an acknowledgement that nothing can be said about the transcendent being. The second is to distinguish between ways in which the transcendent is beyond names, and ways in which it is not, as in the medieval distinction between God-as-he-is-in-himself, and God-as-he-is-in-creatures. The third is to accept the dilemma as a genuine *aporia*, as unresolvable, leading to a discourse of negative theology or *apophasis*.[88] The paradox of transcendence becomes a leitmotif throughout the history of philosophy and reappears in the twentieth century in the guise of skeptical theism.

One of the earliest exponents of *apophasis* is Plotinus (d. 270 CE), whose *Enneads* present a philosophical and cosmological system of causality based upon a hierarchical series of hypostases, ranging from "the one" (*to hen*) to mind (*nous*) and soul (*psyche*). The ultimate goal of human existence is for the individual soul to turn away from the material world and reunite with the ultimate source of emanation, "the one." Plotinus tells us repeatedly in the *Enneads* that "the one" is "beyond being" or "the beyond being" (*epekeina ontos*); the very act of naming delimits this being "beyond being." In Plotinus' words, "The beyond-being does not refer to a something since it does not posit any-thing, nor does it 'speak its name.'"[89] Nor can the one be grasped in human understanding: "It is certainly nothing of the things of which it is the origin, being such, as it were, that nothing can be attributed to it, neither being, nor beings, nor life. It is beyond those."[90]

---

[86] Wolfson 1977b, 249.   [87] Sells 1994, 2.
[88] For a description of *apophasis*, see Sells 1994, 2–3.   [89] Plotinus *Enneads* 5.5.6:11.
[90] Plotinus *Enneads* 6.8:20.

The influence of Plotinus can be felt in a number of early Christian thinkers who emphasize the nothingness of God in the context of apophatic discourse. John Scotus Eriugena (810–77) composed a work entitled *Periphyseon (On the Divine Nature)* in which, drawing upon the work of Pseudo-Dionysius, he emphasizes apophatic discourse in his conceptualization of God. Eriugena's work provides an alternative cosmology to that of Aristotle, one that emphasizes the mystical ideas of divine darkness and the ultimate unification of everything with God. Eriugena begins with a division of nature into two categories: things that are (that can be grasped by the human mind) and things that are not (that transcend human understanding). That which transcends the mind necessarily transcends being as well, thus establishing an isomorphism between ontology and epistemology. Adopting an emanationist scheme, the ontological movement of things from their primordial unity into the world, and back to their source, is reflected in reason itself. The divine nature itself is simple, beyond being, time, and space (although, even using the term "beyond" is problematic in the context of apophatic discourse). God is described as the "ineffable and incomprehensible and inaccessible brilliance of the Divine Goodness which is unknown to all intellects whether human or angelic—for it is super-essential and supernatural—which while it is contemplated in itself neither is nor was nor shall be, for it is understood to be in none of the things that exist because it surpasses all things, but . . . it alone is found to be in all things . . . Hence the inaccessible brilliance of the celestial powers is often called by theology darkness."[91]

God lies beyond all the Aristotelian categories, and thus, like Plotinus, Eriugena argues that God is beyond both being and language: "strictly speaking, the ineffable nature can be signified by no verb, by no noun, and by no other audible sound, by no signified thing."[92] Because God has no essence, there is no "what" which God is, and so even God does not know what He is, since if God knows *what* He is, he is defining himself: "since, being beyond nature, it escapes all comprehension by itself, how much more (will it elude) any defined or definable intellect?"[93] If not even God can have self-knowledge, it should certainly come as no surprise that finite minds cannot know what God is. Ivry notes that the doctrine of negative theology was practiced by Muslim theologians and philosophers alike, believing that understanding a positive attribution as the negation of its privation allows one to retain traditional predications while not formally endorsing them.[94]

The most radical medieval exponent of apophatic thought in the context of a Neoplatonized Aristotelianism is presented by Maimonides who argues in the *Guide* that we must be careful not to attribute to God any predicates that imply or impute to God anthropomorphic or corporeal features. He analyzes both positive attributes and relational terms, arguing that neither is appropriate to predicate of God. In fact, it turns out that we can say very little, if anything, positive *or* negative, about God: *all*

---

[91] John Scotus Eriugena *Periphyseon* 680D–681B.
[92] John Scotus Eriugena *Periphyseon* 460C.   [93] John Scotus Eriugena *Periphyseon* 620D.
[94] See Ivry 2016, 68. Ivry provides a succinct summary of the apophatic tradition among Islamic philosophers.

attempts to describe God fall short. This new understanding of God's incorporeality must be reflected in our language as well, leading us to Maimonides' celebrated theory of divine predication.

Maimonides develops in Part I, chapters 51–60 of the *Guide* an elaborate theory of divine predication, the purpose of which is to claim that linguistic utterances are inadequate to say anything about God. In these chapters, Maimonides presents a tri-fold set of arguments, corresponding to different types of predicates. The first set of predicates comprises positive attributes and attributes of action, which are descriptive of the "ways and characteristics" of the Deity.[95] Maimonides rejects positive attributes, claiming that they are inadequate to describe God. The final group of affirmative attributes comprises actions that an agent has performed. Maimonides describes attributes of action as follows: "A thing is described by its actions . . . this kind of attributes is separate from the essence of the thing described, and therefore, the most appropriate to be employed in describing the Creator, especially since we know that these different actions do not imply that different elements must be contained in the substance of the agent, by which the different actions are produced."[96] Passages in Scripture that seem to describe God's attributes can be re-interpreted in terms of actions that are descriptive of the "ways and the characteristics" of the Deity; from them we infer corresponding mental states similar to those states that humans experience when exhibiting those actions. Just as we attribute the characteristic "mercy" to an individual who exhibits certain sorts of actions that we describe as being merciful, so too do we attribute to God the state of "mercy$_1$" when God exhibits actions that resemble our own merciful actions. Maimonides is quick to point out, however, that the descriptive terms "mercy" and "mercy$_1$" do not mean the same thing. It is only in an attenuated sense that we can attribute to God the attribute of mercy$_1$. All we mean by calling God "merciful" is that God's actions look similar to the sorts of things a merciful human agent would do.

Maimonides' second theoretical point is that the four essential attributes of God—life, power, wisdom, and will—are of one simple essence; all other attributes are to be conceived either as descriptive of divine action, or as negative attributes. However, Maimonides claims that even these four attributes, when predicated of God, are used in an equivocal sense. Believing that God's essence differs from all other essences, Maimonides maintains that even the terms knowledge, power, will, and life are "purely equivocal, so that their meaning when they are predicated of Him is in no way like their meaning in other applications."[97] These equivocal predicates have nothing but the linguistic utterance in common: they "have nothing in common in any respect or in any mode; these attributions have in common only the name and nothing else."[98] Maimonides will conclude in *Guide* 1.59 that only equivocal predication captures the fact that God shares no essential or accidental characteristics in common with humans. God is totally *other* in all respects, and so terms describing God cannot be applied either univocally or amphibolously. Thus, even the four

[95] Maimonides *Guide* 1.54:125. [96] Maimonides *Guide* 1.52:119.
[97] Maimonides *Guide* 1.56:131. [98] Maimonides *Guide* 1.56:131.

attributes noted above (knowledge, power, will, and life) when predicated of God, must be used in a homonymous or equivocal sense.[99]

We come then to Maimonides' third set of arguments that comprises his celebrated theory of negative predication, according to which negative predicates alone bring the mind closer to an understanding of God: "Know that the description of God, may he be cherished and exalted, by means of negations is the correct description."[100] This third piece of Maimonides' theory of divine predication represents the logical culmination of his theory of language.[101] Maimonides theory rests upon Aristotle's theory of negation, which is one of the four types of opposite distinguished in Aristotle's *Categories*. This classification, reproduced in chapter eleven of Maimonides' *Treatise on the Art of Logic*, allows Maimonides to explain that we use the language of opposites, or negative language, to remove from our concept of God attributes that are inappropriate.

Following Aristotle, Maimonides distinguishes between privations and negations in order to explain this procedure. Privations can only be applied to things that could have the predicate in question: e.g., the statement "Zayd is blind" implies that of a class of beings that normally sees, a certain individual Zayd is not seeing. To say that Zayd is blind suggests that under normal conditions, Zayd could have been seeing. Negations on the other hand are applied to things that by nature cannot have the predicate in question. Take, for example, the statement "the wall is blind." Since walls are not the sorts of things that are able to see or fail to see, it makes no sense to attribute either seeing or not seeing to a wall. Similarly, God is not the sort of entity of which anything is or fails to be, and so we can only attribute negations of God. Attributes predicated of God signify "the negation of the privation of the attribute in question."[102] Applying negations of privations to God is a way of reiterating that any positive attribution is simply a category error.

Maimonides concludes that negative predication is the only way to perfect our linguistic utterances with respect to God. Achieving proficiency with negative predication becomes for Maimonides a mark of personal excellence and perfection, and Maimonides presents an epistemological taxonomy according to which "with every increase in the negations regarding Him . . . you come nearer to that apprehension

---

[99] When Maimonides claims that only equivocal predicates can be applied to God, his point is both logical and semantic. Logically, these terms do not function as meaning bearers in a proposition. Semantically, these propositions tell us only what God is not, and nothing about what God is. The only terms that can be used amphibolously are action terms, but here too, Maimonides is careful to note that any analogy between God's actions and our actions is tangential at best.

[100] Maimonides *Guide* 1.58:134.

[101] For more on Maimonides' philosophy of language, see Benor 1995; Stern 2000; Davies 2011; Rudavsky 2010; Stern 2013; Ivry 2016.

[102] Maimonides *Guide* 1.58:136. To take an example, when we say of God that, "God is not temporal," what we mean is that God is not the sort of thing to which temporality either applies or fails to apply. To apply *either* temporality *or* non-temporality to God is to be guilty of a category error. A better way of making this point would be to say, "God is not-un-temporal," emphasizing the uniqueness of God. Because every affirmation about God is to be understood as a negation and not as a privation, it follows that the negation of a weakness does not imply that its opposite power is indirectly attributed to God, but that neither the term nor its opposite applies to God at all. So God is said to be neither weak nor powerful, just as a wall is said to be neither seeing nor blind. God is simply not the sort of being that either has or fails to have any predicate we might want to apply.

than he who does not negate with regard to Him that which, according to what has been demonstrated to you, must be negated."[103] In other words, the individual who describes God in glowing, flowery language is epistemologically further away from God than the individual who recognizes that God cannot be described at all. Maimonides is explicit on this point: whenever a person affirms of God positive attributes, the said person recedes from God's true reality. Ultimately, silence is the only appropriate linguistic response to divine predication: "silence with regard to You is praise."[104]

Nor is Maimonides shy about expounding the implication of his theory with respect to prayers, claiming that exaltations and glorifications of God found in the prayers and poems addressed to God do not constitute logical propositions and hence are meaningless at best, and harmful at worst. The ignorant masses persist in reciting prayers, indulging in language that, if applied to humans, would result in an insult. In fact, Maimonides derides the efforts of poets and psalmists whose attempts to glorify God result, in his words, in "an absolute denial of faith" or "rubbish."[105] The process of affirmative predication is "very dangerous" and can lead to a loss of belief. In one of the most striking passages in the *Guide*, Maimonides warns his reader that one who insists upon positive affirmations has "abolished his belief in the existence of the deity without being aware of it."[106] We shall return in Chapter 9 to the implications of Maimonides' statement.

The untoward ramifications of Maimonides' theory of divine predication cannot be overemphasized. Few philosophers, Jewish or Christian, followed in Maimonides' footsteps. Compare Maimonides' doctrine to the theory of analogy developed by the thirteenth-century scholastic Thomas Aquinas, according to whom predicates can be ascribed relationally (or analogically) to humans and to God. Some commentators have understood Aquinas as arguing that we have no knowledge of God at all, drawing upon his statements to the effect that God is incomprehensible; it is true that Aquinas repeatedly makes the point, for example, that when it comes to God, we cannot know *what* He is, only *that* He is. He offers arguments in many of his works to support the claim that God is not in any genus, and that naming God falls short. In other words, we cannot develop a "science" of God in the way that we can develop a science of things whose essence we can ascertain.[107] By calling God a mystery, Aquinas means that God is not an item in the world like other items; God is not an instance of a kind, nor is God even the one and only instance of a kind; and whatever God's nature is cannot be distinguished from God itself.[108]

What this amounts to is that while we can make true statements about God of the form "God is good" or "God exists," we are seriously in the dark when it comes to understanding what it is for God to *be* perfect, or to *be* good. One implication of this reading is that according to Aquinas, God is not a moral agent in the same way that we are moral agents, and so there can be no explanation of evil on the part of God in the way that we might explain human action. In fact, Aquinas actually denies that

---

[103] Maimonides *Guide* 1.59:138.   [104] Maimonides *Guide* 1.59:139.
[105] Maimonides *Guide* 1.60:141.   [106] Maimonides *Guide* 1.60:145.
[107] Davies 1992, 79; see Thomas Aquinas *Summa Theologica*, question 12.
[108] See Davies 1992, 27.

God is rational, or has reasons, in the way that humans are rational, and so we cannot explain or understand God's actions on a human model.[109]

Unlike Maimonides, however, Aquinas does think that we can truly affirm certain things of God without equivocation, and that we can know that what we say when doing so is true. Although he cites Pseudo-Dionysius regularly, whose emphasis upon the transcendence and unknowability of God is extreme, Aquinas does not move in the direction of Pseudo-Dionysius's apophatic theology.[110] Rather, Aquinas' noted doctrine of analogy is an attempt to drive a middle ground between negative theology on the one hand and total univocity on the other. In contradistinction to Maimonides, Aquinas holds that every act of negation depends upon the prior grasp of an affirmation. He thus assumes that there is a hierarchy of meaningful predications about God, and that our language when applied to God can be meaningful.[111] Thus for example, Aquinas claims that the term "good" when ascribed to God is proportionally greater than when ascribed to humans. According to Aquinas, while the term "good" doesn't mean exactly the same thing in both cases, we can nevertheless draw an analogy between the goodness of God and the goodness of humans. As a result, unlike thinkers in the apophatic tradition, Aquinas will maintain that human beings can, in fact, come to understand and know God, albeit in an attenuated sense.[112]

Maimonides' formulation of an apophatic theology clashed with both the Islamic Ash'arites and Jewish "proto-Kabbalists," both of whom ascribed to God real qualities, including anthropomorphic attributes. Like Aquinas, both Gersonides and Crescas reject the notion of negative predicates as well, arguing that if God is to be intelligible, his attributes must be understood as positive predications. Gersonides criticizes Maimonides' view of homonymous predicates in *Wars* III.3. Gersonides believed that positive predicates could be applied to God literally, because their primary meaning is derived from their application to God, while their human meaning is secondary. He thus attempted to salvage the ability of humans to talk meaningfully about God, claiming that divine predicates are to be understood as *pros en* equivocals rather than absolute equivocals (as Maimonides had argued). What this means is that according to Gersonides, predicates applied to God represent the prime instance or meaning of the term, whereas human predicates are derivative or inferior instances. So, for example, knowledge when applied to God is perfect knowledge and constitutes the standard for human knowledge, which is less perfect than divine knowledge: "the term 'knowledge' is predicated of God (may he be blessed) *primarily* and of others *secondarily*."[113] Gersonides denies that terms have completely different meanings when predicated of God and of humans; it is only because of an underlying commonality of meaning that we can use language meaningfully at all.

Crescas first criticizes Maimonides' theory of negative attributes on two respects: first, that they preclude one's ability to come to know God; and second, that the

---

[109] Davies 1992, 229.
[110] For a study of the importance of Pseudo-Dionysius to Aquinas, see O'Rourke 1992.
[111] See Thomas Aquinas *Summa Theologica*, question 14.
[112] Thomas Aquinas *Summa Theologica*, question 12.   [113] Gersonides *Wars* vol. 2. III.3, 107.

theory is irreconcilable with tradition.[114] He then goes on to reject the traditional distinction between essence and existence, rejecting the views of both Avicenna and Averroes, and inferentially that of Maimonides as well. In *Light* I.III.1, Crescas adopts a position that relies on both positive and negative attributes. The attribute of existence can be predicated of God in a not totally homonymous sense: speaking of the attribute of existence, "the general meaning, however, is that whatever is predicated by existence is not absent. It is in this sense of non-absence that the term is applied to God and to other substances, except that to God it is applied primarily and to other beings subsequently. It is thus clear that the term existence in its application to God and to other beings is not a perfect homonym, but it is a certain kind of ambiguity [i.e., *secundum prius et posterius*]."[115] Nonetheless, Crescas does admit that in some cases, the positive meaning of the attribute amounts to a negation. Hence, the positive meaning of existence is the antithesis of absence, and that of unity is the antithesis of plurality: "so much the more the attribute *priority* which is a mental distinction of His not having been created, *existence* which is an indication of His not being absent, and *unity* which indicates that there is no plurality in His essence."[116]

Crescas in *Light* I:3, 1–6 distinguishes between the essence of God, which is unknowable, and the essential predicates, which are knowable. The essential predicates are inseparable from but not identical with God's essence, in that the one cannot be conceived without the other. The attributes of omniscience and omnipotence may be predicated of God *secundum prius et posterius*, meaning that they are understood both by a priori and a posteriori reasoning. Some of the attributes are negative in meaning, including existence, unity, and eternity. Nonetheless, any rescue attempts cannot ignore the radical nature of Maimonides' linguistic analysis. In an ontology that eschews God's materiality, one in which God is ontologically *sui generis*, it follows that nothing at all can be said of God. Once we recognize with the negative theologian that God inhabits a unique class of one, we realize that human language simply cannot talk about this unique ontological entity, and so, to paraphrase Wittgenstein, one must remain silent. And yet, as we turn to subsequent chapters, medieval Jewish philosophers had much to say about all these issues.

---

[114] Crescas 'Or Adonai I. III.3:23b, quoted in Wolfson 1977.
[115] Crescas 'Or Adonai I. III.3:23, quoted in Wolfson 1977, 319.
[116] Crescas 'Or Adonai I. III.3:24b, quoted in Wolfson 1977, 323–4.

5

God, Suffering, and Omniscience

I Introduction

The question of why the righteous suffer dates back to the *Book of Job* and remains one of the most intractable issues in philosophical theology. Most generally, the very concept of a caring deity who is both omniscient and omnipotent gives rise to a logical dilemma, one that was concretized by Hume in his *Dialogues on Natural Religion*: if God is omniscient, then God knows past, present, and future contingents; if God is omnipotent, then God can actualize any state of affairs; if God is benevolent, then presumably God wishes the best possible state of affairs for God's creatures; and yet we cannot help but recognize the basic fact that the righteous suffer. And so, given the ineluctable reality of human suffering, God is either not omniscient, or not omnipotent, or not benevolent.

The problem of evil thus comprises a number of issues related to divine omniscience and omnipotence: the general problem of logical fatalism, the problem of God's foreknowledge of human events and the relation of this knowledge to free will, and particular theological difficulties centering on the notions of divine providence and retribution. In this chapter, I examine the major philosophical moves made in medieval Jewish philosophy to address these issues. Before turning to the second and third clusters of issues surrounding God's foreknowledge, however, let me first explore the underlying logical dimension of the problem. For it is the logical dimension that underscores the connection between God's omniscience and the domain of temporality. At stake ultimately is how a benevolent, omniscient, and omnipotent creator can allow creatures to suffer.

II The Many Dimensions of the Problem of Divine Omniscience

The general problem of divine omniscience comprises a number of subsidiary problems: the problem of logical fatalism as introduced by Aristotle in his *De Interpretatione* and further developed by the Stoics; the problem of God's foreknowledge of human events and the relation of this knowledge to free will; and particular theological difficulties centering on the notions of prophecy, providence, and retribution.[1] For our thinkers, the question of whether God knows particulars arises out of a clash of two

---

[1] For an introductory survey of the vast primary and secondary literature dealing with issues connected with God's omniscience, the following works should be consulted: Leaman 1995; Kenny 1979; Normore 1982; Rudavsky 2000; Feldman 2009; Nadler 2009.

world views. On the one hand, Jewish philosophers accept an epistemology that identifies knower with object known in certain respects; hence, to claim that God knows events in the sublunar world is to posit at the very least a likeness, if not an actual isomorphism, between God and his creation. On the other hand, as theologians, these thinkers are committed to certain theological presuppositions about the transcendent nature of God that in many instances seems to preclude such a likeness. If God knows future contingents before they have occurred, does God's knowledge affect the contingent nature of human actions? In the *Mishneh Torah*, Maimonides articulated the classic dilemma of free choice vs. foreknowledge in terms of the following dilemma:

Perchance you will say, 'Does not the Almighty know everything that will be before it happens?' He either knows that this person will be righteous or wicked, or He does not know. If He knows that he will be righteous, it is impossible that he should not be righteous; and if you say that He knows that he will be righteous and yet it is possible for him to be wicked, then He does not know the matter clearly.[2]

On this dilemma, either God has foreknowledge, or humans have free will, but not both. Jewish philosophers acknowledge the intractability of this dilemma, inherited already from the rabbis. The primary worry underlying these questions is whether the claim that God's knowledge extends to particulars in the sublunar world is inconsistent with the doctrine of God's unity and inmmutability. Our thinkers will have to explain how it is that God can know particulars in the sublunar world, without this knowledge compromising God's essential nature.

Within the history of medieval thought, two main solutions to the problem of divine foreknowledge presented themselves: (theological) incompatibilism and (theological) compatibilism.[3] The *incompatibilist* holds that God's foreknowledge of future contingents is incompatible with the contingency of these events or states of affairs. We can distinguish further between two forms of incompatibilism. One form of incompatibilism, which I shall term *theological indeterminism*, is that God does not know future contingent events. The theological indeterminist will want to maintain that if God has foreknowledge of future contingent events, then those events cannot be construed as free. Starting with free choice as a given, the indeterminist claims that my freely performing an action precludes God's having foreknowledge of that action. Once God knows in advance what I will do, I have no power to do the opposite of what God knows I will do.[4] Another strand of incompatibilism, *theological determinism*, claims that if God knows future contingent events or states of affairs, then human actions are ultimately determined. Theological determinism

---

[2] Maimonides *MT* 5:10:87b.

[3] In this discussion, I am concerned primarily with theological versions of determinism and indeterminism; we will turn shortly to logical determinism and astrological determinism.

[4] Gersonides and Ibn Daud come closest to this view, trying to safeguard human freedom at the expense of divine omniscience; I will return briefly to both their views in section V, Theological Incompatibilism: Ibn Daud and Gersonides. In this regard, it's worth noting that few Islamic or scholastic philosophers adopt indeterminism. Ockham is one of the few exceptions, but even he "waffles" on the implications for God's knowledge. What I am calling an indeterminist position is sometimes called "strong libertarianism." See for example Gellman 1989.

entails God's infallibility, the notion that God cannot be mistaken about future events. Both the determinists and indeterminists thus agree that if God knows future contingents, then human freedom is constrained by God's knowledge, but they disagree over whether God really does have foreknowledge: indeterminists are committed to human freedom, whereas determinists are unwilling to circumscribe God's foreknowledge. As we shall see below, however, both positions undermine other basic tenets of Jewish belief, most notably prophecy and doctrines of reward and punishment. For this reason, the majority of Jewish philosophers, along with their scholastic contemporaries, adopted a form of compatibilism, claiming that God's foreknowledge of future contingent events in no way impedes human choice.[5]

One reason for the popularity of compatibilism is that it allows for a theory of moral responsibility. Aristotle was the first philosopher to construct a theory of moral responsibility against the backdrop of voluntary action. Already in his early logical work De Interpretatione 9, Aristotle connected moral deliberation to moral responsibility, claiming that agents could not be held morally responsible for their actions if they were not able to deliberate over their actions.[6] The logical dimension of this issue can be traced back to Aristotle's De Interpretatione chapter nine. In this chapter, Aristotle is concerned to safeguard the limits of the Law of the Excluded Middle (LEM) with respect to statements about future contingent events. Aristotle's Law of Excluded Middle states that propositions about the past and present have a definite truth value (either true or false). But in chapter nine, Aristotle limits the scope of LEM, arguing that any statement about a future contingent event is now neither true nor false. If future contingents did have a truth-value, he argues, there would be no human freedom. But Aristotle postulates that we know that future events originate as a result of our deliberation, and so he denies to future contingents a determinate truth-value.

Maimonides echoes this concern of Aristotle's, arguing that if humans have no ability to choose their own actions freely, then "by what right could God punish the wicked or reward the righteous?"[7] If we have no free will, then the doctrine of reward and punishment would be useless, and so moral responsibility is dependent upon freedom of choice. Following Aristotle, philosophers connect the issue of human choice to moral responsibility, and place the problem of divine omniscience in the context of the question of who is ultimately responsible for sinning: humans or God. On a determinist picture, God would ultimately be responsible for human sin, and theories of retribution would presumably be otiose. For this reason, philosophers are driven to work out the relationship between omniscience, free agency, and moral responsibility.

---

[5] A similar point is made about seventeenth-century philosophers. Taking determinism to be the view that "whatever happens in the world is brought about by causes other than itself," seventeenth-century philosophers adopted a compatibilist position with respect to human freedom, namely that "being free is logically compatible with being causally determined." See Sleigh, Chappell, and Della Rocca 1998.

[6] In the Nicomachean Ethics, Aristotle proposed that only voluntary actions are subject to praise/blame. NE 1109b30–5. By a voluntary action, Aristotle means that an action must have its origin in the agent, and the agent must be aware of what it is that s/he is doing or bringing about (NE 1110a–1111b4). For further discussion of the Ethics and On Interpretation, see Rudavsky 2010.

[7] Maimonides MT 5.4:87a.

Furthermore, as Calvin Normore has so succinctly pointed out, the issues under-lying divine omniscience "pose some of the clearest challenges to a philosophical theory of God's relation to time."[8] Another way of articulating the logical cluster of problems is whether past, present, and future, and God's knowledge of past, present, and future, are necessary or contingent. More specifically, if God is present to all of time, and knows all time in one act, what does this imply about the ontological status of the future: if what is future is as available to God as what is past, does it follow that the future is as fixed ontologically as the past?[9] The medieval commentary literature upon Aristotle's sea battle demonstrates the many interpretations given to the ontological status of future contingent events.[10]

Yet another problem has to do with the extent and limits of God's knowledge of particulars in the sublunar universe. In a monism, God is characterized as a unity, unchanging in essence and omniscient. That God knows at least his own essence is reflected in Aristotle's dictum that God is thought thinking itself.[11] Yet once it is claimed that God's knowledge extends beyond his own essence to his creation, a number of problems arise. If it is argued that God knows particular entities, does this compromise either the unity or the immutability of his knowledge, and thus, of his essence? The first would appear to follow from the following considerations. The doctrine of divine simplicity suggests the identity of God's essence and know-ledge. If, however, God's knowledge constitutes a multiplicity, then God's essence would reflect this plurality. The second follows from the fact that if the objects of God's knowledge are subject to generation and corruption, then his essence must change along with changes in the objects of his knowledge. In both cases, the underlying implication is that God's essence has been acted upon or otherwise affected by the objects of his knowledge in much the same way as the human intellect is acted upon by the objects of its knowledge. How to account for divine knowledge while denying, on the one hand, plurality, and on the other hand, the effects of causal activity upon God, becomes a major consideration for Jewish thinkers.

III Suffering, Providence, and *the Book of Job*: Saadiah Gaon, Maimonides, and Gersonides

The *Book of Job*, with its narrative of undeserved suffering, provided medieval philosophers with an opportunity to explain God's role in human suffering. Philo-sophers of all three Abrahamic traditions wrote extensive commentaries to the work. One of the main questions is why God would have inflicted suffering upon an innocent individual: surely, if God is providential, God would do everything to protect individuals from harm. And so commentaries upon Job tend to interpolate theories of providence alongside their theodicy. Job's story is well known: Job is a good person who is tested by God (via Satan), undergoes many physical and

---

[8] See Normore 1985, 4.   [9] Normore 1985, 6.

[10] For a discussion of the relevance of these commentaries upon Jewish philosophers, see Feldman 1982. I shall allude below to Gersonides' commentary upon *De Interpretatione* 9.

[11] Aristotle *Metaphysics* 12.7; 1072b18; cf. also *De Anima* 3.6 431b16, where Aristotle says that the intellect, when it thinks, is the thing it thinks.

emotional trials, and does not give up his belief in God; at the end of the book, God appears to Job out of the whirlwind and chastises him, and the book ends with Job's being rewarded by God.

The *Book of Job* introduces different types of suffering, questioning how to account for the existence of evil in a world that is made by a supposedly benevolent Deity. The problem of evil also reinforces our motif of the tension between Judaism and science, that is between a theological and naturalistic universe. Maimonides addresses the problem of evil in *Guide* 3.11–12. Following the Neoplatonic motif that evil is a privation, Maimonides first claims that most moral evils (those that occur between humans) are the result of either ignorance or the privation of knowledge. Further, using the Islamic philosopher/theologian al-Râzî as a foil, Maimonides claims that there exists much less evil in the world than adduced by al-Râzî.[12] It is only because we view the universe from our limited perspective that we perceive matters as worse than in fact they are; were we to adopt a more holistic view, what Spinoza will later describe as *sub specie aeternitas*, we would realize that humans are but a speck of sand, and that our travails are but a minor chord in the vast orchestra of the universe.

Nevertheless, Maimonides realizes that the masses are unable to attain this lofty detached perspective. Recognizing that a better explanation is needed, Maimonides demarcates three types of evil: metaphysical evil, natural evil, and moral evil. The first type of evil refers back to the ontological makeup of matter itself: it is because we are endowed with matter that we suffer the material infirmities we deem evil. In other words, the very nature of "being a human being" requires that we be subject to generation and corruption, and the latter carries with it all the pains and imperfections we associate with human life. Maimonides adumbrates the strain to be popularized by Leibniz five centuries later in his *Theodicy*, namely that this is the best of all possible worlds. God could not have created a matter with a more perfect nature: material stuff "is generated in the most possible way in which it is possible to be generated out of that specific matter."[13]

Maimonides' second category of evils (natural evils) are those resulting from political upheaval or moral behavior. According to Maimonides, these are relatively rare as well. Again, we can only wonder what Maimonides really thought about the fact that his own family had to flee Cordoba for North Africa, for reasons of political upheaval. It is the third category of evil, what we may call personal or moral evils, that most concerns Maimonides. Here we can hear the strains of Maimonides the physician, admonishing his flock not to overindulge in eating, drinking, sexual licentiousness etc., resulting in personal harm. Maimonides divides personal evils into those we bring upon ourselves physically (diseases of the body), and those we introduce psychically (diseases of the soul). With respect to the first, it is clearly overindulgence that is to blame. Diseases of the soul are a bit more complex. In the first place, Maimonides tells us, overindulgence on the bodily side cannot help but affect our moral temperament, and so that is reason enough to exercise physical restraint. Furthermore, as a result of physical overindulgence, we tend to lust after

---

[12] Abû Bakr Muhammad Ibn Zakariyyâ al-Râzî was an Islamic physician and philosopher who attacked religion by using the example of so much evil in the world. See Pines 1963, for details.

[13] Maimonides *Guide* 3.12:444.

items that will satisfy these physical desires. Were we to eliminate our desires for these luxuries, our souls would cease to suffer needless anxiety and the concomitant evils that accrue upon their pursuit. Hence, it is human will that introduces this third variety of evil.

One of the best opportunities to address the existence of evil occurs in the context of the *Book of Job*. Saadiah Gaon was the first medieval Jewish philosopher to offer an extended commentary on *Job*.[14] Saadiah's two works offer a similar presentation and are written against the backdrop of Kalâm discussions of the problem of evil and suffering.[15] In his introduction to this work, Lenn Goodman notes that the methodology of the Greek sciences, already apparent in Islamic culture, is evident in Saadiah's reading of Job. Saadiah informs us in the introduction that his reading of Job will reflect "what is rooted in the proof of reason."[16] Goodman interprets this to mean that Saadiah's understanding of the book will not violate the demonstrated dictates of human understanding, or the established conclusions of the sciences.[17] Goodman further interprets *Job* 10:22 as providing a merging of Job's cosmography with the scientific schematism of his own day, providing a kind of cosmological theodicy.[18] Saadiah's awareness of the new science is evident in 37:9, where again, in his notes, Goodman claims that Saadiah "brings the cosmology of the sacred text of *Job* into line with the scientific thinking of his day, dismissing the fabular world picture of rabbinic convention and the ancient Hebrew idiom."[19] This tension is reinforced in subsequent works as well, as our thinkers try to provide an account for how an omniscient, omnipotent, and benevolent deity can permit humans to suffer in the natural order.

In Book 5.3 of *Beliefs and Opinions*, Saadiah provides two reasons for the suffering of the righteous: first, God may be punishing the righteous as "penalties for slight failings," or second, the suffering may consist of "incipient trials with which God tests them, when He knows that they are able to endure them, only in order to compensate them for these trials later on."[20] He then elucidates two possible reasons for such a test, citing Job as an example: being (and surviving a test) might allow the righteous to prove their devotion to God, as in the case of Abraham's trial. Furthermore, these tests serve to demonstrate to their fellow human beings their worthiness in having been chosen by God for divine favors.[21]

These points are discussed in greater detail in Saadiah's elaborate linguistic and philosophical commentary on Job, *The Book of Theodicy*, which was most likely written before *Beliefs and Opinions*. In the introduction to his commentary, Saadiah notes three reasons God might permit an innocent person to suffer: for the sake of character building—"discipline and instruction"; as a mode of "purgation and punishment"; and for the sake of "trial and testing."[22] Saadiah emphasizes that it is

[14] See Saadiah 1988, *Theodicy*; Saadiah 1948, *Beliefs*. For a detailed exploration of medieval Jewish commentaries upon the *Book of Job*, including Saadiah, Maimonides and Gersonides, see Eisen 2004.

[15] For extensive discussion of the Islamic background to Saadiah's discussions, see Goodman in Saadiah 1988.

[16] Saadiah *Theodicy* Intro, in Saadiah 1988, 131.   [17] See Goodman, in Saadiah 1988, 147.

[18] Goodman, in Saadiah 1988, 235.   [19] See Goodman, in Saadiah 1988, 380.

[20] Saadiah *Beliefs* 5.3:213.   [21] See Eisen 2004 for detailed discussion of Saadiah's views.

[22] Saadiah 1988, 125–6. For an extensive discussion of these three accounts, as well as a comparison with Thomas Aquinas, see Stump 1997.

not our right to question the ways of God: ultimately, God can do whatever he wishes. Elihu's view, that God causes the righteous to suffer as a test, and rewards them when they endure the trial with patience, is ultimately accepted by Saadiah as reflecting the correct view of the work. Hence, in the case of Job, Job was tested by God, bore the test with fortitude, and according to Saadiah "was assured eternal bliss in the hereafter and granted far more than he had hoped for in this life."[23] Saadiah's theodicy is clearly dependent upon a robust theory of the afterlife, and as we shall see in Chapter 8, Saadiah does in fact provide a theory of physical resurrection of both body and soul.

Maimonides, however, rejected Saadiah's reading of *Job*, claiming that it is not supported by Scripture. In contradistinction to Saadiah, Maimonides provides a more robust theodicy, one in which divine providence, human suffering, and Job's trial form an interdependent unit. Maimonides starts his discussion in *Guide* 3.17 by summarizing five different theories of divine providence.[24] The five theories are:

[T1] Epicurus and his followers who denied God's providence altogether.

[T2] Aristotle who believed that providence extends only to the superlunar (heavenly) sphere but not to the sublunar (natural) sphere.

[T3] the Ash'arites who claimed that every event in the world is predestined by God, thus denying any contingency.

[T4] the Mu'tazilites who believed in limited free will for humans.

[T5] Mosaic Law according to which humans have perfect freedom, while at the same time everything that happens to humans is the result of God's justice.

While we might assume that Maimonides adheres to "Mosaic Law" (T5), I shall argue that Maimonides' own opinion concerning providence is a modification of (T2), which he attributes to Aristotle.[25]

From the perspective of divine omniscience, (T1) represents what we may term a radical atheistic view. On Epicurus' view, everything happens by chance and there is nobody who orders or governs the universe; Maimonides has rejected this position already in his cosmological discussions. On the view attributed to Aristotle (T2), while God's providence pertains only to the eternal spheres, and not to individuals in the sublunar world, providence has provided for the continuation and preservation of individuals by providing them with the appropriate faculties. Every individual has been given "that which the species he belongs to needs," including for example the rational faculty for humans, and so every individual has been provided with a survival mechanism. On Aristotle's view, providence is general and not individual, and does not control the individual minutiae in the sublunar world. Providence does

---

[23] Saadiah 1988, 127. Eleanore Stump summarizes Saadiah's position as follows: "God permits suffering to come to an unwilling innocent, but apparently just for the sake of rewarding him in the after-life for his having endured such suffering." See Stump 1997, 529. See also Eisen 2004, 20–3.

[24] Pines notes that in his delineation of the five theories, Maimonides is very much influenced by the treatise *On Providence* (*De Fato*) by Alexander of Aphrodisias, who is mentioned by name in *Guide* 3.16.

[25] In fact, there is no evidence that Aristotle himself subscribed to the view of providence attributed to him by Alexander and by Maimonides. Furthermore, in Alexander's treatise, the third view is actually attributed to Plato, whereas Maimonides ascribes it to the Ash'arites. Stern discusses *De Fato* and the importance of this treatise for Maimonides' conception of free choice in Stern 1997.

not distinguish, for example, between a stone falling on and killing an ant, and the "drowning of the excellent and superior men that were on board the ship" that went down in a storm. Compare this view to that of the Ash'arite theologians (T3) according to whom nothing is due to chance, for "everything comes about through will, purpose, and governance."[26] On this strictly determinist view, every event in the sublunar world is set into motion by God; in fact, God is the direct cause of all events. There is no possibility, and all events are "either necessary or impossible."[27] Because there is no human choice or freedom, the law is rendered useless. In their attempt to circumvent the uselessness of human deliberation and responsibility, the Mu'tazilites claim (T4) that "man has the ability to act of his own accord" even though God knows future contingent events.[28] Maimonides finds this position problematic as well, arguing that the Mu'tazilites are forced to propose far-fetched explanations for apparent injustices.

Having rejected each of these positions, Maimonides then turns to (T5), the position of the Law ("our opinion"), according to which God has willed that humans have "an absolute ability to act: I mean to say that in virtue of his nature, his choice, and his will, he may do everything that it is within the capacity of man to do, and this without there being created for his benefit in any way any newly produced thing."[29] On this position, God is absolutely just, and so according to (T5) all calamities are deserved. Maimonides, however, is quite explicit that this is not his position and that he will let us know what "I myself believe about this."[30] Maimonides describes his own position as follows:

> (T6)   Divine providence watches only over the individuals belonging to the human species ... but regarding all the other animals, and all the more, the plants and other things, my opinion is that of Aristotle.[31]

Despite the fact that Maimonides tells us that he has not relied on demonstrative argument, but rather on the books of the prophets, his own view differs from (T5). He tells us that this position is "nearer than they to intellectual reasoning." Maimonides' (T6) thus incorporates elements of both Aristotle and the divine law. Remember that while the superlunar orderings on Aristotle's view (T2) occur in accordance with providence and evince a certain "orderly course," everything in the sublunar universe "exist[s] by chance and not through the governance of one who governs," and so is not subject to providence.[32] Maimonides agrees with the first half of (T2) pertaining to the superlunar spheres, but disagrees with the second. Maimonides argues that although providence in the sublunar universe extends to all and only human beings, it does not necessarily reflect divine retribution or reward.

Maimonides distinguishes between general providence, which is provided equally to all members of the human species as part of the natural order, and individual providence, which is provided to individuals according to their merit.[33] Individual

---

[26] Maimonides *Guide* 3.17:466.   [27] Maimonides *Guide* 3.17:467.
[28] Maimonides *Guide* 3.17:468.   [29] Maimonides *Guide* 3.17:469.
[30] Maimonides *Guide* 3.17:469.   [31] Maimonides *Guide* 3.17:471.
[32] Maimonides *Guide* 3.17:466.
[33] See Nadler 2009 for a philosophically astute discussion of Maimonides' theory.

providence is the result of the divine overflow through the Agent Intellect; Maimonides explains that on his view, divine providence is "consequent upon the divine overflow; and the species with which this intellectual overflow is united, so that it became endowed with intellect and so that everything that is disclosed to a being endowed with the intellect was disclosed to it, is the one accompanied by divine providence."[34] In other words, the amount of providence is directly dependent upon the level of intellectual perfection achieved by the agent. Providence is not equal for all individuals, but is "graded as their human perfection is graded."[35] When we are no longer communing with God and have withdrawn our epistemic attention, providence ceases to protect us: "those who are near to Him are exceedingly well protected ... whereas those who are far from Him are given over to whatever may happen to befall them."[36] As we shall see in Chapter 9, only those who have achieved the highest levels of intellectual perfection will enjoy complete providential benevolence.

How then does this elaborate theory of providence apply to Job, who to all appearances suffered needlessly? Maimonides provides in *Guide* 3.22–4 a perfect case study of how his theory of divine providence works in the case of somebody like Job. The story of Job is, in Maimonides' words "extraordinary and marvelous," a "parable intended to set forth the opinions of people concerning providence."[37] The most marvelous and strange part of this story according to Maimonides is that Job is described at the beginning of story not as wise, but only as moral and righteous. To mention a theme to which we shall return in Chapter 9, moral virtues such as righteousness turn out to be necessary but not sufficient for human perfection: intellectual virtue is required as well for human perfection, which leads to providential care. If Job had been wise, or had attained intellectual virtue, then "his situation would not have been obscure for him, as will become clear."[38] The individual endowed with intellectual virtue will understand his/her position, and will not even be tempted by Satan to revile God when one's fortunes turn. Thus, Maimonides sets the stage for utilizing the *Book of Job* as providing scriptural support for his own theory of divine providence.

Maimonides interprets each of Job's "friends" as representative of one of the five theories of Providence adduced above: Job's own position (that evil attends to both the righteous and wicked indiscriminately) is ostensibly identified with the Epicureans (T1); Eliphaz claims that Job deserved everything that happened but we cannot understand the correlations between our actions and our punishment, reflecting a simplistic reading of "the Law" (T5); Bildad's position, that if he did not deserve to suffer in this life, Job will be rewarded in the afterlife, is in keeping with that of the Mu'tazilites (and possibly Saadiah Gaon) (T4); and Zophar, who emphasizes the immutable and absolute will of God, reflects the Ash'arite position (T3). Maimonides pays particular attention to the opinions of the stranger Elihu, suggesting that it is Elihu who introduces an Aristotelian dimension into the Story of Job (T2); this dimension is reflected in (T6) as well. Elihu describes the three previous speeches as

---

[34] Maimonides *Guide* 3.17:472.   [35] Maimonides *Guide* 3.18:475.
[36] Maimonides *Guide* 3.18:476.   [37] Maimonides *Guide* 3.22:486.
[38] Maimonides *Guide* 3.22:487.

"senile drivel" and he introduces the idea of the "intercession of an angel," suggesting that if an angel intercedes for a person during the final moments, said person can be "raised from his fall... and restored to the best of states."[39] This intercession is akin to a moment of prophetic revelation, and is the very experience that Job achieves at the culmination of his ordeal. Unfortunately, Maimonides says very little about this experience, and we learn nothing about who this angel is, what exactly the angel does, and how Job reacts.

Job's recantation, "Wherefore I abhor myself, and repent in dust and ashes," (*Job* 42:6) reflects his newly acquired status that enables him to both understand and endure his situation with equanimity. This twofold ability—understanding and perseverance—brings about his ultimate salvation and the salvation of his family. What Job has learned is to transcend his suffering, and not let it affect his inner being. This lesson is reflective of Maimonides' comments in *Guide* 3.51, to which we turn below. It also reinforces the viewpoint of Elihu, who in Maimonides' view presents the most sanguine view of providence. According to some commentators, Maimonides thus intends to signal to the astute reader that Elihu, and the (esoterically) Aristotelian views on providence, are ultimately presaged in the *Book of Job*.[40]

We shall return in Chapter 9 to the suffering of the righteous, in the context of Maimonides' discussion of human felicity. Let me suggest here, though, that on a naturalistic reading, it is the intellectual overflow from the Agent Intellect that provides the righteous individual with the knowledge to avoid harmful situations. Presumably, if I have sufficient knowledge of weather and oceanic storms, I should know not to embark upon a perilous sea voyage.[41] When I am actualizing my intellectual perfection, and am attuned to the intellectual overflow, I am protected; only when I am distracted does providential protection cease. But more important, Maimonides will claim in *Guide* 3.51 that the truly perfect individual is impervious to suffering. One who is genuinely focused on divine apprehension, and consummately

---

[39] Maimonides *Guide* 3.23:495.

[40] I have suggested (see Rudavsky 2010) that in its emphasis upon the importance of intellectual perfection, Maimonides' theory of divine providence combines elements of Aristotelian naturalism with the Mosaic emphasis upon divine will and volition. At the end of the *Guide*, Maimonides tries to explain why it is that often the righteous (who ostensibly should be most firmly united with the divine overflow) nevertheless experience evil and suffering. Maimonides introduces this discussion in the middle of *Guide* 3.51, sharing what he calls a "most extraordinary speculation" that has just occurred to him. Claiming that divine providence is constantly watching over those who have obtained the intellectual overflow from God, Maimonides emphasizes the point that evil only attends to those who withdraw their attentions from God: "providence withdraws from him during the time when he is occupied with something else." Prophets or excellent persons suffer evil only during times of distraction, the greatness of the calamity being "proportionate to the duration of the period of distraction or to the vileness of the matter with which he was occupied" (ibid.). One who apprehends God and is not distracted, "that individual can never be afflicted with evil of any kind. For he is with God and God is with him" (ibid.). Evil can only befall one who abandons God. Maimonides explicitly states that, "we are cause of this hiding of the face," that we are the cause of the separation between ourselves and God. I shall return to this point in Chapter 9, where we examine Maimonides' claim that calamities are most apt to strike while attending to one's physical needs rather than intellectual apprehension.

[41] One can only wonder about the relevance of this example to Maimonides' own brother David who died at sea. For further discussion of the relevance of this example, see Rudavsky and Rudavsky-Brody 2012; Ivry 2016.

devoted to achieving intellectual perfection, will not be affected by "spatio-temporal suffering"; such an individual has transcended the ordinary sphere of human evils and suffering, and exists on a separate plane altogether. On this theory, Maimonides argues, evil does not actually exist for such an individual. Returning to the motif that evil (like matter) is a privation, Maimonides' point is that one who has perfected the intellectual faculty will no longer be affected by privations.

We turn now to Gersonides' discussion of suffering and providence, presented both in Book IV of *Wars* and in his *Commentary on Job*. More specifically, Gersonides is concerned with two issues: the extent of God's providential activity, and an explanation of the suffering of the righteous. As we have seen, Maimonides argues that individual divine providence extends only to those human beings who have achieved intellectual and moral perfection; providence for other species is only general. Gersonides, however, will maintain that God cannot know particulars *qua* particular, and so Maimonides' solution is unacceptable to him. Gersonides must therefore reframe his views on providence in light of his theory of divine cognition.

In his *Commentary on Job*, which complements book 4 of *Wars*, Gersonides claims (as did Maimonides) that each of the characters in the *Book of Job* represents a different theory of divine providence. Summarizing Maimonides' theory, Gersonides claims that "on Maimonides' theory of providence, divine knowledge does not extend to particulars as particulars."[42] As Feldman notes, Gersonides realizes that his own theory of divine omniscience runs into similar problems, since on his view God does not know future contingents. He does so by distinguishing between divine cognition and divine providence. In his interpretation of *Job*, Gersonides' own position is a restatement of Elihu's theory that providence is not directed to particulars but rather to groups of individuals, or universals.

The problem of evil and providence is revisited in *Wars* IV.1. Gersonides summarizes three general views on providence: the philosophical view of Aristotle according to which there is no individual providence; the traditional Torah view, according to which divine providence extends over each member of the species as humans; and the view of Maimonides, namely that divine providence extends to some but not all individual humans. Gersonides makes use of the *Book of Job* to elucidate the various positions adduced, as well as to develop a theodicy that explains the existence of suffering and evil. Most of Book IV is addressed to the second view. Gersonides takes great pains to explain that his theory of divine cognition does not preclude providence. Arguing that providence is general in nature, Gersonides claims that it primarily appertains to species and only incidentally to particulars of the species. God, for example, does not know the particular individual Levi ben Gershom and does not bestow particular providence on him. Rather, inasmuch as Levi ben Gershom is a member of the species humanity and the species philosopher, he is in a position to receive the providential care accorded to those groups. We shall return to the details of Gersonides' view of divine knowledge below.

---

[42] Gersonides *Wars* vol. 2, IV.7:208. See also Gersonides 1946.

Gersonides then turns to the parallel issue of theodicy. That instances of evil exist is a fact borne out by sense experience, which shows "many righteous people suffering great evils most of their lives and receiving very few benefits ... moreover we observe that some righteous men suffer many evils despite their attempt to avert evils from coming to them, but they are not protected from these evils."[43] How, then, can we account for the suffering of the righteous? Gersonides' discussion must be understood against the backdrop of Maimonides' response, which he found insufficient. In order to account for the existence of human suffering, Gersonides distinguishes between "general providence" that is embedded in nature itself, and "special providence" that pertains to an individual's spiritual perfection: special providence is enjoyed in direct relation to the level of spiritual perfection attained by an individual. Only few individuals achieve the "kind of unity and conjunction with God" that provides individual providence.[44] As noted above, those who are more strongly identified with the Active Intellect receive this communication in a more perfect manner.

But could it not be argued, in contradistinction to Gersonides' position, that God must be either evil or impotent? "Either God (may He be blessed) can arrange it so that a man receives his due reward but He does not attempt to do so, and this would indeed be evil with respect to God (God forbid), or He cannot so arrange this, which also would be an imperfection in God."[45] Gersonides' response is twofold. First, he avers that this is the best of all possible worlds, and that this world exhibits the best possible providential ordering and beneficence for sublunar things.[46] Second, he argues that the benefits of special providence, delegated to only certain individuals, are for the most part deferred to the world to come. What we call "material evils" are the result ultimately of the material constitution of nature itself. In other words, evil is ultimately the result of matter, over which God has no control. Gersonides states that, "evil derives from God only by chance and because of the necessity of matter."[47] Examples are adduced to show that evils are caused by chance, or by matter. The evils that befall humans from the patterns determined by the arrangements of the heavenly bodies are not "essentially [evil] or primarily intended to be [evil]," but rather are chance occurrences not due to God.

Does Gersonides provide a sufficient response to the problem of evil and theodicy? Feldman, for one, claims that Gersonides' philosophy is "the only religious philosophy that can" respond to this problem.[48] As Feldman notes, that God cannot prevent or eliminate them [evil] is not a reflection of His impotence; the fact that they occur is a necessary consequence of the world's being what it is, i.e., material.[49] Nature itself, which is corruptible and a source of imperfection, accounts for evil and suffering. In Chapters 6 and 7 we shall pay more attention to Gersonides' underlying cosmology, which introduces "eternal formless matter" out of which the universe is created.

---

[43] Gersonides *Wars* vol. 2, IV.3:171.   [44] Gersonides *Wars* vol. 2, IV.4:175.
[45] Gersonides *Wars* vol. 2, IV.6:182.   [46] Gersonides *Wars* vol. 2, IV.6:183.
[47] Gersonides *Wars* vol. 2, IV.3:167.   [48] See Feldman's comments in Gersonides *Wars* vol. 2, 149.
[49] See Feldman's comments in Gersonides *Wars* vol. 2, 151. See also Nadler 2009.

IV Theological Compatibilism: Saadiah Gaon, Halevi, and Maimonides

We have seen that the problem of human suffering is ineluctably intertwined with theories of providence as well as theories of human choice. For if divine providence entails a modicum of divine causal agency, if only in God's inclination to protect a creature from harm, or as in the case of Job, to inflict a creature with suffering, then we must consider the extent to which human beings can exercise their own free will in light of these divine inclinations. The topic of human freedom was crystallized as a philosophical conundrum through Jewish contact with Greek and Islamic writings, particularly with Kalâm writings on the antinomies of free will.[50] But this does not mean that the issue had not arisen earlier. The rabbis already faced the theological problem of reconciling human freedom and God's providential care and concern for humans. In the Mishnaic tractate *Avot*, Rabbi Akiba, for example, is said to have taught that, "everything is seen (*tsafui*), and choice (*reshut*) is given."[51] Recognizing the tension between these two concepts, Akiba however does not try to reconcile them.

The writings of Saadiah Gaon and Judah Halevi clearly exemplify the Kalâm preoccupation with the problem of reconciling divine providence with human freedom. In accordance with his Kalâm predecessors, Saadiah sees the problem of divine omniscience as intimately connected to issues of divine justice. Although not stated explicitly as an argument, Saadiah does offer the following considerations to support his contention. He accepts as a given that God has granted to humans free will: "It accords with the justice of the Creator and his mercy towards man that he should have granted him the power and ability to do what he commanded him to do, and to refrain from what he forbade him to do."[52] Saadiah's discussion occurs within the Kalâm context of trying to explicate these philosophical terms.

Kalâm philosophers had fought long and hard over what constitutes a free action. At stake were two sets of questions: first, does freedom of will arise before the action itself, or simultaneously with it; and, second, is God's freedom subject to the same

---

[50] For a detailed discussion of the Kalâm arguments surrounding free will and divine omniscience, see Wolfson 1976. Recent discussion of Kalâm thought can be found in Frank 1992. The actual word for providence is not found in Jewish writings prior to Ibn Tibbon's introduction of the term in the process of translating Maimonides' appropriation of the Arabic term "*tâdbir*." Nor is there a term in Hebrew philosophical language corresponding to the scholastic notion of free will, *liberum arbitrium*. See the discussion by Manekin 1997a, 13ff. Manekin points out that the Hebrew phrase for free choice, *behirah ḥofshit*, does not appear until the fifteenth century, and can be taken as a sign of the influence of scholastic discussions.

[51] *Mishnah Avot*, III.15. For a sustained discussion of Akiba's dictum and its influence upon the rabbis, see Urbach 1975, 255–85. In his recent article on the notion of *ḥaritzut* (diligence) in Jewish thought, Horwitz points out that the rabbis worried how to account for human "diligence" or "effort" in light of fatalism: "if the decree is true, diligence is absurd." See Horwitz's rich article (1997) in which he traces the notion of *ḥaritzut* in Judaic traditional and philosophical texts. The term appears among numerous philosophers, including Ibn Gabirol, Gersonides, Narboni Crescas, and Albo. Horwitz suggests that this epigram could well serve as "antipode" for the views of philosophers, in particular Gersonides, on the issue of human effort versus determinism. We shall return to this notion in Chapter 9, in the context of Gersonides' ethics.

[52] Saadiah Gaon 1972, *Beliefs* 4.2, 119. The Kalâm influences upon Saadiah's discussion are examined in Altmann 1974.

constraints? More specifically Kalâm philosophers debated whether the ability to act must precede the act itself, or whether the ability to act could be said to exist simultaneously with the action in question.[53] On the latter view, supported primarily by the Mut'azilite school, human freedom consisted in the mere act of consenting to an action. Hence, the consent could accompany the action simultaneously without actually causing it. Saadiah rejects this position, claiming that, "The ability [to act] must necessarily exist before the act, so as to give man the [choice of doing the positive] act or abstaining from the act."[54] In line with this characterization, Saadiah further claims that both acting and desisting to act count equally as free actions: "In the same way as when a man's doing a thing constitutes an action, so too his desisting from it constitutes an action."[55] Saadiah's point here is that the term "action" in its full sense implies free choice; even in not choosing, humans are exercising their free will. "I must further explain that man does not perform any action unless he chooses to do it, since it is impossible for one to act if he has no free will or fails to exercise his free will."[56]

Halevi, following Saadiah, rejects as well the necessitarian position that possibility does not exist: "Only a perverse, heretical person would deny the nature of what is possible. If he believed that what will be will inevitably be, he would simply submit, and not equip himself with weapons against his enemy, or with food against his hunger."[57] But the acceptance of possibility is "not incompatible with a belief in Divine Providence."[58] In order to support the compatibility of possibility with providence, Halevi distinguishes between two chains of causation. The first chain is related directly as an immediate expression of the divine will, whereas the second represents an intermediary chain between God and natural events.[59] Based on these two causal chains, Halevi then distinguishes four types of actions: divine actions, which issue forth directly from God; natural actions, which are derived from inter-mediate causes, and unfold naturally, barring any interference; accidental actions, which result not by nature or arrangement, or will power, but by accident; and arbitrary actions, which have their "root in the free will of man."[60] According to Halevi, human actions of will belong to the final category and possess causes which reduce them, chain-like, to the Prime Cause. Reflecting Aristotle's concerns reflected above, Halevi claims that only actions in this latter class are susceptible to praise and blame.

Having established that humans have free will, both Saadiah and Halevi are ready to turn to the issue of divine omniscience, and whether God's knowledge interferes with this absolute freedom. Saadiah's position will be that "the creator (be he exalted) does not allow his power to interfere in the least with the actions of men, nor does he

[53] For a discussion of the implications of this point, see Altmann, note 1 in his 1972 edition of *Book of Doctrines and Beliefs*, 119.

[54] Saadiah Gaon 1972, *Beliefs* 4.3, 118.

[55] Saadiah Gaon 1972, *Beliefs* 4.3, 119. Altmann suggests that Saadiah may have been influenced in this distinction by Aristotle's discussions in the *Metaphysics*. See Altmann's comments in Saadiah Gaon 1972, *Beliefs*, 31 for further discussion of this point.

[56] Saadiah Gaon 1972, *Beliefs* 4.3, 119.   [57] Halevi 1947, *Kuzari* 5.20, 315.

[58] Halevi 1947, *Kuzari* 5.20 315.   [59] Halevi 1947, *Kuzari* 5.20 316.

[60] Halevi 1947, *Kuzari* 5.20 316.

compel them to be either obedient or disobedient."[61] But how can this be, given that God knows future events before they happen? Saadiah, for the first time in medieval Jewish philosophy, crystallizes the dilemma of divine omniscience in the following terms:

Perhaps someone will ask further: 'If God knows that which is going to be before it comes into being, he knows already that a certain person will disobey him; and it is not possible that that person not disobey God, in order that God's foreknowledge prove to be correct.'[62]

Saadiah's solution is straightforward and introduces the position common in later scholastic thought, namely that God's knowledge is not causative. "He who makes this assertion has no proof that the knowledge of the Creator concerning things is the cause of their existence."[63] Importantly for our concerns, his support for this contention rests upon quasi-temporal considerations. Saadiah offers two reasons for rejecting the efficacy of God's foreknowledge. The first reason draws upon the relation between knowledge and causes; if God's knowledge were causative, then according to Saadiah, "they [future contingents] would have existed from eternity, since God's knowledge of them is eternal."[64] We shall return to the implications of this claim when we examine Crescas' adoption of the eternity thesis. Suffice it to say that scholastic philosophers (Crescas included) parted company with Saadiah on this point. Accepting the antecedent of this conditional, most philosophers were willing to accept the consequent as well. Thus, for example, Boethius and Aquinas were willing to argue that precisely because God's knowledge of events is eternal, it follows that God's knowledge is technically not foreknowledge at all but rather eternally existing knowledge. Boethius, for example, states explicitly that God's knowledge, technically speaking, is "the knowledge of a never fading instant rather than a foreknowledge of the 'future.'"[65] Saadiah clearly claims that God knows all things in advance, and in particular, with respect to freely willed actions God "knew in advance that man was going to choose them."[66]

Halevi's support of compatibilism reflects that of Saadiah. Halevi addresses several philosophical objections designed to deny God's knowledge. The first objection, attributed to the Mutakallimûn, suggests that inasmuch as human actions are possible, they are removed entirely from the sphere of divine knowledge. Halevi counters that these actions, although "completely outside the control of Providence," are indirectly linked to it.[67] The second objection concerns the ontological composition of what is possible, and suggests that, "these matters are outside divine omniscience because the absolutely potential is naturally an unknown quantity."[68] Halevi echoes Saadiah's claim that, "the knowledge of a thing is not the cause of its coming into

---

[61] Saadiah Gaon 1947, *Beliefs* 4.4, 120.   [62] Saadiah 1972, *Beliefs* 4.4, 122.

[63] Saadiah Gaon 1972, *Beliefs* 4.4, 122. Compare to Augustine's statement in *De Libero Arbitrio* that God's knowledge does not bring about the event in question.

[64] Saadiah Gaon 1972, *Beliefs* 4.4, 122.

[65] Boethius 1957, book 5, prose 6, 63. We will return below to the doctrine of God's eternal knowledge in the context of Crescas' theory of divine knowledge that incorporates a notion of timelessness much like that of Boethius and Aquinas.

[66] Saadiah Gaon 1972, *Beliefs* 4.4, 122.   [67] Halevi *Kuzari* 5.20:318.

[68] Halevi *Kuzari* 5.20:318.

existence."[69] It is here that Halevi states, along with his Kalâm predecessors, that, "the knowledge of events to come is not the cause of their coming to be, just as the knowledge of things which have been is not the cause of their having come to be."[70] Having established to his satisfaction that human freedom exists, Halevi concludes his discussion with his sixth principle, namely that "Man finds in himself this power of doing evil or avoiding it in matters which are possible for him."[71]

To what extent does human action causally affect God's prior knowledge? Both Saadiah and Halevi interestingly anticipate later scholastic discussions of this issue. Saadiah entertains a possible objection, namely if God knew that a certain person would speak, it is not possible for that person to be silent; in response to this query Saadiah claims that, "we answer quite simply that if that person was to keep silent instead of speaking we should have said in our original statement that God knew that this man would be silent, and we were not entitled to state that God knew that this person would speak."[72] Halevi offers a similar argument, claiming that speaking or being silent is in one's power so long as it is subject to reason and not subject to other accidents.[73] Thus, Saadiah and Halevi both argue for freedom of choice on phenomenological grounds: our awareness of the power we have over our own speech attests to the existence of human freedom. The underlying issue raised by this argument, however, is whether Saadiah and Halevi are willing to accept the implication that divine knowledge is ultimately affected by future contingent actions. In other words, while accepting the dictum that divine knowledge is not causative upon future actions, are they willing to grant that future human actions are to some extent at least causative upon divine knowledge? Neither Saadiah nor Halevi addresses this critical issue, which becomes a focus for subsequent examinations. The full implications of this conclusion will be unpacked when we turn below to the indeterminist position.

Compatibilism receives its fullest expression by Maimonides who deals with this topic in a number of contexts.[74] In *Guide* 3.17, Maimonides states that humans have an "absolute capacity" to act, meaning that they have the choice and will to do "everything that it is within the capacity of man to do." *Guide* 2.48 is more clearly supportive of determinism. In this chapter, human and animal volition are explicitly compared:

Inasmuch as the deity is, as has been established, he who arouses a particular volition in the irrational animal and who has necessitated this particular free choice in the rational animal and

---

[69] Halevi *Kuzari* 5.20:319.   [70] Halevi *Kuzari* 5.20:319.   [71] Halevi *Kuzari* 5.20:326.
[72] Saadiah Gaon 1972, *Beliefs* 4.4:123. Altmann (1974), 31, notes that a similar example can be found in Ghazali, and suggests historical precedents for this example.
[73] Halevi *Kuzari* 5.4:281.
[74] By describing Maimonides as a compatibilist, I am placing myself in the midst of a controversy that has occupied much of recent Maimonidean scholarship. In recent years, scholars have argued over whether an esoteric reading of the *Guide* reveals a determinist or indeterminist stance. Pines and Altmann have argued that with respect to the issue of absolute freedom, Maimonides holds a form of determinism that precludes the ontological uniqueness of human will and intention. They point out, for example, that nowhere in the *Guide* is the doctrine of absolute freedom espoused, nor does Maimonides definitively refute the necessitarianism that runs as a sub-theme throughout the *Guide*. See, for example, Pines 1963 and Altmann 1974. More recently, however, Gellman, Hyman, and Ivry have tried to controvert this determinist reading of Maimonides. See Gellman 1989; Stern 1997; Hyman 1997; Ivry 2016.

who has made natural things pursue their course... it follows necessarily from all this that it may be said with regard to proceeds necessarily from these causes that God has commanded that something should be done in such and such a way.[75]

This passage suggests that human choice is on a par with animal choice. In what follows, I shall argue that very little of human freedom remains once we recognize the force of God's activity in the world. In fact, Maimonides' compatibilism, as defined above, emerges most clearly in the context of his views on God's knowledge of future events and occurs against the backdrop of an examination of the objects of God's knowledge.

Maimonides addresses the issue of God's knowledge of human affairs more fully in *Guide* 3.15–21. In these chapters of the *Guide*, the question of divine omniscience is posed in the context of whether God's knowledge extends to the infinite. Maimonides is concerned with two questions: whether God knows actually existing particulars, and whether God's knowledge extends as well to the domain of possibles. Possibles can refer to those things that are now existing and depend for their existence upon a necessary cause, or to those things which will be brought into existence at a future time.[76] Of these, the latter is of direct concern to us with respect to God's knowledge of future contingents, while the former pertains to God's knowledge of actualized particulars.

The first question for Maimonides is under what conditions God can be said to know concrete particular entities. Maimonides' general position is a modification of the thesis that "He, may he be exalted, knows everything and nothing secret is at all hidden from him."[77] I take the term "everything" to apply literally to *everything*; the question, of course, is whether "everything" includes the domain of particulars. One issue is whether God can know unactualized particulars. Inasmuch as this issue introduces the problem of an immutable deity coming to know what is mutable, Maimonides pays particular attention to the difficulties attending to this issue. As we have seen in Chapter 4, Maimonides emphasizes that the term "knowledge" is predicated equivocally of God and humans, maintaining that God is in no way affected by what he knows. God remains one even though his objects constitute a plurality, and he remains unchanged even though the objects of his knowledge are mutable. These points are reflected in two brief assertions: first, that God's knowledge does not contain plurality, and second, that God cannot acquire at a certain time knowledge he did not possess previously. Since divine knowledge is a priori, it is not affected by the ontological status of objects that results from this knowledge. Hence Maimonides argues that since the objects of God's knowledge do not causally act upon his knowledge, his essence is unaffected by their multiplicity. Although Maimonides' ultimate contention will be that the whole of Being comprises one

---

[75] Maimonides *Guide* 2.48:410.

[76] For a more extensive discussion of these distinctions in Maimonides, and analogous discussion in Averroes, see Rudavsky 1984; 2010. The notion of possibility is connected to the Kalâm theory of admissibility (*al-tâjwiz*) and is fairly complex; it can be pursued in a number of discussions: See Wolfson 1976; Blumberg 1970; Ivry 1986; Rosenberg 1978.

[77] Maimonides *Guide* 3.16:463.

individual, nevertheless his emphasis here is that God is not affected by the underlying plurality of the world.

The second claim, that God's knowledge is unaffected by any change in its objects, is supported in the context of a distinction between absolute and relative nonexistence. Absolute nonexistence is never an object of God's knowledge.[78] Relative non-existents, or future contingents, are possible objects of God's knowledge. It is not impossible, Maimonides claims, that God's knowledge has as its object those "non-existent things about whose being he brought into existence."[79] Maimonides illustrates this with the case of God's knowing that a certain man who is now non-existent, will exist at a future time, will continue to exist for some time, and then cease to exist. "God's knowledge does not increase when this person comes into existence—it contains nothing that it did not contain before." Neither does his knowledge imply plurality or change: "something was produced of which it had been perpetually known that it would be produced in the way it came into existence."[80] However, Maimonides is quick to point out that God's knowledge does not bring about the necessary occurrence of the entity in question: the possible remains possible.

... His knowledge, may he be exalted, that a certain possible thing will come into existence, does not in any way make that possible thing quit the nature of the possible. On the contrary, the nature of the possible remains with it; and knowledge concerning what possible things will be produced, does not entail one of the two possibilities becoming necessary... His knowledge concerning what will happen does not make this possible thing quit its nature.[81]

In other words, given two unactualized states of affairs p and $-p$, God's knowledge that p will become actualized does not affect the possible status of $-p$. Hence, like Saadiah and Halevi, Maimonides asserts that God's knowledge of future possibles does not change their nature; neither is his nature altered by a change in the objects of his knowledge. Maimonides does not, however, attempt to flesh out the logical difficulties in holding such a view.

One way of highlighting the problems inherent in Maimonides' theory of omniscience is to return to his theory of providence. I have already stated that God's knowledge comprises individuals. But to what extent does God's providence extend to individuals? It might be argued that if providence represents the theological ramification of knowledge, then God's knowing individuals *qua* individual can offer to individuals the guarantee of providential care. I submit, however, that these passages are ambiguous with respect to what God actually knows, and hence are equally ambiguous with respect to the efficacy of divine providence.

Ultimately, Maimonides realizes that his compatibilism relies upon a leap of faith. By emphasizing the total otherness of the deity, the incomprehensibility of the divine attributes, and the inability of humans to understand God's knowledge, Maimonides attempts to reconcile the fact that, on the one hand, God has ordered our lives, and on the other hand, human freedom is a prerequisite for moral and religious accountability. This attempted reconciliation reflects the efforts of his predecessors

---

[78] Maimonides *Guide* 3.20:480.   [79] Maimonides *Guide* 3.20:481.   [80] Ibid.
[81] Maimonides *Guide* 3.20:482.

Saadiah and Halevi. All three thinkers share an attempt to argue that God is all-knowing, that contingent states of affairs exist, and that God's omniscience does not preclude this contingency. But, as I have tried to demonstrate, compatibilism contains numerous metaphysical and theological tensions. Let us turn, then, to Jewish philosophical responses to compatibilism, which contain in their formulations a trenchant critique of the very compatibilist position presented by Saadiah, Halevi, and Maimonides.

V Theological Incompatibilism: Ibn Daud and Gersonides

In contradistinction to the compatibilists, both Ibn Daud and Gersonides are deeply committed to the asymmetry of the past and the future. As Feldman has pointed out, this commitment entails that the future is open and indeterminate, whereas the past is closed and determinate.[82] That is, the truth-value of statements about future contingents are as yet undetermined, whereas those about past events are determinately true or false; there are no truth-value gaps in the past. For this reason, many philosophers characterize the "truly possible" in terms of the future alone.[83]

Ibn Daud and Gersonides are the only Jewish thinkers to uphold a form of indeterminism as a solution to the paradox of divine omniscience. Ibn Daud tells his reader that he has undertaken to write his philosophical work *Sefer ha-Emunah ha-Ramah* in response to the problem of free will and omniscience. As he states in his preface, "(Someone) had asked the author, Are the actions of man necessary or does he have choice over them? To answer this question the author stated (this treatise) in one Abstract and three books."[84] The problem is crystallized further in the Introduction where Ibn Daud states the position of those who have difficulty accepting that God punishes those whom he necessitates to sin: "If God, may he be exalted, necessitates him (to commit sins), then how can he punish him for them?"[85]

Ibn Daud answers this quandary with a position not evidenced hitherto in Jewish thought, namely that God's omniscience does not extend to future contingents. His defense of free will is based on the very nature of the possible. In Book II:2, Ibn Daud develops this solution by upholding the domain of genuine possibility. Distinguishing between two types of possibility, he claims that only the first, epistemological possibility, leads to ignorance: "(One kind of) possibility is possibility with respect to ignorance."[86] Ibn Daud adduces two examples of epistemological possibility. The first example, whether the king of Babylonia died today or is alive, is a possibility because we, the men of Spain, do not know this (state of affairs). Rather, both alternatives are equal to us... But since (this) matter in itself is not possible, of necessity one of the alternatives

---

[82] Feldman, 1982, 9; See also Feldman 2009. We saw this position expressed above in the context of Aristotle's sea-fight battle.

[83] See for example Maimonides *TL* ch. 4; Rosenberg 1978.

[84] Ibn Daud 1986, *Sefer ha-Emunah ha-Ramah (The Exalted Faith)*. For a recent study of this work, see Fontaine 1990.

[85] Ibn Daud 1986, *The Exalted Faith*, 1. [86] Ibn Daud 1986, *The Exalted Faith* II.6:96.

is correct, and God, may he be exalted, knows in (cases) like this that one of the alternatives is necessary as it is in itself.[87]

Clearly, such cases are termed possible only because humans do not have sufficient knowledge of the matter at hand; in Ibn Daud's example, the men of Spain simply don't have prior knowledge of the determinate state of affairs that God does know. The second example is astronomical and concerns the future occurrence of an eclipse. To those ignorant of astronomy, eclipses appear to be indeterminate, but to a trained astronomer, and most certainly to God, astronomical events are not "a possibility" because they are known to be determinate, natural events.[88] Once again, the possibility adduced reflects an epistemic deficiency on the part of the knower and not a metaphysically indeterminate state of affairs.

Ibn Daud then distinguishes a second type of possibility; this genuine ontological possibility is one that God himself has created *qua* possible: God "created it as a thing that can bear one or the other of two contrary attributes."[89] The most God knows is that such a thing is possible; even God, however, does not know which of the two possibilities will be actualized. To the "sophist" who argues that this imputes ignorance to God, Ibn Daud replies that, "this is not ignorance" because technically speaking, there is nothing determinate to be known.[90] Not to know *what is-not* does not constitute a deficiency in God's omniscience. And so Ibn Daud feels that he has safeguarded future contingency without limiting God's power to know all that is unknowable.

Intimated but not fully developed by Ibn Daud, indeterminism finds its fullest expression in Gersonides' *Wars*.[91] Gersonides' concerns in *Wars* III are threefold: to determine whether God's knowledge extends to material singular objects, to future contingent objects, and to events. Although Gersonides himself does not always clearly separate these questions, I shall attempt to introduce a number of relevant distinctions into this discussion. The first question deals with knowledge of particular objects and presupposes the following distinction between individuals and particulars: an individual is any object that is capable of unique reference, whereas a particular is a material individual.[92] Hence, the first question in Treatise III can be construed as whether God, an immaterial entity, can know materially constituted objects. The second question is a subset of the first and is concerned with whether God knows possible objects. Although Gersonides does not distinguish in the text between knowing possible events and knowing possible objects, it is important to note that his discussion for the most part centers on the latter.

[87] Ibid.

[88] Ibn Daud 1986, *The Exalted Faith* II.6:96. This example is used by Avicenna but in a different context. For Avicenna, the issue is whether particulars like a lunar eclipse can be known without implying a change in the knower.

[89] Ibn Daud 1986, *The Exalted Faith* II.6:96.

[90] Ibn Daud 1986, *The Exalted Faith* II.6:96. See Fontaine 1990, 13–14 for a discussion of this position.

[91] References to specific articles will be made in the present chapter when relevant; however, the following works should be noted for their treatment of Gersonides' theory of divine omniscience: N. Samuelson 1972; T. M. Rudavsky 1983; Sirat 1969; Touati 1973; Rudavsky 2000.

[92] For further discussion of the difference between individuals and particulars, cf. Feldman's discussion in *Wars* 1987: 89; cf. also Rudavsky 1982; Rudavsky 1993.

In addition, however, Gersonides is concerned with a further problem. Like the majority of his philosophical precursors, Gersonides does assert the existence of contingency in the universe. However, as we will discuss in greater detail in Chapter 7, Gersonides is one of a minority of Jewish philosophers to uphold a theory of astrological determinism, according to which, states of affairs are determined by the heavenly bodies. His teleological cosmology is spelled out in Wars II, in which Gersonides is concerned to explain how divine knowledge operates, and to what extent divine foreknowledge of future contingents affects human choice. Gersonides' major thesis is that divine knowledge is predicated to a great extent upon knowledge of the heavenly bodies, which bodies are in turn "systematically directed toward his [man's] preservation and guidance so that all his activities and thoughts are ordered by them."[93] In support of this teleology, Gersonides argues that the celestial bodies have a purpose. This teleology is reflected by a "law, order and rightness" in the universe, implying the existence of an intellect that orders the nature of things: "you see that the domain of the spheres provides, in the best way possible, for the sublunar world."[94]

Of course, as we all know, astrologers often err in their predictions. One of the most compelling causes lies in human free will: our intellect and choice "have the power to move us contrary to that which is determined by the heavenly bodies."[95] Although Gersonides admits that on occasion human choice is able to contravene the celestial bodies, nevertheless this intervention is rare, and true contingency is a rare state of affairs indeed in Gersonides' ontology.[96] Within this deterministic scheme, Gersonides recognizes a domain of contingency that comprises chance events, possibilities, and human choices. Each of these represents an area that is not subject to the absolute necessity of the stars. Gersonides defines contingent events as those that are devoid of determining causes, as opposed to events that come to pass as a result of their own determinate causes. He goes on to say, however, that contingent events are nevertheless structured.[97] Gersonides' point is that inasmuch as the determination of contingent events occurs on the astral level, these events are ordered. However, their causes are incomplete, and so he will argue that the causes of human volition are not subject to the stars.

Contingent events are reflected most clearly in the domain of human agency. Following Aristotle, Gersonides argues that absolute necessity contravenes human deliberation and will.[98] A similar point is made in Gersonides' super-commentary on Aristotle's De Interpretatione. Arguing that arguments in favor of fatalism destroy

---

[93] Gersonides Wars vol. 2, 2.2:33.   [94] Gersonides Wars vol. 3, 5.3.5:137.
[95] Gersonides Wars vol. 2, 2.2:34.   [96] See Rudavsky 2000.
[97] "We assert that it is already clear that contingent events (be-miqreh ve-hizdamen) have a certain structure, inasmuch as there are already many individuals to whom many good things happen, all of them occurring by chance and it is these who are called fortunate…This necessarily entails that contingent events (le-mah she-be-miqreh) will have a mode of determination and structure. As to what that mode is, I wish I knew!" Gersonides Wars vol. 2, III.2: 95.
[98] "There is little doubt that according to this assumption (determinism) all voluntary affairs connected to will (ratzon) are necessary and there would be no free choice. And this is the lie from which Aristotle fled in the De Interpretatione. In truth there will be no choice since when what is chosen is necessary, the choice is not called a choice, since 'choice' refers to (a situation in which) two parts of a contradictory are possible." The text is found in Altmann 1979–80, "Gersonides' Commentary."

the nature of the possible, Gersonides goes on to state that from fatalism many absurdities result, including the pointlessness of human deliberation. But, he claims, "we need no teacher from whom to learn that deliberation itself and the will is a cause from which many things arise." And furthermore, "this sort of possibility appears in the agent . . . because the agent has free choice and (the power of) decision, so that he can actualize each opposite."[99]

It should be noted that these distinctions are ontologically rooted in events and are not epistemically based. Gersonides is not suggesting that humans, acting out of ignorance of the determining causes of their behavior, believe (falsely) that their actions are based on human volition. Rather, he is claiming that human beings, by virtue of their intellect and will, can overcome the determining influences of their astrological signs. Granted, according to Gersonides, this ability is rare, and real instances of volition are uncommon: "despite the fact that deliberate human choice made out of rational consideration has the power to disrupt this determination, such an eventuality will occur very rarely."[100]

As Manekin has argued, Gersonides has no equivalent for "free choice" or "free will"; the term "behirah" (choice) is more limited in scope, emphasizing the efficacy of human choice in the face of celestial causality.[101] Intellect and will, however, can move humans to do something other than what has been determined from the standpoint of the heavenly bodies. For God has placed within humans purposive reason "so as to move (humans) toward something other than that which has been determined from the aspect of the heavenly bodies, insofar as this is possible to make straight that which chance has convoluted."[102]

Gersonides claims as well that some states of affairs occur by chance. Speaking in Treatise IV of Wars of the origin of evil, Gersonides distinguishes between evils which arise from human choice and those which arise from chance.[103] In these examples, chance events occur without regard to human intention. However, not all chance events occur independently of human agency. In Wars II Gersonides gives the following characterization of a chance event. In describing chance events which are viewed under the mode of indetermination, Gersonides says that characterizations of such events are "analogous to the claim that were we to dig a hole so deep as

---

[99] Gersonides, Supercommentary on Averroes' Commentary on Aristotle's De Interpretatione, chapter 9 (found in the 1562 edition of Aristotelis omnia quas extant opera . . . Averrois Cordubensis in ea opera omnes qui ad haec usque tempora pervenere commentarii . . . cum Levi Gersonidis in libros logicos annotationibus . . . a Iacob Mantino in Latinum conversi. Venetiis, apud Iunctas, MDLXII (vol. I, ff. 82^{vb}K–83^{rb}F). An English translation of this portion of Averroes' commentary and Gersonides' super-commentary has been prepared by N. Kretzmann. The quoted passage is found in 83^{rb}D 46ff.

[100] Gersonides Wars vol. 2, III.2:97.

[101] For a detailed study of Gersonides' theory of free choice, see Manekin 1997a.

[102] Clearly, astrological determinism and human freedom are contradictory states of affairs; however, aside from baldly stating that in some cases human freedom is preserved in the face of determinism, Gersonides does not explain how these two contradictory states can be reconciled. We will return to astrology in Chapter 8.

[103] "Of those misfortunes which arise externally and not from temperament and choice, such as the overturning of a country, earthquakes or lightning, and the like, it is clear that they cause evil only by chance (be-miqreh). For example, a fire may accidentally fall upon a man and kill him, or the earth may envelop its inhabitants who found themselves there by chance" Wars vol. 2, IV.2:160–1.

to make a pit, we would find a treasure—for this is infrequent, i.e., if we were to find a treasure each time that we dug so deeply as to form a pit."[104] The actual occurrence of contingency is fairly infrequent; in fact, human acts of will are the only example of contingency. Since only humans have free will, to ask whether God knows future contingent events is tantamount to asking whether God has foreknowledge of the free actions of humans.[105]

Before stating his own view, Gersonides first examines the positions of his two philosophical predecessors, Aristotle and Maimonides, who represent diametrically opposed positions. According to Gersonides' understanding, Aristotle denied to God knowledge of particulars whereas Maimonides claimed that God in a single act knows all particulars.[106] Gersonides' own position will ultimately reflect his affinities with the Aristotelian position. Having examined the arguments in support of both Aristotle and Maimonides, Gersonides then develops his main argument that an omniscient, immutable deity cannot know changing particulars. The underlying premise in this argument is that all future particular objects are in fact mutable: that is, they change from a state of nonexistence to one of existence. Gersonides claims that an immutable deity cannot be omniscient, if omniscience entails knowing objects that undergo change. In order to demonstrate that in ordinary-knowing situations omniscience and immutability are incompatible, Gersonides raises the following dilemma. Once it is granted that God knows future contingents, one of the two must obtain. Either God knows that, from a set of possibilities, the alternatives that he knows would be generated has been generated. Or God knows that the actualized alternative from a set of possibilities has been generated even though it is different from that alternative which he knew would be generated prior to the generation of this actualized alternative.[107] In other words, given a situation in which (p or $-p$) are both future contingents, one of which occurs at t, the first states that God knows before t and at t that p would be generated, whereas the second states that he knows at t that $-p$ has been generated even though he knew before t that p would be generated.

According to the first horn of the dilemma, God's knowledge is unchanging: He always knew, both before and after t, that p would occur. Gersonides claims that this option allows for error on the part of God. The reason for this, he insists, is that

---

[104] Gersonides Wars vol. 2, II.2:34. Cf. also Gersonides' Supercommentary on Averroes' Commentary on Aristotle's De Interpretatione, chapter 9, 83ʳᵃA 11. 5–10; "a thing is said to be by chance because it is the result of an incomplete cause—e.g., when someone digs a ditch and finds a treasure. For this is classified as that which comes about by chance because he does not dig a ditch of that sort for the sake of that end, and it is not necessary that a man who digs a ditch should find a treasure. And so we say that finding a treasure while he is digging that ditch is by chance."

[105] The problems associated with contingency are discussed briefly by Touati 1973, 377–8. Brief allusions to contingency can be found in Wars vol. 2, II.2:34, "Contingency occurs only with respect to human affairs. In all other things, contingency can be said to occur only insofar as it concerns human beings." Cf. also Wars vol. 2, III.4.

[106] It should be noted that Gersonides' summary of Aristotle's position is based on an interpretation of how Aristotle might have treated the problem of divine omniscience. Any number of passages from the Aristotelian commentators, Themistius, Alexander of Aphrodisias, and Averroes could be used to support Gersonides' characterization of Aristotle.

[107] Gersonides Wars vol. 2, III.2:105.

"since the possibility whose occurrence he foreknew could not have occurred, it could happen in many of these things that what takes place is not the event that God foreknew would happen."[108] In other words, if both p and $-p$ are truly contingent, then $-p$ has as equal a chance of occurring as does p. Hence, it is possible that even though before t God knew that p would occur, in fact $-p$ occurs. According to Gersonides, in such a case what God knows is false.

In short, Gersonides argues that the assumption that God foreknows a future contingent event leads to the unacceptable conclusion that God is fallible. For if an event is truly contingent, it can either occur or not occur. But that means that when God knows that a contingent event will occur, the possibility exists that it will not occur. If it turns out not to occur, then the item that God knew (that the event would occur) turns out to be false. Hence, God is fallible, i.e., God's knowledge is not absolutely certain.

The arguments attributed to Aristotle further support Gersonides' thesis that divine omniscience and immutability are incompatible. In *Wars* III.4, Gersonides lays out the arguments of those Aristotelians who, following certain suggestions implicit in Aristotle, claimed that God does not know particulars. According to Gersonides, the Aristotelian claim that the thesis that God does know particulars is prone to two possibilities: either (4.1) God knows objects before they come to be; or (4.2) God knows them only when they come to be and not before. The former leads, however, to a number of untoward consequences, the most pressing of which is that God's knowledge is related to what does not exist. But this then leads to the following dilemma:

4.3   Either God knows objects according to their nature as contingent beings so that the contradictory of what he knows will be actualized remains a possibility.
4.4   Or God knows which one of these contradictory alternatives will be actualized and its contradictory does not remain possible.[109]

The Aristotelian rejects each of these alternatives as follows: (4.3) leads to the conclusion that God's knowledge of these entities, before they came to be, changes with their coming to be, since both were possibilities before being actualized, but afterwards both possibilities were eliminated. Hence on this reading God's nature is mutable. And the implication of (4.4) is that nothing in this world is a contingent that either may or may not be actualized. Since Gersonides and the Aristotelians are both committed to the existence of contingency, this option is rejected as absurd without further discussion. Having rejected all readings for (4.3), the only possible alternative is (4.2), namely that God knows future contingents only when they come to be. But this position entails that God's knowledge be subject to change; for every time that a new state of affairs occurred, God would acquire a new piece of knowledge. On the basis of these arguments, the Aristotelians, according to Gersonides, concluded that God has no knowledge of particulars. We shall see that Gersonides ultimately espouses a weaker formulation of this conclusion.

[108] Gersonides *Wars* vol. 2, III.2:105.   [109] Gersonides *Wars* vol. 2, III.4:122.

The third and final question concerns the epistemological force of God's foreknowledge. Does it follow from God's knowing a future contingent that it is necessary? In contradistinction to Saadiah Gaon and Halevi, who claimed that God's knowledge does not render the objects of his knowledge necessary, Gersonides will want to maintain that divine foreknowledge and contingency are incompatible. It should be noted that the main force of this controversy centers not upon causal necessity but rather upon epistemological and logical necessity. That is, Gersonides is not concerned in this context with whether God's knowledge itself has causal efficacy over the objects of his knowledge. This question, having to do with the relation between intellect and will, is a separate issue pertaining to the extent of God's creative will. Rather is he concerned with the apparent logical necessity that follows from the infallibility of God's knowledge. In other words, given that God knows *p*, it appears to follow from God's infallibility that *p* cannot fail to be the case, and hence that *p* is necessary.

Gersonides summarizes Maimonides' position, as stated in the *Guide*, as follows: "The divine knowledge of future events does not entail that the predicted event will occur; rather its opposite is still possible."[110] Only by denying the logical force of God's knowledge can Maimonides safeguard the contingency of events. Gersonides rejects Maimonides' arguments on the grounds that they attribute to God the *possibility* of fallibility. Arguing that divine omniscience severely compromises the contingency of the objects of God's knowledge, Gersonides dismisses Maimonides' form of compatibilism. Having rejected Maimonides' attempts to harmonize foreknowledge and contingency, and having upheld the existence of contingency in the universe, Gersonides adopts the one option left to him, namely that God does not know future contingents.

According to Gersonides, God knows that certain states of affairs may or may not be actualized. But insofar as they are contingent states, he does not know which of the two alternatives will in fact be actualized. For if God did know future contingents prior to their actualization, there could be no contingency in the world.[111] Echoing Ibn Daud, Gersonides claims that God's inability to foreknow future contingents is not a defect in his knowledge:

The fact that God does not have the knowledge of which possible outcome will be realized does not imply any defect in God. For perfect knowledge of something is the knowledge of what that thing is in reality; when the thing is not apprehended as it is, this is error, not knowledge.[112]

In this fashion, Gersonides concludes, the problem of divine omniscience is resolved in favor of indeterminism. With respect to future contingents, God knows their ordered nature or essence, and he knows that they are contingent, but he does not know which alternative will become actualized. Two interpretations of this position suggest themselves. The first is that what God knows are the individual forms or concepts of particulars. That is, when a sufficient number of general properties are known, God can be said to know the particular in question. According to this

---

[110] Gersonides *Wars* vol. 2, III.2:102. [111] Gersonides *Wars* vol. 2, III.4:116.
[112] Gersonides *Wars* vol. 2, III.4:118.

interpretation, since every object represents a unique instantiation of an individual concept, knowledge of a particular consists in being able to read off the predicates obtained in the individual concept of that particular. It is unlikely for a number of reasons that Gersonides had this interpretation in mind, however. First, it presupposes that it is possible to refer uniquely to a particular by this process of descriptive specifications without any reference to material specification. Gersonides, however, does feel that even though material composition of an object is accidental, it must enter into the description of the object in question.[113] Since God could not materially individuate the particular, he could not have referential knowledge of the particular in question. Furthermore, unable to individuate an object on the basis of its matter, God could not know whether the description in question referred to one object alone: in other words, God would be unable to ascertain whether the description in question were satisfied by only one member, or whether a number of objects shared the same description. Finally, this interpretation appears to rule out contingency. For if God can read off all the predicates contained in an individual concept, and these predicates are determinate, wherein lies the room for contingency?

A second interpretation of the phrase is that what God knows are the universal causes of particulars. Insofar as particulars represent instances of these causes, God can be said to know particulars. This view was developed earlier by Avicenna, whose views Gersonides might have known.[114] In other words, according to Avicenna, God's knowledge extends only to the domain of genera and species; God knows individual persons, for example, only through knowing the species man. Although Gersonides does not explicitly mention Avicenna, various aspects of Avicenna's theory are present in his own theory of divine omniscience. For like Avicenna, Gersonides would like to argue that God knows universals and only indirectly does his knowledge pertain to particulars. What God knows are the constitutive properties of concepts; these properties are then applied indirectly to particulars.

Feldman notes that the indeterminacy of God's knowledge, which many might consider the "most radical of Ralbag's doctrines," is explicitly mentioned even in his interpretation of *Genesis* 18:20. In this passage, Gersonides tells us that God was *about to see* whether the residents of Sodom and Gomorrah had actually sinned; until they do so, his knowledge is incomplete, "for it was possible for them to do otherwise than what God knows of them." The passage is worth quoting in full, since it reflects

---

[113] Gersonides does feel that objects are individuated on the basis of their constitutive matter. For further elaboration of this point, cf. Rudavsky 1982.

[114] Avicenna's theory of divine omniscience, propounded in a number of works, is summarized by Ghazâlî in his *Tahâfut al-Falasîfah*; both Avicenna's theory and Ghazâlî's comments are presented by Averroes in his *Tahâfut al Tahâfut* as follows: "...and as to those who believe that he knows things besides himself (and this is the theory which Avicenna has chosen) they believe that God knows other things in a universal knowledge which is not differentiated through past, future and present although, nevertheless, Avicenna affirms that not the weight of a grain escapes God's knowledge either in earth or in the heavens, since he knows individual things in a universal way...they say that God does not know the accidents of Zaid, Amr and Khalid and that he knows only men in general, through a universal knowledge." Since Gersonides refers to so few contemporary writers by name, the problem of citing influences upon him is difficult. It is likely, however that he was aware of various texts in which Avicenna's views were expounded. For a discussion of this point, cf. C. Touati 1973, 38ff.; Vajda 1957, 8, 267.

Gersonides' ability to weave his philosophical position into the context of a biblical commentary:

The Torah teaches us here something remarkable about God's knowledge of things, a point that has eluded all our predecessors whose writings are available to us. It is this. Whatever God knows of (human) deeds here on earth may be different from what men actually do. For what God knows of human actions is that which is appropriate for them to do according to the astral patterns that He has arranged...However human choice prevails over this pattern in their actions deriving from the heavenly patterns...He knows these deeds insofar as they are knowable, and this is in their being ordered and determinate. However, in the sense in which they are contingent, there cannot be any knowledge of them, for if there were knowledge of them, they would not be contingent.[115]

Hence, contingency has been retained with no apparent sacrifice of omniscience. In an apparent attempt to mediate between the mutually contradictory views of Aristotle and Maimonides, Gersonides adopts the best of both sets of arguments, claiming that, "there is no alternative but to say that God knows particulars in one respect but does not know them in another respect. But what these respects are, would that I knew!"[116]

VI The Challenge of Determinism: Crescas on Divine Knowledge and Possibility

We have now examined both compatibilism and incompatibilism; both theories present their own set of problems. Incompatibilism in particular limits the extent of God's knowledge of future contingents. Feldman notes that no philosopher before Gersonides had "so explicitly and consistently denied God's knowledge of human actions."[117] These sorts of limitations on God's knowledge led Crescas to posit what Feldman has described as a "theological determinis[m] of the compatibility variety."[118] On Feldman's reading of Crescas, although human actions, including future acts, are determined by God's knowledge, these actions are not absolutely necessitated. In this section, I shall argue that Crescas has abandoned compatibilism in favor of determinism, that is, that Crescas has so compromised the domain of possibility and of future contingency that he no longer permits a genuine sense of freedom. In other words, I claim that for Crescas the future is as fixed as is the past: there are no indeterminate events, and hence contingency has been eliminated.

Crescas' stated goal in *Light of the Lord* is to examine those arguments of the philosophers, and that of Gersonides in particular, which threaten the following three principles, which are necessitated by tradition:

---

[115] See Feldman's discussion of this text in Gersonides *Wars* vol. 2, 299.
[116] Gersonides *Wars* vol. 2, III.4:117.
[117] See Feldman's comment in Gersonides Wars vol. 2, 299. Perhaps the one philosopher who comes closest to Gersonides' indeterminism is Ockham.
[118] Feldman 1982, 6. For recent studies of Crescas' doctrine of free will, see as well S. Feldman 1984; Feldman 2009; C. Touati 1974; A. Ravitsky 1981–2; Rudavsky 2000.

The infinite science of God: "The first, that his knowledge, may he be exalted, encompasses the infinite."[119]

God's foreknowledge: "The second, that his knowledge, may he be exalted, extends over that which does not (now) exist."[120]

The non-causative power of omniscience: "His knowledge, may he be exalted, extends over the (disjunctive) parts of the possible, without changing the nature of the possible...."[121]

In standard scholastic fashion, Crescas lists arguments both for and against the three principles, with the intention of supporting the former. The philosophical arguments against divine omniscience that concern Crescas include the following four. First, if God knows all events, then God is being perfected by this knowledge, but God cannot be affected by matters in the world. Second, if God's mind becomes identical with things known, God will become a multiplicity. Third, because particular things are temporal, and whatever relates to time is an accident of motion, it follows that whatever is not described in terms of motion will not know particulars. And finally, the whole notion of divine science is untenable given the existence of evil.[122] Other more specific objections are raised against God's prescience as well. For example— Can God's knowledge be infinite? Can the infinite be comprehended? If knowledge requires that its object exists, how can God know what doesn't exist? Does not God's knowledge of future contingents require a change in God—before they occur he knows them as future, and after that as past? These philosophical worries are summarized by Crescas as follows:

...if his knowledge were of the attainment of one of the parts of the possible, and its contradictory remained possible, as would appear to be the case here, then when that one part has been attained, the possible will have vanished, and his knowledge will be of it (alone), and his knowledge will have undergone change. And since the intellect (according to the philosophers) becomes constituted as a substance out of what it knows, it would be necessarily implied that his essence undergoes change, and that is perfectly absurd.[123]

Because Gersonides exemplifies a paradigm of the philosophical stance, Crescas turns to Gersonides' claim that God knows particulars only through their general order; that God knows only that certain things are possible; and God does not know of the happenings of one of the possible sides, even a posteriori, for knowing it would occasion a change in God. Setting out to refute this doctrine, Crescas offers several arguments against Gersonides' position. First, he argues that if God does not know particulars *qua* particular, then what he does *not* know is infinite, and what he *does* know is finite. Second, if God does not know which possibility will be actualized, he is ignorant of most of the happenings of the world. And finally, Crescas asks, can God be said to know the past on this theory? If not, then God is ignorant of most of human history.[124]

---

[119] Crescas *'Or Adonai* II.1.1:28b. Unless otherwise noted, the references in this section of Crescas *'Or* are to my translations of the 1866 Hebrew edition. A recent translation of Book II of *Light* can now be found in Manekin 2007.

[120] Crescas *'Or Adonai* II.1.1:28b.   [121] Ibid.   [122] Crescas *'Or Adonai* II.1.2:29b–30a.

[123] Crescas *'Or Adonai* II.1.2:29a.   [124] Crescas *'Or Adonai* II.1.2:31a.

Crescas' own theory is presented as a response to what he sees as deficiencies in Gersonides' position. He first claims that our knowledge is derivative, whereas God's knowledge is active and causal.

from his knowledge and the concept of his will the objects known acquire existence, while our knowledge is emanated and acquired from the objects known by means of the senses and the imagination.[125]

That is, humans derive their knowledge from sense data, whereas God knows every event *ab initio*: as Feldman puts it, "what God knows he in some sense makes."[126] This qualitative difference between human and divine knowledge, reminiscent of Maimonides' distinction, enables Crescas to solve several problems. First he claims that knowledge of things adds nothing to God, for God is causal and creative, whereas things are dependent upon God:

If that proposition is accepted, inasmuch as it imparts existence and essence to the things other than himself, he most evidently does not become constituted as a substance out of something other than himself, and his knowledge of (things other than himself) does not necessitate a plurality in his essence.[127]

God knows things not because he knows himself, but *eo ipso*; it is through his knowledge that they exist.[128] So too, knowledge does not impute to God multiplicity, because again God is the cause and knows them as many without being many himself. It is in the context of the first question, which implies a change from future to past, that Crescas' determinist stripe is introduced. Does this temporal change from future to past affect God's essence? Crescas responds that because God knows before the occurrence of an event that it will happen, God's essence does not change when the event actually occurs. But how can we call a thing possible if God knows before its occurrence how it will happen? It is here that Crescas upholds determinism in order not to minimize in any way God's knowledge. Crescas attempts to distinguish two senses of contingency, arguing that a thing may be necessary in one way and possible in another.[129]

when we reason analogously from our knowledge to his knowledge, we have no escape but to suppose that the (disjunctive) part which he knows is possible in some respect and necessary in some respect, and that from the standpoint of its being necessary no change will occur in his knowledge and his essence, while from the standpoint of its being possible the nature of the possible will not be denied of possible things.[130]

This distinction is based on Avicenna's distinction between three types of possibility: the necessary in itself, the possible in itself, and the possible in itself but necessary from another. The second category comprises the "purely possible": what may or may not exist, and does not fully capture Crescas' notion of contingency.[131] Rather, Crescas argues that events known by God, although "possible in themselves,"

[125] Crescas *'Or Adonai* II.1.4:32b.   [126] Feldman 1982, 13. See also Feldman 2009.
[127] Crescas *'Or Adonai* II.1.4:32b.   [128] Waxman *Crescas*, 109.
[129] Crescas *'Or Adonai* II.1.4:33a.   [130] Crescas *'Or Adonai* II.1.4:33a.
[131] Crescas *'Or Adonai* II.1.4:33a. See Chapter 4 for Avicenna's trifold distinction.

nevertheless are necessary with respect to their causal history. In other words, if God knows p, then the truth value of p is determinate and "is necessary in terms of its causes."[132] Giving the analogy of a man's knowledge, which does not change the nature of the possibility of the thing known, so too does Crescas argue that the knowledge of God does not change the nature of the possibility in question. "Thus, the knowledge of God, may he be blessed, in the respect that (his) choice occurs in it, does not entail necessity in his essence, and does not change the nature of the possible at all."[133]

In Book II principle 5, chapter 1 of *Light*, Crescas turns more specifically to the problem of free choice. What is the connection between choice and possibility? Crescas is unequivocal that free choice presupposes possibility: "if there did not exist the nature of the possible, man's actions would be necessary."[134] He offers five arguments in favor of the existence of possibility and seven arguments against the existence of possibility.[135] The last is most relevant to us and suggests that if God's knowledge extends to particulars, then if possibility exists, this would preclude God's prescience. Crescas' solution, adduced earlier but developed more fully now, is that the possible exists in some respects and in other respects not. The possible exists "only in regard to itself." That is, when regarded from the perspective of causality, it does not exist as possible. Crescas argues that natural phenomena are "possible in themselves and necessary with respect to their causes."[136] What this means is that from the perspective of its causal history, every event is necessary. Only in light of human epistemological weakness (viz., our inability to know this causal history) can an event be said to be possible. As necessary, events can be foreknown; as possible per se, they are "*qua possibile*." Crescas goes on to suggest that what is necessary before its existence is not possible. That is, "it is not possible from the perspective of its knowledge, but it is possible from its own perspective."[137] In other words, if God knows that I will do an action at a future time, then my doing that action is determined from the perspective of God's knowledge. Even though from my own perspective, I may still do the opposite, from God's perspective it is not possible for me to do the opposite. Hence, from "the perspective of God's knowledge," I am not free with respect to performing future actions.

To the extent, then, that ontological differences between past and future have vanished, so too has contingency vanished. Human freedom exists no more in light of God's knowledge, and compatibilism has been replaced with a thoroughgoing determinism.[138] In order to counter the claim that he has eliminated human freedom altogether, Crescas in II.5.3 distinguishes between acts that are compelled and those that are caused. Only in the former case can we say that the agent was not responsible for the action. In the latter, even though the action is caused, the agent according to Crescas nevertheless chooses to bring the action about, and so it is voluntary.

---

[132] Feldman 1982, 17; see Crescas *'Or Adonai* II.1.4:33a.   [133] Crescas *'Or Adonai* II.1.4:33a.

[134] Crescas *'Or Adonai* II.5:45b.   [135] Crescas *'Or Adonai* I.5.1:45b–47b.

[136] Crescas *'Or Adonai* II.5:48a. The following passages are discussed in Harvey 1998.

[137] Crescas *'Or Adonai* II.5.3:48b.

[138] Feldman suggests that contingency has vanished because "whatever is eternalized has become past, and thus necessary, at least in the sense of being irrevocable and unpreventable." See Feldman 1982, 25.

A voluntary action is accompanied by a feeling of joy, or assent, which underscores its voluntary nature. Hence, Crescas argues, actions can be both causally determined and also voluntary.[139]

The temporal and ontological conflation of past and future is evidenced even more strikingly in Crescas' description of God's knowledge as timeless. By "timeless," Crescas means that God's knowledge is outside the domain of time altogether. Equating divine foreknowledge with the knowledge of present events, Crescas states that, "the science of God is beyond time, his knowledge of the future is like his knowledge of things existing which does not necessitate compulsion and necessity in the nature of things."[140]

That this position reflects analogous theories of eternity found in scholastic thought has not escaped notice. The most trenchant difficulty with this view has to do with the elimination of possibility; it is this issue that has not been resolved by these attempts. For, as Feldman has argued, the timelessness theory entails a world in which "all the episodes in the history of the universe have already been written."[141] These events cannot be other than what God already knows they are. More specifically, let us return to Crescas' statement that God's knowledge of future events is *like* that of present events. We know present events to be temporally necessary: to adopt Aristotle's language discussed above, while they are occurring they are necessarily occurring. By conflating present and future events, Crescas has eliminated the metaphysical openness of the future and reduced it to the necessity of the present. Any remaining possibility is "in the mind of the actor," as it were, and not in the event itself. And so the very doctrine of timelessness removes any vestige of contingency from the world.

VII Conclusion

We are now in a position to summarize and assess our findings. Jewish philosophers grappled with the tensions resulting from two traditions: on the one hand, a metaphysical system in which God was conceived as a unity, unchanging in essence, and all-knowing; and on the other hand, a tradition which claimed that God is intimately involved with a mutable world of possible entities. Does God's knowledge extend to this world of possibles? If not, then it might be claimed that God's knowledge is deficient—that is, that God's unawareness of the realm of the possible represents a deficiency in his nature. If his knowledge does extend to the sublunar realm of possibility, then it might be argued that the possible must give way to the necessary—that is, that God's knowledge precludes the existence of the possible.

---

[139] For a discussion of this move on the part of Crescas, see Feldman 1982, 27.

[140] Crescas 'Or Adonai II.5.3.

[141] Feldman conflates the views of Boethius, Aquinas, and Crescas into what he terms the "BAC Theory." What these three theories share in common is that God, being an eternal rather than a temporal being, has a "timeless knowledge of temporal facts such that events apparently future are really present, at least to him; and that this cognition in no way annuls the inherent contingency in statements about future contingencies" Feldman 1982, 21.

In answer to the questions raised at the beginning of this section, compatibilists attempt to uphold both omniscience and the genuineness of the future. Saadiah and Halevi laid the groundwork for Maimonides' compatibilism. Maimonides upholds God's omniscience in the face of numerous objections, claiming that God knows both concrete and unactualized particulars. Concrete particulars are known even though they are individuated by corporeal matter, and unactualized particulars, or possibles, are known even though they do not yet exist. On this view, God is not affected by what he knows. Maimonides attempts to forestall any objections with respect to the epistemological inconsistency of such a solution by emphasizing God's equivocal nature; because of the equivocal nature of the term knowledge when applied to God and man, the same consistency cannot be expected of both domains. An uneasy balance between God's omniscience and the logical and epistemological implications of such knowledge has therefore been achieved, but only at the expense of sacrificing the meaning of the term knowledge when it is applied to God.

On the other hand, Ibn Daud and Gersonides attempt to explain how God can know future contingents without this knowledge affecting the contingency of the objects known. Both argue that foreknowledge coupled with infallibility precluded the contingency of the objects of God's knowledge. Unable to adopt a compatibilist solution, Ibn Daud and Gersonides therefore uphold a form of incompatibilism in an attempt to preserve the existence of contingency in the world. Claiming that only a very small class of actions are truly contingent, Gersonides in particular argues that God's knowledge pertains to those actions only insofar as they are ordered and not *qua* contingent. That is, according to Gersonides, God knows particulars only as universals and not in their particularity. This knowledge is then transmitted to the prophet in the form of universal conditional statements. The prophet instantiates these statements and is able to apply them to future contingent events. I have argued, however, that this analysis does not adequately account for the conditional nature of prophecies.

For these and similar reasons, determinists such as Crescas have attempted to salvage what remains of divine omniscience. I have argued, however, that the end result is a truncated sense of future contingency. On Crescas' reading, God knows in a timeless fashion those events which occur necessarily with respect to their causes, but which appear to be possible to one not familiar with the causes in question. By equating knowledge of future events with that of the past and present, Crescas has obliterated the difference between future and past. In so doing, Crescas returns full circle to Aristotle's sea battle. Aristotle recognized the importance of positing an ontological difference between future events on the one hand, and past and present events on the other. Without this difference inherent in the very nature of reality, Aristotle felt that he could not give an adequate account of human action, deliberation, and responsibility.

Crescas' own student Joseph Albo reflected this point when he criticized his teacher's theory of free will. Summarizing Crescas' position, Albo's reaction is that it is "very close to the view that all things are determined and that the possible does not exist. For since the things are necessary considered in relation to their causes, if God knows the causes, they are actually necessary."[142] Albo's point is that on Crescas'

---

[142] Albo 1946, *Sefer ha-'Ikkarim* IV.1:7.

theory, future events cannot come into existence in any other way than in fact they *do* come into existence: "there is no thing that may equally be or not be when considered in relation to its causes."[143] In other words, having given up that *p* may "equally be or not be," Crescas has eliminated the definition of a free action. Albo, therefore, finds Crescas' determinism unacceptable on the grounds that it has eliminated the openness of the future, and by implication human freedom.

[143] Albo 1946, *Sefer ha-'Ikkarim* IV.1:8. See also Weiss 2017.

6
Creation, Time, and Eternity

I Introduction

Of the many philosophical perplexities facing medieval Jewish thinkers, perhaps none has challenged religious belief as much as God's creation of the world. No Jewish philosopher denied the centrality of the doctrine of creation to Jewish belief. Jews were enormously affected by Scripture and in particular by the creation account found in *Genesis* I–II. But like their Christian and Muslim counterparts, Jewish thinkers did not always agree upon what qualifies as an acceptable model of creation. In the context of this topic, perhaps the most important phrase of Scripture is *Bereshit*, "in the beginning." The very term *Bereshit* designates the fact that there was a beginning, i.e., temporality has been introduced if only in the weakest sense that this creative act occupies a period of time.[1] But medieval Jewish philosophers thinking about creation were influenced as well by Aristotle's model of an eternally existing world. When trying to prove that the world was created by God in time, philosophers who wanted to support a biblical theory of creation in time had to reject Aristotle's position that time is infinite. Creation theory is thus embedded in the larger context of the ontology of time.

Aristotle and the Kalâm atomists represent two diametrically opposed ways of approaching the issue of continuity versus discreteness of time.[2] Aristotle's theory of time reinforces a cosmology supportive of an eternally existing universe, thus obviating the need for a creator. Although Aristotle's eternity thesis is often regarded as the target of medieval philosophers, both Dhanani and Langermann suggest that it was possibly Galen rather than Aristotle who posed an equal if not greater threat.[3] In contrast to Aristotle, both Greek and Islamic atomists denied the continuity of time, and posited the existence of discrete time atoms, thus undermining the very assumption that things "persist" through time.[4] Like Aristotle, Galen was famous for

---

[1] Cf. Neher 1976, 50: "The primordial element is 'time' itself. Creation was manifested in the appearance of time. This time is entirely new. That is the significance of the verb *bara'*."

[2] See Furley 1967. The contemporary relevance of these texts is discussed in White 1992.

[3] Dhanani (1994) is interested primarily in the Mu'tazilites of Basra, and he emphasizes the link between Kalâm and Epicurean minimal parts. Langermann will argue further that "Epicurean teachings are reported in the master's name in the Galenic corpus," in Langermann 2009: the point being that Galen was an important vehicle for the transmission of Epicurean atomism to Islamicate culture.

[4] Kalâm atomism differs from its Greek atomist precursors in two important respects. First, as we shall see in greater detail below, atoms in Kalâm thought are construed as unextended, sizeless points, as opposed to Greek atoms, which were thought to be indivisible yet with extension. Second, the Kalâm theologians introduced an occasionalist tinge to their doctrine, arguing that these atoms are destroyed and recreated at every instant by the deity. One might imagine the Kalâm atomist agreeing with McTaggart's (1978)

having denied creation and emphasizing a self-contained natural order that eschewed a creator; because Galen was careful to reject atomism, the Islamic Kalâm theologians might have gravitated toward atomism as an effort to develop an alternative world view to the Galenic.[5] Given Galen's staunch anti-atomist views, Langermann suggests that "it is not beyond the realm of the possible that Galen's notion of *minima*, and not just his reports concerning his atomist opponents, had some influence upon the Mutakallimûn."[6]

This chapter examines medieval Jewish responses to the many challenges posed by both Aristotelian and Kalâm views of time as they occur against the backdrop of issues connected with the creation of the world.[7] It should be noted that rabbinic Jews did not for the most part concern themselves with time as a general construct.[8] As Sacha Stern notes, Maimonides was "one of the first rabbinic philosophers to conceive of time as an entity in itself and structure of reality, and to engage in systematic philosophical discussions about it."[9] Maimonides rejects Kalâm ontology in favor of Aristotle, but then must consider the implications of this ontology for creation. Maimonides was preceded in this tension by Saadiah Gaon, who struggles with the implications of the Kalâm atomistic theory, especially with regard to creation. By the fourteenth century, we find both Ḥasdai Crescas and Joseph Albo rejecting Aristotelian views, and returning to positions reflective of Kalâm ontology, most notably having to do with the theory of vacuum or void.[10] In general, I shall argue that these thinkers are committed to reconciling traditional Jewish beliefs with what they feel are the strongest points in Aristotle in an attempt to explain the existence of the universe in time. Further, in contradistinction to recent scholars who suggest that the question of time is not the primary concern of Maimonides in this

conclusion that ultimately both time and things are unreal; all that exist are individual discrete time (and space) atoms. For a discussion of different types of atomism and their implications, see Sorabji 1983, 350ff.

[5] Pines was not able to identify any one particular text or tradition as the source of the distinctive atomisms of the Kalâm. See Pines 1997. H. A. Wolfson (1976) mentions Galen's *On the Elements* (Galen 1996) in the context of Isaac Israeli who discusses at length both Galen's theory of minimal parts as well as Mutazilite atomism, in his own *Book of the Elements*.

[6] In this context, Isaac Israeli holds a pivotal role. The second part of Israeli's *On the Elements* deals with Galen. After presenting Galen's theory of *minima*, Israeli provides a lengthy exposition and rebuttal of atomism (he even mentions al-Nazzâm by name). After a long discussion, Israeli attempts to reconcile Galen and Aristotle. For more on Isaac Israeli, see Rudavsky 2000; Langermann 2009, 287. Galen's discussion can be found in Galen 1996. De Lacy traces the Arabic transmission of this work on pp. 20–5.

[7] For extended discussion of these issues, see Rudavsky 2000; ibid. 2009, 388–433.

[8] The contrast between Judaic and early Greek interest in time and temporality is quite stunning. I have argued elsewhere that early Jewish texts evinced little interest in time as a category in and of itself, whereas Greek texts on the other hand provided a rich and fertile layer of discussion. See Rudavsky 2000. For a detailed comparison of the rabbinic and Greek views of time, see Stern 2003. Stern's goal is to "draw a contrast between the Greek notion of time and its absence in ancient Jewish culture" (Stern 2003, 91), arguing that "their [the rabbis] apparently infrequent use of the Greek concept of time reveals a fundamentally different cultural background that to some extent they were unwilling, or unable, to shed" (Stern 2003, 99). See also Kaye 2018.

[9] Stern 2003; Glasner 2015, 88.

[10] Recent scholars have traced the criticism of Aristotelian physics back to fourteenth-century Jewish thinkers such as Gersonides and Abner of Burgos. See discussions in Eisenmann and Sadik 2015; Glasner 2015.

controversy, I shall argue that issues of temporality are critical to understanding the theory of creation both in Maimonides, as well as in subsequent Jewish philosophers.

As we shall in the next section, Aristotle posits an eternal universe in which time is potentially, if not actually, infinite.[11] That is, Aristotle argues that since there can be no "before" to time, neither time nor the universe was created. Jewish philosophers, however, almost without exception are committed to the belief that God created the universe but also inclined to accept certain aspects of Aristotle's science, as reflected in his theory of time and the universe. So when they consider whether the world was created by God in time, Jewish philosophers must deal critically with Greek and Islamic philosophical notions of time, infinity, and cosmology. By understanding the notion of creation and how an eternal, timeless creator created a temporal universe, we may begin to understand how the notions of eternity and time function within the context of Jewish philosophical theories of creation. In this chapter, we shall examine Neoplatonic, Kalâm, and Aristotelian attempts to think critically about creation.

II The concept of Time: Greek and Rabbinic Background

For reasons having to do as much with contemporary theological concerns as with pedagogical research, modern biblical scholars have devoted much time trying to uncover a "theory of time" in the Hebrew Scriptures. The enterprise has been fraught with frustration, however, and has not reached a scholarly consensus. That linguistic analysis of biblical temporal terms has yielded little fruit is obvious, especially in light of the ostensible lack of significant discussion in Scripture having to do with time per se. The word 'et is the most important word in biblical Hebrew for time and tends to mean the moment or point of time at which something happens.[12] The point of time can change over into a longer period of time. Other words used for time indications include mo'ed, zeman, 'olam, and yom. The term zeman occurs only three times in the latest period (Nehemiah 2:6; Esther 9:27, 31) and means, like mo'ed, appointed day. By Mishnaic times, the term zeman takes over and it is the most commonly used term in medieval texts.[13] But the rabbis were not philosophers and were not interested in elucidating a philosophical theory of time per se. With the exception, perhaps, of Ecclesiastes, there is very little speculation of a specifically metaphysical nature in biblical texts, little awareness of time as a metaphysical construct. Even in the Sefer Yeẓirah, which contains numerous references to space, little mention is made of time.[14]

What we do find in biblical and rabbinic texts is a model of time that emphasizes life cycles. Given the pre-eminence of ritualized events in Judaism, the marking of time assumes overwhelming importance in the rabbinic period. Inasmuch as the rabbis are equally concerned with the daily rituals and events, which are performed at specific times, so the exact determination of temporal demarcations, e.g., "day,"

---

[11] Aristotle's discussion of the eternity of the universe is contained in several places, most notably De Caelo 1, Physics 8.1, and Metaphysics 12.6. For a recent discussion of these and other relevant passages, see Sorabji 1983, 276ff.

[12] Jenni 1962, 643.   [13] Barr 1962, 117–18.   [14] See Stern 2003; Sorabji 1983, 133.

"twilight," "cycle," becomes of paramount importance in rabbinic literature.[15] The importance in this context of liturgical time cannot be overemphasized.[16] The religious calendar orients celebrants in time through the use of regularly repeated rituals; this temporal system structures the life of the community.[17] Such time is not just chronological time but is connected with repetitions: temporal repetition is one essential attribute of ritual. Calendars are not restricted to purely practical functions, that is, to refer to points in time and to time durations. They also represent a process of human cognition in which the experience of time is conceptualized, structured, and comprehended. "Calendars make sense of the dimension of time by imposing a rational, human structure upon it. Calendars represent at once a way of describing time and of establishing conceptual order amidst a seemingly disordered world."[18] But as Stern has noted, although the importance of timing is critical to rabbinic law, it is difficult if not impossible to abstract an independent notion out of these calendrical discussions. Even the calendar, Stern notes, is "not necessarily a scheme for measuring time, nor does it necessarily imply the existence of an abstract time dimension."[19]

A complete account of theories of time in the Greek philosophical tradition is beyond the scope of this chapter.[20] Nevertheless, several motifs and arguments emerge that are extremely influential upon subsequent medieval Jewish discussions. Plato's influence can be felt in his most explicitly cosmological dialogue, the *Timaeus*, a work that has helped to shape medieval cosmology and cosmogony. In the *Timaeus*, Plato distinguishes between eternity (*aionios*) and everlastingness (*aidios*): everlastingness is "the nearest approach to eternity of which sensible things are capable."[21] Plato distinguishes further between the sphere of eternity and that of time.[22] What Plato calls the Living Being is identified with the domain of pattern or forms, and is eternal and hence not subject to time. The world-soul and the world-body, which characterize the world of becoming, cannot be eternal because they comprise "motion"; hence, the Demiurge makes them a "moving likeness of eternity." Time is then defined as a likeness of eternity, which is the measure of the world-soul and world-body, or more specifically an "everlasting likeness" moving according to number.

When time actually comes into being, however, is a problematic issue. In *Timaeus* 38b, Plato suggests that inasmuch as time came into being with the heavens, it would appear that before creation there is no time: "Be that as it may, Time came into being together with the Heaven, in order that, as they were brought into being together, so they may be dissolved together."[23] Other early passages in the *Timaeus* suggest that time itself was created along with the cosmos as a whole.[24] But later passages in the

---

[15] See for example Mishnah 1:1 9b.   [16] See Higgins 1989, 232ff.
[17] Robbins 1997, 73.   [18] Stern 1996, 104.
[19] Stern 2003, 137. Kaye (2018) tries in fact to provide such an account of time in rabbinical works.
[20] For a succinct overview of theories of time in Greek philosophy, see Sorabji 1983.
[21] See Lloyd 1976, 138.   [22] Plato *Timaeus* 37c-d.
[23] Plato *Timaeus* 38b. Although in general I follow the translation in Cornford, I have replaced his term "ever-existent" with the term "everlasting" for the Greek word *aidios*.
[24] See for example: "Concerning the whole Heaven or World...it has come to be" (Plato *Timaeus* 28b); "at the same time that he ordered the Heaven, he made...Time" (37d); "For there were no days and nights, months and years, before the Heaven came into being; but he planned that they should now come to be at

dialogue support the interpretation that time may pre-exist the creation of the heavens. In contradistinction to those passages adduced earlier that suggested *ex nihilo* creation, other passages suggest that time existed, in some ontological measure, before creation.[25] If we take seriously Plato's definition of time as "a likeness moving according to number," which is aligned with the creation of the heavenly spheres, and if we emphasize the importance of these celestial spheres with respect to the measure of time, then it is not possible that time pre-exist the creation of the heavens. It is here that the discontinuity between time and space appears most explicitly in the *Timaeus*. For unlike time, which is the measure of motion, place (*chora*) is the necessary precondition for the coming into being of motion. And so while it is perfectly possible for *chora* to pre-exist the creation of the heavens, it is not possible for time to so pre-exist.

Aristotle turns to issues of creation and time against the fabric of Plato's *Timaeus*. For Aristotle, the prime example of time and motion is the relation between time and the circular motion of the heavens. Time is therefore construed in terms of a circle, measured by the circular motion of the heavens.[26] In *De Caelo* 1.10, he summarizes the positions of his predecessors, in particular that of Plato, who claimed that the cosmos had a beginning but is everlasting. Aristotle presents a number of arguments against Plato, arguing that a universe that is ungenerated and indestructible at all times is not capable of nonexistence; he rules out the possibility in which things exist for an infinite time and then cease to exist for an infinite time.[27] Aristotle then applies these and other considerations to Plato's arguments in the *Timaeus*, arguing that it is impossible for something to be once generated and yet indestructible.[28]

The eternity of the cosmos is integrally related to Aristotle's conception of time. In answer to the question whether time was generated, Aristotle develops further Plato's notion of the instant or "now" (*to nûn*) as a basic feature of time. The instant is defined as the middle point between the beginning and end of time. Since it is a boundary or limit, it has no size and hence cannot be considered to exist: it is a durationless instant. Since instants do not in and of themselves exist, it might be argued that time itself does not exist. That is, the past and future do not now exist, and the present "now" is not a part of time since, as we have already noted, it is sizeless. Because the extremity, or limit, of time resides in the instant, Aristotle claims that time must exist on both sides of it: "Since the now is both a beginning and an end, there must always be time on both sides of it."[29] In *Metaphysics* XII.6, Aristotle claims that there can be no "before" or "after" if time does not exist, for both terms imply the existence of relative time. "For there could not be a before and an after if time did not exist."[30] For these reasons he insists that time must be uncreated.

the same time that the Heaven was framed" (37e); "In virtue, then, of this plan and intent of the god for the birth of Time, in order that Time might be brought into being..." (38c); "Now so far, up to the birth of Time..." (39e).

[25] See for example Plato *Timaeus* 39e3; 38e3–5; 34b-c; 53a; 69b.
[26] See Whitrow 1988, ch. 1 for further details.
[27] See Aristotle *De Caelo* 281b:33.   [28] Aristotle *De Caelo* 283a:30.
[29] Aristotle *Physics* VIII.1 251b ff.   [30] Aristotle *Metaphysics* XII.6 1071b ff.

Aristotle's emphasis upon an ungenerated cosmos is reinforced in his analysis of the relation between time and motion.[31] This characterization is developed further in his classic discussion on time in *Physics* IV.10–14. Having asked of time whether "it belongs to the class of things that exist or that of things that do not exist,"[32] he rejects various considerations which might lead one to think that time does not exist. Time, he claims, is connected with movement. This leads to a definition of time in terms of the movement of the "now": "When we do perceive a 'before' and an 'after,' then we say that there is time. For time is just this—number of motion in respect of 'before' and 'after'... time is only movement in so far as it admits of enumeration... Time then is a kind of number."[33]

Aristotle then stipulates two important qualifications to his characterization of time in terms of movement. First, he points out that "not only do we measure the movement by the time, but also the time by the movement, because they define each other."[34] Further, he argues that time is the measure not only of motion but of rest as well. "For all rest is in time. For it does not follow that what is in time is moved, though what is in motion is necessarily moved. For time is not motion, but 'number of motion': and what is at rest also can be in the number of motion."[35] We shall return to the importance of this passage in section VI below when we examine Crescas' critique of Aristotle.

The last important Greek philosophical school to influence Jewish discussions of time and creation is Neoplatonism, which was largely based on the writings of Plotinus and Proclus. As noted in Chapter 2, the work of Plotinus was transmitted in a variety of ways, most notably through the *Theology of Aristotle* (a paraphrase of books 4, 5, and 6 of the *Enneads*), and through doxographies. Plotinus' distinction between time and eternity is carried out against the background of both Plato's characterization of time in the *Timaeus* as the "moving image of eternity," as well as Aristotle's description of time in *Physics* IV as the measure of motion. The main distinction in Plotinus is between that which is outside of time altogether, and that to which temporal predicates apply.[36] In contrast to the Aristotelian view, Plotinus and his followers develop a theory of time that does not depend upon external objects and their motion for its existence. On this view, the essence of time is not motion but rather duration. In *Enneads* 3.7 Plotinus rejects the view that makes time dependent upon physical motion. Rather, he connects it with the "the Life of the Soul in a motion of change from one stage of life to another."[37]

Plotinus defines eternity as

A life which remains always in the same state, always having the whole present to it—not one thing now and then another, but everything at once, and not different things now, and afterward different things, but a part-less completion, as if all things existed together in a single point, and never flowed forth, but remained there in the same state, and did not change, but were always in the present, because none of it has gone by, nor shall it come to be, but it is just what it is.[38]

---

[31] See Aristotle *De Caelo* I.9 279a 15 ff.   [32] Aristotle *Physics* IV.10 217b32.
[33] Aristotle *Physics* IV.11 219b1–2.   [34] Aristotle *Physics* IV.12 220b15; *Physics* IV.12 220b15.
[35] Aristotle *Physics* IV.12 221b8.   [36] See Gerson 1994, 116.
[37] Plotinus *Enneads* 3.7.11, 263.   [38] Plotinus *Enneads* 3.7.3, 255.

In this important and influential definition, we note that eternity always has the whole present to it; it is changeless, always present. Eternity is "all at once, and is everywhere full yet unextended."[39] Plotinus is ostensibly aware of the dilemma of speaking about eternity using temporal predicates. Because eternity always is, it never "is not" and cannot be other than it is. In contrast to eternity, then, time represents the domain of incompleteness. Temporality reflects the image of the eternal. For Plotinus, time is a function of the movement of the life of the soul: it is "the product of the spreading out of life."[40] Time is dependent upon soul, and so upon the return of the soul to the One, time itself will disappear. But the origin of time, and the soul, is unclear in Plotinus. Originally time "was not yet time, but it too was at rest in Eternity."[41] Due, however, to the "officious nature" of world-soul, the world-soul moved away [and down] from eternity, and time moved with it; in this move away from Eternity the world-soul "produced time as the image of eternity" when it produces the sensible world in imitation of the intelligible world.[42] What is interesting about this myth of generation is that in the beginning, time was both in eternity and yet distinguishable from it. Plotinus does not explain what accounts for the initial discontent of the soul, nor does he explain why time moves along with the soul away from eternity.

The individual who enabled medieval Jewish philosophers to incorporate Aristotle's model into a theological context is John Philoponus, whose works contain a refutation of Aristotle's theory of the eternity of the world from the perspective of theories of the infinite. John Philoponus' major work *Contra Aristotelem* has been lost and survives only in quotations from Simplicius' commentaries on Aristotle's *De Caelo* and *Physics*.[43] In this work, Philoponus hopes to demonstrate the creation of the world by arguing that Aristotle's assumption of eternal motion leads to untenable conclusions. Philoponus' works were known to Arabic philosophers, and were transmitted by the Islamic school of Kalâm, through Saadiah Gaon, to eleventh- and twelfth-century Jewish and Christian philosophers.[44] For this reason, his arguments are of crucial importance to understand theological attempts to refute Aristotle's eternity arguments, which are based on a theory of the infinite.

In his *Contra Aristotelem*, Philoponus presents two sets of arguments in support of creation, both of which are directed against Aristotle's eternity thesis. According to Simplicius, Philoponus assumes as axiomatic that "it is impossible for an infinite number to exist in actuality or for anyone to traverse the infinite in counting and that it is also impossible that anything should be greater than the infinite, or that the infinite should be increased."[45] From this axiom he argues as follows. Imagine an infinite series of transformations that has taken place among the four elements. In an eternal world, these transformations would constitute an infinite series. But, using

---

[39] Plotinus *Enneads* 3.7.3, 255.   [40] See Lloyd 1976, 143.
[41] Plotinus *Enneads* 3.7.11, 262.   [42] Ibid.
[43] For a detailed discussion of the history and transmission of these texts, see Davidson 1987, 86ff.; Sorabji 1983, 197ff. Some of Philoponus' relevant texts can be found in Philoponus 1987.
[44] For a history of this transmission, see Davidson 1987, 86–116. Davidson notes at least thirteen medieval discussions that draw upon Philoponus' position that the infinite cannot be traversed.
[45] Philoponus 1987, 144.

Aristotle's characterization of infinity, it is clear that an infinite number cannot exist actually or be traversed. So in an eternal world, the infinite series of transformations could never be completed and the particle now known to exist could never in fact have come into existence.[46] Further, imagine that the scenario were expanded to the spheres. If the motion of the heavens is without a beginning, and if spheres revolve at unequal periods of revolution, then it is necessary that the sphere of Saturn has rotated with an infinite number of revolutions; but on this celestial model, the sphere of Jupiter must have rotated with nearly three times more revolutions, the sun with thirty times more revolutions than Saturn, and that of the fixed stars more than ten thousand times more. But, Philoponus, argues, "if it is not [even] possible to traverse the infinite once, is it not beyond all absurdity to assume ten thousand times the infinite, or rather the infinite an infinite number of times?"[47] Hence, he concludes that the circular motion of the heavens is not eternal but must have had a beginning.

III Harmonizing Jerusalem and Athens: Time and creation in Philo

Philo's discussions about creation were influenced by Platonic, Aristotelian, and Stoic ideas, as well as by the Jewish sources available to him in Hellenistic Alexandria. Philo is not an original philosopher, but rather a highly competent student of the entire range of the Greek philosophical tradition available to him. As stated in a number of his works, Philo characterized his mission as one of assimilating the wisdom of the Greek philosophers with his Jewish heritage. His genius, as depicted by Runia, was to "select, modify, amplify, refine and synthesize this great mass of material and place it in service of an elaborate religious-philosophical worldview."[48] Although Philo rarely makes mention of Plato by name, nevertheless echoes of Plato's works resonate throughout Philo's corpus, particularly when he discusses the issue of creation.

Philo's presentation of creation occurs in several works, but most notably in his treatise *On the Creation of the Cosmos According to Moses*, in which he tries to show that both *Genesis* and Plato's cosmogony share similar philosophical features. Philo depicts Moses as an author who not only had reached "the very summit of philosophy" but had also been instructed "in the many and most essential doctrines of nature by means of oracles."[49] Turning to the issue of why and when God created the cosmos, Philo rejects the view that the cosmos is "ungenerated and eternal" on the grounds that it would not only impute idleness to God, but further that it would eliminate the doctrine of Providence. To present the world as uncreated leaves God

---

[46] Philoponus 1987, 145. See Davidson 1987, 88. Philoponus expands this argument, claiming that "... if on the one hand the ascent (*anodos*) took place *ad infinitum*, complete things would not precede the incomplete, and the actual not the potential; but if on the other hand <the motions> are limited <in number>, then the first <motion> which evidently exists together with the universe, has made a beginning which starts from something actual and complete for the subsequent motions" Philoponus 1987, 145.

[47] Philoponus 1987, 146.   [48] Runia 1986, 23.   [49] Philo 2001, *Creation* 49.

with nothing to do.[50] The cosmos is, according to Moses, generated, in contradistinction to God who is unchanging and ungenerated. According to Philo's reading of Genesis, Moses says that God fashioned the cosmos in six days in order to provide order. But God was not needful of a length of time, since God "surely did everything at the same time."[51] Creation is thus envisaged as an instantaneous process.

But what does Philo mean when he claims that time itself (chronos) began with the ordered cosmos? If he allows that matter existed before the cosmos, then he must allow for a "before" before creation; but, on the other hand if, as he claims, creation is simultaneous, then there can be no "before."[52] The major question has to do with whether God is the producer of the beginningless matter. Most recently, Runia has argued that Philo's conception of time is compatible with both simultaneous creation and eternal creation. In the former case, creation takes place as a temporal event, and involves a beginning of time. In the latter case, there is no creation of time, but creation reflects the dependence of the cosmos upon God.

The discussion of time in the treatise Quod Deus Immutabilis Sit (On the Unchangeableness of God) emphasizes a number of motifs pertaining to God and time. First, Philo emphasizes that for God nothing is future: "nothing is uncertain or future to God."[53] Furthermore, God is the "maker of time" as well, for God is depicted as "the father of time's father, that is of the universe...thus time stands to God in the relation of a grandson."[54] And finally, reminiscent of Plato's Timaeus 37d, Philo characterizes God's eternity in contradistinction to temporality: "God's life is not a time, but eternity, which is the archetype and pattern of time; and in eternity there is no past nor future, but only present existence."[55]

Philo reiterates in a number of passages the view that time is dependent for its existence upon the ordered movement of the cosmos. In Legum Allegoriae (Allegorical Interpretation), for example, Philo argues that inasmuch as every period of time is a collection of days and nights, which are brought about by the sun's movements, it follows that "time is confessedly more recent than the world."[56] Philo then continues by saying that "it would therefore be correct to say that the world was not made in time, but that time was formed by means of the world."[57] Similarly in de Opificio Mundi (On the Creation of the Universe) 26, he claims that time did not exist before the cosmos, but came into existence either with the cosmos or after it; it is therefore either as old as or younger than the cosmos. Reflecting the Stoic definition of time as a measured space,[58] or duration, Philo argues that "...there was no time before the cosmos, but rather it either came into existence together with the cosmos or after it. When we consider that time is the extension of the cosmos' movement, and that there could not be any movement earlier than the thing that moves but must necessarily be established either later or at the same time, then we must necessarily

---

[50]   See Sorabji 1983, 250, for discussion of the "idleness" argument.
[51]   Philo 2001, Creation 49.
[52]   See Sorabji 1983, 209 for a discussion of the various scholarly views on this issue.
[53]   Philo 1960d, Unchangeableness of God 5.30:25.   [54]   Ibid.   [55]   Ibid. 5.32:27.
[56]   Philo 1960a, Allegorical Interpretation I.2:149.   [57]   Ibid.
[58]   This Stoic definition is explicitly stated in Philo 1960c, Eternity of the World 4:4: "and time, they [the Stoics] say, is what measures its movement."

conclude that time too is either the same age as the cosmos or younger than it. To venture to affirm that it is older is unphilosophical."[59]

Attempting to accord his view with that of Scripture, Philo maintains further that Moses does not take the term "beginning" in a temporal sense but rather in a numerical sense. Commenting on *Genesis* I, Philo interprets the verse to refer to a beginning according to number, rather than a temporal beginning. Time cannot be separated from the cosmos itself; so, it should be understood "numerically," since there is a close relation between number and order.[60] That time did not exist before the creation of the world is evidenced in a number of passages. In this regard, Philo follows Aristotle's conception of time as connected with motion. Philo presents the purpose of the heavenly bodies as giving us temporal measure and quantitative measure: to give the "right times for the annual seasons"; and "for days and months and years, which indeed have come into existence as the measure of time and also have generated the nature of number."[61] In this latter case, Philo claims that time makes manifest number: "from a single day the number one is derived, from two days two... and from infinite time the number that is infinite."[62]

Finally, mention must be made of the treatise *Aeternitate Mundi* (*Eternity of the Universe*), in which Philo adduces Greek philosophical considerations to prove the eternity of the cosmos based on the eternity of time. If time is uncreated, so too must the world be uncreated. Since time is what "measures the movement of the universe... the world is coeval with time." But time itself has no beginning or end; the very words "was" and "ever" indicate time, and so it is absurd to suggest that there was a time in which time did not exist. And so Philo concludes the argument by stating that "it is necessary that both [time and the cosmos] should have subsisted from everlasting without having any beginning in which they came into being."[63] What are we to make of this argument? Runia provides compelling evidence to the effect that Philo does not in fact subscribe to the view expressed by this argument, as evidenced by his use of the Mosaic account of creation.[64]

IV Neoplatonic Cosmology: Creation as Emanation

When we turn to the Neoplatonist tradition epitomized by Isaac Israeli and Ibn Gabirol, we find a cosmology superimposed onto an emanation scheme derived ultimately from Plotinus. When we turn to Isaac Israeli, we find operative many of these cosmological ingredients adduced above. Of Israeli's many surviving works, the *Book of Definitions* and the *Book of Substances* comprise the main sources of Israeli's philosophical ideas. His best-known work, the *Book of Definitions*, deals with definitions of philosophical, logical, and other terms.[65] The *Book of Substances* has survived only in

---

[59] Philo 2001, *Creation* 53.   [60] Philo 2001, *Creation* 156.   [61] Philo 2001, *Creation* 60.
[62] Ibid., 61.   [63] Philo 1960c, *Eternity of the World* 52–5:221.
[64] For extensive analysis of Philo's theory of time, see Runia 1986, 218ff.
[65] The entire treatise exists in Hebrew and Latin translations; only a portion survives in the original Arabic. It opens with an account of Aristotle's four types of inquiry (whether, which, what, why) and an elaboration of al-Kindi's definitions of philosophy.

incomplete fragments of the original Arabic.[66] Finally, the *Chapter on the Elements* (the *Mantua Text*) exists only in manuscript, at Mantua.[67] From this text, we learn that Israeli based his view of creation and the series of emanations on an earlier text known as *Ibn Ḥasdai's Neoplatonist*.[68]

Israeli's philosophical cosmology describes the various stages of being as a series of emanations, or hypostases, from the intellect. The intellect itself is constituted by the union of first matter and first form, which are created by the power and will of God, who brought them into existence *ex nihilo*. Israeli thus upholds the notion of creation *ex nihilo* in the case of the first three hypostases, while adopting the Plotinian concept of emanation for the others. But, unlike Plotinus, Israeli maintains in the *Book of Definitions* that each hypostasis acquires more shadows and darkness, out of which the next hypostasis emanates. The shadow accounts for its loss of strength.

In *Book of Substances*, Israeli argues against the opponents of the theory of creation, presumably those Aristotelian followers who support an eternal universe. According to Israeli, these followers erroneously attribute change to God rather than to the world. Employing the language of *ex nihilo* creation, Israeli superimposes a theory of creation upon his Neoplatonic scheme. We thus have "a combination of creation *ex nihilo* with emanation."[69] God's creation is an act of will that extends to the top hypostasis of First Form and First Matter. He then inserts an extra stage, that of "simple substances," between God and universal first intellect, perhaps, as suggested by Altmann, to "facilitate the adoption of the concept of creation within the framework of Neoplatonic metaphysics."[70] In short, Israeli attempts to combine both metaphors by claiming that the shadow is the new substance; the essence or light is not what emanates. Unfortunately, Israeli is seemingly unaware of the contradiction between maintaining that emanation is both the passing of the essence and the passing of a shadow.[71]

Whereas Plotinus described intellect as emanating directly from the One, Israeli, following his pseudo-Aristotelian source, interposes two simple substances—first matter and first form or wisdom—between the Creator and intellect as representing the first hypostasis or emanation from the Godhead.[72] Soul follows intellect in this triad of hypostases and is divided into a higher phase and a lower one: the latter of which Israeli calls nature.[73]

---

[66] Discovered by A. Borisov and edited by S. M. Stern, this work seems to have been written in Arabic characters, though the extant manuscripts are in Hebrew script. See Altmann and Stern 1958, 80.

[67] Attributed to Israeli by Altmann and Stern, this text is a commentary on a work by Aristotle. The *explicit* says that the aim of the text is to explain the words of the philosopher by way of arguments and proofs. See Altmann and Stern 1958, 118.

[68] Ibid., 119.   [69] Jospe 2009, 102.

[70] See Altmann and Stern 1958, 163, quoted in Jospe 2009, 102.

[71] As in Plotinus, emanation does not imply change; the source remains unaffected. Plotinus used this fact to explain how multiplicity arises from unity; however, because Israeli introduces a notion of creation, he cannot do the same. Instead, he tries to harmonize the two motifs. Hence, Israeli ignores Plotinus' important distinction of the two moments in emanation: the pure uninformed moment, and the turning back to the source in contemplation.

[72] Altmann and Stern 1958, 159.

[73] Other Neoplatonic sources also equate the sphere with nature. There is no warrant for this in Plotinus—he only identifies nature with the vegetative soul. Following his pseudo-Aristotelian source,

The doctrine of atomism is clearly expressed in Israeli's *Book on the Elements*. In this work, Israeli is concerned to define the term "element," out of which the sublunar world is composed. In the context of this discussion he combats the atomistic theory of both the Mu'tazilites and the Greek philosopher Democritus, and attempts to prove that a line is not composed of points. Israeli is not a systematic thinker, and he does not develop his key concepts. However, from fragments scattered throughout his works, we can pull together a number of definitions and concepts that pertain to his view of time and infinity. Israeli introduces the discussion in the context of discussing Galen's definition of the term element. According to Israeli, by "element" Galen means "the minimum part of a thing,"[74] echoing Aristotle's use of the term. He then introduces a fictitious interlocutor who suggests that by "part" he means "those parts into which a body is divided naturally and of which it is composed, just as a body is divided into surfaces and surfaces into lines and lines into points."[75] But Israeli rejects the mathematization of atoms by arguing that the union of two points can be conceived in two ways: either the totality of the one unites with the totality of the other, or a part of one comes in touch with a part of the other:

you may say either that the point when it is connected to another point is a conjunction of whole with whole, or a part with a part. But if you say that the conjunction of one point with another is a conjunction of whole with whole, then the two points will form one point and their place will be one place, for the whole of the one is the whole of the other, seeing that neither of them has extension nor is there between them any difference. And the same will hold true of the third point and the fourth and the others after it to infinity. And if the conjunction of one point with another is as part with part of the other, then the division and dissection of the point would necessarily follow, but this would do away with his claim that the point is indivisible.[76]

In the first case, there is no distance between the two, and so the result would be a point; in the second case, a contradiction results—a partial union of atoms, which are *ex hypothesi* spaceless and devoid of parts. In either case, mathematical points cannot produce an extended body.[77] Israeli therefore concludes that inasmuch as bodies cannot be composed of atoms that are both indivisible and unextended, nor can they be composed of atoms that are indivisible and extended: it is not appropriate to postulate the existence of indivisible magnitudes. Further, in the Mantua text, Israeli notes, reflecting Plotinus' *Enneads* 3.7.11, that in the sphere itself there exists neither

---

Israeli transfers Aristotle's divisions of the individual soul (rational, animal, vegetative) to the universal soul, giving us three hypostases of soul, to which he adds as a final quasi-spiritual substance the "sphere" or heaven, representing the Plotinian hypostasis of nature. Altmann and Stern cite many examples of how this scheme can be seen in his writings; it also occurs in *Ibn Ḥasdai's Neoplatonist* and the *Long Theology*.

[74] See Israeli 1958, *Sefer Yesodot* II.3–8, 40: "After we have reached this point in our treatise and have explained all that the philosopher has said concerning the essence of the elements and its limits . . . it is now incumbent that we mention in the second part what Galen says and his beliefs on this; and this is that Galen's view was similar to the philosopher and said that the element is the minimum part of a thing."

[75] Israeli 1958, *Sefer Yesodot* II.3–5, 43.

[76] Israeli 1958, *Sefer Yesodot* II.12–17, 43. The final point of this argument is that we cannot speak of indivisible magnitudes.

[77] This argument can be found in Aristotle *Physics* VI.1 231b, 2–5; Aristotle *De Generatione et Corruptione* I.2, 316b, 14–18; Aristotle *Metaphysics* XIII.8 1083b, 13–16.

place nor time. None of the simple substances require place or time, nor are they "in time or place but they are the place for time and place."[78] Israeli reflects the sentiment expressed in Pseudo-Empedocles that "the soul is the place of the world, and not the world its place."[79]

Echoes of Israeli's Neoplatonic cosmology can be found in Ibn Gabirol's *Mekor Ḥayyim* as well. As we saw in Chapter 2, Ibn Gabirol's most creative and influential contribution in *Mekor Ḥayyim* comprises his hylomorphic conception of matter. Ibn Gabirol's purpose is to show that all substances in the world, both spiritual and corporeal, are composed of matter and form. How are form and matter interrelated? Gabirol's ambivalence is reflected in two alternative responses. On the one hand, he argues that form and matter are mutually inter-defined, and are differentiated only according to our perspective of them at a particular time; accordingly, both are aspects of simple substance. On the other hand, he emphasizes the complete opposition between matter and form, suggesting that each possesses mutually exclusive properties that render a reduction of one to the other an impossibility.[80]

In this work, there exists a hierarchy of different kinds of place, some spiritual, and others physical. God represents the infinite place (space), whereas simple corporeal place occupies the lowest rung of the hierarchy. In *Meqor Ḥayyim* II.14, Ibn Gabirol defines space (*makom*) as "the contact between two bodies,"[81] and distinguishes two types: corporeal and spiritual space. In III.32 Ibn Gabirol argues that whether or not an entity occupies place depends upon the ontological makeup of its foundation. Hence, whatever is simple and spiritual does not occupy place, whereas corporeal entities do occupy place. Ibn Gabirol further notes that while simple substance can function as a "spiritual place" for spiritual forms, the same does not hold of corporeal forms: "of whatever functions as corporeal place for something, it is not possible that many things can inhere in it simultaneously."[82]

Ibn Gabirol raises the issue of the infinite divisibility of matter and substance in treatise two of *Mekor Ḥayyim*, in the context of working out his ontologies of matter and form. Although he does not mention Zeno by name, his analysis pertains to the ultimate divisibility of the parts of substance, reflecting issues raised by Zeno. Having maintained that each composite of substance is composed of that of which it was put together, and since the parts of the quantity of the substance in question are all similar, Ibn Gabirol asks whether the ultimate constituents of reality are divisible or indivisible.[83] In posing this question, Ibn Gabirol reflects the concern of the Mutakallimûn who had argued for the ultimate indivisibility of matter. Ibn Gabirol

---

[78] Israeli *Mantua Text* in Altmann and Stern 1958, 127.

[79] This reference is given by the editor in Altmann and Stern 1958, 126.

[80] Ibn Gabirol 1926, *Mekor Ḥayyim* 4.2.

[81] Ibn Gabirol 1926, *Mekor Ḥayyim* 2.14:73. This definition is reiterated in 2.15: place (*maqom*) is "one body in another body."

[82] Ibid., 3.37:98.

[83] Ibn Gabirol 1926, *Mekor Ḥayyim* 2.16:94. Schlanger notes that Ibn Gabirol is posing the problem of atomism here, and hopes to prove that there is quantity only where there is substance. He also notes that this entire discussion of atomism in chapters 16–19 was omitted from the Falaquera edition presumably because he was not interested in this discussion. See Ibn Gabirol 1970, 86, for further discussion of these passages. See also Pessin 2013.

presents a number of arguments designed to support the divisibility of parts and concludes that "the part in question between the parts of the quantity of the world is divisible, and it is clear to me that it is divided into substance and accident."[84] In response to his disciple who presents an argument in favor of infinite divisibility, Ibn Gabirol responds by distinguishing between two types of divisibility, arguing that we may not be able to detect divisible parts beyond our senses, but nevertheless they do exist.[85]

Ibn Gabirol concludes that "the smallest part in question is not non-divisible, for we cannot find an indivisible part; and it is clear as well that the part in question between the parts of the quantity of the substance of the world is composed of substance and accident."[86] In this discussion, Ibn Gabirol has posited the infinite divisibility of substance on the grounds that there is quantity only where there is substance. "I concede now in a clear and certain manner the continuity of the totality of the substance with the totality of quantity."[87] Ibn Gabirol's contention is that extension and indivisibility pertain to two different kinds of being: the former is associated with matter, and the latter with spirit. It is impossible to reduce the one to the other. Hence, matter cannot be composed of indivisible, spaceless atoms.[88]

We turn now to Ibn Gabirol's theory of creation in both *Mekor Ḥayyim* and *Keter Malkhut*, both of which emphasize God's divine will. This will resides in the intermediary sphere between finitude and infinity: the finite and infinite intersect in the divine will. In part III of *Mekor Ḥayyim*, Gabirol offers fifty-six arguments to demonstrate the existence of a substance intermediate between God and substance. Speaking of the intelligible substance, the disciple asks, "Tell me whether the forms of these substances are finite or infinite; if they are finite, how they can have the being of an infinite force; if they are infinite, how something finite in act can issue from them."[89] Ibn Gabirol's response requires aligning form with the creative will: in and of itself, form is identical with will. It is only when it enters into creative act with matter that it becomes finite. In other words, both form and will, that is to say the force that produces these substances, are finite by virtue of their effect and infinite by virtue of their essence. But the will is not finite by virtue of its effect except "because the action has a beginning and so follows the will; and it is infinite by virtue of its essence for it does not possess a beginning. And inversely, we say of the intelligible substance that it has a beginning because it is caused, and that it has no end for it is simple and not temporal."[90] Hence, the process of creation is seen as the projection of infinite form upon finite matter, and the retention on the part of matter of a part of this infinite form. Theoretically, were form able to exist independently of matter, it would be infinite and not finite. An even more interesting question concerns the finitude of matter: if matter were able to exist independently of form, would it be infinite as well? No, for it contains within itself the grounds for finitude.

---

[84] Ibn Gabirol 1926, *Mekor Ḥayyim* 2.18:84.
[85] The text for this argument is found in *Mekor Ḥayyim* 2.18:84–5.
[86] Ibn Gabirol 1926, *Mekor Ḥayyim* 2.18:85.   [87] Ibn Gabirol 1926, *Mekor Ḥayyim* 2.19:87–8.
[88] See the discussion in Efros 1917, 44,53.   [89] Ibn Gabirol 1926, *Mekor Ḥayyim* 4.20.
[90] Ibn Gabirol 1926, *Mekor Ḥayyim* 3.57.

So that although form is allied with finitude, Ibn Gabirol reserves the possibility of speaking of the infinity of form.

Finally, we turn to the difficult question concerning the role of will in creation. From comments within *Mekor Hayyim*, Ibn Gabirol apparently either wrote or intended to write a separate treatise on divine will; in any event, the notion of Will plays a central role in his cosmogony. Gabirol posits the doctrine of divine will as both creative and ultimate unity; it is both the origin of multiplicity and yet itself one.[91] Will is the necessary medium between God and creation. Will is described as both identical with Divine intelligence or essence, and as creatively productive of universal form and matter, although in some contexts it is productive of form alone. In the former case, it is inactive, and is identical with Divine intelligence; in the latter case, it is finite and not identical with Divine essence. From God's will as activity are created all things. Thus will is both united to and separate from the absolute unity of God.[92]

The question, then, is how to understand the relation that exists between God's essence and God's will when will is active. Is will a hypostasis separate from God, or does it acquire a being of its own? In other words, is will or intellect superior? Schlanger has argued that for Ibn Gabirol, God's will is superior to intellect, yielding a radical voluntarism. Schlanger goes as far as to suggest that God's will is distinct from God's essence as an independent, autonomous entity.[93] Activity is what accounts for the distinction between will and the Divine essence. But inasmuch as the will is itself repose, how does it traverse everything and become movement? Ibn Gabirol responds that

This problem is beyond our research, for it is one of the most difficult in the understanding of the will. But what you must know is that the will penetrates everything without movement and acts in everything, outside of time, by its grand force and its unity. And if you wish to comprehend this more easily, think of the action of the intellect and the soul without movement and outside of time; and represent to yourself the diffusion of the light, sudden, without movement and current of time.[94]

Reflecting the discrepancies discussed earlier with respect to matter and form, Gabirol's discussion of will is thus fraught with tension; this tension reverberates in his discussion of creation as well. Again, the question is whether Gabirol's concept of will rules out a standard Neoplatonist emanationism. In his elaborate poem *Keter Malkhut* (*The Kingly Crown*), wisdom (*hokhmah*) and will (*hefez*) are presented as distinct hypostases: "Thou art wise, and from Thy wisdom Thou didst send forth a predestined will (*hefez mezuman*) and made it as an artisan and craftsman to draw the stream of being from the void."[95] In this work, then, Gabirol appears to postulate a voluntary creation out of nothing. But in *Meqor Hayyim*, matters are less clear. In several passages, Gabirol suggests that creation occurs outside of time. "It is necessary that the First Author achieve its work outside of time."[96] Speaking of simple substances and their actions, he asks "How much more grand must be the

[91] McGinn 1992, 87.   [92] Ibn Gabirol 1926, *Mekor Hayyim* 5.37.
[93] Schlanger 1968, 277–8.   [94] Ibn Gabirol 1926, *Mekor Hayyim* 5.39.
[95] Ibn Gabirol 1961, *The Kingly Crown* IX.   [96] Ibn Gabirol 1926, *Mekor Hayyim* 3.4.

force of God which penetrates all things, exists in all things and acts on all things outside of time."[97] Talking about the difference between matter and will, he says that the will acts outside of time, without movement. That is, the action of the will has for its effect the simple substances, which are outside of time, while the simple substances have for effects corporeal substance that is in time. "The will produces outside of time the being in matter and intelligence, that is to say it produces the universal form which sustains all the forms."[98] But in other passages, he describes creation as a necessary emanation.[99]

In answer to the question whether matter and form are eternal or not, Ibn Gabirol gives an ambivalent response: "matter issues from non-matter and form from non-form."[100] When describing the yearnings of matter, Gabirol argues that inasmuch as matter was created bereft of form, it now yearns for fulfillment. However, in other contexts, he asserts that matter subsists not even for an instant without form.[101] In this latter case, matter is and always was united with form. Additionally, Gabirol offers two accounts of the actual process of creation. According to *Mekor Hayyim* 5.42, universal matter comes from the essence of God, and form from the divine will; whereas according to *Mekor Hayyim* 5.36–8, both were created by the divine will.

From this brief synopsis, it is clear that Ibn Gabirol's cosmology differs from standard Muslim Neoplatonism in two important respects: in his concept of form and matter, and in his view of will. In his conception of matter, Gabirol has incorporated both Aristotelian and Stoic elements, the latter possibly from having read Galen. It has been suggested that the notion of spiritual matter may have been influenced by Proclus' *Elements of Theology*. Unlike Gabirol, however, Proclus does not maintain that universal form and matter are the first simple substances after God and will. It is more likely that on this point Gabirol was influenced by both Pseudo-Empedocles and Isaac Israeli, both of whose views on matter and form are very similar to those of Gabirol. Second, we have seen that Gabirol places great importance upon primacy of will in the creative act. Will represents the nexus of finite and infinite: of time and eternity. Finally, it is clear that Ibn Gabirol is grappling with a notion of infinity that takes into account not only the quantitative dimension of measure, but the qualitative as well. This twofold sense of infinity is developed in greater detail, particularly by Christian scholastics, and culminates in Spinoza's famous *Letter on the Infinite*.[102]

V Kalâm and Anti-Kalâm Arguments for Creation

We have discussed in Chapter 2 the transmission of Philoponus' works by the Islamic school of Kalâm, through Saadiah Gaon, to eleventh- and twelfth-century Jewish and Christian philosophers.[103] The major figure in this transmission was al-Ghazâlî,

---

[97] Ibn Gabirol 1926, *Mekor Hayyim* 3.15.   [98] Ibn Gabirol 1926, *Mekor Hayyim* 5.37.
[99] See for example Ibn Gabirol 1926, *Mekor Hayyim* 5.41:43.
[100] Ibn Gabirol 1926, *Mekor Hayyim* 4.15.   [101] Ibn Gabirol 1926, *Mekor Hayyim* 5.42.
[102] See Rudavsky 2000, for further discussion of Spinoza's theory of infinity.
[103] For a history of this transmission, see Davidson 1987, 86–116. Davidson notes at least thirteen medieval discussions that draw upon Philoponus' position that the infinite cannot be traversed.

whose work was known to Jews through translations, and whose presentation of Kalâm atomism in his *Maqâsid al-Falâsifa* (*Aims of the Philosophers*) may have been quite influential. In contradistinction to Aristotle, whose ontology implies continuity, and requires an abiding substrate to change matter,[104] the underlying Ash'arite (Kalâm) ontology can be described in terms of occurrences, or events, in space and time with space/time coordinates. This occasionalist ontology has no room for events and causes inasmuch as time itself is "an arbitrary convention of correlating coincident or simultaneous events."[105] On this Kalâm picture, the world appears as a set of synchronic time-slices, and movement from one to another state of the world is orchestrated by God, who recreates the world anew at each instant. More specifically, the main features of Islamic atomism can be summarized as follows: creation divides up into atoms of matter, qualities, space, and time. Every event can be analyzed into discrete moments, completely independent of one another, and brought together by the will of God. Qualities exist only for a single instant, and substances persist by a process of continuous recreation at each instant.[106] On an occasionalist model, there is no necessary connection between cause and effect other than what God has ordained, and the Aristotelian notions of time, change, and motion have been abandoned in favor of a robust theory of divine omnipotence, which eschews any laws of nature or laws of causality independent of God's power. Without God's continuous intervention, no object would continue to exist from one instant to the next.[107]

The metaphysical implications of temporal atomicity with respect to "thingness" are quite stark. Temporal atomicity simply means that time is made up of discrete instants that do not coalesce and cannot be indefinitely sub-divided. In general, atomicity implies inter-atomic vacua. For example, if the physical world is made up of discrete atoms of matter, then between any two material atoms there has to be a vacuum. Similarly, if time is atomistic, then between any pair of discrete instants there must be a vacuum. The two postulates that time and space are both atomic, taken with certain other postulates, imply a doctrine of temporal occasionalism. This implies that nothing exists continuously and without interruption. Any perceptual object that we observe at any instant is what it is at the exact instant we observe it and only at that instant. Because time is a series of serial moments, it follows that accidents must be created anew at every moment. Aristotle's notion of a continuous temporal stream has thus been replaced by discrete discontinuous instants.[108] In this world of events, there are no Aristotelian substances, no natures, no forms, or essences.

Both the Aristotelian and atomist positions were available to Jewish thinkers, the majority of whom sided with Aristotle against atomism. By the time of Isaac Israeli, in the ninth century, Kalâm atomism was as influential as the atomism of Democritus. Ben Shammai speaks of a "Jewish Mu'tazilism," the roots of which we can trace to Judah Halevi and Abraham Ibn Daud.[109] Judah Halevi (1075–1141) was

---

[104] See Aristotle *Physics* II.7 198a-b; VIII.8; Aristotle *Posterior Analytics* II.95a22-b-12.
[105] See Sabra 2006, 207.   [106] See Pines 1997, 2.
[107] For discussion of the importance of the doctrine of divine omnipotence to Kalâm ontology, see Rudavsky 2000.
[108] For additional examples, see El-Bizri 2007.
[109] See the recent synthesis in Ben Shammai 1997, 115–48.

clearly influenced by Kalâm atomism, and in particular by al-Ghazâlî.[110] Notably, al-Ghazâlî's attitude toward the philosophical tradition is one of harsh criticism, and yet he integrates into his thought various aspects of the same philosophical tradition that he outwardly rejects. This dialectical approach to philosophy can be found in Judah Halevi's major work *The Kuzari* as well: like al-Ghazâlî, Halevi excoriates the philosophers (and in particular the atomists) while at the sametime adopting their rationalist methodology. Ibn Daud is not only the first Jewish Aristotelian, as evidenced in his philosophical work *The Exalted Faith*, but he made extensive use of both Avicenna and al-Ghazâlî. Mauro Zonta suggests that Ibn Daud's main source for Avicenna may in fact have been al-Ghazâlî.[111]

Maimonides provides a useful overview of these Kalâm views in *Guide* 1.71–6.[112] Maimonides summarizes Kalâm theory in terms of eleven premises. The first premise posits the existence of indivisible atoms which are unextended and yet when combined form extended bodies. The second premise postulates the existence of a vacuum and states that according to Kalâm theologians, "vacuum exists and that it is a certain space or spaces in which there is nothing at all, being accordingly empty of all bodies, devoid of all substances."[113] The unstated Kalâm argument, already intimated in Aristotle, is that in order for atoms to be individuated one from the other, there must be space between them, which is "atom-less," or void of body. In order to account for motion, the void must therefore exist. The third premise applies the metaphysics of space to that of time and introduces the existence of indivisible time atoms. Finally, the eleventh premise pertains directly to the problem of infinite divisibility and states that the existence of the infinite in any mode is impossible. From these premises, Maimonides tells us, the Kalâm atomists deduce a number of consequences which deny the possibility of motion and which hearken back to Zeno's paradoxes of motion. These consequences lead ineluctably to postulating the beginning of the world. As we shall see below, both Maimonides and Saadiah reject these arguments on both metaphysical and epistemological grounds.[114]

Saadiah Gaon incorporated Kalâm influences into *The Book of Doctrines and Beliefs*.[115] In his chapter on creation, Saadiah presents eight arguments for the creation of the world that can be divided into two groups of four arguments each: the first group proves that the world must be finite (i.e., not eternal), and the second group that the world was created *ex nihilo* and not out of a pre-existent matter. His fourth proof of creation "from time" draws upon John Philoponus' first proof of creation and is based on Philoponus' premise that no infinite can be traversed. Saadiah argues that if the present instant is infinite, then it is never possible to traverse the very instant in which we find ourselves. So too, it would not be possible to traverse any other infinite instant in order to reach the point we now inhabit.

---

[110] Krinis notes several lines of influence between the two. See Krinis 2013.

[111] See Zonta 2000; see also Eran 2008.

[112] H. A. Wolfson discusses the question of the transmission of Kalâm thought into Jewish philosophy fairly extensively in 1976, 82ff.; see also Schwarz 1991.

[113] Maimonides *Guide* 1.73:195–6.

[114] For an analysis of other influential Kalâm arguments, see Davidson 1987, 117–53.

[115] In this chapter, unless otherwise noted, Saadiah's text will be based on Altmann's English translation found in Saadiah Gaon 1972.

But we know that we have in fact reached this present point in time. It follows, therefore, that the time we have to traverse is finite.[116]

Having argued that proof of the traversal of past time supports his postulating the finitude of time, Saadiah then applies the argument to the traversal of future time as well. Saadiah raises a possible objection to the argument, attributing to an anonymous heretic a variation of Zeno's paradoxes of motion: the heretic claims that inasmuch as any distance is infinitely divisible, the fact that a person can travel from one point to another demonstrates that the infinite can be traversed.[117] How can Saadiah account for traversing an infinite distance, without abandoning his argument for the finitude of time? Saadiah focuses upon Kalâm solutions to the problem based on the notion of the leap. The Kalâm philosopher al-Nazzâm, for example, introduced the notion of the leap as a response to Zeno.[118] Believing in infinite divisibility, but eschewing atomism, al-Nazzâm adopted the idea of infinitely divisible leaps in order to explain how we can traverse an infinity of sub-distances. On this theory, any journey involves a finite number of variably short leaps.[119]

Rejecting this Kalâm position as untenable, Saadiah proposes his own solution, one that reflects Aristotle's distinction between actual and potential infinity as mediated through the works of John Philoponus.[120] Saadiah argues that Zeno's

---

[116] The actual text of the argument is presented in Saadiah Gaon, *The Book of Doctrines and Beliefs*: "I know that time is threefold: past, present, and future. Although the present is shorter than any instant, I take the instant as one takes a point, and say: If a man should try in his thought to ascend from that point in time to the uppermost points, it would be impossible for him to do so, inasmuch as time is now assumed to be infinite and it is impossible for thought to penetrate to the furthest point of that which is infinite... The same reason will also make it impossible that the process of generation should traverse an infinite period down to the lowest point so as ultimately to reach us. Yet if the process of generation did not reach us, we would not be generated, from which it necessarily follows that we, the multitude of generated beings, would not be generated and the beings now existent would not be existent. And since I find myself existent, I know that the process of generation has traversed time until it has reached us, *and that if time were not finite, the process of generation would not have traversed it*" Saadiah *Doctrines* 1972, 56.

[117] Saadiah Gaon, *Doctrines*: "It has come to my notice that a certain heretic in conversation with one of the Believers in the Unity of God, objected to this proof. He said 'It is possible for a man to traverse by walking that which has an infinite number of parts. For if we consider any distance which a man walks, be it a mile, or an ell, we should find that it can be divided into an infinite number of parts." In Saadiah *Doctrines* 1972, 57.

[118] Maimonides describes al-Nazzâm's theory of the leap in greater detail in *Guide* 1.73, prop. 3. See also the discussions in Dhanani 1994; Sorabji 1983, 385ff.

[119] Sorabji 1983, 388.

[120] See Ivry 1986a, 74: "Before every temporal segment there is (another) segment, until we reach a temporal segment before which there is no segment, i.e., a segmented duration before which there is no segmented duration. It cannot be otherwise—if it were possible, and after every segment of time there was a segment, infinitely, then we would never reach a given time—for the duration from past infinity to this given time would be equal to the duration from this given time regressing in times to infinity; and if (the duration) from infinity to a definite time was known, then (the duration) from this known time to temporal infinity would be known, and then the infinite is finite, and this is an impossible contradiction." Al-Kindî's argument then continues as follows: "Furthermore, if a definite time cannot be reached until a time before it is reached, nor that before it until a time before it is reached, and so to infinity; and the infinite can neither be traversed nor brought to an end; then the temporally infinite can never be traversed so as to reach a definite time. However, its termination at a definite time exists, and time is not an infinite segment, but rather is finite necessarily, and therefore the duration of body is not infinite, and it is not possible for body to be without duration. Thus, the being of a body does not have infinity; the being of a body is, rather, finite, and it is impossible for body to be eternal."

paradox is sophistical in that it fails to note that "the infinite divisibility of a thing is only a matter of imagination, but not a matter of reality."[121] If, Saadiah argues, the infinite traversal had occurred in the past in the imagination alone, the paradox would be valid. But since the process of generation has traversed real time and reached us, it "cannot invalidate our proof, because infinite divisibility exists only in the imagination."[122] In answer to this paradox, then, Saadiah distinguishes between actual and potential traversal. Traversing a finite spatial distance is not the same as traversing infinity, because in this case there *is* no actual infinity, but only an infinitely divisible finite distance.

While Saadiah availed himself of several Kalâm atomistic views, Maimonides is even more articulate in his rejection of Kalâm atomism. Maimonides is quick to point out that the Mutakallimûn, even more than "the cleverest philosophers," have "no knowledge at all of the true reality of time."[123] He does not present a counter-argument, however, and is content to rely upon an *ad hominem* statement, which will be amplified in *Guide* 2.13, in the context of discussing creation. Now whether (and which) Mutakallimûn actually endorsed the very atomistic conception of time as described by Maimonides is itself problematic.[124] But Maimonides was certainly on *terra firma* to infer an atomistic theory from other doctrines that predominate in the writings of the Mutakallimûn. Further, he may have believed that such a conception follows from the first premise, according to which every body is composed of indivisible atomic parts. In accordance with Aristotle's view that distance, time, and local motion must be proportionate,[125] it follows that if time were infinitely divisible, the particles that these thinkers took to be atomistic would have to be infinitely divisible as well.

In *Guide* I.74.7, Maimonides points out that whoever wishes to demonstrate the creation of the world in time must use Kalâm assumptions in order to rule out infinite regress. For from the hypothesis that the world is eternal, it follows that many imaginary infinite series can be postulated. Those who postulate the eternity of the universe believe both "that an infinite may be greater in number than another infinite," and congruously that "an infinite number of revolutions may be greater than another infinite number of revolutions."[126] Having rejected the infinite in all its guises, the Mutakallimûn are able to reject the hypotheses of the eternalists. Against the first argument, Maimonides emphasizes the distinction made by Aristotle between actual and potential, and between essential and accidental infinite. The second argument is dismissed by his saying that "all these things are mere fictions and have no reality."[127] The major thrust of Maimonides' rejection of the Kalâm arguments, however, is contained in *Guide* 1.71. Maimonides' general contention is that these arguments "are derived from premises that run counter to the nature of existence that is perceived."[128] Maimonides himself adopts the theoretical stance of an eternalist and tries to argue for creation using Aristotle's own premises, rather

---

[121] Saadiah Gaon *Doctrines*. Altmann notes that the term imagination (*wahm*; *maḥshavah*) is sometimes used by the Arabic philosophers in the sense of "potentially." See Altmann 1972, 57.
[122] Ibid.   [123] Maimonides *Guide* 1.73.3:196.
[124] See Schwarz 1991, 177.   [125] Maimonides *Guide* 1.73.3:196.
[126] Maimonides *Guide* 1.74.7:222. See H. A. Wolfson's discussion of these arguments in 1976, 427ff.
[127] Maimonides *Guide* 1.74.7:222.   [128] Maimonides *Guide* 1.71:182.

than those of Kalâm. In this way, he feels, the shaky metaphysical ground of Kalâm metaphysics is obviated.

VI Aristotelian Models of Creation: Maimonides, Gersonides, and Crescas

We turn now to those views of creation and time that are most influenced by the Aristotelian corpus. Maimonides, Gersonides, and Crescas all present theories that reflect a clear peripatetic influence, either supportive or critical of Aristotle's views. And yet all three thinkers are writing in the context of *Genesis*, and so the question is how to reconcile Aristotelian and Neoplatonic science with Scripture. Is it possible to adopt "pieces" of Aristotelian cosmology and ontology without jeopardizing basic Judaic beliefs? We turn now to this set of topics.

Maimonides' theory of creation is presented in *Guide* 2.13–30. In *Guide* 2.13, Maimonides describes three opinions on creation, and then in *Guide* 2.32 he describes three opinions on prophecy, stating that "the opinions of people concerning prophecy are like their opinions concerning the eternity of the world or its creation in time."[129] Is the word "like" supposed to posit a one-to-one correspondence between the two sets of opinions? If so, can Maimonides' own position be linked with any one set of correspondences, or is his allegiance split? In answer to these questions, interpreters have suggested every possible combination of opinions, and have offered every possible strategy for determining which is Maimonides' own view.[130] In this chapter, I shall not enter the Maimonidean taxonomy controversy per se. My main concern, rather, is to elucidate the theory of temporality that evolves out of his discussion of creation. I shall, in the course of my discussion, however, offer evidence from Maimonides' discussion of temporality to support the contention that Maimonides' doctrine of the creation of the world incorporates important elements of Aristotelian eternity. In arguing thus, I clearly align myself with scholars who see in the *Guide* an esoteric text addressed to the intellectual elite. My own interpretation is that Maimonides recognizes internal difficulties with the view of Scripture having to do with issues of time, but that in the absence of definitive demonstrative argument in support of Aristotle, he is forced to an epistemological stance that incorporates both Platonic and Aristotelian elements.

In *Guide* 2.13 Maimonides states the three standard views on creation. The main features of these three views, characterized as the Law of Moses (Scriptural), Platonic, and Aristotelian, can be summarized as follows:

> 5.1 *The Scriptural view:* that the universe was brought into existence by God after "having been purely and absolutely nonexistent"; through his will and his volition, God brought into "existence out of nothing all the beings as they are, time itself being one of the created things";[131]

---

[129] Maimonides *Guide* 2.31:360.
[130] Representative interpretations can be found in Klein-Braslavy 1986; Davidson 1979; W. Z. Harvey 1981c; Hyman 1987; Kaplan 1977; Rudavsky 2010; Stern 2013. Ivry (2016) provides a useful summary of these many different interpretations.
[131] Maimonides *Guide* 2.13:281.

5.2 The Platonic view: that inasmuch as even God cannot create matter and form out of absolute nonexistence (since this constitutes an ontological impossibility and so does not impute impotence to God), there "exists a certain matter that is eternal as the deity is eternal ... He is the cause of its existence ... and that He creates in it whatever he wishes."[132]

5.3 The Aristotelian view: that matter cannot be created from absolute nonexistence, concluding that the heaven is not subject to generation/corruption and that "time and motion are perpetual and everlasting and not subject to generation and passing-away."[133]

Each of these positions carries with it both metaphysical and theological implications. [5.1] clearly postulates creation after absolute nonexistence and states that before creation there was sheer nonexistence. It is thus incompatible with the eternity of time.[134] And so [5.1] incorporates four distinct propositions: that God brought the world into existence after absolute nonexistence; that he did so through his will and volition; that he did so not from anything; and that time is created.[135] [5.3] can be seen as postulating an eternally beginningless universe. Finally, [5.2] postulates both a creator as well as an eternal substance out of which the universe is created. That is, it represents a version of eternal creation, adopting features of both [5.1] and [5.3].

Maimonides specifies several observations concerning the relations among these three characterizations. First, contrary to those who "imagine that our opinion and his [Plato's] opinion are identical,"[136] Maimonides is quick to disabuse those who are tempted to posit a connection between [5.1] and [5.2]. The Platonic view, he states, cannot be substituted for Mosaic doctrine, even though there appear to be superficial similarities—most notably the postulation of a creator—between the two. Secondly, Maimonides' attitude toward the relation between [5.2] and [5.3] is ambiguous and ultimately dismisses [5.2] as not worthy of serious consideration on the grounds that if Aristotle can be refuted, so too can Plato's theory be disqualified as a justifiable creation theory. Having dismissed [5.2] as a weaker version of [5.3], he argues that the Scriptural account is no *more* flawed than is the Aristotelian account. Then, pointing to the possibility of [5.1], coupled with its Mosaic (and Abrahamic) sanction, Maimonides argues that the very plausibility of Scripture suggests the non-necessity of Aristotle.

In Chapter 25, Maimonides lays out several pragmatic reasons as well for supporting [5.1] over [5.2] and [5.3]. The most important of these is that [5.3] would destroy belief not only in the Law but in miracles and prophecy as well:

the belief in the way Aristotle sees it—that is, the belief according to which the world exists in virtue of necessity, that no nature changes at all, and that the customary course of events cannot be modified with regard to anything—destroys the Law in its principle, necessarily gives the lie to every miracle, and reduces to inanity all the hopes and threats that the Law has held out.[137]

---

[132] Maimonides *Guide* 2.283.   [133] Maimonides *Guide* 2.13:284.
[134] See Harvey 1981c, 289, n. 9, for further discussion of this point. See also the extensive discussion by H. A. Wolfson 1973, 207–21.
[135] See the discussion of these four propositions in Hyman 1987, 49ff.
[136] Maimonides *Guide* 2.13:284.   [137] Maimonides *Guide* 2.25:328.

Maimonides is quick to point out, however, that [5.2] is not nearly as devastating: the opinion of Plato would "not destroy the foundations of the Law and would be followed not by the lie being given to miracles, but by their becoming admissible."[138] Why, then, does Maimonides not accept the authority of [5.2]? The main reason, he tells us, is that the Platonic view has not been demonstrated: "In view of the fact that it has not been demonstrated, we shall not favor this [Plato's] opinion, nor shall we at all heed that other opinion [Aristotle's], but rather shall take the texts according to their external sense."[139] It would appear, then, that [5.1], the Scriptural account of creation of the universe out of absolute nonexistence, is Maimonides' final view.

Sara Klein-Braslavy argues however that ultimately Maimonides upholds a skeptical stance and does not ascribe to any of the three positions.[140] Inasmuch as Maimonides has clearly questioned the demonstrability of each of these views, she suggests that Maimonides' ultimate position is one of epistemological skepticism: the human intellect is simply unable to resolve the issue. Disagreement in matters of metaphysics occurs in cases when demonstrative arguments are not available.[141] So too, when the evidence is conflicting and unsupported by sound Aristotelian demonstration, the only justifiably rational stance, on this reading, is to withhold one's belief until such time as adequate demonstration becomes possible.

The importance of Aristotelian demonstration to this skeptical contention cannot be over-emphasized. According to Maimonides, Aristotle did not claim to have a demonstrative proof for the eternity thesis; Aristotle himself considered his proofs in support of eternity to be "mere arguments" as opposed to logical demonstrations.[142] Although he is quick to point out that Aristotle "does not affirm categorically that the arguments he put forward in its favor constitute a demonstration" for the eternity thesis, Maimonides clearly disagrees with the Mutakallimûn who attempted to demonstrate the impossibility of such a claim. Rather, Maimonides states that "it seems that the premise in question is possible—that is, neither necessary... nor impossible... "[143] Aristotle himself, he points out, only considered his theory to be probable and not necessary: "Now to me it seems that he [Aristotle] does not affirm categorically that the arguments he put forward in its favor constitute a demonstration. The premise in question is rather, in his opinion, the most fitting and the most probable."[144] It is because he was lacking demonstrative arguments that Aristotle had to "buttress his opinion by means of the fact that the physicists who preceded him had the same belief as he."[145] For Maimonides, Aristotle's proofs for eternity constitute not "a cogent demonstration" but rather dialectical arguments, and so cannot be regarded as indubitable support for the eternity thesis.[146]

---

[138] Maimonides Guide 2.25:328.   [139] Maimonides Guide 2.25:329.

[140] See Klein-Braslavy 1986. For additional discussions of epistemological and metaphysical skepticism in Maimonides, see the essay by Pines 1979; Kogan 1985 summarizes some of the other interpretations regarding Maimonides' own view of creation in his essay. A response to Pines can be found in Davidson 1992-3. See also Rudavsky 2010; Davies 2011; Ivry 2016; Halbertal 2015.

[141] See the discussion of this point in Kraemer 1989.

[142] Maimonides Guide 2.15:291.   [143] Maimonides Guide 2. Intro: 241.

[144] Maimonides Guide 2. Intro: 240.   [145] Maimonides Guide 2.15:290.

[146] Maimonides Guide 2.15:293. For a careful study of the importance of demonstration to Maimonides' discussion of creation, see Kraemer 1989, 64–76.

Let us summarize our discussion to this point. With respect to creation, Maimonides maintains that "God's bringing the world into existence does not have a temporal beginning, for time is one of the created things."[147] Maimonides does not want to suggest that time itself is eternal, for "if you affirm as true the existence of time prior to the world, you are necessarily bound to believe in the eternity [of the world]."[148] But neither will he claim that the creation of the world is a temporally specifiable action, for on the Aristotelian definition of time, the world must be beginningless in the sense that it has no temporal beginning. While supporting on an exoteric level the Scriptural reading of creation, on an esoteric level Maimonides is suggesting that an Aristotelian theory of time (which he accepts) is more consistent with an eternity model of the universe. This reading is reinforced by Maimonides' analysis of the term be-reishit, to which we shall return below.

Like Maimonides, Gersonides is concerned with whether time is finite or infinite, as well as with whether the creation of the world can be said to have occurred at an instant. Unlike Maimonides, however, Gersonides' discussion includes the physical manifestation of time and matter, as well as the theoretical implications of temporality. Having posited that the world was created at an initial instant of time by a freely willing agent, Gersonides must decide whether the world was engendered out of absolute nothing or out of a pre-existent matter. His examination, therefore, focuses upon the concept of matter underlying creation. In Wars of the Lord VI.1.2, Gersonides hopes to refute Aristotle's eternity thesis by showing that the infinity of time and motion fail as exceptions to Aristotle's own finitistic universe.[149] In order to reject Aristotle's eternity thesis, Gersonides must demonstrate the finitude of time. To this end, he first makes a number of observations pertaining to the general characteristics of time.

In Wars VI.1.2 Gersonides lists three views of his predecessors who discussed the creation of the world. The first, that the world comes into existence and passes away an infinite number of times, has been associated with the rabbis as well as with certain ancient philosophers.[150] The second view, that the world was generated only one time, is associated with two sets of proponents: first is the version of Plato that the world was created one time out of some thing; the second is the view attributed to the Kalâm and to Maimonides, that the world was created out of absolute non-existence; and the third view is the eternity thesis of Aristotle, that the world is eternal and hence has not been created.[151]

Gersonides' critical refutation of Aristotle's eternity thesis introduces the motif of time and its relation to motion. In contradistinction to Aristotle who postulated the eternity of time and motion, Gersonides will insist that both time and motion are finite. Gersonides hopes to refute Aristotle's eternity of the world by showing that the

---

[147] Maimonides Guide 2.13:282.   [148] Ibid.

[149] For an examination of the underlying logical moves implicit in Gersonides' attack, see Feldman 1967.

[150] In De Caelo I.10 Aristotle associates this view with Empedocles and Heraclitus. It is also found in Genesis Rabbah 3:7 and 9:2.

[151] Gersonides Wars vol. 3, VI.1.2:219.

infinity of time and motion fail as exceptions to Aristotle's own finitistic universe.[152] According to Gersonides, Aristotle offered at least nine arguments in support of the eternity thesis: of these, three have to do with temporality. Aristotle's first argument has to do with the nature of time in general, the second is based on the nature of the "instant," and the third is based on the nature of temporal language. Gersonides' statement of Aristotle's first argument can be summarized as follows: If time came to be, it would have come to be in time. But this would imply a time before the original time. Since time is inseparable from motion and motion is connected to the moved object that moves in a single, continuously circular motion, it follows that time too is continuous. Hence, time must be eternal.[153] This argument is based on those aforementioned passages in which Aristotle argues that since time is defined in terms of motion, there can be no time without motion.[154]

Aristotle's second argument, as stated by Gersonides, is based on his definition of the instant as the middle point between the "before" and "after" and goes as follows: If time came to be, there would have to be an actual instant at which it came to be. But this would entail there being a potential instant before the present instant was actualized. But every part of time has only potential existence, and so no such instant could exist. Hence time could not come to be.[155] The main thrust of this argument, as presented by Gersonides, is that in order to account for the coming into existence of any present instant, there must exist a prior actual instant; but in the case of the first instant, there could be no prior instant, actual or potential. The third argument, based upon the second, takes into consideration the nature of temporal language. Whoever tries to speak about the coming into existence of time must utilize words that imply temporality before the existence of time itself. But these references would imply that time exists prior to its coming into existence. Time must therefore be eternal.[156]

Other arguments in favor of eternity are taken from Aristotle and center for the most part on the nature of motion, the impossibility of a first motion, the incorruptibility of the heavens, and the impossibility of a void.[157] Gersonides concludes his summary of Aristotle's arguments with two general comments that link the metaphysical considerations to those of a more theological nature. Gersonides offers the suggestion that ultimately what may have motivated Aristotle to support the eternity thesis were theological considerations based on the nature of the deity. First, echoing Maimonides' "Why not Sooner" argument discussed above, he argues that it would be inappropriate to suggest that the deity causes at one time rather than at another. Furthermore, it is not appropriate that the deity exist independently of the world, which functions as the object of God's self-conception. And finally, Gersonides reminds us, as did Maimonides, that Aristotle himself did not regard his arguments

---

[152] For an examination of the underlying logical moves implicit in Gersonides' attack, see Feldman 1967, 113–37; Feldman 2010.

[153] This reconstruction of Gersonides' understanding of Aristotle's argument is based on the text in Gersonides Wars vol. 3, VI.1.3.

[154] A similar argument is propounded in Physics 4.12. In Physics 4.12, Aristotle demonstrates that inasmuch as time is the measure of motion, those things that are subject to generation and corruption are necessarily in time.

[155] Gersonides Wars vol. 3, VI.1.3:224–5.   [156] Gersonides Wars vol. 3, VI.1.3:226–9.

[157] See the arguments listed in Gersonides Wars vol. 3, VI.1.3:224–30.

in favor of eternity as demonstrations, but rather as containing fewer doubts than other arguments.[158]

In order to reject Aristotle's eternity thesis, Gersonides must demonstrate the finitude of time. To this end, he first makes a number of observations pertaining to the general characteristics of time that will affect his argument. Time, Gersonides argues, falls in the category of continuous quantity. We speak, for example, of the parts of time as being equal or unequal; time itself is measured by convention as opposed to by nature; and its limit is the "instant" which itself is indivisible.[159] Echoing Aristotle, Gersonides points out that time cannot be comprised of "instants" because the instant measures time, but is not a part of time. Unlike time, which is divisible, the instant is indivisible.[160] Further, Gersonides claims that time can be construed both as separate from its substratum and as residing in it. That time resides in its substratum is demonstrated from the fact that it has distinguishable parts: that is, present time is distinguished from both past and future time. Were these parts not distinguishable, argues Gersonides, then any part of time would equal the whole of time. Hence, time must reside in that which it measures. At the same time, it is separable from any substratum; for if it were in its substratum, there would be as many times as there are substrata. But we know that there is only one time and not a multiplicity of times. Hence time must not reside in its substratum.[161]

According to Gersonides, time is partly potential and partly actual. Aristotle had argued that the past, in being a potency, was infinite. Gersonides however claims that potency refers only to the future and not to the past.[162] If the past were potential, then, Gersonides argues, contrary possibilities would inhere in the past as well as in the future; this however is absurd, since we know that the past has already occurred.[163] Hence, Gersonides concludes that only future time carries within itself potency. As we will discuss further in the next chapter, these comments are consistent with his statements elsewhere regarding the nature of future contingents.[164]

Having shown to his satisfaction that time is finite, Gersonides must now refute the original arguments proffered by Aristotle in support of the infinity of time. Aristotle's first argument was that since all generation must take place in time, there can be no beginning to time. Hence phrases like "beginning of time" have no referent. Gersonides, however, refutes this argument by distinguishing two types of generation. The first he bases on Aristotle's notion of a change from contrary to contrary and takes place in time. The second, however, is what Gersonides terms absolute generation and is atemporal; that is, it is instantaneous and does not take place in time. It is in this second sense that Gersonides argues that time was generated. Before this absolute generation, there was no time. Phrases such as "beginning of time," Gersonides argues, must be understood in an equivocal sense.[165]

---

[158] Gersonides Wars vol. 3, VI.1.3:300.

[159] The various characteristics of time are elaborated in Gersonides Wars vol. 3, VI.1.10:270ff.

[160] For a discussion of this point, see Staub 1982, 30.

[161] Gersonides Wars vol. 3, VI.1.10:271-2. Aristotle's arguments can be found in Physics 4.10-14.

[162] Gersonides Wars vol. 3, VI.1.10:273.   [163] Gersonides Wars vol. 3, VI.1.10:274.

[164] Gersonides' notion of the contingency of the future is elaborated in Wars 3, in the context of the issue of divine omniscience. For further discussion of this issue, see Rudavsky 1983; Samuelson 1972.

[165] Gersonides Wars vol. 3, VI.1.21:359-60. See Feldman 1967, 134-5 for a discussion of these pages.

Aristotle's second objection centered on the notion of the instant as the limit between the past and future. In answer to this argument, Gersonides makes a number of points. To Aristotle's objection that we cannot imagine an "instant" before which there is no time, Gersonides claims that there are many truths that we cannot imagine (just as many imaginable things are not true). Reminiscent of the Kalâm controversy over the doctrine of admissibility, Gersonides' point is that the non-imaginability of a claim is not a sufficient condition for rejecting its truth.[166]

But Gersonides' rejection of Aristotle's eternity thesis, and his support of creation, do not commit Gersonides to a theory of creation *ex nihilo*. Arguing that creation out of nothing is incompatible with the facts of physical reality, Gersonides adopts a version of the second view, adopting a Platonic model of matter drawn ultimately from the *Timaeus*. The opening verses of *Genesis* I are used to distinguish two types of material reality: *geshem* and *homer ri'shon*.[167] Totally devoid of form, *geshem* is the primordial matter out of which the universe was created. Since it is not informed, it is not capable of motion or rest; and since it is characterized by negation, *geshem* is inert and chaotic.[168] This primordial matter is identified with the "primeval waters" described in *Genesis* I.2. However, Gersonides points out that *geshem* does not itself exemplify absolute non-being, but rather is an intermediary between being and non-being.[169]

In contrast to *geshem*, *homer ri'shon* (first matter) is the second type of reality. *Homer ri'shon* is understood in the Aristotelian sense as a substratum that is allied to form. *Homer ri'shon* is inferior to form and hence cannot be known in itself. It contains within itself the potentiality to receive forms, yet has no actuality of its own.[170] Inasmuch as it does not contain its own actuality, *homer ri'shon* is not an ontologically independent entity. Gersonides refers to this *homer ri'shon* as "the matter that does not keep its shape."[171] In *Wars* VI.2.7 Gersonides compares this matter to darkness, for just as darkness is the absence of light, so too this matter represents the absence of form or shape.[172]

---

[166] Gersonides *Wars* vol. 3, VI.1.21. For a description of the Kalâm notion of admissibility, see Maimonides *Guide* 3.15. See the following works for a critical analysis of Maimonides' exposition: Blumberg 1970; Ivry 2016.

[167] Gersonides *Wars* vol. 3, VI.1.17:330. For general discussions of Gersonides' theory of creation and matter, see Feldman 1975; Feldman 2010.

[168] Gersonides *Wars* vol. 3, VI.1.17:330-1. For further elaboration of these arguments, see Feldman 1975, 394-5.

[169] Gersonides *Wars* vol. 3, VI.1.18:372.   [170] Gersonides *Wars* vol. 3, VI.1.17.

[171] Gersonides *Wars* vol. 3, VI.1.17:329-30; cf. also Gersonides *Wars* vol. 3, VI.2.7: "there was body which does not preserve its shape, from which the upper and lower (waters) came to be."

[172] This cosmological principle plays a crucial role in Gersonides' astronomy. In an important study of the chronology of Gersonides' works, Glasner (1996) has argued that the notion of a "matter that does not keep its shape" is essential for Gersonides' "eccentric cosmology" in a number of ways: it explains why the movements of the different planets do not interfere with each other; it solves the problem of the contact between an eccentric orb and the orbs above or below it; and it solves the problem of the center of motion. More specifically, Gersonides agrees with his predecessors that each of the astral bodies occupies its own celestial sphere, with the stars all residing in one sphere. He further rejects as untenable the view that there exists a diurnal sphere deprived of stars that carries the world in one simple movement. But how do we account for the interaction between these spheres? The celestial spheres are concentric and contiguous, and in principle we might expect that they move in unison. However, as Gersonides has already pointed out, each has its own proper movement, and often these movements are in conflict. In order to account for the independence of each sphere, Gersonides argues that between each sphere there exists a fluid body that

Gersonides has thus presented an ambitious account of the finitude of time, one that attempts to refute the eternity thesis while at the same retaining a sense of "initial instant" that remains true to Aristotle. Let us turn now to two critics of Gersonides, namely Crescas and his student Joseph Albo, both of whom reflected the fourteenth century backlash against Aristotelian natural philosophy. In the fourteenth century, in part as a result of the Condemnations of 1277, Christian scholastics (e.g., Thomas Bradwardine; Jean Buridan) began to question the basic premises of Aristotelian physics, and suggest non-Aristotelian alternatives. One of the most pervasive results of the Condemnation of 1277 was that it encouraged alternatives to Aristotelian natural philosophy.[173] More specifically, the condemned propositions directly affected theories of place, the void, and plurality of worlds, thus giving way to new ways of thinking which helped usher in the new science. We have seen that according to Aristotle, the ultimate sphere has no movement other than that of rotation, its fixed center belonging to the absolutely immobile body earth. But this view threatened scholastic notions of omnipotence; that is, it suggested that not even God was able to displace the immobile center of the universe. The Condemnation of 1277 thus targeted those propositions that imputed to God any limits. The two propositions most important to this new way of thinking were proposition 34, "*Quod prima causa non posset plures mundos facere*," and proposition 49, "*Quod Deus non possit movere celum motu recto. Et ratio est, quia tunc relinqueret vacuum.*"[174] As John Murdoch has argued, these two propositions represented the foundation of the whole edifice of Aristotelian physics. Their being declared anathema implicitly demanded the creation of a new physics that would be acceptable to Christian reason.[175]

determines the movements of the spheres. This body, uninformed and without movement of its own, is described as "the matter that does not keep its shape" and lies between the spheres of the astral bodies. Its function is to assure the motion of the celestial bodies and precludes the possibility of one planetary motion affecting another: "it is clearly appropriate that there be [enough] fluid between the spheres of one planet and the spheres of another such that a motionless layer may remain in its midst to make sure that the motions are not confused." Gersonides compares this diaphanous body to the bones of an organic animal that make possible movement of the animal. In *Wars* V.1. Gersonides tries to compute the thickness of these fluid layers. Glasner argues, further, that Gersonides' theological and astronomical projects are interrelated: "Gersonides' theology and astronomy are deeply involved with each other through the hypothesis of the body that does not preserve its shape. The existence of this body before the creation of the world is a basic premise of Gersonides' theology; its existence between the celestial spheres is a basic premise of his cosmology and essential for the justification of his eccentric astronomy. Thus, the introduction of the concept of the body that does not preserve its shape was a breakthrough for both projects" Glasner 1996, 41. See also Glasner 2015.

[173] For an extensive discussion of the importance of the Condemnation of 1277 upon medieval science, see Grant 1982. See also Chapter 3, where the significance of the condemnations was discussed.

[174] See Murdoch 1991. Proposition 34 reads "That the first cause could not make many worlds." Proposition 49 reads "That God could not move the heavens with rectilinear motion, and the reason is that a vacuum would remain." See also Grant 1997.

[175] The question of the extent to which the condemnation of 1277 causally affected the development of late medieval and early modern science is itself problematic, and has recently been revisited. While Duhem argued for a strong causal relation, recent scholars have been reluctant to posit a straightforward causal connection. For discussion and summary of recent views, see Murdoch 1991; Grant 1997; Aertsen, Emery, and Speer 2001.

In exploring the consequences of these condemnations, scholastic philosophers were encouraged to develop concepts contrary to Aristotelian physics and cosmology. With respect to the topic of place/space, philosophers became increasingly interested in the properties of the vacuum, e.g., the idea of a completely empty space. Proposition 49 led to speculation about the existence of multiple universes. Prior to the condemnations, scholastic philosophers considered the impossibility of multiple worlds against the backdrop of Aristotelian arguments that outside the world there cannot be any place because there are no bodies; and there cannot be a void, because a void is a place where there could be a body where there is presently no body.[176] Inasmuch as these arguments were linked to the issue of God's omnipotence as well, it became increasingly popular to argue that God's creative omnipotence allowed for the creation of multiple worlds. For example, God was said to create multiple worlds, each with its own center. On the supposition that God did make other worlds, it was argued that empty space would intervene between them. So that God could create a vacuum between worlds, certainly God could create vacua within the world.[177]

Against the backdrop of these scholastic condemnations, Crescas too sought to demolish the Aristotelian natural philosophy, albeit for theological rather than purely naturalistic reasons. His rejection of Aristotle's theories of place and the infinite forms part of an extended attempt to weaken Aristotle's hold upon Jewish philosophy. Harvey suggests that Crescas' work was "perhaps connected in some way with the pioneering work in natural science being conducted at the University of Paris."[178] Even in the absence of definitive evidence of causal interaction between Crescas and the scholastics, at the very least, it is clear that Crescas is embroiled in precisely the same set of scientific issues that occupied scholastic philosophers after the Condemnation of 1277.

In light of this increasingly anti-Aristotelian (and *ipso facto* anti-Maimonidean) stance, the fourteenth century witnessed an attitudinal shift toward atomism.[179] Al-Ghazâlî's *Incoherence of Philosophy* (*Tahâfut al-Falâsîfa*) was translated before 1411 by Zerahyah ha-Levi Saladin. Al-Ghazâlî's continued popularity can be explained in part by the fact that he provided ammunition in defending the theological positions of Jewish anti-Aristotelians. The fourteenth century was witness to what Zonta calls a sort of "'Jewish Ghazalism' based upon al-Ghazâlî's works" in that many aspects of his thought were employed for defending similar aspects of Jewish religious tradition.[180]

Whether Ḥasdai Crescas actually employed al-Ghazâlî's work as one of the undeclared sources of *Light of the Lord* remains a source of contention.[181] It is not inconceivable that Crescas was drawn to al-Ghazâlî's work because of its straightforward anti-Aristotelianism, an antagonism that Crescas shared for similar theological reasons. As Shlomo Pines notes, the historian who seeks to place Crescas within the tradition of Arabic–Jewish philosophy cannot afford to ignore the many

[176] Duhem 1985, 442.   [177] Grant 1997, 537–40.   [178] W. Harvey 1998, 23.
[179] For a discussion of the anti-Maimonidean turn in the fourteenth century, see Rudavsky 2010.
[180] See Zonta 2007.   [181] See Wolfson 1929, 11–16. See also Harvey 1998.

analogies between Crescas' physics and the theories that, in the Islamic orbit, were designated as Platonic.[182] For example, Crescas rejects the Peripatetic concept of *prima materia*. For Crescas, matter exists independently of form; it is actual and extended.

One important implication of Crescas' rejection of Aristotelian theory has to do with his postulating the existence of the vacuum. According to Crescas, place is prior to bodies: in contradistinction to Aristotle's conception of place, space for Crescas is not a mere relationship of bodies but is the "interval between the limits of that which surrounds."[183] Space is construed by Crescas as an infinite continuum ready to receive matter. Because this place or extension of bodies is identified with space, there is no contradiction in postulating the existence of space not filled with body, i.e., the vacuum.[184] Crescas, in fact, assumes that place is identical with the void, on the grounds that "place must be equal to the whole of its occupant as well as to [the sum of] its parts."[185] Harvey has characterized four parallels between Crescas' concepts of space and time. First, space and time are both defined as "continuous quantity" as opposed to discrete quantity. Second, both are defined as separate from physical objects; both would continue to exist even if there were no physical objects in the universe. Third, both are supposed infinite, as reflected in the description of space as an "infinite magnitude." And finally, both the place and time of a given thing are conceived as intervals.[186]

Crescas' theory of space has important ramifications with respect to his conception of the infinite as well. In order to postulate the infinity of space, time and number, Crescas must refute Aristotle's theory of the infinite. Crescas' general contention is that Aristotle's arguments are all victim to a common fallacy in that they assume that one can argue against the existence of the infinite from the analogy of the finite. Crescas, however, will want to maintain that the assumptions one makes about the finite are inapplicable to the infinite—the infinite and finite are qualitatively different and cannot be compared.[187]

Crescas' characterization of time occurs in *Light* Part I, in the context of elaborating Maimonides' summary of Aristotle's twenty-five metaphysical propositions.[188] According to Crescas, time is not tied to motion. Crescas allows for the spheres to be both immaterial and corporeal: so too with terrestrial matter—matter and quantity are inseparable and ontologically primary, and so we have no need for prime matter/ corporeal form compound. On this view, matter exists partially informed of its own nature. As we have noted above, the actuality of matter is one of the great metaphysical issues dividing Atomists from Aristotelians, and on this issue at least,

---

[182] See Pines 1997.   [183] Crescas *Light* I.1.2, in Wolfson 1929, 195.
[184] For a detailed analysis of Crescas' conception of space, see H. Wolfson 1929, 38–69. See also H. Davidson 1987, 253ff.
[185] Crescas *Light* I.1.2, in Wolfson 1929, 199.
[186] See W. Harvey 1998, 6–7 for elaboration of these points.
[187] See H. Wolfson 1929a, 42.
[188] This discussion occurs in Crescas *Light* Part I.2.11 and I.1.15 in H. Wolfson 1929, 282–91. Recent discussions of Crescas' theory of time and its relation to Aristotle can be found in the following works: W. Harvey 1981a; W. Harvey 1981b; Schweid 1970; and H. Wolfson 1929.

Crescas clearly aligns with the atomists. Pines goes so far as to suggest that Crescas' non-Peripatetic views "take place within a definite Islamic philosophical tradition."[189]

Proposition fifteen, as was introduced and discussed already by Maimonides, pertains to time and is summarized by Crescas as follows:

Proof of the fifteenth proposition which reads: 'Time is an accident that is consequent on motion and is conjoined with it. Neither one of them exists without the other. Motion does not exist except in time, and time cannot be conceived except with motion, and whatsoever is not in motion does not fall under the category of time.[190]

This statement, which is taken directly from Maimonides, is then contrasted with Aristotle's own definition: "Aristotle defines time as the number of priority and posteriority of motion."[191] In Part II of *Light*, Crescas turns to a critical evaluation of this Aristotelian conception of time, replacing Aristotle's definition with his own, namely that time can measure rest as well.[192]

Crescas makes several important points. The first is that time can measure rest as well as motion. Second, time can be measured by rest as well as by motion. And finally, time exists only in the soul. The first two points are captured in Crescas' revised definition of time: "the correct definition of time is that it is the measure of the continuity of motion or of rest between two instants."[193] In this definition, Crescas retains Aristotle's and Maimonides' notion of time as a "measure" or "number." However, Crescas adds the important qualification that time is the measure not only of motion or change, but of rest as well. We should remember in this context that although Aristotle did allow that time could measure rest, he did not amplify this suggestion.

Crescas then goes on to say that the genus most appropriate to time is magnitude. Inasmuch as time belongs to continuous quantity and number to discrete quantity, if we describe time as number, we describe it by a genus, which is not essential to it. Time is "indeed measured by both motion and rest, because it is our conception of the measure of their continuity that is time."[194] On this basis, Crescas concludes that "the existence of time is only in the soul."[195] It is because humans have a mental conception of this measure that time even exists. The continuity of time depends only upon a thinking mind, and is indefinite, becoming definite only by being measured by motion. Were we not to conceive of it, there would be no time.

In an interesting gambit, Crescas uses Aristotle's arguments against an absolute beginning to motion (in *Physics* VI.5.23a 236aff.) in order to uphold an infinite series of causation. Appropriating Aristotle's dictum that there can be no first part of

---

[189] Pines 1997, 98. For the sources used by Crescas, which included the Hebrew translation of Averroës' Long Commentary on the *Physics*, as well as the paraphrase of Aristotle's account in Averroës' Middle Commentary on the *Physics*, see Wolfson 1929, 8–9.

[190] Crescas *Light* I.1.15, in H. Wolfson 1929, 283.

[191] Crescas *Light* I.1.15, in H. Wolfson 1929, 285.

[192] Crescas *Light* I.2.15, in H. Wolfson 1929, 287–9.

[193] Crescas *Light* I.2.15, in H. Wolfson 1929, 289. For a discussion of the term *hitdabequt* and whether it means duration or continuity, see W. Harvey 1981a, 47. In this chapter, I follow Harvey's suggestion to translate the term *hitdabequt* as continuity.

[194] H. Wolfson 1929, 289.   [195] Ibid.

motion, because every object that is moved must have already been moved, Crescas maintains that "it is not inconceivable, therefore, that the infinite line [in question] should meet the other line in a finite distance with a finite motion, and this may be accounted for by the fact that the extreme beginning of motion must take place in no-time."[196] In his parting company with generations of Aristotelians who had used the denial of an infinite series of causes to postulate the necessary existence of a prime mover, Crescas therefore will have to resort to other arguments to postulate the existence of God.

The implications of Crescas' theory of time are apparent when we turn briefly to his discussion of creation in *Light* III.1. Without entering into the intricacies of this technical discussion, several important points can be made. Crescas takes as his point of departure the doctrine of creation *ex nihilo*. First, he summarizes the three arguments Gersonides gave in behalf of his thesis that the world was created out of a pre-existent matter. In direct response to Gersonides, Crescas is adamant that both the matter and form of the universe derive directly from God.[197] Unlike for his predecessors, however, creation *ex nihilo* for Crescas is a non-temporal concept. Crescas tries to show that eternal creation is a plausible doctrine even in the context of creation *ex nihilo* by exploring the notion of divine omnipotence. God's power is infinite in the sense that God's acts are not temporally limited. Inasmuch as God acts under no constraints, when God creates the world, he is able to create something that is infinite in duration, or eternal. It is in this sense that Crescas claims that the world is both eternal and created.[198]

Crescas first summarizes various arguments that were given in support of eternal creation. The first argument reiterates the connection between time and motion, and states that if time exists it must be eternal, for otherwise it would be existent prior to its existence as the measure of motion, which is absurd.[199] The second argument pertains to the nature of the instant ('*ata*). It claims that if time came into existence, it would follow that the instant would have no "before," which is an absurdity. Just as a point divides a line into "prior" and "posterior" so too the instant divides time into "before" and "after."[200] In response to this argument, Crescas follows the precedent of Gersonides who distinguished two types of instant. Not every instant divides past from future; just as a point can serve as the beginning of a line, Crescas argues that an "initial instant" can serve as the absolute beginning of time without implying a prior temporal unit. On the basis of this distinction, Crescas is able to posit an initial instant that marks the creation of time. Crescas then claims that "God created and brought forth the universe at a definite instant."[201] That is, that the universe has a temporal beginning.

Although Crescas posits an initial instant to creation, this does not mean that he rejects the doctrine of eternity altogether. In III.4, he rejects Maimonides' contention

---

[196] Crescas *Light* I.1.2, in H. Wolfson 1929, 213.   [197] Crescas '*Or Adonai* III.1.5:69a.
[198] Crescas' argument is contained in '*Or Adonai* III.1.5:69a. For a critical discussion of these arguments, see Feldman 1980, 304ff.
[199] Crescas '*Or Adonai* III.1.1:61b–62a.
[200] See Crescas *Light* III.1.1:62b. For further discussion of this version of the argument, see Davidson 1987, 24.
[201] Crescas '*Or Adonai* III.1.5:70a.

that the world has a temporal beginning, claiming that it is based on the mistaken Aristotelian equation of time and motion. Because he has already abandoned this Aristotelian conception, Crescas is able to argue that the notion of "creation" of the world does not refer to a temporal beginning. Rather, for Crescas, the world is both eternal and created: because time and motion are not interconnected, Crescas is able to adopt a position that on Aristotelian grounds appears to be self-contradictory.[202] Scholars have worked hard to offer an interpretation of Crescas that preserves both. Feldman, for example, offers an alternative reading of Crescas, one which interprets eternal creation as "the continuous and limitless creation by God of an infinite series of worlds, each of finite duration. Thus interpreted, eternal creation implies eternal creativity: it is not the product that is eternal but the activity of creation."[203] We are not to understand creation as a single event in which time begins "after" not having existed. Eternity does not pertain to temporality but to the never-endingness of time. The world is both eternal and created.[204]

Crescas' student Joseph Albo incorporates Maimonides' discussion of pre-existent matter into his own examination of creation, which is couched in the context of developing a theory of time. Albo is one of the first Jewish philosophers to espouse the view that time is a phenomenon of the imagination, a motif introduced by Crescas and recurring in Spinoza. Albo's discussion of time, contained in his work *The Book of Principles*, occurs in the context of demonstrating that God is independent of time. For Albo, God's independence of time comprises both eternity and perpetuity and is upheld as a basic principle:[205]

The third dogma is that God is independent of time. This means that God existed before time, and will exist after time ceases, therefore his power is infinite. For everyone who is dependent upon time is necessarily limited in power, which ends with time. Since, therefore God is not dependent upon time, his power is infinite.[206]

By God's priority Albo means that nothing was prior to God, not even non-existence; God has always existed "in the same way without change."[207] Similarly God's eternality means that nothing is posterior to God, not even time. For if time outlasted God either *a parte ante* or *a parte post*, then God would exist at one instant of time and not at another; this, of course, would undermine God's necessary existence. These comments lead Albo to examine the nature of time and creation more closely. God's eternality holds, he claims,

even if by time we mean unmeasured duration conceived only in thought, existing always, both before the creation of the world and after its cessation, but without the order apparent from the motion of the sphere, since the sphere was then neither in motion nor existent.[208]

---

[202] Crescas 'Or Adonai III.1.4 66a–68b. Commentators have tried to make sense of Crescas' apparently contradictory theory. For further discussion of this theory of creation, see Feldman 1980, 289–320; Schweid 1970, 44.

[203] Feldman 1980 317.   [204] Schweid 1970, 44.

[205] Albo 1946, *Sefer ha-'Ikkarim* vol. I, I.15:130.

[206] Albo 1946, *Sefer ha-'Ikkarim* vol. II, II.18:108–9.

[207] Albo 1946, *Sefer ha-'Ikkarim* vol. II, II.18:109.

[208] Albo 1946, *Sefer ha-'Ikkarim* vol. II, II.18:110.

Only measured time cannot exist without motion. Time itself, according to Albo, is not dependent upon motion and even preexisted the world. This non-Aristotelian motif is developed more fully. In another context, Albo compares the commandments to time inasmuch as both time and commandments are not actual existents:

[just as] time is not an actual existent, for the past is no longer here, the future is not yet, and the present is merely the now which binds the past to the future. The now itself is not real time, since it is not divisible, whereas time is divisible, pertaining as it does to continuous quantity. The now is related to time as the point is related to the line. Time is therefore not an actual existent, and yet it gives perfection of existence to all things existing in time.[209]

Albo then distinguishes between "plain time" and "the order of time" as follows:

Our rabbis are of the opinion that time in the abstract is such a duration. Time measured or numbered through the motion of the sphere they call "order of times", not simply time. According to this there are two species of time, the one is numbered and measured by the motion of the sphere, to which are applicable the terms prior and posterior, equal and unequal. The other is not numbered or measured but is a duration existing prior to the sphere, to which the words equal and unequal do not apply.[210]

Whereas plain time is neither numbered nor measured, the order of times is numbered and measured by the motion of the diurnal sphere. In contrast to ordered time, plain time is eternal duration. Albo then raises two perplexities pertaining to time. The first puzzle is whether time originates in time or not. The solution is that although time has no origin and does not come to be in time, the "order of time" originates in time.[211] The second puzzle concerns the instant: "The now (ha-'atah), it is said, divides the past from the future. There is therefore a time before the first now, and hence time and the sphere are eternal."[212] Albo's answer, relying on his twofold notion of time, is that Aristotle's argument refers only to the "order of times" and not to "plain time": plain time in which there is no motion "has not the elements prior and posterior, and it is not subject to measure because measure cannot apply to time without motion. The terms prior and posterior apply to it [plain time] only figuratively and loosely."[213]

VII Scripture, Philosophy, and the First Instant of Creation

In previous pages, we have seen the many ways in which Jewish philosophers have tried to incorporate a scientific model in talking about creation. We are now in a position to explore some of the theological implications embedded in these philosophical discussions. I suggested in the introduction to this chapter that the phrase *Bereshit* designates the fact that there was a beginning. But positing a beginning instant carries with it assumptions about what preceded this instant, and how this

---

[209] Albo 1946, *Sefer ha-'Ikkarim*, vol. III, III.27:259.
[210] Albo 1946, *Sefer ha-'Ikkarim*, vol. II, II.18:110–11.
[211] Albo 1946, *Sefer ha-'Ikkarim*, vol. II, II.18:111.   [212] Ibid.
[213] Albo 1946, *Sefer ha-'Ikkarim*, vol. II, II.18:111–12.

"pre" instant is reflected in Scripture. The following passage from *Genesis Rabbah* provides an appropriate springboard for examining some of these implications. In this commentary upon *Genesis*, we find the following statement:

["And there was evening and there was morning," (Gen. 1:3)] Said R. Judah b. R. Simon, "Let there be evening is not what is written here, but rather 'and there was evening.' On the basis of that formulation we learn that the sequence of time had already been laid out." Said R. Abbahu, "on the basis of that same formulation we learn that the Holy One, Blessed be he, had been engaged in creating worlds and destroying them prior to the moment at which he created this one. Then he said, "This is the one that pleases me, but those did not please me."[214]

This paragraph became the focus of profound philosophical speculation among Jewish philosophers wishing to ground their analysis of Scripture in scientific legitimacy. A number of pressing questions emerged from this passage: first, how does one's understanding of Rabbi Judah's phrase "sequence of time" (*seder zemanim*) affect one's interpretation of the temporality of creation in *Genesis* I.1? Second, what is the status of the existence of time before day four when the temporal markers were created? And finally, how is time measured in these first three days of creation? In short, these questions crystallize the attempt of Jewish philosophers to reconcile rabbinic dicta and sentiments with an Aristotelian theory of time.[215] Inasmuch as their interpretations of Rabbi Judah's words serve as a revealing litmus test for the theological implications of their metaphysics of time, let me end this chapter with a brief examination of their discussions.

The first question is the subject of Maimonides' commentary on the phrase *Bereshit*, the first words of *Genesis* I.1 Why does Scripture start with the phrase "In the beginning God created..."? In order to explain the sense of "beginning" being used in this context, Maimonides turns in *Guide* 2.30 to an interpretation of the two terms *tehilah* and *reshit*, both of which can mean "start" or "beginning." Maimonides distinguishes between the two on the basis of causal priority.[216] An event *e* can specify an event/state of affairs *A* as being causally prior to *B* in one of two ways: first, When *A* is a part of *B*, and second, when *A* is not a part of *B* but rather appears simultaneously with it. In both cases the term *tehilah*, or causal beginning, can be used. In contradistinction, the term *reshit* refers not to a temporal priority of *A* to *B*, but rather to its ontological genesis.[217] On this basis, Maimonides is able to allow for an interpretation of the phrase *Bereshit* in such a way as to accord with eternal creation. The proposition *bet* in the phrase *Bereshit* is not, on this reading, a temporal indicator, but rather fixes the event in question ontologically: it refers not to a temporal beginning but to an underlying ontological state. So that when we read the statement in *Genesis* I.1 ("*Bereshit bara' 'Elohim*" = "in the beginning God created"), we should understand it to describe a nontemporal event, one which specifies that God is the creator of the universe, that is, its ontological ground of Being, or what Harvey describes as the continuous ontic dependence of creation on

---

[214] Neusner 1985, 33.   [215] Klein-Braslavy 1975.   [216] See Klein-Braslavy 1975, 115.
[217] For further elaboration of this point, see Harvey 1981b, 296; Klein-Braslavy 1987, 81–2, 86–7.

the creator. On this interpretation, *Bereshit* refers to a "principle" in the sense of the Greek *arché*.[218]

Having postulated the non-temporal mode of creation, Maimonides is able to interpret those rabbis who understood the Creation account in *Genesis* to postulate a domain of temporality before the creation event. That is, in order to explain how there can be "one day," at the beginning of creation, when the temporal indicators, i.e., the sun and moon, were not created until the fourth day, Maimonides quotes both Rabbis Judah ben Simon and Abahu to support his contention that "time existed prior to the existence of this sun."[219] Recognizing that their statements support an eternity thesis, Maimonides adopts two separate strategies. The first is simply to recognize that their comments imply that "the order of time necessarily exists eternally *a parte ante*. That, however, is the belief in the eternity *a parte ante* of the world, and all who adhere to the Law should reject it."[220] In other words, one strategy is simply to recognize that these sages were supporting a version of eternal creation and hence to reject their interpretation.

Maimonides' second strategy is to subsume their comments as corollaries of those of Rabbi Eliezer. In II.13, Maimonides refers to Rabbi Eliezer, whose commentary on creation postulates creation by means of pre-existent matter. Maimonides depicts this commentary as admitting "the eternity of the world, if only as it is conceived according to Plato's opinion."[221] Interestingly enough, Maimonides does not respond directly to Eliezer's statement; his only response to it is to claim that it may "confuse very much indeed the belief of a learned man who adheres to the Law. No persuasive figurative interpretation with regard to it has become clear to me."[222] Uttered by an individual who is generally not at a loss for interpretative prowess, for whom the "gates of interpretation" are rarely if ever closed, Maimonides' stance suggests that he himself is not as uncomfortable with Eliezer's statements as one might expect.[223] If so, then Maimonides' second strategy with respect to Rabbis Judah and Abahu is similar to his attitude toward Eliezer. Maimonides claims that their comments are "only the counterpart of the passage in which Rabbi Eliezer says, "Wherefrom were the heavens created."[224] Inasmuch as Maimonides is not bothered by the latter, so too can it be inferred that he is not bothered by the former. Note that Maimonides seemingly discredits these rabbinic comments altogether by questioning the authority of the speakers: "To sum up: you should not, in considering these points, take into account the statements made by this or that one."[225] Here Maimonides seems to be

---

[218] See Harvey 1981b, 296. In his *Commentary on the Guide* 2.30, Narboni comments upon Maimonides' distinction between two meanings of "first": For Narboni the term *hathala* connotes the idea of efficient cause. Second, Narboni looks at the passage where Maimonides says that to take the term *rei'shit* in the sense of initial instant introduces eternity of the world, since by definition an instant separates anterior from posterior. Thus, one cannot take the expression *Bereshit* in this temporal sense since the instant would have been preceded by another instant. According to Narboni, Maimonides conceded to the vulgar creation *ex nihilo* whereas in reality he knew that time, which is the number of movement, is eternal. In other words, when Maimonides writes that creation of beings accompanied that of time, he knew that the world had been created in time since he established a connection between time and created beings. See Hayoun 1989, 150.

[219] Maimonides *Guide* 2.30:349.   [220] Maimonides *Guide* 2.30:349.

[221] Maimonides *Guide* 2.26:331.   [222] Maimonides *Guide* 2.26:331.

[223] See Klein-Braslavy 1988, 235–8, for further discussion of this point.

[224] Maimonides *Guide* 2.30:349.   [225] Maimonides *Guide* 2.30:349.

suggesting that in considering the issues of time and creation, one ought not to be misled by the opinions of sundry rabbis. If this is so, what sense, then, should we make of Maimonides' overt espousal of [5.1] on the basis of Mosaic authority? At least [5.2] and [5.3] have other considerations in its favor. But if the sole basis for [5.1] is authority, then Maimonides seems to be undermining its very plausibility.

In an apparent attempt to deflect the strength of the eternity thesis, Maimonides suggests that the worry underlying Rabbi Judah's passage really can be understood in terms of the metaphysics of time, namely the difficulty with "the notion that time existed prior to the existence of this sun."[226] In order to account for this worry, Maimonides gives an allegorical explanation, suggesting that the term "heavens" (shamayim) is sometimes called "firmament" (raqi'a) which comprises the spheres and the celestial lighters. On this interpretation, the luminaries were created with the entire shamayim on the first day but not suspended until the fourth day. The stars as well as the sun and moon are situated within the firmament of the heaven. Presumably, then, days one, two, and three could be measured by these temporal markers. Technically, however, Maimonides interprets the creative act as a simultaneous creation of heaven and earth, and so the demarcation of days subsequent to creation represents a gradual unfolding of differentiation within creation.[227]

Gersonides deals with Rabbi Judah's dicta both in Wars VI.2.8, and in his Torah Commentary. Gersonides first turns to the term Bereshit, which is seen to have many meanings, only one of which refers specifically to temporality. Bereshit can mean priority in order, priority in degree, or priority in cause and in nature.[228] Accepting the precept that time existed from the instant of creation and not before—"the generation of the universe by God occurred in no time"[229]—Gersonides reflects Maimonides and states that everything described in the first six days of creation was actually created together, that is, simultaneously.[230] On Gersonides' interpretation, the term "day" does not reflect temporal temporality but rather causal priority: the term "day" is used "to indicate the priority of some existent things over others."[231] Gersonides then reiterates the point that, inasmuch as all things were created simultaneously, the supralunar spheres were actually created on the first day, and so their light was available to account for the demarcation of days one through three.[232]

In part because they have already rejected the Aristotelian equation of time and motion, Crescas and Albo have less trouble accounting for Rabbi Judah's dicta. We have seen that for Maimonides, time as well as the celestial spheres were created. If, however, as Crescas believes, time is independent of motion, and exists prior to the

---

[226] Maimonides Guide 2.30:349.

[227] See Maimonides Guide 2.30:350: "Accordingly everything was created simultaneously; then gradually all things became differentiated."

[228] Gersonides Wars vol. 3, VI.2.2:430. Gersonides returns to this distinction in his Torah Commentary. These different ways of understanding "beginning" reflect Aristotle's discussion in Categories 2.1a–4a 25ff.

[229] Gersonides Wars vol. 3, VI.2.8. See also Gersonides Wars vol. 3, VI.1.18: "Prior to the creation of the world there was no time at all." This point is reiterated in his Torah Commentary, 21.

[230] Gersonides Wars vol. 3, VI.2.8:446. Again, the point is repeated in his Torah Commentary, 21.

[231] Gersonides Wars vol. 3, VI.2.8:446-7. Gersonides gives as examples the movers of the heavenly bodies which are prior in cause to the heavenly bodies, and the heavenly bodies which are prior in cause to the nature of the elements.

[232] Gersonides Wars vol. 3, VI.2.8:447-8.

creation of the world, then the spheres can be in time even before the creation.[233] This is the import of Crescas' interpretation of Rabbi Judah's statement. In contradistinction to Maimonides who had to interpret this statement figuratively, Crescas is able to adopt its literal meaning: "... the passage of Rabbi Jehudah, son of Rabbi Simon, which reads: 'It teaches us that the order of time had existed previous to that,' may be taken in its literal sense."[234] To Rabbi Judah ben Simon's related dictum that the order of time pre-existed creation, Albo is quick to point out that Rabbi Judah really meant that the time which is measured by the motion of the sphere is called "order of times" and is contrasted to time "simply" which has no priority, posteriority, or order.[235] Because the phrase "order of times" applies only to time which is correlated to motion, Albo argues that Rabbi Judah's statement implies that time existed prior to the fourth day of creation. But Albo recognizes that ultimately this solution does not resolve the issue. Quoting the famous rabbinic passage that one must not explore what is above, below, before, and behind, Albo accedes that he has not really explained "how there can be a duration before the creation of the world which has in it neither prior nor posterior."[236] Or as Harvey has succinctly argued, Albo has not succeeded in explaining how, *within* the "order of times," there can be a first instant which has no "before."[237]

Let us turn finally to the fifteenth-century thinker Isaac Arama (1420–94), who in his sermons combines philosophical and theological motifs with creative ingenuity. In dealing with *Genesis* I, Arama addresses all three of our original concerns. Starting with the question how could there have been a day, that is a unit of time measurement, before the fourth day when the luminaries were created, Arama first notes the two main views of time, that of Aristotle and that of Maimonides. He agrees with Maimonides that, "the beginning of time and the beginning of creation exist as one and the same."[238] Given this position, he must explain how time could possibly preexist the fourth day of creation. Arama resolves the conundrum by introducing a notion of time that is not tied to spherical motion, but rather to motions that already existed prior to the fourth day.[239] Arama argues that the spheres were created on the second day but started their movement on the fourth day when the sun and moon were introduced. Although according to Arama the sun and moon were created on the first day, they were not actually suspended until the fourth day, which demarcates the commencement of motion.[240]

But then Arama offers another solution to the problem of time before the fourth day in the context of Crescas' theory. This second solution is based upon Maimonides' basic contention that there is a basic connection between time and movement of the spheres. We have seen that Arama is not willing to accept Maimonides' position that time exists from the first day on because the sphere was already created on the first day. According to Arama, spherical motion begins on day four. So he says that the time of days one to four can be construed as "complete time" only in the mind of

---

[233] See Wolfson 1929, 633.   [234] Wolfson 1929, 291.
[235] Albo 1946, *Sefer ha-'Ikkarim* vol. II.18:113.   [236] Albo 1946, *Sefer ha-'Ikkarim* vol. II.18:112.
[237] Harvey 1981a, 223.   [238] Arama *'Aqedat Yitzhaq* III.24b.
[239] See Heller-Wilensky 1956, 118.
[240] Klein-Braslavy 1975, notes the influence of Averroës upon Arama.

God. Time turns out to be an image in God's soul.[241] "Although it is known that time cannot be created at all without the motion of the spheres, nevertheless Scripture will not, because of this, refrain from describing it in terms of the future. For God speaks and Moses writes... For insofar as complete time exists in God's wisdom... Scripture mentions it and defines it even before it becomes into existence in its final description."[242] Arama's point here is that Scripture has recorded the creation of time retrospectively.

On this basis, then, Arama distinguishes between two types of time: complete, or natural, time, (zeman shalem) which is connected to spherical motion; and incomplete time (zeman bilti shalem), which is not tied to spherical motion but rather connected to other forms of motion.[243] In an interesting analogy drawn from Ibn Rushd, Arama claims that it does not make sense to argue that those who do not experience spherical movement do not experience time: imagine, for example, individuals imprisoned in a cave since childhood, who have not experienced natural time since they have not experienced spherical motion of the heavens. Arama argues that nevertheless, they experience other motions and hence time, by way of inference.[244] Using this example, then, Arama resolves the original dilemma, seeing the existence of time as a distinction between before and after. When this distinction between before and after is made, time in the incomplete sense exists.

How, then, do we even recognize the first day as day number one, that is, as the first day? Arama claims that light was created after a measure of dark, and then continues this analogy to other days as well. That is, the existence of time is not dependent upon the existence of the motion of the spheres, but upon the existence of any motion in general. On the first three days, there is only incomplete time, and only on day four is there complete time, which is time predicated upon day and night.[245]

Arama finally turns to Rabbi Judah's dicta. According to Arama, the order of times precedes not the creation of the world but only the fourth day, preceding the creation of the luminaries. The order of times preceding the luminaries was that of "incomplete time," which is not tied to planetary motion.[246] Arama tries to find support for these two solutions in Bereshit Rabba III and offers the following interpretation of Rabbi Judah's words. According to Arama, Rabbi Judah teaches that time can be estimated without the motion of the spheres, hence supporting the position that time exists after creation but before the fourth day. Creation brings with it the concept of prior and posterior, and so it contains the "order of time." The term "day" refers not to an exact measured time, but rather to a concept of a definite duration of time, which is independent of the movement of the spheres. While rejecting the views of Maimonides, Crescas, and Albo, Arama continues to postulate a concept of time before the fourth day.

[241] Klein-Braslavy 1975, 125.   [242] Arama 'Aqedat Yitzhaq III.24b–25a.
[243] Arama 'Aqedat Yitzhaq III.24b.   [244] See Arama 'Aqedat Yitzhaq III.24b for this example.
[245] Klein-Braslavy 1975, 123; see Arama's discussion in 'Aqedat Yitzhaq III.24a and III.26a.
[246] Arama 'Aqedat Yitzhaq III.25a. See Heller-Wilensky 1956, 119.

7

Philosophical Cosmology
The Nature of the Universe

I Introduction

The preceding chapters have focused upon the nature of God and God's creation of the world. We now turn to a more careful examination of the natural order, including in this chapter the heavenly bodies and in Chapter 8, human beings. The heavenly bodies play an important role in ancient and medieval cosmology, natural philosophy, metaphysics, medicine, and theology. Two rival geocentric cosmologies, those of Aristotle and of Ptolemy, competed for acceptance in the medieval world and affected related issues in natural philosophy. Works of Aristotle and Ptolemy influenced medieval views on astrology as well, as philosophers considered the causal efficacy of the heavenly bodies upon the sublunar world.

In this chapter, we focus upon the ingredients that comprise the universe, both superlunar and sublunary. The superlunar cosmology includes the heavenly bodies, and any effects they may have upon the sublunary world, which comprises the natural order. We finally must say something about those events that, contravening the natural order, fall into the general category of miracles. How, in a natural order ruled by law, can we account for miracles? The theological acceptance of miracles provided our thinkers with a particular challenge: how to reconcile Aristotelian science, which rules out supernatural events, with a tradition that includes many examples of miraculous events.

II Astronomy and Cosmology Conceived Broadly

In the medieval world, two rival cosmologies, those of Aristotle and Ptolemy, competed for acceptance. Influenced by Aristotle's physical and natural works, many cosmologists followed Aristotle rather than Ptolemy in their quest to provide a comprehensive theory of the universe. The formative classical texts included Aristotle's *De Caelo*, supplemented by relevant passages from the *Metaphysics*, *Physics*, and *De Generatione et Corruptione*. Plato's *Timaeus* and commentaries upon *Genesis* presented an additional dimension to this corpus. Historian of science Pierre Duhem notes the first clear definition of the subject matter of astronomy in Plato, as reported by Simplicius in his Commentary.[1] Assuming in principle that the motion

---

[1] Duhem 1913, vol. I, 103.

of celestial bodies is uniform, circular, and perfectly regular, Plato then poses to the mathematicians the following problem: What uniform circular motions are convenient to be taken as hypotheses in order to save the appearances presented in the wandering planets?[2]

That cosmology and astronomy comprised separate disciplines was already explicitly indicated in early textual traditions. In his commentary upon Aristotle's *Physics*, for example, the Greek commentator Simplicius reflected the longstanding tradition of distinguishing between the two, stating that cosmology considers the physical substance of the heavenly bodies, while astronomy is concerned with the mathematical relations, distances, and movements among these bodies. In the Aristotelian cosmology, the universe is a finite sphere whose center is at the earth and bounded by the sphere of the fixed stars. Nine primary concentric spheres (in turn divided into subsidiary spheres) rotate around the earth; these spheres form a compact whole, much like the skins of an onion, with no vacuum. First came the other three terrestrial elements, water, air, and fire. Surrounding the sphere of fire were the crystalline spheres in which were placed the seven planets: the moon, Mercury, Venus, the sun, Mars, Jupiter, and Saturn. Beyond the last planet came the fixed stars, identified with the sphere of the "prime mover," and then nothing. The sphere of the moon separated the universe into the sublunar, or terrestrial, region, and the superlunar or celestial region.[3]

Outside its boundary nothing existed, and neither body, location, nor time could exist beyond the stellar sphere. Within the confines of the universe were two regions—the celestial and the terrestrial—whose physics and constitution were radically different from one another. In the celestial realm, which extended from the moon to the outermost sphere, heavenly bodies move in eternal, unchanging circular motions; the fifth element or *aether* was immutable and constituted the heavens. The terrestrial realm comprised the four elements. Motion in the sublunar realm was an effect of a prior cause: thus, motion was ultimately eternal, since there could not be a temporal beginning to motion. While the first mover, or god, caused the universe to move through desire, each of the planets had its own unmoved movers that acted as final causes or objects of desire to affect the movement of their spheres. These spheres affected each other mechanically as well; because in the Aristotelian universe no void could exist, they had to be in contact with one another. Yet Aristotle was obscure on the question of how the mechanical effects of planetary spheres on each other related to the operations of unmoved movers as well as to the Unmoved Mover. The notion of fifty-five counteracting spheres was introduced to discount the effects of this mechanical effect.

The superlunar heavens differed in composition from the sublunar bodies in that the former were composed of a single incorruptible element, *aether*, while the earth comprised the four elements. One of the purposes of *aether* was to account for the movements of the celestial bodies, which Aristotle argued could not move in the same way as did the terrestrial elements. For according to Aristotle, elements in the sublunar realm were subject to the four kinds of change, while elements composed of *aether* only underwent one kind of change, eternally uniform motion in a circle. Another reason was that the four terrestrial elements could not account for the vast distance between the earth and the outermost sphere; only an element not subject to contraries, Aristotle argued, could exist sufficiently long to fill this space.[4]

Aristotle provides few details about his concentric system of orbs.[5] Aristotle nested all the spheres concentrically while at the same time prevented the motions of the orbs of the outer planets from affecting the motions of the orbs of the inner planets; he achieved this by incorporating contrary motions into the very structure of his system. In *De Caelo*, he deals with the question of whether the equal and uniform motions of two oppositely directed orbs were contrary motions. But can a circular motion have a contrary? Based on these passages in *De Caelo*, Grant argues that "the motions of the counteracting spheres would not qualify as contrary motions."[6]

The ultimate source of motion in this Aristotelian system is the unmoved first mover.[7] But did this agent move the first moving sphere as an active, efficient cause, or as a passive, final cause? Aristotle had attributed to all the celestial spheres a mover, the ultimate source of motion being god-like. Medieval thinkers, however, introduced immobile created intelligences to explain celestial motion. These separate intelligences move the orbs with both intellect and will. Each sphere has a soul or internal moving source; in the medieval period, these were often identified with angels.[8]

In a number of important works, Aristotle laid the groundwork for the theory that these celestial bodies were responsible for the growth and sustenance of sublunar entities. In the *Physics*, for example, Aristotle argues that motion is the primary cause of change. In order to explain both generation and corruption, we need two different motions, different in speed. The sun's motion along the ecliptic provides this twofold motion in that it both advances and retreats. Thus, "every time" is measured by a period.[9] Thus, the sun's movement produces a cyclical interchange between elements. Even time gets its continuity from the circular movement of the sun. The second Aristotle passage is from *Meteorologica*, which covers phenomena in the upper reaches of the sublunar region, such as comets and the Milky Way. The efficient cause of these phenomena is the sun, while the material causes are the four elements.

Gad Freudenthal notes that Aristotle's separation of the cosmos into two distinct realms in which different natural laws obtain remained the source of persistent difficulties for his followers. Aristotle's introduction of the notion of a fifth body, or aether, which separated the superlunar from the sublunar spheres, raised the intractable problem of how the heavenly bodies could influence the sublunar realm. Peripatetic thinkers introduced two new non-Aristotelian notions—the notion of a "divine force" of the stars' rays, and the Neoplatonic idea of an "overflow" from the "separate bodies" associated with the planets—to account for this influence.[10] Consider,

---

[4] Aristotle *De Caelo* I.2–4; II.4.

[5] Aristotle *Metaphysics* 12.8 is one of the only places in which he does so.

[6] Grant has provided extensive discussion of the movements of the celestial spheres. See Grant 1997, 285.

[7] Aristotle *Metaphysics* 7.7; *Physics* 8.6.

[8] See for example Maimonides *Guide* 2.6. For further discussion of these angelic substances, see Ivry 2016.

[9] Aristotle *Physics* 336b 12–14.   [10] Freudenthal 2000, 336–7.

for example, the enormously popular treatise *De Radiis* by Islamic philosopher Abû Yûsuf Ya'qûb ibn Ishâq al-Kindî (?c. 800–70). Translated into Latin (the original Arabic is lost), this treatise presented the theory that causal action of the sublunar world originated from the astral world of stellar influence. On al-Kindî's model, every star emits rays of a different type, providing a celestial harmony in which all events, past, present and future, are inscribed.[11]

As we move into the medieval period, two rival cosmological systems vied for acceptance: the Aristotelian homocentric theory in which the stars and planets were carried around on concentric spheres; and the Ptolemaic theory in which the planets were carried around by a system of eccentric and epicyclic spheres. Although Aristotle's works comprised the foundation for science, and for astrology, for several thousand years, other texts were equally influential, including both Neoplatonic and Stoic texts, as well as of course Ptolemy's *Tetrabiblos*. But tensions centered on the metaphysical status of mathematical theories in science. On the one hand, the universe, as described by Aristotle in *De Caelo*, was a material entity based on the laws of physics, while on the other hand, mathematical astronomy made use of geometrical devices that violated these very physical laws. More specifically, both Aristotle and Ptolemy agreed that there must be a plurality of spheres to account for the motion of each planet. These spheres, as we have seen, were nested contiguously. On Aristotle's model, there was a series of concentric orbs, each moving in a natural, uniform, circular motion, all sharing the earth as a common center. Ptolemy, however, recognized that Aristotle could not account for variations in the observed distances of the planets. This recognition led to the postulating of an alternative cosmological scheme.

In his two astronomical works the *Almagest* and *Hypothesis of the Planets*, Ptolemy argued that the planets were carried about by a system of eccentric and epicyclical spheres. In the *Almagest*, Ptolemy had proposed that his astronomical theory was merely a method the purpose of which was to "save the appearances," or account for the observed phenomena.[12] His *Hypothesis of the Planets* provided the mechanical explanation for his system. Ptolemy's *Hypothesis* was not translated into Latin during the Middle Ages, and it is not clear how its ideas reached Western Europe; presumably through works translated from Arabic, although the precise treatises are not yet known. Roger Bacon was one of the first scholastics to present a serious evaluation of the cosmological utility of Ptolemy's system, although he himself seems to have inclined toward Aristotle's theory. Bacon's description of material eccentrics and epicycles was the one most widely adopted during the Middle Ages.[13]

On Ptolemy's model, each concentric planetary orb contained at least three partial eccentric and epicyclical spheres. That this system of eccentric and epicyclical spheres contravened the concentric spheres of Aristotle was not lost upon Ptolemy or his followers. In particular, Ptolemy's insistence that partial eccentric orbs had centers other than the earth violated Aristotle's dictum that all celestial spheres move around the earth with uniform motion. And yet, most medieval astronomers

---

[11] See al-Kindî 1974; Travaglia 1999.   [12] Ptolemy *Almagest* 13.2.
[13] See Hackett 1997.

found that Ptolemy's system did a better job of "saving the appearances" of astronomical data. As Grant has argued, "the medieval conflict between the Aristotelian and Ptolemaic systems centered on efforts to demonstrate that eccentric and epicyclical orbs did not imply consequences that were subversive and destructive of Aristotelian cosmology and physics."[14] In other words, medieval philosophers were faced with a dilemma: either they could reject the earth's centrality and abandon a vital part of Aristotelian physics in the name of astronomical and mathematical purity, or they could accept a cosmology that was untenable from the perspective of the astronomers.

Ptolemy thus tried to account for the complex motion of the wandering planets by introducing new models that subordinate physics to mathematics, thus widening the gap between the two. By the end of the fourteenth century, most scholastics came to assume the truth of material eccentrics, including Duns Scotus, Aegidius Romanus, Durandus de Saint-Pourcain, and especially Pierre D'Ailly, who offered a spirited account and support of the system in his *14 Questions on the Sphere of Sacrobosco*. Ptolemy's *Almagest* thus became the most important treatise on astronomy for the next 1,400 years.

But as noted by Tahiri, the *Almagest* was "the first important Greek scientific work to be successfully disputed."[15] The trouble began when Ptolemy attempted to explain celestial mechanics within the framework of Aristotle's cosmology. He was not able to account for how a frictionless sphere could move another frictionless sphere, for example, if they were both revolving around the same center. This raised a number of questions among Islamic scholars: could the celestial bodies have properties that contradicted their originally defined natures? But the problems with Ptolemy were so complex that it took generations for Islamic scholars to understand and resolve them.

The earliest serious critique of Ptolemy's astronomy was presented by Ibn al-Haytham (Alhazen, *c.* 1039), one of the first Islamic scientists who, in his *al-Shukûk 'ala Batlamyus* (*Doubts about Ptolemy*), attacked the inconsistencies in Ptolemy's arguments. Al-Haytham objected to Ptolemy's lunar model, which he saw as unduly complex. Noting that Ptolemy's equant model of planetary motion was inconsistent with his theory of uniform circular motion, he argued that Ptolemy had not succeeded in "saving the phenomena."[16] Al-Haytham's influence soon spread throughout Arabic Spain.

In Islamic Spain, Maimonides echoed the views of the Islamic philosopher Ibn Bâjja ("Avempace," *d. c.* 1139) who rejected the epicyclic theory on the grounds that a point on an epicycle does not move toward the center, away from the center, or around it. According to Maimonides, the eccentric model is contrary to Aristotelian principles; to this he adds the criticism that these centers are not all below the sphere of the moon, but must participate in the motions of the planetary spheres. But Maimonides was equally unhappy with the abandonment of Ptolemy's models by the Aristotelian school. In response to this quandary, Maimonides took refuge in epistemological skepticism.

---

[14] See Grant 1987, 195.   [15] Tahiri 2008, 197.   [16] Goldstein 1980, 137.

Having rejected Aristotle's analysis, Maimonides presents his own version in *Guide* 2.24. His main thesis is that the underlying premise of Ptolemy's *Almagest*, namely that "everything depends on two principles; either that of the epicycles or that of the eccentric spheres or on both of them," is untenable. Maimonides' own contention is that these two principles are "entirely outside the bounds of reasoning and opposed to all that has been made clear in natural science."[17] In other words, Maimonides rejects Ptolemaic astronomy on the grounds that it conflicts with Aristotelian physics. The first principle is rejected on the grounds that the existence of epicycles implies that the "epicycle rolls and changes its place completely," hence undermining the Aristotelian dictum that things in the heavens are immovable. He then offers other considerations, in the name of the Islamic astronomer Abu Bâkr, against accepting the doctrine of epicycles. Following this analysis, Maimonides presents the following theoretical perplexity:

> If what Aristotle has stated with regard to natural science is true, there are no epicycles or eccentric circles and everything revolves round the center of the earth. But in that case how can the various motions of the stars come about? Is it in any way possible that motion should be on the one hand circular, uniform, and perfect, and that on the other hand the things that are observable should be observed in consequence of it, unless this be accounted for by making use of one of the two principles, or of both of them? This consideration is all the stronger because of the fact that if one accepts everything stated by Ptolemy concerning the epicycle of the moon and its deviation toward a point outside the center of the world and also outside the center of the eccentric circle, it will be found that what is calculated on the hypothesis of the two principles is not at fault by even a minute... This is the true perplexity.[18]

That Maimonides characterizes an astronomical conundrum as the "true perplexity" in a work whose raison d'être is devoted to defusing perplexities has not escaped scholars, and has functioned as one of the keys to understanding Maimonides' esotericism.[19]

The twelfth-century Islamic astronomer al-Bitrûjî was critical of epicycles and eccentrics as well, and tried to replace them with a homocentric theory, but this proved to be a disaster, as pointed out by Gersonides. Gersonides was one of the most noted astronomers of his time, and contributed detailed astronomical tables, calculations, and inventions to the papal court in Avignon. Gersonides dismissed al-Bitrûjî's models and introduced new theories to account for planetary motion. In his astronomical treatise, Gersonides accepted the equant model while exploring additional configurations not found in Ptolemy.[20] Although Gersonides wrote no scientific works as such, scientific discussions were included in his philosophical works. Gersonides' major scientific contributions were in the area of astronomy; his works were known by his contemporaries, both Jewish and Christian. Gersonides' astronomical writings are contained primarily in book 5, part 1 of *Wars*. The astronomical parts of *The Wars* were translated into Latin during Gersonides' lifetime.[21]

---

[17] Maimonides *Guide* 2.24:322.
[18] Maimonides *Guide* 2.24:326–7. The underline is my addition.
[19] See Langermann 2008; Rudavsky 2010; Ivry 2016.   [20] See Goldstein 1974, 33ff.
[21] Although the astronomy chapters were conceived as an integral part of the work, they were omitted in the first printed edition of *The Wars*, and have survived in four manuscripts. In the 136 chapters of book 5,

Gersonides' reliance upon and consummate knowledge of mathematics, coupled with his belief in the accuracy of observations achieved by the use of good instruments, distinguished Gersonides from his Jewish philosophical predecessors. Because of this rootedness in empirical observation bolstered by mathematics, Gersonides believed that he had the tools to succeed where others had failed, particularly in the area of astronomy. Unlike Maimonides, Gersonides was determined to harmonize astronomy and physics: "In its perfection this investigation [astronomy] belongs to both sciences—to mathematics because of the geometric proofs, and to natural philosophy because of the physical and philosophical proofs."[22]

That Gersonides clearly considered his own observations to be the ultimate test of his system is explicit from his attitude towards Ptolemy. The importance of empirical observation cannot be underestimated, he claims, and he values his own observations over those of others. "We did not find among our predecessors from Ptolemy to the present day observations that are helpful for this investigation except our own,"[23] he says in describing his method of collecting astronomical data. Often his observations do not agree with those of Ptolemy, and in those cases he tells us explicitly that he prefers his own. Gersonides lists the many inaccuracies he has found trying to follow Ptolemy's calculations. Having investigated the positions of the planets, for example, Gersonides encountered "confusion and disorder" which led him to deny several of Ptolemy's planetary principles.[24] He does warn his colleagues, however, to dissent from Ptolemy only after great diligence and scrutiny. It is interesting to note that Gersonides briefly discusses, and then dismisses, the heliocentric model of the universe before rejecting it in favor of geocentrism.[25]

Gersonides is perhaps best known for his invention of the Jacob's Staff. This instrument, which he called *Megalle 'amuqot* (*Revealer of Profundities*) and which was termed *Baculus Jacob* (*Jacob's staff*) by his Christian contemporaries, is described in detail in chapters 4–11 of *Wars* 5.1. The material contained in these chapters was translated into Latin in 1342 at the request of Pope Clement VI and survives in a number of manuscripts. Gersonides' instrument was used to measure the heights of stars above the horizon and is described by Goldstein as follows: "the instrument consisted of a long rod along which a plate slides. To determine the angular distance between two stars, one places the staff in front of one eye with the other eye directed toward the sky, and then with the cross-plate lines up the two stars on either side of the plate. The ratio of the size of the plate in relation to its distance from the eye as measured on the staff provides the distance between the stars."[26]

Gersonides was interested in other instruments as well, including the astrolabe for which he suggested several refinements, and the *camera obscura*. This latter instrument was used by him for making observations of eclipses. Gersonides also applied

---

part 1 of *The Wars*, Gersonides reviews and criticizes astronomical theories of the day, compiles astronomical tables, and describes one of his astronomical inventions. In recent years, selections of these chapters have been edited and translated by B. Goldstein (1988).

[22] Gersonides *Wars* 1.13.   [23] Gersonides *Wars* vol. 5, 1.3:27, in Goldstein 1985a.
[24] See Goldstein, 1988, 386.
[25] Gersonides *Wars* vol. 5, chapter 51, in Goldstein 1985a; see also his Commentary on *Deuteronomy*, 213c.
[26] For further details, see Goldstein 1985a.

the principle of the *camera obscura* to make a large room into an observing chamber, taking advantage of the image cast by a window on the opposite wall.[27] Chapter 99 of Book 5, part 1 contains astronomical tables commissioned by several Christian clerics. As well as comprising a general explanation of the tables, Chapter 99 contains instructions on how to compute the mean conjunction and opposition of the moon and sun; a method for deriving the true conjunction or opposition of the moon and sun; a computation of solar time; and a discussion of eclipses, with tables for position of the moon for each day.[28]

In Book 5, part 2 of *The Wars*, which was included in most manuscripts, Gersonides deals with technical, albeit nonmathematical, issues in astronomy, such as the interspherical matter, topics concerning the diurnal sphere, the Milky Way and the movements of the planets, and how the sun heats the air. In Book 5, part 3, Gersonides examines a number of additional topics, such as the Aristotelian question of how many celestial spheres are needed to explain the movements of the heavenly bodies, and whether the velocities of the heavenly bodies are related by a commensurate number.[29]

In this context, Gersonides addresses Ptolemy's theory of cosmic distances based on a system of nested spherical planetary shells. As we saw in Chapter 6, he introduced a fluid layer ("the matter that does not keep its shape") between two successive planetary shells so that motion of one planet would not affect the motion of the planet adjacent to it. Gersonides then computed the planetary distances according to three separate theories.[30]

In short, Gersonides sees the ultimate function of astronomy is to understand God. Astronomy, he claims, can only be pursued as a science by "one who is both a mathematician and a natural philosopher, for he can be aided by both of these sciences and take from them whatever is needed to perfect his work."[31] Astronomy, he tells us, is instructive not only by virtue of its exalted subject matter, but also because of its utility to the other sciences. By studying the orbs and stars, we are led ineluctably to a fuller knowledge and appreciation of God. Astronomy thus functions as the underpinnings of the rest of the work.[32]

III Astrology and the Heavenly Bodies: Greek and Secular Antecedents

The influences of both Aristotle and Ptolemy are apparent in the controversy over astrology as well. As noted by Lemay, "astrology, during all of that time, formed an indispensable and intimate part of physical science and cosmology."[33] The vehement condemnation of astrology, starting in the late twelfth century, by leaders of all three Abrahamic traditions, should give us pause. The condemnation of astrology among the church schoolmen is well known. By 1277, numerous propositions concerning

---

[27] These and other topics are discussed in Goldstein 1985b. See also Feldman 2010.
[28] See Goldstein 1974, for details of this table.   [29] Gersonides *Wars* vol. 3, 5.3.
[30] Gersonides *Wars* vol. 3, 5.3.   [31] Gersonides *Wars* vol. 5, 1.1:23, in Goldstein 1985a.
[32] See Gersonides *Wars* vol. 3, 5.14:192, where Gersonides extols the science of astronomy as the apex of the sciences.
[33] Lemay 1987, 58.

astrology were condemned by Bishop Tempier in the Latin west. Lemay sees the Condemnations of 1277 as reflective of "a genuine revulsion against the Western dependence on the Arabs in the field of science and natural philosophy since the beginning of the twelfth century."[34] These included the following propositions:

94 (195)   That fate, which is a universal disposition, proceeds from the divine providence not immediately but by the mediation of the movement of the heavenly bodies

104 (143)   That by different signs in the heavens there are signified different conditions in men both of their spiritual gifts and of their temporal affairs

105 (207)   That in the hour of the begetting of a man in his body and consequently in his soul, which follows the body, by the ordering of causes superior and inferior there is in a man a disposition inducing him to such and such actions and events. This is an error unless it is understood to mean "natural events" and "by way of a disposition"

106 (206)   That anyone attribute health and sickness, life and death, to the position of the stars and the aspect of Fortune, saying that if Fortune is well-aspected to him he will live, and if not, he will die

154 (162)   That our will is subject to the power of the heavenly bodies

156 (161)   That the effects of the stars on free will are hidden.[35]

Major scholastic figures who discussed astrology during the period before and after the Condemnations included Albertus Magnus (c. 1193–1280), Roger Bacon (c. 1214/20–c. 1292) and Thomas Aquinas (1225–74). Albertus Magnus saw astrology as a valid and useful science, but argued that human reason and will were free from stellar control. Similarly, in his Opus Maius, Roger Bacon accepted the influence of the stars on the body but not on the soul. In part four of Opus Maius he cites Aristotle, Avicenna, Ptolemy and the noted Arabic astrologer Abû Mâ'âshar as authorities with respect to judicial astrology, recognizing that the heavenly bodies do assert an influence upon natural events. He denies, however, that this influence imposes absolute necessity upon human will.[36] The very listing of these propositions is evidence of the popularity of astrological prediction not only among the general populace, but among the schoolmen as well.

But astrology was attacked by Jewish philosophers a century or so earlier. Maimonides' trenchant rejection of astrology occurred against a culture that, at least prima facie, did not eliminate either natural or judicial astrology from theoretical considerations. In his Letter on Astrology, addressed to the rabbis of southern France, Maimonides adduces several sorts of considerations in opposition to astrology.[37] For our purposes, however, the very fact that Maimonides was called upon to legislate upon this issue is evidence of the popularity of astrology among twelfth-century Provençal Jews. But, as scholars of Jewish philosophy are well aware, Maimonides'

---

[34] Lemay 1987, 71.   [35] Mandonnet 1908, 175ff.
[36] See Hackett 1997; Bacon 1928, Opus Maius part 4.
[37] For details of this letter, see Maimonides 1926; Marx 1934–5; Rudavsky 2010.

letter had little effect. Barely a generation later, Gersonides' works evince an explicit belief in astrology. Take, for example, the following statement from his *Prognostication for 1345*:

Levi ben Gerson said: By experience and much investigation it became clear to the ancients that changes in this lower world emanate from the stars, more so for the human species than for the other composite [substances].

Therefore it is necessary to look at the implications [of the stellar influences] for the future so that [this investigation] will direct men to take counsel concerning evil so that it will not occur, and concerning good so that it will occur, as perfectly as possible. This is the entire fruit of the science of judgments, and in this way it is possible for a man to change what is implied by the decree of the stars, namely, [first,] things related to free will and, second, [things dependent on] divine providence...[38]

Can we account for both the attraction and repulsion generated by the view that the heavenly bodies had direct causal efficacy upon human events in the sublunar world? In 1955 the scholar Lynn Thorndike reminded us that "during the long period of scientific development before Sir Isaac Newton promulgated the universal law of gravitation, there had been generally recognized and accepted another and different universal natural law, which his supplanted. And that universal natural law was astrological."[39] The validity of nativities depended on the underlying assumption that the natural order was governed and directed by the movement of the heavens and the celestial bodies, and that humans were also naturally under their rule. Thorndike takes issue with those who argue that it was Newton who introduced the idea of universal laws of becoming and change as "an entirely new and seminal idea which was destined to revolutionize the natural sciences." According to Thorndike, "surely astrology had for centuries before believed in universal laws which governed particular events."[40]

The Stoic concept of universal "sympathy," which is so fundamental to causal and ethical theory, was to become the first axiom of philosophical astrology—the idea that natural signs revealed the ordered nature of the cosmos and provided information and materials for living accordingly. But no texts actually associate the Stoics Zeno or Cleanthes with astrological divination. The most famous case is that of Chrysippus' example that "if someone is born at the rising of the Dog Star, he will not die at sea," found in Cicero's *De Fato*.

Greek astrology most likely developed in the second century BCE and reflected several seminal texts in Aristotle. Aristotle and astrologers agreed: that the heavens and celestial bodies were incorruptible and unchanging; that their motions were regular and eternal, circular and perfect; that all the sublunar processes corresponded to the movements and positions of the heavenly bodies; and most important for our purposes, that the heavenly bodies were responsible for all meteorological phenomena, caused tides, affected all generation on earth, formed gems of underground rocks, etc.

---

[38] Gersonides *Prognostication*, quoted in Goldstein and Pingree 1990, 11.
[39] Thorndike 1955, 273.   [40] Ibid., 275.

Aristotle thus provided the intellectual basis for the view that the heavenly region excelled over the terrestrial. In *De Caelo* and other works he provided a series of arguments contrasting the eternal, incorruptible, uniform circular motions of celestial bodies with the natural, non-uniform and finite rectilinear motions of the four elementary terrestrial bodies.[41] Other important passages include *De Generatione et Corruptione* II.10, a fundamental text for those who tried to justify astrology in the scholastic tradition; and *Meteorologica*, where he discusses phenomena in the upper reaches of the sublunar region, where the Sun is given pride of place.

Ptolemy built on Aristotle's distinction, assuming that "a certain power emanating from the eternal ethereal substance is dispersed through and permeates the whole region of the earth, which throughout is subject to change."[42] The behaviors of the sun and moon exemplified this influence.[43] Depending on a complex set of relationships, planets and stars could cause either beneficial or harmful effects; by a combination of observation and theory, it was possible to know when and where these effects would occur.[44] Thus Ptolemy argues that if we know the movements and natures of celestial bodies, and we can deduce scientifically the qualities resulting from a combination of these factors, we should be able to predict both weather and human character.[45] Freudenthal notes that this justification of astrology on the basis of natural science permitted astrologers to maintain that their discipline was not opposed to the claims of science.[46] Furthermore, the relative positions of the planets to one another (their aspects) play an important role: "Then too, their [the planets'] aspects to another, by meeting and mingling of their dispensations, bring about many complicated changes."[47]

Ptolemy's position was quite compatible with the Stoic supposition of a universal harmony and sympathy. As noted above, the Stoic theory of astrological influence rested on the belief that the universe was a single organism, all of whose material parts interrelated through the activity of a cosmic spirit: the cosmos is a unified regulated system in which all being was interlinked. Stoic influences include a certain power (*dunamis*) that emanates from the aether, causing changes in the sublunar elements. The effluence from the sun and moon affect both animate and inanimate things, while the planets and stars have their effects as well. In referring to what he calls the "astrologization of the Aristotelian doctrine" in the Middle Ages to explain the influence of the sun upon sublunar existents, Freudenthal refers to the divine force by virtue of which reflected rays of light generate heat, and notes that this divine force may be traceable back to the Stoic theory of *pneuma*.[48] We thus find in the ancients the main ingredients for a philosophical, naturally grounded theory of astrology according to which the heavenly bodies exerted a causal influence upon events in the sublunar world.

By the mid-twelfth century, the basic works of astronomy and astrology had been translated from the Arabic, including works of Aristotle, Ptolemy, and Abû

---

[41] See Aristotle *De Caelo* 1.3.270b1–14; *Metaphysics* 1074b.1–14; *NE* 6.7.1141b.1–2.
[42] Ptolemy 1940, *Tetrabiblos* 1.2, 5–7.   [43] See Ptolemy 1940, *Tetrabiblos* 1.7.
[44] Ptolemy 1940, *Tetrabiblos* 1.11–13.   [45] Ptolemy 1940, *Tetrabiblos* 1.2.
[46] See Freudenthal 2000.   [47] Ptolemy 1940, *Tetrabiblos* 1:2, 8–9.
[48] See Freudenthal 2000, 43.

Mâ'âshar. That the sun and moon both affect natural cycles and events on earth is unequivocal and represents a classic paradigm of natural astrology. The calculations of natural astrology overlapped those of astronomy, and could be utilized for practical purposes such as fixing the calendar. According to astrologers, each planet and sign of the zodiac has its own character, power and attributes. Inasmuch as the characters of the planets and the signs of the zodiac are opposed to each other, they are engaged in a perpetual power struggle. Thus the position of the planets and their interrelation with the signs of the zodiac, regulate the fate of both individuals and nations. From the perspective of medieval scholars, astrology was construed and accepted as a science from the second to the seventeenth centuries.

Two questions arose concerning the coherence of judicial astrology. The first had to do with the extent to which the celestial bodies exerted an influence over human events in general, or more particularly, over those actions that entail human choice. The second question had to do with the extension of judicial astrology to universal historical events, which by their nature subsumed the individual. But judicial astrology became controversial for religious authorities, for while judicial astrology was derisively dismissed in the Bible, identified with idolatry and pagan star worship,[49] on the other hand it was an accepted science that permeated ordinary life.

In the Latin West, we find newly invented labels taken from the Arabic: science of the stars (scientia stellarum) refers to both astronomy and astrology, dealing with the entire heavens; "science of the movements" (scientia motuum) dealing with astronomy; and "science of the judgments" (scientia iudiciorum) for judicial astrology.[50] These terms can be traced to the opening lines of Abû Mâ'âshar's Introductorium Maius in Astronomiam (Introduction to Astronomy), which was translated into Latin by John of Seville in 1133, and quoted by Albertus Magnus in his Speculum Astronomiae. Abû Mâ'âshar's work in astrology provided for Latin scholars a new terminology for distinguishing astronomy from judicial astrology. Abû Mâ'âshar defined astrology as the "knowledge of the effects of the powers of the stars, at a given time, as well as the future time." Not until the thirteenth century was a distinction made between them, when astrology was shifted to refer to the applied physical sciences.

IV Astrology in the Jewish world

Let us turn now to the contentious role of astrology in Jewish thought. Most Jewish philosophers supported natural astrology, the view that the celestial bodies affect sublunar life and existence to some extent. The calculations of natural astrology overlapped those of astronomy, and could be utilized for practical purposes such as fixing the calendar. The real question, then, concerns the coherence of judicial astrology, that is, the extent to which the stars and planets exerted an influence over human events in general, or more particularly, over those actions that entail human choice.

---

[49] See 2 Kings 17:16; 2 Kings 23:5; Jeremiah 7:18; Jeremiah 8:2; Jeremiah 10:2; Jeremiah 44:17–19; Isaiah 14:12; 47:13; Amos 5:26.
[50] Lemay 1987, 64.

On the one hand, judicial astrology was derisively dismissed in the Bible, identified with idolatry and pagan star worship. Two passages in Scripture explicitly prohibit the study of the stars: *Deuteronomy* 4:19 "Beware, when you look up into the heavens and see all the host of the heavens, the sun, moon and stars, that you do not let yourselves be allured into paying homage to them," and *Deuteronomy* 17:3 "[one who has] paid homage to them [alien gods] namely, the sun, or the moon, or the whole host of the heavens, which I prohibited." Other passages, as noted above, indirectly deplore the science of astrology.

On the other hand, astrology was recognized as an accepted science that permeated ordinary life. In rabbinic texts, there are passing references to divination by means of planets. The rabbis were especially ambivalent about the role played by astrology. Most Talmudic sages recognized the role played by the celestial bodies in determining human affairs, as evidenced by numerous Talmudic passages that attribute astrological consultation in approving terms. Every person was seen to have a patron star (*mazal*) that determined his destiny. On occasion, natural events could be traced to astrological signs: further, individuals born under a specific planet were said to exhibit the qualities popularly assigned to that planet.

The effect of these astrological motifs can be seen explicitly in perhaps one of the most influential works in medieval Jewish cosmology, the *Sefer Yeẓirah*, a mystical commentary upon *Genesis*. Early Jewish philosophers, faced with a variety of philosophical cosmogonies—Kalâm, Aristotelian, Neoplatonic—commented extensively upon *Sefer Yeẓirah*, possibly because it offered what they considered an "authentic Jewish response, compatible with at least some of the philosophic theories, to the question of cosmogony."[51] As we move into the philosophical literature of the twelfth century, astrological references proliferate. Many philosophers considered astrology as a genuine science. These included, in addition to the *Sefer Yeẓirah* commentaries of Saadiah Gaon, Shabbetai Donnolo, and Solomon ibn Gabirol, and the works of such thinkers as Abraham ibn Ezra and Abraham Bar Ḥiyyah. Maimonides is the most vehement opponent of astrology, seconded by Joseph Albo in the fourteenth century. Ibn Ezra and Halevi represent, along with Ibn Daud, the culmination of Jewish philosophy in the twelfth century; of the three, Ibn Ezra is the most unabashed supporter of astrology.

Contained in the *Sefer Yeẓirah* is an elaborate cosmological scheme that can be summarized briefly as follows. The twenty-two letters of the Hebrew alphabet, along with the ten *Sefirot*, the numbers one to ten, comprise the foundation of the creation process. The first four *Sefirot* stand for the power of God, the transmutation of divine spirit into air, the emergence of water from air, and the emergence of fire from water. *Sefirot* five through ten describe the six possible dimensions or directions of the created universe. The twenty-two letters are the "foundation letters" out of which the universe is created by an intricate process of combination and permutation.

In order to actuate this creation process, the letters are grouped into "three books," that is, groups of letters grouped according to their special functions. The first group, the "mother letters" *'alef, mem* and *shin*, are the prime constituents of everything else

---

[51] Jospe 1990, 376.

in the universe. The "doubles," which include *bet, gimel, dalet, kaf, peh, resh,* and *tav,* become the basis for the creation of the planets. And the "simples," which comprise the remaining twelve letters, constitute the twelve months of the year, as well as the twelve signs of the zodiac, which are associated with the twelve vital organs of the human body.[52]

In the context of this cosmological description, then, we see that several astrological passages emerge as the basis for subsequent commentary. The first includes such topics as the relationship of the seven Hebrew consonants that take a *dagesh* to the seven planets and seven days of the week: "Seven Doubles: BGD KPRT of Foundation, he engraved them, he carved them, he permuted them, he weighed them, he transformed them, And with them he formed, Seven planets in the Universe, Seven days in the Week, Seven gates in the Soul, male and female."[53] Each of the letters corresponds to a specific heavenly sphere, day of the week, and psychological characteristic. The letter *kaf,* for example, is associated with the planet Venus, with Wednesday, and with the "left eye in the Soul."[54] Each letter, then, can be used to influence the part of the body with which it is associated. The second astrological section pertains to the twelve simple consonants with which "He formed twelve constellations in the Universe, twelve months in the Year, and twelve directors in the Soul, male and female."[55] The signs of the zodiac are associated with the twelve Hebrew lunar months (rather than with the position of the sun as in Western astrology). A final astrological passage has to do with the power of the *teli.* The twenty-two letters form a triad which is represented by the dragon (*teli*), the sphere, and the heart.[56] This dragon has extraordinary astrological powers.[57]

These astrological passages in the *Sefer Yezirah* have given rise to a rich commentary tradition. Both Saadiah Gaon and Shabbetai Donnolo wrote extensive commentaries upon *Sefer Yezirah,* emphasizing astrological passages in this work. Saadiah Gaon wrote an Arabic commentary in the late ninth or early tenth century.[58] Another influential commentary, called *Sefer Ḥakhmoni,* was written by the Italian physician Shabbetai Donnolo (913 to after 982).[59] While a full examination of this commentary tradition is beyond the scope of this study, let me emphasize one passage that especially interested philosophers. This is the passage mentioned above, having to do with the threefold reading of the term "*sefer*": "He created his world by three *sefarim, s-f-r-, s-f-r,* and *s-f-r-.*"[60] This passage reappears in many philosophical contexts. Saadiah's commentary canonizes the reading, which is adapted by many subsequent thinkers.

---

[52] For a succinct study of the *Sefer Yetzirah,* see Scholem 2007, 782–8. A translation of the work can be found in Kaplan 1997.

[53] *Sefer Yetzirah* 4:6.   [54] *Sefer Yetzirah* 4:11.   [55] *Sefer Yetzirah* 5:3.

[56] *Sefer Yetzirah* 6:1. "He set them in the Teli, the Cycle, and the Heart."

[57] From the mention of the *teli,* Pines suggests that the astronomical views of the group within which the *Sefer Yetzirah* originated may have been influenced by Syriac Christian milieu. Cf. Pines 1989, 111.

[58] See the following editions of Saadia Gaon's commentary: *Sefer Yetzirah 'im Perush Rabbenu Sa'adia ben Yosef Fayyumi (Ga'on),* Arabic text edited with Hebrew translation by Yosef Kafih (Jerusalem 1972); *Commentaire sur le Sefer Yesira,* translated by Mayer Lambert (Paris, repr. 1986).

[59] Donnolo's commentary can be found in *Il Commento di Sabbatai Donnolo sul Libro della Creazione,* ed. D. Castelli Firenze, 1880 (Heb. Sec). Selected passages and critical discussion can be found in Sharf 1976.

[60] *Sefer Yetzirah* 1:1.

He created the world by three things, writing, number and speech ... I interpret *sefer* as writing as it says (*Daniel* 1:4): "To teach them the writing and language of the Chaldeans". *Sfar* means quantity and number, as it says about Solomon (II *Chronicles* 2:16): "After the numbering which David his father has counted."[61]

The third would be *sippur*, which Saadiah Gaon does not bother to mention, presumably because it was so obvious. Saadiah then continues to explain the three in terms of speech, writing, and thought.[62]

Interestingly enough, Halevi interprets the reference further; stripping it of mystical or poetical nuance, Halevi "was the first to interpret the three *sefarim* of our passage in light of a basic doctrine of Aristotelian rationalism: the unity of the subject, act, and object of intellection."[63] In *Kuzari* 4:25, Halevi refers to *Sefer Yeẓirah*, "the 'Book of Creation' by the Patriarch Abraham," and explains the terms *s'far*, *sefer* and *sipur* in terms of will, writing and speaking. In the case of God, the three are a unity inasmuch as God's will, speech, and act are one and the same. With respect to humans, however, the three are non-identical: "Man's will, writing and word are marks of the thing, but not the nature of the same."[64]

Ibn Gabirol refers to *Sefer Yeẓirah* indirectly in *Mekor Ḥayyim* in the following passage: "And so we shall say that the composition of the world arose from the arrangement of number and letters in the air."[65] The allusion is not fleshed out, however, and the implications of creation by number and letters are not developed further. In his poems, however, Gabirol is more explicit. In his poem *Shokhen 'Ad*, recited by some Sephardic communities on *Rosh Hashanah*, Ibn Gabirol refers to the *Sefirot* as well as to the *'Ein-sof*: "he decided to reveal the set of ten *Sefirot*/And he wrote Ten corresponding to them in the *'Ein-Sof*."[66] He refers as well to the "three books":

> He who dwelleth forever, exalted is he alone from of yore
> Solitary in his royal grandeur is he, and there is none by his side
> From the light in which he is cloaked he fashioned the universe
> In the manner of the three sealed books.[67]

From these lines, it is clear that the universe is an emanation from God, or more specifically from the light in which God is cloaked. The three sealed books may very well refer to the three books in *Sefer Yeẓirah*, corresponding to the letters *s/f/r*, namely *sofer*, *sipur*, and *sefer*. Zangwill suggests as well that they may refer to *Meqor Ḥayyim* 5.62 in which Gabirol compares Form to the script, and Matter to

---

[61] Saadiah Gaon *Commentary* (ed. Kafih), 35–6; quoted in Jospe 1990, 389.

[62] For a history of subsequent commentaries and appropriation of Saadiah's conception, see Jospe, 1990, 390ff.

[63] Cf. Jospe 1990, 394, for an elaboration of this identification and its importance for subsequent epistemological and psychological doctrines in Maimonides.

[64] Halevi *Kuzari* 4:25. The apparent uniqueness of Halevi's reading is discussed in Jospe 1990.

[65] See Ibn Gabirol *Mekor Ḥayyim* 2:21.

[66] In his 1982 article, Idel suggests the existence of ten *Sefirot* above the usual set of *Sefirot*. Pines suggests that it is these *Sefirot* which are mentioned by Ibn Gabirol in his poem "*Shokhen 'ad me-'az*"; see Pines 1989, 123, for a discussion of this point.

[67] Ibn Gabirol, "*Shokhen 'ad me-'az*," in Yarden 1973, vol. 1, 9.

the tablet upon which the writing is engraved. On this reading the *sefarim* refer to entities which are accountable for the creation of the universe, namely, Will, Form, and Matter; these in turn may be compared to the three agencies involved in the writing of a book—the scribe, script, and scroll—again alluding to *Sefer Yeẓirah*.[68]

Gabirol's masterpiece poem *Keter Malkhut* incorporates the basic elements of Ptolemy's *Planetary Hypotheses*: a series of concentric spheres around the earth, with the five planets, moon and sun, the Zodiac, and a ninth diurnal sphere that imparts motion to all the other spheres. In *Cento* X, the earth is described as an orb with the moon and four elements encircling it. The moon excites new events in our world every month, but Gabirol cautions that "Always her own Creator's will she heeds," noting that astrological influences are subject to divine will.[69] *Cento* XII describes the lunar eclipse, which again shows that "a Judge keeps them controlled/ Who raiseth one and brings another low." Gabirol then mentions the *Teli*, the mythological serpent that swallows heavenly bodies and causes their eclipse. The sun was created as a time-keeper:

> What mind could grasp thy greatness, how the Sun
> To be a timekeeper Thou hast designed
> To count the days, as into years they run,
> Each instant fixed, each period defined;
> And make the fruit-trees bud, beneath the bland
> Spell of Orion's band/And genial Pleiades, for richest yield.[70]

After describing Jupiter, Mars, and Saturn, Gabirol turns to the Zodiac, whose signs have a power to affect sublunar events:

> And power resides
> In those signs, whence that potency doth flow
> That each created thing can wield below
> Each after its own kind.[71]

The signs of the Zodiac function as "mansions palatine" to the planets. In all these passages, Gabirol emphasizes that the influences that flow through the planets to the sublunar sphere do so at the will of their Creator.[72] In *Cento* XXIV Gabirol introduces a tenth sphere, "the sphere of mind—Intelligence, the palace court most nigh/ Unto Thyself." This tenth sphere, which serves as the location of intelligence, is Gabirol's own introduction. From this sphere, the stuff of souls and angels ("psyches of highest rate") is made.[73]

By the twelfth and thirteenth centuries, most philosophers supported at least a weak form of natural astrology. Take for example Abraham Bar Ḥiyya who represented the thorough integration of astrology into the Jewish world view, due to the work of a number of Hispano-Jewish thinkers, including Abraham ibn Ezra, Judah Halevi, and Bar Ḥiyya himself. Y. Tzvi Langermann argues that within eleventh- and

---

[68] See Pessin 2013 for discussion of these passages.   [69] Ibn Gabirol *Keter Malkhut* Cento XI.
[70] Ibn Gabirol *Keter Malkhut* Cento XVI.   [71] Ibn Gabirol *Keter Malkhut* Cento XXII.
[72] See Loewe 1979, 184.
[73] Ibn Gabirol, *Keter Malkhut* Cento XXV; see a similar discussion in *Meqor Ḥayyim* V.1.

twelfth-century Hispanic Jewry, astrology provided the "chief mechanism for rational/ naturalist explanations of the concepts and phenomena of concern to religious thought."[74] Maimonides is the most vehement opponent of astrology, seconded by Joseph Albo in the fourteenth century.

As we have noted in Chapter 2, Abraham ibn Ezra's astrological works form the largest bulk of his scientific output and cover all the main branches of astrology, including textbooks, specialized treatises on nativities, elections, interrogations, medical astrology, and general astrology. This corpus consists of the following works: *Reshit Ḥokhmah*; *Mishpetei ha-Mazzalot*; *Sefer ha-Te'amim*; *Sefer ha-Moladot*; *Mivḥarim*; *She'elot*; *Me'orot*; and *Sefer ha-Olam*. He rewrote many of these works and offered different versions of them.

Ibn Ezra's major astrological work *Reshit Ḥokhma* (*Beginning of Wisdom*) was completed in approximately June 1148 in Beziers (Provence). Conceived primarily as a textbook explaining the basic tenets of astrology, the work is divided into ten chapters dealing with three main subjects: general description of the fixed stars, zodiac constellations, and their astrological characteristics; general description of the planets and their astrological characteristics; miscellaneous astrological concepts. Ibn Ezra considered it his chief astrological work and referenced it often. *Sefer ha-Te'amim* (*Book of Reasons*) was composed shortly after *Reshit Ḥokhma* in order to explain the underlying astrological reasons for the raw data; it appeared two years later in a second, and quite different, version.

In the second version of his *Sefer ha-Te'amim*, Ibn Ezra draws a sharp distinction between astronomy and astrology. The former is endowed with "clear scientific status" in contrast to the latter that is demoted to the rank of an "art" that relies on analogy or proofs that derive from experience.[75] Ibn Ezra believed that all beings in the sublunar world were influenced by the configurations of the stars and the zodiac, and most humans were enslaved by the power of the planets. He introduces the new term *hokmat ha-mazzalot* (wisdom of the stars) to refer to the science of the zodiacal signs. That the celestial powers affect human affairs is stated explicitly in *Reshit Ḥokhma*: the moon, for example, "influences every deliberation and the beginning of any task." If, for example, the moon is in ascendancy and its circumstances favorable, "anything which one may start at that moment will meet with success."[76]

Ibn Ezra's biblical commentaries invoke astrological themes as well. In discussing why the Israelites made the golden calf, for example, Ibn Ezra appeals to astrological explanations: "The astrologers say that the great conjunction of the two upper bodies was in the constellation of Taurus. This is a lie. The conjunction took place in Aquarius. According to the science of astrology, this is Israel's constellation. Many have tested this secret, generation after generation. I too have seen this to be the case."[77] What this means is that Israel's luck improves when the heavenly upper bodies are propitiously aligned in Aquarius. We shall return to the significance of this view below.

---

[74] Langermann 1999, 29.   [75] Sela 2003, 93.   [76] *Reshit Ḥokhma*, chapter 8:215.
[77] *Exodus* 31:18, in Ibn Ezra 1988, vol. 2, 663.

In an extended comment to *Exodus* 3:15, Ibn Ezra lays out his cosmological scheme, which includes an astrological component. Adhering to the standard medieval distinction between three worlds (the lower world, middle world, and upper world), he focuses upon the celestial objects in the middle world: the five ministering stars (Mercury, Venus, Mars, Jupiter, and Saturn), the sun and moon, and the stars that make up the constellations, which are a level above the five planetary objects. Ibn Ezra describes the order of the constellations and then maintains that "the inhabitants of the lower world are affected by them in accordance with their makeup." There are one hundred and twenty possible conjunctions in each one of the three hundred and sixty degrees. It is due to the irregular movements of the planets that "different things happen to man's body and certainly to his fortune in this lower world." Further, man's soul as well "receives power from above in accordance to the arrangement of the ministers, that is, the arrangement of each 'minister' *vis à vis* the great hosts at the time of a person's birth."[78]

Reflecting the doctrine of climatology found in Ptolemy's *Tetrabiblos* II, Ibn Ezra argues that individuals having similar horoscopes, but living in different climates, or having different nationalities, will meet distinct fates. In a number of texts, Ibn Ezra says that climate is a strong variable in the determination of astrological forecasts. The only exception to strict astrological determination occurs when one "cleaves to and is protected by a power that is higher and more powerful than the stars."[79] As an example of intervention on the part of divine providence, Ibn Ezra gives the example of a river destined (by the stars) to overflow and destroy the inhabitants of a certain town. If the people in that town turn to God with all their hearts, God might "put it into their hearts" to leave the city on the very day that the river overflowed, "as is its nature." It turns out that the river flooded the city, but the people were saved. In this case, "Now God's decree was not altered and He saved them."[80] And so Ibn Ezra maintains that astrological determinism can work in conjunction with providence to avert an evil decree. But still Ibn Ezra has not accounted for human action, and the extent of human possibility, within the context of astrological determinism.

V   Astrological Determinism and Human Freedom: Ibn Ezra, Maimonides and Gersonides

We have emphasized the allure represented by astrology, rooted in both Aristotelian and Ptolemaic science. Yet astrology provides a challenge to Jewish belief, which emphasizes moral responsibility and human choice. Does astrological determinism circumscribe human freedom; that is, to what extent can an individual exhibit free choice in light of astrological determinism? The issue is even more complex than the straightforward problem of divine omniscience, providence, and human freedom, for even God's providence can be seen as answerable to the astrological configurations; and if God is subject to the celestial order, how much more so for humans. More specifically, God's providence and omnipotence may be seriously challenged and

---

[78] *Exodus* 3:15, in Ibn Ezra 1988, vol. 2, 89–90.
[79] E.g., *Ecclesiastes* 1:12; *Psalms* 87:5–6; *Exodus* 25:40; Ibn Ezra 1988, 701.   [80] Ibid., 702.

undermined by the claim that the heavenly bodies autonomously shape the earth and determine the fate of both its natural environment and its creatures. Philosophers sympathetic to astrology in all three traditions had to grapple with the challenge to human freedom, and had to provide responses to more libertarian positions that upheld modal possibility and human freedom.

The importance of mastering the passions in order to circumvent the influence of the heavenly bodies was emphasized by a number of thinkers.[81] Recognizing the importance of stellar influences upon human destiny, Ibn Ezra emphasizes that some humans are immune from the decrees of the heavenly bodies. The ability to contravene astral decree is broached in his introduction to *Reshit Hokhmah*, in which he argues as follows:

The fear of the Lord is the beginning of wisdom (*Psalms* 111:10); that is the foundation... furthermore, the fear of the Lord protects him from the ordinances of heaven and their dominion on the earth (*Job* 38:33) all the days of his life... Now I shall begin to explain the ordinances of heaven (*Job* 38:33), employing the method of astrology as the ancients have experimented generation after generation.[82]

In this passage, Ibn Ezra emphasizes not only the "ordinances of heaven and their dominion," but also that humans who follow the proper regimen are protected from these ordinances. More specifically, though, it is the science of astrology that permits knowledge of impending disaster, and thus enables humans to take appropriate precautionary measures. One way for humans to free themselves of the dictates of the stars is by perfecting themselves spiritually. This motif is developed in a number of contexts. Noting several biblical passages (e.g., *Isaiah* 63:17; 1 *Kings* 18:37), which imply that humans have no free will, Ibn Ezra counters these passages by claiming that "every intelligent person has the power to choose good and the bad."[83] Take for example the case of Noah: "One should not argue and ask, 'How can God change the laws of heaven?' For lo and behold the account of Noah shows this to be the case."[84] What's interesting in this passage, of course, is the conflation of astrological determination and divine providence.

In his comments on *Exodus* 3:15, Ibn Ezra adopts a deterministic stance and admits that a human being's soul "receives superior power in accordance to the configuration of the planets." But then he concedes that if the soul grows wise, it "will share the secrets of the angels and will be able to receive great power from an upper power that received it from the light of the angels. The person will then cleave to God the glorious."[85] As long as a Jew is engaged in study of Torah, he is linked to a spiritual realm that is superior to the stars. In this way, Jews can liberate themselves from stellar decrees.

The wisdom of the soul, and its ability to contravene astrological decrees, thus becomes a crucial underlying motif for Ibn Ezra and is embedded in a larger mechanism of overriding of the stars. In his introduction to *Sefer ha-Moladot* Ibn Ezra notes that "universal [astrological] judgments override particular [astrological]

---

[81] See Rudavsky 2010 for discussion of these traditions.   [82] Ibn Ezra 1939, intro.
[83] *Yesod Morah* in Ibn Ezra 1995, 100.   [84] Ibid., 99.   [85] Ibn Ezra 1988, vol. 2, 90.

judgments, with respect to which I now present eight rules."[86] These universal judgments arise from a study of "superior science," by which he means a comprehensive science comprising the most general laws of nature. Only by studying this more theoretical science can the student of astrology recognize that "universal judgments" can on occasion override "particular judgments."[87] Because of the intricacy of this science, and the fact that universal judgments must be balanced against the particular judgments, astrologers are known to make mistakes: "every scholar learning the science of the zodiacal signs who is not acquainted with the superior science will sometimes be found to have made erroneous astrological judgments."[88]

Ibn Ezra distinguishes two types of wise soul: one who is a "scholar in the science of the zodiacal signs" and one who "trusts in God with all his heart." Although both can avoid disasters, it turns out that the latter is more protected than the former:

Likewise, he who trusts in God with all his heart, God ... will, for him, bring about the proper causes to save him from any harm prognosticated in his horoscope. Therefore, there is no doubt that the righteous person is more protected than the scholar regarding the judgments coming from the stars, since sometimes the scholar's acuteness of judgment will be faulty...[89]

A scholar, for example, might combine his astrological expertise with medical knowledge. First, he casts a horoscope and prognosticates the future astrological event that will cause him physical harm (e.g., coming down with fever). Then he combines this knowledge with his medical knowledge to neutralize the decree; by applying the theory of the four humors, and maintaining the balance in his body, for example, he can avoid the fever. In his commentary on *Exodus* 23:25, Ibn Ezra writes

Note that what befalls human beings depends on the alignment of the planets and what their arrangement indicates at the time of a person's birth. But this can be averted. If a person who is born under an arrangement of the planets that determines that he will have a physical makeup that is unable to beget children cleaves to God, then if he truly cleaves to God, the revered God will strengthen the power of this man's kidneys and see to it that his sperm functions properly so that he will be able to have children.[90]

Thus on Ibn Ezra's view, if we observe the Torah, we can circumvent the causal efficacy of the heavenly bodies. Similarly, in *Exodus* 6:3, in the context of discussing the secret meaning of the name *El Shaddai*, Ibn Ezra turns to the relationship between the soul and God. If the soul

is wise and recognizes the works of God, both those done without an intermediary and those done via an intermediary and if the soul forsakes the pleasures of this lowest world and separates itself from them to cleave to God the glorious, should there be at the time of the birth of such a person an arrangement of the stars indicating that evil will befall this man on a certain day, the God to whom this man cleaves will set the chain of events in such a way that this man

---

[86] Ibn Ezra *Sefer ha-Moladot*, in Sela 2003, 347–8.
[87] Sela 2003, 147; note that Ptolemy makes the same point in *Tetrabiblos*.   [88] Ibid.
[89] Ibid., 173.   [90] In Ibn Ezra 1988, vol. 2, 517.

is saved from the evil that was destined to befall him. Similarly, if it is in the arrangement of the stars that this man be sterile, God will make him virile and he will sire children.[91]

Based on these examples, we can posit a hierarchy in which astrological determinism is ultimately overshadowed by divine providence. Ultimately, it is God, utilizing the heavenly bodies, who determines a person's future. By following the Torah, a person can mitigate the evil decree, and God might intervene on his behalf, and contravene the astrological determination. Although Ibn Ezra has not attacked the issue of free will head-on, he at least hints that, at least in the case of a pious Jews, human actions are not fully determined.

But the rabbis found Ibn Ezra's support of astrology troubling, and as a result, they forwarded to Maimonides a letter in which they articulated their fears that astrological doctrines threatened to undermine belief in divine providence. The rabbis quote the *responsa* of Rabbis Sherira and Hai who distinguished two types of astrologers. The first (representing hard astrology) attributes all human actions to the stars: even "a man's movements and even his inner thoughts depend on the stars." These astrologers do not acknowledge God's role at all in the human order, and so they (according to the rabbis) are therefore eliminated from consideration.[92] The second type of astrologer maintains that humans can contravene the stars—a person can "by means of his knowledge, overcome what has been predetermined by the stars."[93] In this form of soft determinism, both the causal power of the stars and the power of human will are maintained.

Taking the hard view of astrology adduced earlier (see above), namely that "the decrees of the stars and of the zodiacal constellations are as one of the natural processes that obtain in the world since the day when God created man," the rabbis conclude that such a view "deters people from believing in the Torah and slams the door before those who put their faith in prayers."[94] Such a position (hard astrological determinism) reinforces the futility of human action and "destroys the foundations of faith by positing astrology as an immovable peg."[95] The rabbis therefore ask of Maimonides whether the astrologers in fact know the future, and whether it is possible to protect oneself from evil by asking the advice of an astrologer. After quoting a series of examples taken directly from Ibn Ezra's *Sefer ha-Moladot* (par 8), they ask: "can a scholar [well-versed in astrology] know [in advance] the beginning of all the afore-mentioned future calamities?"[96] The Provençal scholars formulate their misgivings about astrology in its hard version: that "the belief that the course of events in the world is entirely predetermined since creation induces people to think that prayer is futile."[97]

As we have seen above, according to Ibn Ezra, the only way to avoid the decrees of the stars is to circumvent them. But "natural forces" can trump astrological decrees as well. As an example of how universal judgments can trump particular ones, Ibn Ezra offers the following example:

If somebody embarks on a ship in the cold season and the sea becomes tempestuous, he will not survive, even though he took the precaution of assuring that in the ascendant

---

[91] *Exodus* 6:3, in Ibn Ezra 1988, vol. 2, 134.   [92] Ibn Ezra *Queries*, in Sela 2004, 99.
[93] Ibid., 101.   [94] Ibid., 103.   [95] Ibid., 105.   [96] Ibid., 107.   [97] Ibid., 143.

[of the horoscope] there be Jupiter and Venus, which are favorable stars. For natural power is a universal power, and the particular [configuration of the stars] that he selected will be of no avail for him.[98]

In this case, evidently, there was no reason for divine providence to intervene, presumably because the individual was totally absorbed in the astrological configuration solely (and not in Torah study?). Although the rabbis do not quote Ibn Ezra's shipwreck example directly in their letter to Maimonides, it is interesting that Maimonides uses a similar example in his own discussion of providence.

Interestingly, Maimonides never mentions Ibn Ezra's position. In his own *Letter on Astrology*, addressed to the rabbis of southern France, Maimonides adduces several sorts of considerations in opposition to astrology.[99] For Maimonides, the real philosophical issue concerns the relation *between* judicial and natural astrology. In other words, from the very real influence of the celestial beings upon sublunar reality, the question is whether judicial astrology can be postulated. In Maimonides' mind, it is this issue that directly affects theories of divine providence, retribution, and free will.

In the context of setting out his theory of divine providence, Maimonides gives the following example to support his position that divine providence watches only "over the individuals belonging to the human species" and that "divine providence is consequent upon the divine overflow":

If, as he states, the foundering of a ship and the drowning of those who were in it and the falling-down of a roof upon those who were in the house, are due to pure chance, the fact that the people in the ship were on board and that the people in the house were sitting in it is according to our opinion, not due to chance but to divine will in accordance with the deserts of those people as determined in His judgments...[100]

Maimonides' point is that divine providence is directed toward those who have perfected their intellect, and hence in his mind it is clear that those who went down with the ship were not protected by providence. It is tantalizing to speculate what Ibn Ezra might have thought of Maimonides' analysis; if we follow the logic of Ibn Ezra's theory, he too might have agreed that had those who embarked on a sea journey engaged in study of Torah, they might not have perished. Ultimately though, Maimonides' critics did not find this response any more acceptable than that of Ibn Ezra, for it left unanswered the issue of why the wise and righteous in fact can be seen to suffer.[101]

Gersonides approaches this issue from a slightly different perspective. His astral determinism is explicitly developed in two contexts: in Book II of *Wars* he interweaves astrological motifs into his discussion of divine providence and prophecy, while in Book V astrology occupies a central role in the context of his cosmological speculations. Langermann emphasizes the teleological nature of astrology for Gersonides, its

---

[98] Ibn Ezra *Sefer ha-Moladot*, in Sela 2003, 349.   [99] See Marx 1926; Lerner 1968.
[100] Maimonides *Guide* 3.17:472.
[101] As noted in Chapter 5 in the context of divine providence, one cannot help think of Maimonides' own brother who died at sea. See Rudavsky and Rudavsky-Brody 2012; Ivry 2016.

chief merit being its ability to provide "teleological explanations for the wide variety of stellar motions that are observed to take place."[102] Gersonides disagrees with Maimonides over the ultimate purpose of the celestial bodies. For Maimonides, it was not possible that a greater entity, the heavens, would exist for the sake of the sublunar universe. Gersonides disagrees, maintaining that it is not inappropriate that the more noble exist for the less noble. The stars, he argues, exist for the sake of things in the sublunar world. More explicitly, the heavenly bodies are designed for the benefit of sublunar existence, and they guarantee the perpetuation of life on earth.

This teleological cosmology is spelled out in Wars II, in which Gersonides is concerned to explain how divine knowledge operates, and to what extent divine foreknowledge of future contingents affects human choice. His major thesis is that divine knowledge is predicated to a great extent upon knowledge of the heavenly bodies, which bodies are in turn "systematically directed toward his [man's] preservation and guidance so that all his activities and thoughts are ordered by them."[103] In support of this teleology, Gersonides argues that the celestial bodies have a purpose. This teleology is reflected by a "law, order and rightness" in the universe, implying the existence of an intellect that orders the nature of things: "you see that the domain of the spheres provides, in the best way possible, for the sub-lunar world."[104]

However, Gersonides must be able to account for individual variety in the sublunar realm. Inasmuch as stellar radiation is the means by which stellar influences are conveyed, the wide variety of mixtures of stellar radiation guarantees a sufficient variety of "influences" on terrestrial processes. The movers emanate from God who is construed as the "First Separate Intellect."[105] They are ordered in a rational system that governs the sublunar domain. If there were no one first intellect, Gersonides argues, the rational order we see in the heavens would be the result of chance, which is unacceptable. The agent intellect thus functions as the link between these celestial bodies and human affairs. The kinds of information it transmits are of an astronomical type, as evidenced in the following example: "it [the agent intellect] knows how many revolutions of the sun, or of the diurnal sphere, or of any other sphere [have transpired] from the time at which someone, who falls under a particular pattern, had a particular level of good or ill fortune..."[106] Gersonides goes on to explain that the information transmitted is of a general nature and does not pertain to the individual qua particular. The agent intellect serves as the repository for information communicated by the heavenly bodies. The patterns revealed in this communication between agent intellect and diviner (astrologer, prophet) are from the heavenly bodies, which themselves are endowed with intellects and so "apprehend the pattern that derives from them."[107] Each mover apprehends the order deriving from the heavenly body it moves, and not patterns that emanate from other heavenly bodies. As a result, the imaginative faculty receives the "pattern inherent in the intellects of the heavenly bodies from the influence deriving from them."[108] This influence derives from the position of the heavenly bodies "by the ascendant degree or the dominant

---

[102] Langermann, in Gersonides Wars vol. 3, 506.   [103] Gersonides Wars vol. 2, II.2:33.
[104] Gersonides Wars vol. 3, V.3.3:137.   [105] Gersonides Wars vol. 3, VI.2.10:272.
[106] Gersonides Wars vol. 2, II.6:53.   [107] Gersonides Wars vol. 3.
[108] Gersonides Wars vol. 2, II.6:64.

planet [in a particular zodiacal position]".[109] However, inasmuch as the heavenly bodies do not jointly cooperate with one another in this process, it is possible for the communication to be misconstrued.

Of course, as we all know, astrologers often err in their predictions. One of the most compelling causes lies in human free will: our intellect and choice "have the power to move us contrary to that which is determined by the heavenly bodies."[110] Although Gersonides admits that on occasion human choice is able to contravene the celestial bodies, nevertheless this intervention is rare, and true contingency is a rare state of affairs indeed in Gersonides' ontology. Gersonides presents an argument to show that human choice guided by reason can subvert the celestial bodies despite their general ordering of our lives. The heavenly bodies can order human affairs either by virtue of their difference of position in the heavens, or from the difference of the bodies among themselves. Astral bodies, however, will affect different individuals in different ways; they can also affect an individual differently at different times; and finally, two or more bodies can affect a single individual, resulting in multiple influences that can have contrary effects. Gersonides notes that humans can contravene these effects: God has provided humans with "the intellectual capacity that enables us both to act contrary to what has been ordered by the heavenly bodies and to correct, as far as possible, the [astrally ordained] misfortunes that befall us."[111] Nevertheless, he assures us that whatever happens by chance is "determined and ordered according to this type of determinateness and order."[112] Outdoing even Plato's hierarchical structuring in *Republic* IV, Gersonides argues that the ultimate perfection and ordering of society is due to astrological influence.[113]

The treatise *Prognosticon de conjunctione Saturni et Jovis et Martis* was started by Gersonides (possibly at the request of Pope Clement VI) and completed by his Latin translator, Peter of Alexander, and Levi's brother, Solomon. This work is a prediction based on the conjunction of Saturn and Jupiter to take place in March 1345. Gersonides himself died in 1344, a year before the event in question. In his prognostication, Gersonides predicts that there will be "extraordinary evil with many wars, visions and miraculous signs"; "Diseases and death, and the evil will endure for a long time"; "the absence of good, pleasure and happiness for most of the inhabited world"; "the spilling of much blood and increasing enmity, jealousy, strife, famine, various diseases, drought and dearth."[114] The Black Death, which arrived in Europe in 1347, was thus provided with numerous astrological credentials. The official statement of the medical faculty of the University of Paris, presented to the king in 1348, reported on the conjunction of Saturn and Jupiter in the house of Aquarius on March 20, 1345, which was seen to spread "death and disaster."

VI Miracles: Natural or Supernatural?

We turn now to our final question, namely how to understand miracles within the context of a naturally ordered universe. The very nature of a miracle suggests the

---

[109] Ibid.   [110] Gersonides *Wars* vol. 2, II.2:34.   [111] Gersonides *Wars* vol. 2, II.2:35.
[112] Gersonides *Wars* vol. 2, II.2:35.   [113] Gersonides *Wars* vol. 2, II.2:36.
[114] Goldstein and Pingree, 1990.

overturning of the natural order, and so miracles raise the important philosophical question: whether it is epistemically and ontologically possible to hold that the natural order of things is preserved while at the same time admitting the possibility of exceptions. To say of an event that it is *natural* means that it obeys fixed laws such that even occasional anomalies or deviations may be accounted for in strictly natural terms. To say that something is *miraculous* means that it contravenes fixed laws in a way that cannot be accounted for in strictly natural terms, but introduces an element of divine will.[115] As Roslyn Weiss has pointed out, any world view that accommodates miracles is not a world governed by the necessity of natural law: things subject to divine will cannot be natural, nor can they be "just like" natural things.[116] Most Jewish philosophers accept the veracity of miraculous events as providing evidence for God's intervention in the natural order. But to what extent is this intervention even possible? The topic of miracles renders more potent the struggles between Judaism and science. In this section, we shall briefly examine several attempts to explain the role played by miracles, ending with a famous passage in *Joshua*, which serves as paradigm example of a miraculous event.

For a philosopher who sees no limits to God's omnipotence, miracles are simply an example of God's volitional will intervening in the natural order. God's unbridled power was established already by al-Ghazâlî in *The Incoherence of the Philosophers*, his extended diatribe against the philosophers. Al-Ghazâlî provided an occasionalist explanation of miracles, arguing in effect that *all* events, insofar as they reflect the continuous recreation of the world, are miracles. It is the philosophers, he avers, that are at a loss to explain causality: "Whoever renders the habitual courses [of nature] a necessary constant makes all these [miracles] impossible."[117] Claiming that the philosophers have nothing but constant conjunction to justify their belief in causality, al-Ghazâlî rejects the Aristotelian theory of cause and effect, replacing it with God's continuous recreation: the apparent connection between "effects" and their "causes" is "due to the prior decree of God, who creates them side by side."[118]

Saadiah Gaon and Judah Halevi do not question the possibility of miracles. Saadiah discusses miracles in *Beliefs* III.4–5. He defines miracles as a change in the essence of the elements, and all of his examples are taken directly from the Bible. Based on Kalâm occasionalist principles, Saadiah sees no contradiction in God's being able to change any entity's behavior. While he emphasizes that under normal conditions the elements do follow universal laws and possess fixed essences, these essences can be changed intentionally by God. How then, does one distinguish between true and false miracles? Saadiah suggests that we must confirm the supposed miracle for its veracity: both the miraculous occurrence and the doctrine it confirms must be subjected to scientific scrutiny. Saadiah warns that nothing that clearly

---

[115] Manekin has argued in a recent article that Maimonides has two operative notions of will, eternal will and novel will, and that these affect his concept of "naturally caused action." On this reading, naturalism rules out supernatural things or events, but does not exclude the notion of ongoing divine activity. According to Manekin, Maimonides recognizes a class of divine phenomena that "are not explicable with reference to the stable nature of things," such as miracles. See Manekin 2008, 192–3.

[116] See Weiss 2007, 14, for further discussion of the implications of these characterizations.

[117] Al-Ghazâlî 1977 *Incoherence* Part II.17, Intro, 166.

[118] Al-Ghazâlî 1977 *Incoherence* Part II.17, 171.

contradicts intellectual judgment may be accepted as a miracle. We have already noted several contexts in which Halevi rejects rational or intellectual judgment in favor of experience. And so, too, in the case of miracles, the fact of miracles is upheld by the immediate authenticity of the event in question (*Kuzari* I:5); divine revelation is itself an example of such a miracle.

In a similar vein, Crescas provides another way of thinking about miracles. Crescas' return to an occasionalist ontology provides him with an effective way of explaining miraculous events that contravene the natural order. Once the "intrinsic order of nature" is denied, miracles turn out to be no different ontically than "natural" events.[119] So too, for Crescas, the world is continually recreated by the divine will, and so every event in the world turns out to be a perpetual miracle. As Eliezer Schweid puts it, "the miracle is not an aberration of nature, rather it precedes nature."[120] We shall see a similar point made (below) by Isaac Abravanel.

Both Maimonides and Gersonides struggle to provide an account of miracles that accords with an Aristotelian view. Much of Maimonides' discussion centers on the notion of "possibility." According to Aristotle's cosmology, no change can take place in the superlunar sphere. In *Guide* 3.15 Maimonides struggles with the problem of defining the limits of the "possible." Part of his struggle has to do with whether God can perform miracles at will. Clearly an incorporeal deity cannot act in time, since the temporal domain pertains to matter. Furthermore, since creation is perfect,[121] no new volition can arise in God leading Him to introduce something new. And so Maimonides mentions in II.29 the sages' view that miracles have been integrated into nature at the time of creation. Miracles are on this view "the product of natural causes rather than suspensions in the laws of nature."[122]

Not surprisingly, although Maimonides affirms the theoretical possibility of miracles, he does not interpret them all literally. In agreement with Aristotle's view that no change can take place in the (eternal unchanging) heavens, he interprets all miracles involving celestial bodies figuratively.[123] Even in the sublunar sphere, Maimonides appears to agree with Aristotle: is God unable to introduce even small changes in nature, such as lengthening a fly's wing? "But Aristotle will say that He would not wish it and that it is impossible for Him to will something different from what is; that it would not add to His perfection but would perhaps from a certain point of view be a deficiency."[124]

In Maimonides' early writings, both miracles and natural events are said to take place in accordance with the preordained nature of things. Maimonides embraces in *Commentary on the Mishnah* the rabbinic view that miracles are rare but not supernatural phenomena, and are already embedded into the natural order during the act of Creation. The best known, and most-quoted, discussion of miracles occurs in the context of explaining the splitting of the Red Sea. In the context of explaining what is meant by human volition and its relation to divine volition, Maimonides

---

[119] See Crescas *Light* 2, prop. 3:2.   [120] Schweid 2007.
[121] See passages in *Guide* 2.13.28.29.
[122] Kreisel 1984, 109. Kreisel provides a detailed analysis of miracles in medieval Jewish thought. See also Ackerman 2009.
[123] Kreisel 1984, 111.   [124] Maimonides *Guide* 2.22:319.

explains that the splitting of the Red Sea was already written into the natural order, as it were.[125] What we or Scripture are tempted to describe as miraculous turns out to represent the actualization of a nature that was determined at the beginning of creation. None of these actions are *contrary* to nature, and hence there are no "supernatural" miracles. Concomitant with the disavowal of miracles is the view that events unfold according to a natural, regular order, and there is no room for actions that represent a violation of this order. As put succinctly by Langermann, the author of the *Commentary on the Mishnah* was convinced that natural science could account for all phenomena and rejected miracles on the grounds that the supposedly miraculous events can be explained naturalistically.[126]

Maimonides revisits the issue of miracles in his *Medical Aphorisms,* in the context of a sustained critique of Galen. Both he and Galen are concerned with the limits of God's creative powers. On Maimonides' reading, Galen used the example of eyebrow and eyelash hair to support his claim that God has created the best possible state of affairs, and could not have created any other state of affairs: because this is the best possible world, some things are inherently impossible for God. That eyebrow and eyelash hairs do not grow overly long, as does facial hair, reflects God's purpose in providing a teleological order to nature. Galen used this example to drive a wedge between the view of Moses, and that of the philosophers, claiming that while according to "the faith of Moses" all things are possible for God, the Greek philosophers claimed that "there are certain things inherently impossible." Galen argued that "if God had wished a thousand times a thousand that this hair should be so, it would never have been so if He had let it grow from soft skin. Had He not planted the roots of the hair in a hard body, they would not have remained erect and rigid in spite of His command."[127] Galen's point is that given the best possible state of affairs (one in which eyebrows can only grow to the proper length if embedded in hard cartilage), it follows that even God could not have coaxed eyebrows from soft skin.

Maimonides agrees with Galen's claim that according to Moses, "to God everything is possible," and asserts that according to Moses, "something can suddenly exist in a manner contrary to the laws of nature, such as the transformation of a staff into a snake, and of dust into lice."[128] Maimonides attributes to Scripture the view that it is possible for God to change the nature of any creation.[129] This ability depends solely on God's divine will. Maimonides defines miracle as "the coming into existence of something which is outside its normal and permanent nature."[130] He then distinguishes two types of miracles: those that include an instantaneous transformation, like the transformation of a staff into a snake, or water into blood; and those that attribute to an object characteristics that it normally doesn't have, like the simultaneous

---

[125] In PH 8, 87, Maimonides states that "[divine] volition occurred during the six days of Creation, and [since then] all things act continuously in accordance with their natures... Therefore the sages insisted that there was a prior volition, during the six days of Creation, for all the miracles which deviate from custom and which have come about or will come about as has been promised. At that time the natures of those things were determined in such a way that what has taken place in them would take place. When it takes place at the time it is supposed to, something new is presumed to occur, but that is not so."
[126] Langermann 2004, 150.   [127] Maimonides *MA* 25.62:438.
[128] Maimonides *MA* 25.64:441.   [129] Maimonides *MA* 25.64:441.
[130] Maimonides *MA* 25.64:442.

hardness and softness of manna. According to Maimonides, the eternity theorist cannot account for these latter cases, because on the eternity model, God's divine will cannot exert an influence upon matter: "All this results from the arrangement of matter over which the Lord, blessed be He, can exert no influence."[131] In fact, as Langermann notes, once again, these miracles do not necessarily violate the natural order: it is "the regularity of natural processes, but not the rules that limit the scope of these processes," that has been violated.[132] And so God *can* make it be the case that the hair of the eyebrows grow beyond a certain length, or that dust be converted to lice, or water to blood, etc., because none of these examples are *contrary* to nature. We can imagine a natural process occurring instantaneously, rather than over a period of time, but acceleration of a natural process is not itself tantamount to a supernatural event.[133] And so neither the early halakhic works, nor the *Medical Aphorisms*, present a theory of supernatural miracle that necessarily violates the natural order.

The *Guide* reflects an apparent shift from a totally deterministic, naturalistic order to one that ostensibly makes room for at least the *possibility* of miracles. On the one hand, Maimonides accepts Aristotle's view that God will not change the laws of the universe. This position is articulated already in *Guide* 2.11, in which Maimonides clearly states that God creates directly the first Intelligence, and through successive natural emanations, the Intelligences create the rest of the universe. Maimonides then notes in *Guide* 2.13 several "naturally impossible events," among them that God by his free will brought into existence out of nothing all the beings as they are, and that the heaven was generated out of nothing after a state of absolute nonexistence. See also *Guide* 2.28, in which Maimonides suggests that miracles are impossible; the works of the deity are perfect as they are and permanently established as they are, "for there is no possibility of something calling for a change in them."[134] Since creation is already perfect, no new volition can arise in God's leading to create something new.[135] On the other hand, several passages in the *Guide* evince evidence for the recognition of the *possibility* of miracles. For example, Maimonides tells us in *Guide* 2.25 that not accepting creation *ex nihilo* would violate one's belief in miracles. He ostensibly upholds the assumption of the temporal creation of the world as the only one that allows for miracles. Note that whereas in *Medical Aphorisms*, Maimonides used creation to establish the existence of miracles, in the *Guide* he uses miracles to uphold the veracity of creation.

How, then, does Maimonides reconcile the notion of miracles (the existence of which are intimated in *Guide* 2.19 and 2.25) with the Aristotelian naturalism espoused in *Guide* 2.11, 2.13, and 2.28? One way is by claiming that although miracles are voluntary acts of God, nevertheless they are predetermined at the time of creation, and do not indicate a *change* in God's will or wisdom. A miracle represents a unique

---

[131] Maimonides *MA* 25.65:443.   [132] Langermann 2004, 160.

[133] Interestingly, the same point is made by al-Ghazâlî in his *Tahâfut*: "why does our opponent declare it impossible that matter should pass through these different phases in a shorter period than is usual, and when once a shorter period is allowed, there is no limit to its being shorter and shorter … and eventually arrive at the stage of being a miracle of a prophet" al-Ghazâlî 199.7, 327.

[134] Maimonides *Guide* 2.28:335.

[135] For further discussion of this point, see Kreisel 1984.

occurrence of an event that can still be understood within the causal nexus. On this reading, the *Guide* reinforces the idea already suggested in *Commentary on the Mishnah,* and *Medical Aphorisms,* namely, that miracles do not represent the abrogation of the laws of nature. In *Guide* 2.29, Maimonides states (in accordance with the Sages) that when God created the primary parts of the universe (the heavens and first matter), God impressed upon them their various natural properties, which contained the very characteristics that would make them produce anomalies at various times in the future. What we might be tempted to call "miraculous events" are already contained in embryo in nature, and will be revealed to the prophet shortly before they occur. God does not need to initiate the miracle when it occurs, nor does the prophet need to do anything special to bring about a miracle: when God warns the prophet about an impending natural event, that event "is effected according to what was put into its nature when first it received its particular impress."[136] On this reading, a prophet plays much the same role as the natural scientist: the prophet must possess the information necessary to predict that a certain anomaly will occur. Thus, for example, part of Moses' prophetic excellence was in knowing that the Red Sea would part at a certain time, enabling the Israelites to cross on dry land. All the other miracles, he tells us, "can be explained in an analogous manner."[137] On this reading, Maimonides accepts both the permanence of natural laws and the possibility of a particular, temporary change, but this temporary change is itself part of natural law.[138]

Clearly, however, there are certain things that even God cannot do. What criteria do we use to determine the limits of God's possibility? In *Guide* 1.73, Maimonides committed himself to the conclusion that the intellectual faculty determines the realm of possibility, and that whatever was imaginable was *ipso facto* possible. But in *Guide* 3.15, he juxtaposes imagination against intellect: "Should this be verified and examined with the help of the imaginative faculty or with the intellect . . . Is there accordingly something that permits differentiation between the imaginative faculty and the intellect?"[139] If imagination provides the criterion for divine possibility, then God can do anything imaginable; but if the intellectual faculty provides the criterion, then the possible turns out to be only what is logical and rational. There is no way, Maimonides concludes, to determine which of these two tests is operative. Maimonides lists a number of impossible states of affairs that he claims are agreed "according to all men of speculation": these include the coming together of contraries at the same instant and place; the transmutation of substances; that God should bring into existence an entity like Himself, or annihilate Himself, or become a body, or change.[140] Reflecting these counter-instances to what God can do, Maimonides lays down a general limiting principle on God's ability to perform miracles: "there are impossible things whose existence cannot be admitted."[141] Hence, God cannot produce just any miracle that He pleases: There are limits to what God can do, although, as Maimonides is quick to note, such a limit "signifies neither inability nor deficiency of Power on his part."[142]

---

[136] Maimonides *Guide* 2.29:345.   [137] Maimonides *Guide* 2.29:346.
[138] See Kasher 1998, for further discussion of this point.   [139] Maimonides *Guide* 3.15:460.
[140] Maimonides *Guide* 3.15:460.   [141] Maimonides *Guide* 3.15:461.
[142] Maimonides *Guide* 3.15:461.

Maimonides both naturalizes and subjectivizes many so-called miracles described in Scripture, claiming that the events in question occurred in the agent's mind and not in reality. Take for example, Jacob's wrestling with God, or Balaam's ass speaking. In both these cases, Maimonides reminds us that the event in question happened in a vision of prophecy and not in reality, thus undermining the objective status of the event.[143] Other miraculous accounts are reduced to natural events as well, as in the case of Daniel's surviving in the lions' den.[144] In the case of the Revelation at Sinai, Maimonides offers the reader several ways to understand the miracle: either as a prophetic vision rooted in intellectual apprehension, or as a prophetic vision that incorporated sight as well, or one that incorporated hearing as well. "Choose whatever opinion you wish," says Maimonides,[145] signaling that even this event is not necessarily rooted in objective fact. Again, in the case of explaining the extraordinary lifespan of certain individuals, Maimonides gives us the option to explain such an anomaly either naturally or supernaturally: "only that individual who is mentioned lived so long a life, whereas the other men lived lives that had the natural and usual duration. The anomaly in the individual in question may be due either to numerous causes attaching to his nutrition and his regimen or is due to a miracle and follows the laws thereof."[146] In all these cases, Maimonides is providing his readers with different ways of understanding miracles, depending on their intellectual sophistication: the "vulgar" will cling to the supernatural interpretation that reinforces God's willfully transforming the natural order, whereas those initiated in philosophy and science will recognize that none of these events contravenes the natural order.

Gersonides' approach to miracles is more radical than that of Maimonides. He first provides a general description of miracles, and then shows that a prophet was involved in each of the miracles recorded in Scripture. But who is the immediate agent of these "exceptions" to the natural order? For Gersonides, the agent is not God but rather the Active Intellect. More specifically, Gersonides provides an argument to the effect that God is incapable of performing miracles, on the grounds that God does not know the order of future contingents and so is unable to "implant specific miracles in the order in response to particular historical situations."[147] He thus concludes that miracles are providential acts performed by the Active Intellect; they result from the divine will only in the attenuated sense that God created the world order. As Kreisel summarizes, Gersonides' theory "reflects an attempt to maintain the naturalism of the philosopher's world view, while continuing to uphold the traditional Jewish belief in a special providence operating directly in history."[148]

Consider, for example, Gersonides' interpretation of the miracle recounted in Joshua and Isaiah. In their respective examination of the relation between science and religion, medieval philosophers often used *Joshua* 10:12–14 and *Isaiah* 38:7–8 as proof texts to support their Scriptural hermeneutics, but to different ends.[149] The text

---

[143] Maimonides *Guide* 2.42.   [144] Maimonides *Guide* 2.6.   [145] Maimonides *Guide* 1.21.
[146] Maimonides *Guide* 2.47:408.   [147] Kreisel 1984, 124.   [148] Kreisel 1984, 126.
[149] That the Copernican system ran counter to the world view presented in Scripture is well known. One of the most pressing problems centered on how to interpret the alleged miracle expressed in *Joshua* 10:12–14. By denying the alleged miracle of the sun standing still in the sky, supporters of Copernicanism ran the risk of denying God's intervention in the natural world, leaving no room for Divine intervention and presence in the natural order. See Vermij 2002, 242.

from *Joshua* 10.12 reads as follows. Joshua and his men are worried that there will not be sufficient time to defeat the five Amorite kings, and so Joshua prays to God to extend the day:

Joshua addressed the Lord; he said in the presence of the Israelites: 'Stand still, O sun, at Gibeon, O moon, in the Valley of Ajalon!' and the sun stood still and the moon halted, while a nation wreaked judgment on its foes... thus the sun halted in mid-heaven, and did not press on to set, for a whole day. (*Joshua* 10:12–13)

The text in *Isaiah* 38:7–8 provides similar astronomical issues. Isaiah assures King Hezekiah that the Lord will heal him and stand by him, and Hezekiah asks for a sign. The text reads as follows:

And this is the sign for you from the Lord that the Lord will do the thing that He has promised. I am going to make the shadow on the steps, which has descended on the dial of Ahaz because of the sun, recede ten steps. And the sun's [shadow] receded ten steps...

Both these miracles posed a particular problem for rationalists who found it hard to accept such a collapse of celestial order, and tried to attribute the arrest of the sun to natural or semi-natural causes. For these philosophers, the underlying question became whether the heavenly bodies could have actually stopped in their tracks, implying a complete suspension of the natural order, or might there not be some natural explanation of the phenomenon.

In his early *Commentary to the Mishnah* (*Avot*), Maimonides uses the Joshua proof text to reiterate the principle that nature was created together with the potential for certain changes, some of which appear as miracles, but actually are woven into the fabric of natural events. As an example, Maimonides gives the following case: "On the fourth day, when the sun was created, it was granted the potential to stand still as Joshua commanded it. The same applies with regard to the other miracles."[150] On this reading, it appears that the sun actually did stand still, but that its standing still was itself an anomalous event prefixed in the natural order. But in *Guide* 2.35, however, Maimonides suggested that only Moses' miracles were visible to all the people. But how does this compare to the Joshua example, in which all Israel apparently witnessed the stoppage of the sun? Maimonides resolves the discrepancy by claiming that Joshua's miracle did not occur in front of "all Israel" but only in front of some Israelites. Further, he argues that the event in question was temporary. Maimonides focuses on the words "for a whole day" to mean "the longest day that may happen," suggesting that "it is *as if* it said that the day of Gibeon was for them *as* the longest of the days of the summer that may occur there."[151] Maimonides thus undercuts the supernaturalist interpretation of this event, according to which the sun actually stopped in its tracks and the entire celestial order was abrogated (in which case the entire world would have been witness to the event). Rather does he suggest that *perhaps* the "sun stood still" only in the minds of the soldiers, for whom the day "was

---

[150] Maimonides *CM* Avot 5:5:131.
[151] Maimonides *Guide* 2.35:368: emphasis is mine.

for them *as* the longest of days"; that is, it was *in their minds*, the longest day of summer, but not in actuality.

Gersonides provides a similar but even more radical interpretation of this example. His discussion indirectly influenced that of Galileo in the seventeenth century. In his treatment of the miracle quoted in Isaiah, Galileo quotes Paul of Burgos who explained that the miracle actually occurred not in the sun but on the sundial. Goldstein makes a convincing case that Galileo's brief remarks are based on Magalhaens's *Commentary on Joshua:* "here we find extensive citations of all the texts mentioned by Galileo."[152] The very position that Galileo quotes is found in Gersonides' commentary on these cases. In the case of Joshua, Gersonides argued that the miracle in question was that the Israelites defeated their enemies while the sun seemed to maintain the same altitude; he adds that miracles do not involve the abrogation of natural law. The Hezekiah case is more involved. Gersonides argues that "this miracle took place in the shadow and not in the Sun." He argues that clouds that move under the sun sometimes cause the rays of the sun to be displaced, and that some vapors under the sun caused the shadow to return ten steps.[153] The main point here is that according to Gersonides, the miracle could not have occurred in the superlunar world, but only in the sublunar world: it was the shadow, and not the sun, that was displaced, due to the intervention of a cloud or vapors that caused a shadow at the appropriate time.[154] To be sure, though, Galileo's goals were different from those of his predecessors: as noted by Goldstein, "for them the interpretation of Scripture was the goal, whereas for Galileo the principal aim was to demonstrate the consistency of these Biblical passages with the Copernican system.[155]

Clearly, Gersonides' account of miracles was exceedingly radical, placing most miracles into the naturalistic realm. In the fifteenth century, we witness a backlash to Gersonides' account in the work of Isaac Abravanel (1437–1508). Abravanel had no patience with the naturalism and "hyper-rationalism" of the Jewish Aristotelians. In his work *Mifalot Elohim (The Works of God)*, Abravanel defines a miracle as "the existence of a thing, or its destruction, without its natural causes and conditions, and which is produced by the intention and will of one who intends and wills."[156] Abravanel stresses the *intention and will* of the agent, namely God. That the one who wills is God and not the Agent Intellect is stated emphatically in his commentary on Job: the belief in the Agent Intellect "was truly an obstacle and a stumbling-block before the Israelites."[157] As we shall see in Chapter 9, medieval philosophers made use of the doctrine of the Agent Intellect to explain prophecy. Abravanel excoriates them, claiming that "this implied for them that prophecy was a natural matter, with the result that they denied the words of the prophet Isaiah ... there is no escaping the fact that prophecy comes from Him (may He be blessed) by means of a particular, simple volition in miraculous fashion."[158]

---

[152] Goldstein and Pingree 1990, 15.   [153] Goldstein and Pingree 1990, 8.
[154] Goldstein and Pingree 1990, 8.   [155] Goldstein and Pingree 1990, 15.
[156] Abravanel 1988, *The Works of God* [English selection] in Frank, Leaman, and Manekin 2000, 278.
[157] Abravanel *Commentary on Joshua* in Frank, Leaman, and Manekin 2000, 275.
[158] Abravanel *Commentary on Joshua* in Frank, Leaman, and Manekin 2000, 275. See Chapter 9 for further comments.

Reflecting similar distinctions in late scholastics, Abravanel recognizes three types of miracles: those that are similar to natural phenomena (e.g., the ten plagues); those that are supernatural (Noah's Flood; Sarah's pregnancy); and those that are contrary to nature (splitting of the Red Sea; manna). In the third type of miracle, the event in question is "contrary to nature"; that is, the event occurs contrary to natural law. The splitting of the Red Sea, and the formation of walls of water, represents an "exception to the fluid nature of water."[159] For Abravanel, Gersonides' "naturaliza- tion" of the Joshua miracle is "sheer heresy," as Feldman puts it. It is a case according to Abravanel, of "Gersonides' philosophical and scientific biases getting the better of his commitment to the Torah." In response to Gersonides' worry about global catastrophes occurring if the sun and moon were to stop moving even for an instant, Abravanel responds that God can easily arrange to have all the heavenly bodies stop such that nothing untoward would happen on earth.[160] Feldman points out that Abravanel's discussion centers on God's omnipotence: "If God can do anything that is logically possible, and if the domain of logical possibility is quite extensive, as it is, then there is no logical reason why God has to be bound to the laws of nature."[161] Only if God and Nature are identified is there a real problem with miracles.

By the seventeenth century, however, Gersonides' radical reinterpretation of mir- acle was becoming more accepted. Galileo used Gersonides' text in the seventeenth century as an example of how biblical hermeneutics can reconcile Scripture with the new heliocentric science. Galileo first points out that the literal interpretation of Scripture is not always correct, as evidenced for example by the fact that statements in Scripture imply that God has a physical body, which we know is not literally true. Second, the literal interpretation of Scripture is incorrect when it conflicts with physical truths that have been conclusively proved. This is because the function of Scripture is not to provide us with scientific truths. In effect, Galileo will want to argue that because God's presence in the world belies a separation between religion and science, in theory it should always be possible to reconcile the two.

With respect to the example in Joshua, Galileo argues in his letter to the Grand Duchess Christina that under the Ptolemaic system, the example "in no way can happen."[162] According to Galileo, if Joshua had wanted the day to be lengthened, he should have ordered the sun to accelerate its motion in such a way that the impulse from the *primum mobile* would not carry it westward. On the Ptolemaic system, therefore, we must reinterpret Joshua's words: "given the Ptolemaic system, it is necessary to interpret the words in a way different from their literal meaning."[163] A fringe benefit of Galileo's heliocentric interpretation is that he is able to give a clever reading of the next phrase, namely that the sun stood still "in the midst of the heavens" (*Joshua* 10:13). Classical theologians have had a difficult time with this

---

[159] See Feldman 2003, 71.   [160] Abravanel 1988, *Mifalot* 10.9:251.
[161] See Feldman 2003, 81.   [162] Galileo 1989, *Letter* 114.
[163] Galileo argues that if the sun stops its own true motion, the day becomes shorter and not longer and that, on the contrary, the way to prolong it would be to speed up the sun's motion; thus, to make the sun stay for some time at the same place above the horizon, without going down toward the west, it would be necessary to accelerate its motion so as to equal the motion of the Prime Mobile, which would be to accelerate it to about three hundred and sixty times its usual motion. Galileo *Letter* 115.

statement, for if it meant that the sun was at the meridian, there would be no reason for a miracle at the time of Joshua's prayer; but if the sun were setting when Joshua asked for cessation of movement, it is not clear how to explain the phrase "in the midst." Galileo's interpretation is that by "in the midst of the heavens" we should understand that the sun is at the center of the celestial orbs and planetary rotations, in accordance with Copernican heliocentrism. Thus at any hour of day, we can say that the sun stands "at the center of the heavens, where it is located."[164]

Similarly, concerned to free philosophy and the study of nature from what he saw as the shackles of theology, Spinoza held controversial views on how to read and evaluate statements in Scripture. These views were embedded in his methodological concern with truth, and with scientific truth in particular. In the *Theological Political Treatise*, Spinoza postulates the incommensurability of religion and science: the authority of the prophets carries weight only in matters concerning morality and true virtue. In other matters, their beliefs are irrelevant. By removing theology from the domain of truth-functionality, Spinoza paves the way for the independence of philosophical (and scientific) truth on the one hand, and religious doctrine on the other. Note that this move paves the way to denying "truth" in the religious sphere altogether. Truth is associated with reason, with philosophical reflection, and does not pertain to what we find in Scripture, which as noted above, is associated with the imaginative sphere.[165] Although Maimonides and Gersonides had laid the groundwork for the naturalization of miracles, Spinoza's reading of the Biblical miracles is even more radical in his categorical denial of supernatural occurrences, including both magic and miracles. Spinoza is clear that "nothing happens contrary to nature, but nature maintains an eternal, fixed and immutable order."[166] More specifically, nothing happens in nature "that contradicts its universal laws."[167] Not even God can contravene these laws, since God/Nature observes those laws. Thus any apparent miracle, according to Spinoza, is simply an event the causes of which are unknown to our intellect.

It is in this context that Spinoza's elaboration of Joshua's role as a prophet must be understood. In contradistinction to Galileo who tried to grant Joshua the benefit of the doubt, Spinoza's conclusion is that we cannot expect scientific knowledge of the prophets. According to Spinoza, Joshua was a simple prophet who, confronted with an unusual natural phenomenon, namely "excessive coldness of the atmosphere," attributed to this phenomenon a supernatural explanation. Joshua had no knowledge of astronomy, nor should we attribute to him such knowledge; he believed, as did the others in his time, that "the sun moves around the earth, that the earth is at rest, and that the sun in fact stood still for a period of time."[168] For Spinoza, then, there is no room for interpretative hermeneutics: the Bible must be interpreted literally.

---

[164] Galileo 1989, *Letter* 118.

[165] In the *Ethics*, Spinoza discusses the notion of truth in detail, and elaborates three distinct epistemic levels of truth, which he articulates in terms of imagination, reason, and intuitive science. According to Spinoza, the knowledge of the first kind (imagination) is the cause of falsity, whereas knowledge of the second and third orders is necessarily true. Spinoza goes on to argue in the demonstration to *Ethics* 2:41 that the first kind of knowledge concerns all those ideas that are inadequate and confused.

[166] Spinoza 2001, *Treatise* 6.73.   [167] Spinoza 2001, *Treatise* 6.73–4.

[168] Spinoza 2001, *Treatise* 2.26.

He has no patience for either the literalists or those who, having learned to philoso-
phize and recognize that the earth moves rather than the sun and that the sun does
not move around the earth, "make great efforts to derive this from this passage even
though it obviously will not permit such a reading."[169]

"Do we have to believe that the soldier Joshua was a skilled astronomer, that a
miracle could not be revealed to him, or that the sun's light could not remain above
the horizon for longer than usual without Joshua's understanding the cause? Both
alternatives seem to me ridiculous."[170] "Knowledge of science and of matters spiritual," Spinoza reminds us, should not be expected of prophets.[171] In fact, on Spinoza's
reading, Joshua was totally ignorant of the scientific explanation for this event. In
chapter six, Spinoza returns to the topic of Joshua in the context of his naturalization
of miracles. He gives a socially contextual explanation of why Joshua might have
offered the explanation we find in *Joshua* 10, arguing that the Hebrews adapted their
description of the event in question in order to "persuade the gentiles who adored the
sun" that the sun answers to a higher order than just natural law, namely "that the
sun operates under the government of another deity at whose command it had to
change its natural regular movement."[172] For this reason, the Hebrews "conceived of
the thing happening in a totally different way from how it actually occurred, and that
is how they reported it."[173]

According to Spinoza, Scripture cannot be accommodated to the new sciences.
Scripture could not be regarded as a source of knowledge; and because it is neither a
philosophical nor a scientific work, the rational methods used by these latter disciplines simply cannot be applied to Scripture. Scripture provides only moral guidance
and piety, not even moral truth, and certainly not scientific or mathematical truth. By
pushing the views of Maimonides, Gersonides, and Ibn Ezra to their logical extreme,
Spinoza thus destroyed the carefully constructed hermeneutic methodology introduced by his Jewish predecessors.

---

[169] Spinoza 2001, *Treatise* 2.26–7.   [170] Spinoza 2001, *Treatise* 2.27.
[171] Spinoza 2001, *Treatise* 7.86–7.   [172] Spinoza 2001, *Treatise* 6.81.   [173] Ibid.

8

On Immortality and the Nature of the Soul

I Introduction

In general, problems associated with personal identity and individuation occurred for Jewish philosophers within the context of cosmological and psychological concerns. Starting with Ibn Gabirol's characterization of a universal hylomorphism and continuing throughout the Jewish Neoplatonic tradition, Jewish philosophers were concerned with the ultimate composition of particular entities, and whether matter is sufficient to particularize these entities. More specifically, these issues incorporated a number of interrelated issues regarding the relation between the soul and body, human perfection, and the doctrine of the afterlife.

Jewish theology presents no clearly elaborated views either on the relationship between body and mind, or on the nature of the soul. The soul is in some vague sense seen as separate from the body, but details are not forthcoming; nor do the rabbis accept the gnostic idea, exemplified already in Plato, that the soul is imprisoned in the body.[1] The Greek philosophers more clearly delineated the relationship between mind and matter, or body and soul. For Aristotelians, form and matter are not technically *parts* in the sense, for example, that letters comprise the *parts* of a word.[2] Aristotle had already set out some of the differences that distinguish form and matter from other types of parts in that they are not physically separable, with the possible exception of the human soul.[3] The Neoplatonists, however, have no compunction against viewing matter and form as parts of a composite. As Plotinus had noted, two hylomorphic parts can and in fact do occupy the same place at the same time "as a whole"—Socrates' form is in the same place as Socrates' body.[4] The identity of soul does not change if the body loses parts. Further, even though no two material parts can exist in the same place, nonetheless the soul can occupy the same place as a body; in fact the whole soul occupies each part of the body.

The Neoplatonic emanation scheme forced philosophers to offer an explanation for the very existence of material entities: how, within an ontology that emphasizes the unity of the whole of substance, does one account for the proliferation of entities

---

[1] Ivry points out that the rabbis believed that the soul is in some sense separable from the body: see *Genesis* 2:7; Ta'anit 22b; *Genesis Rabbah* 14:9. See Ivry 2007.

[2] See Aristotle *Metaphysics* 7.17 1041b11ff.   [3] Aristotle *De Anima* III.5.

[4] See Plotinus *Enneads* 4.ii.1:35–6.

within a predominantly nonphysical hierarchy?[5] On the other hand, the Aristotelian emphasis upon the hylomorphic construction of the human being as an indistinguishable body/soul composite raised questions about how, if at all, we can speak of an immortal soul.

Concomitant with the issue of immortality is the connection obtaining between human intellect and the Active Intellect, as characterized by Avicenna and Averroës.[6] Medieval philosophers took seriously the question of whether the soul retains its individuality upon separation from the body; in other words, whether immortality is personal or general. As we shall see in Chapter 9, both the doctrine of reward and punishment, and ultimate human felicity, are predicated upon individual immortality of the soul.

In these final two chapters, we turn to the cluster of issues associated with the nature of the soul, and the implications of these theories upon moral theory. Chapter 8 focuses upon the following issues: what is the soul, and how is it related to the body; if the soul is part of the body, does it perish along with the destruction of the body, or does a part of the soul survive; if part of the soul is immortal, can it acquire new knowledge after death; is the body resurrected in the world to come, or is salvation purely spiritual; if salvation is spiritual, are rewards and punishments in the world to come spiritual as well, or are they material? I shall first present two Neoplatonic views of soul, typified by Isaac Israeli and Ibn Gabirol, and then turn to the more Aristotelian-influenced views of Maimonides and Gersonides. In Chapter 9, we return to the ramifications of soul in the context of moral and political thought. And finally, we must explore the role of the prophet as both moral and political leader. For the majority of our thinkers, the prophet represents that individual who has achieved the highest level of moral, intellectual, and political perfection; the prophet reflects the model of Plato's philosopher-king. Our philosophers' responses to these interrelated issues reflect the attempt once again to reconcile traditional Jewish beliefs with the naturalistic views set forth by the ancient Greek philosophers.

II Matter, Form, and Soul: Isaac Israeli, Solomon ibn Gabirol, and Maimonides

In Chapter 2, we briefly discussed the enormous influence of Neoplatonism upon medieval Jewish philosophy. More specifically we mentioned the impact of the Islamic

---

[5] These ontological concerns carried with them theological ramifications that were manifested in the examination of God's knowledge of these particulars. For if the majority of Jewish philosophers were wont to argue that God is an immaterial Being and not subject to change, then how can he know the world of changing, material particulars? Concomitantly, if these particulars are in some way individuated on the basis of their matter alone, then in what sense can God individuate them? And if God cannot individuate particulars, how can he bestow providence upon them? For, within the medieval Jewish tradition, divine providence is bestowed only upon individuals who satisfy certain criteria, that is, moral and intellectual qualities. A helpful discussion of this problem can be found in H. A. Wolfson 1959, 390ff.

[6] The "Active" (or "Agent") Intellect is a term that refers back to Aristotle's actual intellect as described in De Anima 3.5. The term was transmitted to Jewish and scholastic writers through Islamic philosophers, and it came to represent not only a part of the human soul but the domain of Divine intellectual cognition as well. We will discuss this term more extensively below.

school of Neoplatonism most notably through the *Theology of Aristotle* (in both the long and short versions), doxographies, and the pseudographical work *Ibn Ḥasday's Neoplatonist*, preserved almost in its entirety in a Hebrew translation incorporated into Ibn Ḥasday's text *Ben ha-Melech ve-ha-Nazir* (*The Prince and the Ascetic*).[7] Nowhere is the influence of this work realized more strongly than in Israeli's conceptions and theories of soul. In *Book of Definitions*, Israeli provides definitions of soul, wisdom, and intellect in accordance with standard Neoplatonic cosmology. This scheme is reproduced in both *Book of Substances* and *Chapter on the Elements*, but in the *Book on Spirit and Soul*, a work presumably written for a Jewish public, Israeli amplifies his characterization by incorporating biblical passages to supplement his account.

In general, Israeli describes the various stages of Being as a series of emanations, or hypostases, from the Intellect; the Intellect itself is constituted by the union of first matter and first form, which are "created" by the power and will of God. Israeli thus upholds the notion of creation *ex nihilo* in the case of the first three hypostases, while adopting the Plotinian concept of emanation for the rest. Israeli distinguishes three cosmological processes. The first, creation *ex nihilo*, is used only for Intellect that is created from matter and form, and is due to an act of power and will. The second process, emanation, is the logical and necessary order through which spiritual substances emanate. The third process accords with the causality of nature, or creation from something already existent, and reflects the way corporeal substances are caused. Hence, the more perfect substances are created without the mediation of intervening stages—nothing stands between them and the creator. Israeli presents two schemes of emanation.[8]

Whereas Plotinus described Intellect as emanating directly from the One, Israeli, following his pseudo-Aristotelian source, interposes two simple substances—first matter and first form—between the Creator and Intellect as representing the first hypostasis. First matter is described as "the first substance which subsists in itself and is the substratum of diversity,"[9] whereas first form is described as "impregnating first matter" and is identified with "the perfect wisdom, the pure radiance, and clear splendor!"[10]

Intellect represents the second hypostasis and is divided into three kinds. The first is active intellect, "the intellect which is always in actuality." The second, potential intellect, is found in the soul. And the third intellect, which refers to the actualization in the soul of the potential intellect by perception, is termed by Israeli "second intellect." This latter intellect refers to the actualization in the soul of the potential intellect by way of sense perception, and is distinct from the intuitive knowledge of intellect. As noted by Altmann, it is not entirely clear how Israeli distinguishes between wisdom and intellect. Intellect contains the totality of forms and knows

---

[7] S. M. Stern traces the history and influence of this treatise, offering a reconstruction of the text (Stern 1961, 58–120). Ibn Ḥasday's treatise *Ben ha-Melech ve-ha-Nazir* is a Hebrew adaptation of the Arabic book *Bilawhar wa-Yudasaf*, which goes back to the legend of the Buddha. A complete translation of Ibn Ḥasday's work can be found in Stern 1961, 102ff.

[8] See Rudavsky 1997, 153 for details of Israeli's ontology.

[9] Israeli *Mant. S.*, in Altmann and Stern 1958, 119.   [10] Ibid.

them by an act of intuitive self-knowledge, so it does not seem possible for there to be a level of knowledge superior to it. In the *Book of Substances*, however, it appears that matter and form or wisdom have no existence apart from Intellect.[11]

Soul follows Intellect in this triad of hypostases and is divided into a higher phase and a lower one, which Israeli calls "nature." Other Neoplatonic sources also equate the sphere with nature. There is no warrant for this identification in Plotinus, who only identifies nature with the vegetative soul. Following his pseudo-Aristotelian source, Israeli transfers Aristotle's divisions of the individual soul to the universal soul, giving us three hypostases of soul, to which he adds as a final quasi-spiritual substance the "sphere" or heaven. The *Book of Substances* describes the three souls (rational, animal and vegetative) as the forms (specificalities) of the three stages of living beings (humans, animals, plants). Strangely enough, Israeli does not shed much light on the nature of the three universal souls beyond making them mere replicas, on a macrocosmic scale, of the tripartite division of the particular souls familiar from Aristotle's *De Anima*.[12] The sphere, or heaven, is the last of the "simple substances" and is an addition to the three souls. It holds an intermediate position, acting as a bridge between the spiritual and corporeal worlds. It has a lasting existence, but is not purely spiritual because its light is the least in brightness (since it comprises matter). Composed of the fifth element, it is "unaffected by growth and decrease, coming to be and passing away," and has a "lasting existence."[13]

Israeli amplifies the role of the soul in achieving purification, which will become a major theme in chapter nine. The three stages of ascent described in Israeli's texts are taken from Proclus' *Alcibiades*. Like the Islamic Brethren of Purity (*Ikhwân al-Safâ*), Israeli adopts Proclus' theory of the three stages of purification, illumination, and union. The bliss of the highest stage is, in Israeli's view, tantamount to the bliss of paradise. In this way, he links traditional Jewish eschatology with Neoplatonic mysticism. The first, purification, is a turning away from passions of the lower soul. The human soul now contains little of darkness, or the shells associated with materiality. The second stage, illumination, corresponds to wisdom. The soul acquires true knowledge of external things. And finally, in union, the human soul becomes spiritual and intellectual as the rational soul is raised to the level of Intellect. This final union with wisdom (*devekut*) can, according to Israeli, be achieved even when the soul is still in the body.[14] Robinson suggests that herein "a Jewish eschatology is first developed out of Neoplatonic ideas and images."[15] This theory of purification and the soul corresponds to Israeli's conception of philosophy as a drawing near to God, as far as is possible for human beings. This ideal of *imitatio Dei*, which hearkens back to Plato's *Theatetus*, plays an important role in biblical and Talmudic thought as well.[16]

---

[11] Israeli's discussion occurs in his *Book of Definitions* s. 4, II 33–54, found in Altmann and Stern 1958, 36–9.

[12] Israeli *Book of Substances* 5.12r, in Altmann and Stern 1958, 91; 165.

[13] Altmann and Stern 1958, 166–7.   [14] Altmann and Stern 1958, 193.

[15] For a summary of major theories of soul in medieval Jewish thought, see Robinson 2009, 529.

[16] For a history of this important notion of love of God (*amor dei*), in Jewish philosophy, see Vajda 1957.

The Neoplatonic tenor of Israeli's conception of soul is echoed in Ibn Gabirol's works as well. We have already, in Chapter 6, examined Ibn Gabirol's hylomorphic ontology according to which all substances in the world, both spiritual and corporeal, are composed of matter and form. Unlike Aristotle, Gabirol postulates the existence of spiritual matter, which underlies incorporeal substances. Even intellects, souls, and angels are composed of matter and form. The pre-eminence of matter as epitomized in the human being is already prefigured in his treatise on practical morality, *Tikkun Middot ha-Nefesh*. This work was written in 1045 in Saragossa, and is available in the original Arabic, as well as in a Hebrew translation by Judah ibn Tibbon dated 1167. In *Tikkun Middot ha-Nefesh*, to which we return in Chapter 9, the qualities and defects of the soul are described, with particular emphasis upon the doctrine of the Aristotelian mean. This mean is supported by biblical references, as well as by quotations from Greek philosophers and Arab poets. One original element in this work is Gabirol's connection between the moral and physiological makeup of the human. That is, each of twenty personal traits is correlated to one of the five senses. Hence, the body as well as the soul must participate in the person's aspirations toward ultimate felicity. In effect, Gabirol delineates a complete parallel between the microcosm as represented by the human being and the macrocosm that is the universe.

The contrast between the microcosm and the macrocosm, as well as between matter and form, and body and soul, finds its fullest expression in *Sefer Mekor Hayyim*. Chapters 2 and 6 alluded to Gabirol's hylomorphic ontology, the details of which we can now expand. According to Ibn Gabirol, types of matter are ordered in a hierarchy that corresponds to a criterion of simplicity: general spiritual matter; general corporeal matter; general celestial matter; general natural matter; and particular natural matter. Individual matter is associated with prime matter, which lies at the periphery of the hierarchy, thus epitomizing the very limits of being.[17] Each level of matter is increasingly coarser, so to speak, than its predecessor.

In strict accordance with his ontology, Gabirol insists that the universe, at all levels, is made up of matter and form. Like bodily ones, intelligible substances too are necessarily composed of matter and form: there is a non-sensible substance that serves as "matter" for corporeal nature. In both the sensible and intelligible realm, matter is never found without form. In Book IV of *Mekor Hayyim*, adopting two arguments found already in Plotinus' *Enneads* 2.4.4, Ibn Gabirol demonstrates that matter and form exist in simple, intelligible substances. Gabirol's first argument is there must be a common substratum to account for the unity of the intelligible realm, where the individual forms provide the diversity.[18] Gabirol's second argument depends upon the notion that if simple substances were composed of form alone, they would lack any substratum. The root of diversity in spiritual substances is matter: "diversity is not a property of theirs except on account of the matter which supports them."[19]

How are form and matter interrelated? Gabirol's ambivalence toward this question is reflected in two alternative responses. On the one hand, he argues that form and matter are mutually inter-defined and are differentiated only according to our

---

[17] Ibn Gabirol *Mekor Hayyim* 5.4.   [18] Dillon 1992, 49.   [19] Ibn Gabirol *Mekor Hayyim* 4.1.

perspective of them at a particular time; accordingly, both are aspects of simple substance. On the other hand, he emphasizes the complete opposition between matter and form, suggesting that each possesses mutually exclusive properties that render a reduction of one to the other an impossibility.[20]

On the basis of these passages, it emerges that Gabirol privileges the material over the formal. Just as divine essence is prior to will, so too can it be argued that matter is prior to form. As Sarah Pessin has pointed out, matter is the "purest, most simple pre-formal manifestation of Being in each thing... it is the manifestation in each thing of that which is closest to Divine Essence because most devoid of formal determination and (hence) plurality."[21] It is universal matter that underlies everything and that has primacy over everything, even form. The importance of this characterization cannot be overemphasized.[22] Pessin suggests that "the material essence is to be identified with the Being *simpliciter*—the indeterminate existential foundation... that Intellect emanates forth to all substances first and foremost."[23] On this existentialist reading, each substance has a pure existential foundation as its first matter, or first essence. This existential foundation is the very universal matter that is identified with God's essence. Inasmuch as any indivisible unit must be of a spiritual nature, once we begin to speak of spiritual matter, we leave the issues of quantity and matter behind. Gabirol therefore envisions the possibility that all of the world might exist in a point and that extension is not essential to matter.

In Chapter 6 we examined Gabirol's arguments for the infinite divisibility of matter; we can turn now to his arguments for the divisibility of form. Gabirol clearly asserts that both finitude and divisibility pertain to form. Further, Gabirol claims that "the form is seized by the senses as finite. In effect, the form is finite for it is the limit of the body."[24] Form is the principle of divisibility as well. Clearly, what distinguishes the finitude of both matter and form is the fact that they are mutually interdependent: in this context finitude signifies not so much the sense of spacial limitation as ontological dependence.

We are now in a position to characterize more fully Gabirol's conception of God, who is conceived as infinite. By infinite in the qualitative, or substantive, sense, Gabirol has in mind a totally independently existing entity, one that requires no ontological support. An infinite being possesses no form (4.6), is not divisible (3.3), and is not subject to change (3.6). Interestingly enough, Gabirol says little about infinity itself, but rather devotes considerably more time to divine will which resides in the intermediary sphere between finitude and infinity: the finite and infinite intersect in the will. Speaking of the intelligible substance, the disciple asks, "Tell me whether the forms of these substances are finite or infinite; if they are finite, how they can have the being of an infinite force; if they are infinite, how something

---

[20] Ibn Gabirol *Mekor Ḥayyim* 4.2.   [21] Pessin 2013, 91.
[22] See Brunner 1997, 278.   [23] Pessin 2013, 120.
[24] Ibn Gabirol *Mekor Ḥayyim* 4.20; See also Ibn Gabirol *Mekor Ḥayyim* 5.28. In answer to how it is that forms are unities, and duality convenes to matter, the Master offers a number of explanations, among which we find the following: "The second property of matter is multiplicity and divisibility; this because the form divides and multiplies because of the matter; and matter possesses this property because of a second one which is half of two..." Ibn Gabirol *Mekor Ḥayyim* 5.11.

finite in act can issue from them."[25] Ibn Gabirol's response requires aligning form with the creative will: in and of itself, form is identical with will. It is only when it enters into creative act with matter that it becomes finite. In other words, both form and will, that is to say the force that produces these substances, are finite by virtue of their effect and infinite by virtue of their essence. But the will is not finite by virtue of its effect except "because the action has a beginning and so follows the will; and it is infinite by virtue of its essence for it does not possess a beginning. And inversely, we say of the intelligible substance that it has a beginning because it is caused, and that it has no end for it is simple and not temporal."[26]

Based on this characterization, it is clear that matter plays an important role in the personification not only of the human being, but of the Deity as well. This is not to say that Ibn Gabirol portrays God as per se material, but rather that Ibn Gabirol comes very close to identifying the Supreme Intellect as matter.[27] In order to underscore the importance of this point, let me turn to Ibn Gabirol's related terms *Kavod* (= *glory*) and *Keter Malkhut* (= *divine throne*). The term *Kavod* has had a long history in Jewish literature, acquiring a technical philosophical significance in the writings of Saadiah Gaon. Pines and Freudenthal have both explored the notion of *Kavod* in Saadiah Gaon's *Sefer Yeẓirah* (*Book of Creation*). Freudenthal claims that "the mystics' view of divine immanence and their conception of *kavod* as an intermediate between God and world can ultimately be traced back to Stoicism."[28] More specifically, Freudenthal maintains that *Kavod* can be identified with the Stoic notion of *pneuma*.

That Stoic thought underlies the understanding of modern science has been argued by a number of scholars. H. A. Wolfson had already suggested that Spinoza's hypothesis that God is material can be found in the Stoics.[29] In a similar vein, Peter Barker has surveyed the transmission and use of Cicero's book *On the Nature of the Gods* in sixteenth- and early seventeenth-century discussions of the substance of the heavens.[30] More recently, Freudenthal has suggested that Stoic physics was "one of the great achievements of ancient natural philosophy. Its fructifying effects on early modern science have only recently begun to be appreciated."[31]

Returning to Ibn Gabirol, we see that it is precisely this second difference between Saadiah and the Stoics that has been further eroded. Pines has demonstrated that several formulations in which Ibn Gabirol states the view that God and his Will are immanent to the entire physical world are literal paraphrases of Saadiah's *Commentary*.[32] The "second air" in Saadiah's *Commentary* reappears in Ibn Gabirol as a grade of intellect.

---

[25] Ibn Gabirol *Mekor Ḥayyim* 3.57.   [26] Ibn Gabirol *Mekor Ḥayyim* 3.57. See also 4.19.

[27] In the following discussion, I am very much influenced by Sarah Pessin's analysis (2013). This identification is made explicit of course in Spinoza's *Ethics*.

[28] Freudenthal 1996, 133.   [29] See Wolfson 1959.   [30] Barker 1991, 137–54.

[31] Freudenthal 1996, 113–36. The relevance of this notion of *pneuma* becomes apparent when we turn the historical transformation of this notion from Saadiah to Ibn Gabirol. Freudenthal suggests that the doctrine of immanence in Saadiah, and its frequent association with an omnipresent "air" ("the second subtle air" in Saadiah) as the intermediary between God and the world, are of Stoic origin. Intellect itself is the first substance and fount of unspecified Being in all things, while the second air stands in the same relation to God as does a human's life to intellect.

[32] See Pines 1989, 122–6.

Pessin has argued persuasively that this "second air" is akin to Gabirol's own universal matter, a matter that is "identifiable with the most sublime moment of Universal Intellect itself, the first substance and fount of unspecified Being in all things."[33]

The importance of *Kavod*, and its identification with Intellect, is reflected as well in Ibn Gabirol's elaborate religious poem *Keter Malkhut* (*Throne of Glory*). In *Mekor Hayyim*, Gabirol had already intimated that "Matter is as if the throne of unity, and Will, the giver of form sits in it and reposes above it."[34] In canto 24 of *Keter Malkhut*, Ibn Gabirol locates the *Apiryon* (= canopy, chamber) of the divine Glory within the sphere of Intellect, thus intimating that the incorporeal sphere of the Intellect is the realm of the *Kavod*.[35] Leaving behind the *Kavod*, Ibn Gabirol turns in canto 26 to the Divine Throne (*Kisse ha-Kavod*), which lies at the outermost limits of the supernal world. Canto 29 of *Keter Malkhut* tells us that the soul is derived from the radiance of the divine *Kavod*. In *Mekor Hayyim*, Ibn Gabirol likewise describes the Divine Throne as the realm of "the Mystery and the Foundation." Scholars have associated these two terms with Universal Form and Matter. Matter is thus associated with *Yesod*, or the seat (*cathedra*) of the One, upon which rests the Will as it imparts Form. Form and Matter are both superior to the Universal Intellect and as such they represent the fundamental principles of existence which issue from the First Essence.

As in standard Neoplatonic texts, the ultimate purpose of human existence is the return of the soul to its source. Gabirol modifies the standard Neoplatonic picture by claiming that when the soul attaches itself to the Will, it returns to the world of Universal Intellect and thus reaches the Source of Life. "Your intellect should distinguish most clearly matter from form, form from will, and will from movement. For if you do this, your soul will be purified, and your intellect will be enlightened and will penetrate to the world of intellect."[36] In order to achieve this level of perfection, humans must distance themselves from sensible things and turn themselves toward God. Only by turning from material existence toward will is spiritual perfection achieved.

But can humans acquire knowledge of the Divine Throne? In part, the answer depends upon how we translate the "*ad*" in *Keter Malhut* canto 26 "*ve'adav yagia ha-sekhel ve-ya'amod.*" If we read the word "*ad*" as inclusive, then the human intellect can, in theory, penetrate the Throne. This reading is reinforced in *Mekor Hayyim* 5.35, where Ibn Gabirol describes form and matter as "two closed gates," which the intellect finds difficult to enter. Ibn Gabirol does allow for the exceptional individual to attain knowledge of both Universal Matter and Form through philosophy. But God, or First Essence, cannot be known: the Divine Throne "marks the boundary between what is knowable and what lies beyond human ken."[37]

In this section, I have argued that Ibn Gabirol's cosmology differs from standard Greek and Islamic Neoplatonism in two important respects: in his concept of form and matter, and in his view of will. In his conception of matter, Gabirol has incorporated both Aristotelian and Stoic elements, the latter possibly from having read Galen. We now turn our attention to Maimonides, whose eclectic theory of

---

[33] Pessin 2013, 141.   [34] Ibn Gabirol *Mekor Hayyim* 5.42.   [35] See Tanenbaum 2002, 64.
[36] Ibn Gabirol *Mekor Hayyim* 5.43.   [37] Tanenbaum 2002, 68.

body/soul relation reflects an uneasy accommodation between Neoplatonic, Aristotelian, and Judaic elements. While it is not unlikely that his ambivalence stems in part from his medical activities, his views are deeply rooted in Neoplatonic ontology and cosmology.[38] I shall argue that Maimonides' extreme ambivalence to bodies and corporeality affects much of what he has to say about human behavior.

Unlike many of his Islamic and scholastic contemporaries, Maimonides does not develop the notions of matter and form into a cohesive theory. His characterization of matter and form, albeit sketchy, combines elements taken from both Neoplatonic and Aristotelian ontology. As we saw in Chapter 6, the Neoplatonists emphasized matter as the source of privation, evil, and all moral transgressions, while the Aristotelians supported a scientific study of matter as the underlying principle of generation and corruption. As ontological principles, matter, form, and privation are what render sublunar existence intelligible. Maimonides accepts in many of his discussions Aristotle's hylomorphic ontology, according to which matter and form combine to create a single compound entity: on a hylomorphic ontology, matter and form are always combined, and can never exist apart from each other. But Maimonides follows the Neoplatonists in positing matter as the cause of evil, thus introducing a value component into his ontology.

Maimonides mentions the creation of prime matter in *Guide* 1.28, when he explains the meaning of the Biblical terms referring to divine limbs that appeared in the account of the intellectual apprehension of Moses, Aaron and the elders of Israel: "for what they apprehended was the true reality of prime matter, which derives from Him ... He being the cause of its existence ... "[39] From this statement it is clear that prime matter derives from God. In *Guide* 2.17, Maimonides returns to the topic of prime matter, reiterating that it was brought into existence out of nothing, that it is everlasting, and it does not exist devoid of form. The hylomorphic composition of individual things is described further in *Guide* 2, prop. 22, as follows: "Every body is necessarily composed of two things and is necessarily accompanied by accidents. The two things constituting it are its matter and its form; and the accidents accompanying it are quantity, shape and position."[40] That matter is the principle of possibility is expressed as follows: "Whatsoever is something in *potentia* is necessarily endowed with matter, for possibility is always in matter."[41] The passivity of matter as contrasted to the activity of form is emphasized as well: "Matter, as you know, is always receptive and passive, if one considers its essence, and is not active except by accident. Form, on the other hand, is in its essence always active, ... and is passive only by accident."[42] These characterizations of matter and form in terms of activity and passivity, actuality and potentiality, reflect standard Aristotelian terminology.

---

[38] Ivry suggests that Maimonides' view of matter is essentially Platonic rather than Aristotelian, and is particularly indebted to Plotinus, who shared with the gnostics a negative view of matter. Ivry suggests that Maimonides "had a dim view of the physical, and thus material, dimension of life in general." He disparaged sex, particularly in the female, and saw the material principle as a "veil" separating us from God. See Ivry 2016, 172–3.

[39] Maimonides *Guide* 1.28:61.   [40] Maimonides *Guide* 2. Intro: 238.

[41] Maimonides *Guide* 2. Intro: 239.   [42] Maimonides *Guide* 1.28:61.

This hylomorphic ontology is tinged with Neoplatonic elements that are reflected in Maimonides' extended commentary upon the analogy developed in *Proverbs*: I include a selection as follows:

All bodies subject to generation and corruption are attained by corruption only because of their matter... The nature and true reality of matter are such that it never ceases to be joined to privation; hence no form remains constantly in it, for it perpetually puts off one form and puts on another. How extraordinary is what Solomon said in his wisdom when likening matter to a married harlot (*Proverbs* 6.26), for matter is in no way found without form and is consequently always like a married woman who is never separated from a man, and is never free. However, notwithstanding her being a married woman, she never ceases to seek for another man to substitute for her husband, and she deceives and draws him on in every way until he obtains from her what her husband used to obtain. This is the state of matter...[43]

Matter is a strong veil preventing the apprehension of that which is separate from matter as it truly is. It does this even if it is the noblest and purest matter, I mean to say even if it is the matter of the heavenly spheres. All the more is this true for the dark and turbid matter that is ours. Hence whenever our intellect aspires to apprehend the deity or one of the intellects, there subsists this great veil interposed between the two. This is alluded to in all the books of the prophets; namely that we are separated by a veil from God and that He is hidden from us by a heavy cloud, or by darkness or by a mist or by an enveloping cloud, and similar allusions to our incapacity to apprehend Him because of matter... And though that great assembly was greater than any vision of prophecy and beyond any analogy, it also indicated a notion; I refer to His manifestation... in a thick cloud. For it draws attention to the fact that the apprehension of His true reality is impossible for us because of the dark matter that encompasses us and not Him... for He... is not a body.[44]

In this important set of passages, Maimonides introduces many themes that permeate the *Guide*. Echoing the Neoplatonic dictum that matter is the root of all evil, Maimonides urges humans not to follow their bestial or material nature, since it is matter that stands in the way of human perfection. Maimonides tells us that matter acts as a veil, a barrier, to human knowledge of God, suggesting that ultimately no human can achieve knowledge of God. Solomon's parable is expanded further in light of the inherent corruptibility of matter. Just as a harlot is never satisfied with just one man, so too Maimonides construes matter as constantly flitting from one form to another; and just as a harlot is responsible for indulgence and vice in a man, so too is matter seen as the principle of evil and decay in humans.[45]

Having claimed that matter is a veil that prohibits the ultimate apprehension of formal reality, Maimonides goes on to argue that evil, and in particular its material instantiation, represents a privation, or lack: "all the evils are privations with which an act is only connected in the way we have explained: namely, through the fact that God has brought matter into existence provided with the nature it has—namely a nature that consists in matter always being a concomitant of privation, as is known."[46] What does it mean to say that the material instantiation of evil is a privation? This

---

[43] Maimonides *Guide* 3.8:430–1.   [44] Maimonides *Guide* 3.9:436–7.
[45] For further discussion of the misogynist tone of these passages, see Kellner 1998; Rudavsky 2010.
[46] Maimonides *Guide* 3.9:440.

statement has ontological as well as ethical significance. Ontologically, Maimonides is suggesting that ultimately matter has no positive existence, while from a value perspective matter accounts for human evil, weakness, and deviancy.

Maimonides did not leave us an extended treatise or treatment of the soul, and so his views must be pieced together from a variety of sources, including the *Guide*, the *Mishneh Torah, Perek Ḥelek*, and the *Eight Chapters*. On the topic of the soul, and the ethical issues arising out of his conception of soul, Maimonides was very much influenced by al-Fârâbî, who combined Aristotelian cosmology and psychology with Neoplatonic metaphysics and Platonic political thought. Al-Fârâbî's work *Aphorisms of the Statesman (Fusûl al-Madanî)* introduced Maimonides to many of these elements.[47] Following standard Aristotelian psychology as reflected in al-Fârâbî, he claims that there are five parts of the soul: nutritive, sentient, imaginative, appetitive, and rational.[48] Among powers of the soul, two are of special significance: imagination and reason. The imagination is described in numerous passages in the *Guide*,[49] and we will discuss its importance more fully in Chapter 9, when we turn to prophecy. In brief, the imaginative part is that which preserves the impressions of sensibly perceived objects after they vanish from the immediacy of the senses that perceived them. The imaginative power puts together many impossible things, and so must be approached carefully. The rational part is that power by which humans perceive intelligibles, deliberate, acquire the sciences, and distinguish between base and noble acts.[50] It is what distinguishes humans from other species, and that is the faculty to which the scriptural verse "let us make man in our image" refers. The function of the rational faculty is to rule all the parts of the body in such a way that all the other parts acquiesce to reason.[51] The rational faculty is thus "very noble indeed," and includes both theoretical and practical powers. By means of the theoretical intellect, humans know "the essence of the unchanging beings."[52] Since the soul is the form of a body possessing life, it is inseparable from the body in the same way that form is inseparable from matter. It is indivisible and specific to its species. Following al-Fârâbî, Maimonides draws an extended analogy between soul and body on the one hand, and soul-practitioner and physician on the other hand. The sickness of the soul, claimed al-Fârâbî, consists in its doing wicked and ugly deeds. In order to treat the soul, the statesman and king requires "knowledge of the soul as a whole, the parts of the soul, the defects and vices which are liable to affect it and every part of it. . . . "[53] So too, we find Maimonides commenting that a healthy soul is one that "always does good and fine things and performs noble actions," whereas a diseased soul "always does bad and ugly things and performs base actions."[54] Just as the physician who cures the body must have a perfect knowledge of the body, so the soul-practitioner

---

[47] The work *Fusûl* is cited by Maimonides' pupil and is referenced by Maimonides in his Aphorisms. Like al-Fârâbî, Maimonides tells us that psychology is a necessary preparation for the study of ethics, and for the study of Law. See al-Fârâbî 1961; see also al-Fârâbî 2001.

[48] Maimonides *EC* 1.61. Maimonides' description of the parts of the soul also follows al-Fârâbî's *Fusûl*, which itself is clearly modeled after Aristotle's *Nicomachean Ethics* 1.13 1102a–b. See al-Fârâbî 1961, *Fusûl* 1.6:29.

[49] See for example, Maimonides *Guide* 2.36:369ff.; 1.73:206–12; 1.52:114; 2.12:280.

[50] Maimonides *EC* 1:63.   [51] Maimonides *Guide* 1.72:191.   [52] Maimonides *EC* 1:63.

[53] Al-Fârâbî 1961, *Fusûl* 1.4:28.   [54] Maimonides *EC* 3:65.

who improves its moral qualities must have a perfect idea of what makes the soul sick and what preserves its health.

III Immortality and the Active Intellect: Halevi, Maimonides, and Gersonides

The doctrine of the Active Intellect, introduced by Aristotle, plays an important role in both Islamic and Jewish medieval theories of immortality, which were couched against the backdrop of Aristotle's enormously influential work *De Anima*. In the *De Anima*, Aristotle claims that "intellect understands all things" (*nous panta noei*), unlike perception, which is limited by empirical data, the senses, etc:

> And in fact mind as we have described it is what it is by virtue of becoming all things, while there is another which is what it is by virtue of making all things: this is a sort of positive state like light; for in a sense light makes potential colors into actual colors. Mind in this sense of it is separable, impassible, unmixed, since it is in its essential nature activity.... When mind is set free from its present conditions it appears as just what it is and nothing more: this alone is immortal and eternal... and without it nothing thinks.[55]

In this enigmatic passage Aristotle seems to postulate the existence of an Active Intellect that is separable from the Passive Intellect and primarily responsible for the intellectual activities of the human mind. This leads Aristotle to conclude that intellect is unmixed (pure potential), separable from the body (since it does not have a bodily organ of its own, unlike perception), unaffected by what is being known, and reflexive in a way that perception is not. Further, Aristotle claims that intellect is not entirely passive (like perception), but part of it is active, reflecting our own intellectual activity.[56] The passive part of our intellect cannot account for how thinking begins, what sets it off in the first place; according to Aristotle, we require an active principle to bring about the process of thinking. Hence, the Active Intellect is introduced to explain what brings about, or actualizes, thinking. But what is it and what does it do? These two questions turn out to be two of the most puzzling conundra in Aristotelian scholarship. Aristotle draws upon the analogy of light in *De Anima* 430a16–18. Just as we need a medium (air) for us to see, so too we need a medium in order to understand. Just as air makes something seen, or see-able, so too the Active Intellect makes intelligibles "think-able"; it is the medium between the thing thought (*noeton*) and the Passive Intellect.

Aristotle's theory of the Active Intellect became popular among medieval Islamic and Jewish philosophers for several reasons: first, it provided the springboard for theories of philosophical psychology and immortality of soul. Further, it raised questions concerning the personal nature of immortality. The Active Intellect contains no memories, no thoughts or emotions, no personality, no individuality; all these are contained in the passive intellect, which dies along with the body. And so in an important sense, survival of the soul *qua* Active Intellect has nothing at all to do with *me*. But what theological mileage can we derive from Aristotle's "immortality"

---

[55] Aristotle *De Anima* 3.5:10–25.   [56] Aristotle *De Anima* 430a15.

thesis if what is most true and essential about the individual is not preserved? Is this type of immortality at all useful for a theological system of reward and punishment? Is immortality itself personal or general? Does the Active Intellect allow for particularity, or is it a "general, indivisible" in which we all share? Jewish and Islamic philosophers grappled with these questions in trying to provide a theological theory of immortality that incorporated Aristotelian science.

Avicenna and Averroës provided different accounts of the soul, Active Intellect, and immortality. In general, Islamic philosophers took Aristotle's theory of Active Intellect and folded it into a cosmology presided over by a "first being" who is pure intellect. Active Intellect stands at the end of the long chain of these celestial intelligences.[57] It serves as the link between God and human beings: as the giver of forms, it plays a crucial role in human knowledge as well as prophecy, and serves as a foundation for immortality. For Avicenna, the soul is more than an organizing principle of the body; it is a subsistent entity in its own right, with its own substantial being.[58] The human intellect is an immaterial substance, and needs a body as a tool to reach perfection. Human souls do not antedate a body, but are temporally originated. But how, then, do we account for the immortality of the soul? Avicenna claims that upon the death of the body, the soul retains its individuality in virtue of its substantiality; the very fact that the soul was born with a particular body, and shared all the experiences of that body, is sufficient to individuate the soul personally. As McGinnis puts it, "the soul can and does survive the body's death, continuing to carry on an intellectual existence wholly disassociated from the body."[59] This emphasis upon the importance of the body affects Avicenna's notion of Active Intellect as well. Once the human soul is free of the body, it is able to access the intelligibles in the Active Intellect immediately and without mediation. Avicenna thus provides us with a true substance dualism—the material body and immaterial soul—in which both substances work very closely together.

In contrast to Avicenna, the roles of the material and agent (or active) intellects are more problematic for Averroës. Arguing that both the material and agent intellects are incorporeal and separate from the body, Averroës claims that they cannot be individuated by the body, leading to a view according to which both intellects are indistinguishable for all human knowers.[60] Averroës thus introduced the doctrine of "monopsychism" as it has come to be known, namely a view of the unicity of the intellect, according to which the material and the agent intellect are separate substances, and yet one for all human knowers. On this view, there is no personal immortality, only impersonal or general immortality. Averroës' basic idea is that immortality is a state attained through intellectual activity and achievement but is non-individual. The radical Aristotelians were attracted to Averroës' psychological

---

[57] The human potential intellect is situated immediately after the active intellect in this hierarchical scheme. The role of the Active Intellect, in this scheme, is to lead the human (potential) intellect from a state of potency to one of actuality. When the human intellect achieves this actualized existence, it enters a state of perfection known as "conjunction" with the Active Intellect. This state of conjunction is normally achieved at death, and hence is associated with immortality. The Active Intellect was also associated with the phenomenon of prophecy, and in some cases (e.g., Avicenna) with the cause of existence itself.

[58] Black 2007, 309.   [59] McGinnis 2010, 129.   [60] Black 2007, 321.

theory according to which the human intellect is capable of attaining immortality by means of intellectual conjunction with the Active Intellect.[61]

One of the most straightforward descriptions of the role played by the Active Intellect in immortality occurs in Book Five of Halevi's *Kuzari*. In response to the king's request to the Ḥaver (the spokesperson for the Jews) for a summary of the views of the philosophers, Halevi provides a complete summary of matter and form, soul and body, the tripartite division of the soul, culminating with Avicenna's theory of Active Intellect. In this summary, the soul is characterized as the form or entelechy of the body, more specifically the primary perfection of the body.[62] The soul, according to the "philosophers," is characterized as potential intellect, because "it resembles matter which forms the connecting link between nothingness and actuality."[63] Halevi summarizes several arguments of the philosophers proving that the soul is real, indivisible, incorporeal, and distinct from the body. Reflecting Avicenna, he describes the soul as "a substance with an existence of its own, endowed with angelic attributes and divine substantiality."[64] He then turns to a proof that there exists a spiritual substance, or Active Intellect, "distinct from the body, which stands in the same relation to the soul as the light to the eye, and as soon as the soul is separated from the body, it is united to that substance."[65]

The king finds this narrative compelling, but Halevi, through the Ḥaver, then goes on to critique this theory, focusing in particular upon the very piece of conjunction that Avicenna and his followers found so seductive. Why should we need "such artificial theories" asks the Ḥaver, especially inasmuch as they are incapable of proof or refutation? What sense can we make of such anomalies as forgetting, acquiring, and losing knowledge prior to death? And how do these theories account for the fact that philosophers are not self-conscious during sleep; that they are subject to forgetfulness (like ordinary mortals)? Philosophers, according to Halevi, are highly overrated, but in fact they are "full of doubts" and we should not pay too much attention to their theories.[66] Halevi, through the Ḥaver, thus rejects the entire theory of Active Intellect.

Not surprisingly, in contradistinction to Halevi, the Active Intellect plays a more important role in Maimonides' discussion. We saw above that according to Maimonides, only part of the soul—the intellectual part—is properly immortal. When separated from the body, the immortal part of the individual, and not the entire soul per se, enjoys a special sort of existence akin to the Active Intellect. Maimonides' main discussion of this issue is contained in the *Guide*, as well as in *Treatise on Resurrection*.[67] In *Guide* 1, 41, Maimonides distinguishes three meanings for the term *nefesh*, or soul, and suggests that only in the third sense, that is, as a rational intellect, can the soul be considered immortal. However, the soul that survives after death is not like that a person has when alive, for the former enjoys a separate existence after death and is a distinct ontological reality:

---

[61] Feldman 1992, 331.   [62] Halevi *Kuzari* 5.12:260.   [63] Halevi *Kuzari* 5.12:263.
[64] Halevi *Kuzari* 5.12:267.   [65] Halevi *Kuzari* 5.12:267.   [66] Halevi *Kuzari* 5.14:273.
[67] See the recent translation of this treatise by Halkin in Maimonides 1985a.

For that which comes into being at the time a man is generated is merely the faculty consisting in preparedness, whereas the thing that after death is separate from matter is the thing that has become actual and not the soul that also comes into being; the latter is identical with the spirit that comes into being.[68]

In this passage Maimonides seems to be suggesting that when separated from the body, the immortal soul enjoys a special sort of existence akin to the Active Intellect. For, like the Active Intellect, this soul has no personal features. But if there are no such personal features, how are immortal, incorporeal souls individuated? Maimonides does not expressly address this issue, as will Gersonides. We can only infer his view from what he has to say about his predecessors. Some contextual evidence suggests that Maimonides favors Ibn Bâjja's doctrine of the unity of intellect. For inasmuch as what remains of one soul is neither the cause nor the effect of another, Maimonides suggests that "all are one in number," as Ibn Bâjja was wont to suggest.[69] This interpretation is supported by Guide 2, prop. 16, in which Maimonides states that multiplicity is ultimately founded upon materiality.

In whatsoever is not a body, multiplicity cannot be cognized by the intellect, unless the thing in question is a force in a body, for then the multiplicity of the individual forces would subsist in virtue of the multiplicity of the matters or substances in which these forces are to be found. Hence no multiplicity at all can be cognized by the intellect in the separate things, which are neither a body nor a force in a body, except when they are causes and effects.[70]

Regardless of whether this proposition is read as a metaphysical or an epistemological claim, it upholds the contention that, inasmuch as immortal souls have no causal or motive features, they (unlike the heavenly spheres) are not individuated after death.[71]

Ultimate human perfection consists in the active contemplation of eternal truths. Since all other faculties are connected to the body, nothing remains to preserve these faculties when the body dies. Maimonides rejects the eschatological view that the world to come will come into being only when this world passes out of existence. Why did the sages call the afterlife "the world to come"? The world to come exists now, he tells us: it is called the world to come only because human beings "will enter into it at a time subsequent to the life of the present world in which we now exist with body and soul—and this existence comes first."[72] But Maimonides does not expound upon the sort of existence to be enjoyed in the world to come, which depends in no large measure on whether the body ultimately is resurrected and reunited with the soul. Maimonides' views on physical resurrection are complex, and beyond the scope of this chapter.

We turn now to Gersonides who approaches the issue of individuation and immortality somewhat differently than did his predecessors. In answer to these questions, Gersonides first summarizes four representative positions as follows:

---

[68] Maimonides Guide 1.70:174. For extended discussion of this passage, see Ivry 2016.
[69] Maimonides Guide 1.74:221. For the importance of Ibn Bâjja, see Altmann 1965.
[70] Maimonides Guide 2, prop. 16:237.   [71] See Wolfson 1929, 108.
[72] Maimonides MT 8.8:91a.

The view of Alexander of Aphrodisias, according to whom the material intellect is in the individual soul in its entirety; this intellect is "nothing but a disposition, that is, a passive receptor. In contrast, the "other intellect" is identified with the divine Agent Intellect, which is eternal and totally separate from humans. This latter intellect represents the total intellectual cognitions acquired by an individual and is to some extent immortal.[73]

The view of Themistius, according to whom the material intellect itself is a "separable intellect that is neither generated nor corruptible"; in other words, the material intellect is incorporeal and eternal, and ultimately identifiable with the Agent Intellect.[74]

The view of Averroës is a conflation of I and 2 in that the material intellect is a separate substance and identified with the Agent Intellect, but "insofar as it attaches itself to the human soul, it is a disposition and has a potentiality for knowledge." That is, both the Agent Intellect and the material intellect are ultimately one and the same in all men.[75]

The view of the "moderns", according to whom the material intellect is "a separable intellect that is generated essentially but not from something else."[76]

Inasmuch as Gersonides' own position reflects that of Alexander, he raises a number of objections to the other accounts. A full examination of these arguments is beyond the scope of this chapter; I should, however, like to examine briefly those arguments that pertain most directly to our topic of personal vs. general immortality.

Against Themistius' position that the Agent and material intellects are equivalent, Gersonides raises the following sorts of objections. First, he argues that Themistius' position is unable to account for the individuation of persons on the grounds that separate forms cannot be numerically individuated:

[Material] form is individuated in so far as it is manifested by different subjects, so that, for example, this form of Reuben is numerically different from the form of Simon. If this were not so, one and the same form would be both knowledgeable and ignorant at the same time on the same point.... But this is utterly absurd. And so individuation of this form can be accounted for on Alexander's hypothesis, but this is not the case on Themistius' hypothesis, for separate substances cannot be numerically individuated, except if they differ as species, as has been demonstrated by arguments proper to this subject.[77]

Gersonides' point can be restated as follows. If both Reuben and Simon share the same material form, and this form is reflected in their cognitive abilities, then when Reuben knows *p* and Simon is ignorant of *p*, it follows that one and the same material form both knows and fails to know *p*. Hence, Gersonides concludes that there must be another way to individuate these cognitive processes.

Themistius attempted to minimize such difficulties by claiming that Alexander is unable to account for the identity of the act of knowing and that which is known. Gersonides, however, responds that Themistius' gambit is insufficient on the grounds

[73] Gersonides *Wars* vol. 1, 1.1:110.   [74] Gersonides *Wars* vol. 1, 1.1:110.   [75] Ibid.
[76] Ibid.   [77] Gersonides *Wars* vol. 1, 1.2:114–15.

that epistemological identity does not necessarily presuppose that the intellect be a separate form, as Themistius insists. Rather, Gersonides supports Alexander's attempt to account for this identity on the grounds that cognition need not be of particulars, but can be of general natures that are identified with the material intellect.

Gersonides then turns to various considerations that undermine the Averroist position, according to which the same material intellect is found in all persons. He first points out that, in Averroës' position, two things that have different definitions would be numerically one. But this according to Gersonides is absurd on the grounds that "it is evident that the definition and essence of the Agent Intellect differ from that of the material intellect. But if we were to claim that the two are identical, then two things of different natures would be numerically identical, which is absolutely absurd. For it is impossible for them to be one in species; all the more so is it impossible for them to be numerically identical."[78] And if, as Averroës claims, the material intellect is identical with the Agent Intellect, then one of two situations must arise: either "insofar as it is conjoined with us it is numerically one . . . or, insofar as it is conjoined with us it is numerically many."[79] Gersonides argues, however, that both options are untenable. The first is rejected on grounds similar to those used previously against Themistius; namely, that the very same intellect would be both knowledgeable and ignorant with respect to the same question.[80]

The second option raises a number of problems having to do with individuating particulars. Most important, Gersonides raises the important issue of the separability of these separate forms:

The separate forms differ from other forms because they differ only qualitatively, whereas material forms differ among themselves both qualitatively and quantitatively. Qualitative diversity, for example, is illustrated in the sentence, The form of a horse is different from the form of an ass. Quantitative diversity, for example, is illustrated in the sentence, The form of this horse is different from the form of a second horse. Accordingly, since the material intellect can be diversified quantitatively . . . it is thereby not separate; for a separate form is not multiplied according to the diversity of subjects of which it is the form. But it has been alleged that the material intellect is identical with the Agent Intellect, which is separate. This is absolutely false.[81]

What Gersonides has in mind in this passage is that, on the view that the Agent Intellect is numerically diverse when conjoined to humans, there would be no individuating principle to account for this diversity except on quantitative grounds; but inasmuch as quantitative considerations do not apply to the Agent Intellect and individuation must at least take into account material features, it follows that the Agent Intellect cannot be numerically diverse. Gersonides therefore rejects Averroës' position.

Finally, the "modernist" view, according to which the material intellect is generated but not from anything else, is rejected for a variety of reasons. For example, this view propounds two separate generations for an individual, one for the individual intellect and another for its body. But this entails that one man be actually two insofar as his parts exist independently. Gersonides rejects this position as well on the

[78] Gersonides Wars vol. 1, 1.4:134.   [79] Gersonides Wars vol. 1, 1.4:137.
[80] Gersonides Wars vol. 1, 1.4:138.   [81] Gersonides Wars vol. 1, 1.4:138.

grounds that, when there is no unity between the parts of the definition, the defined entity is actually two things.

The import of Gersonides' critique of his predecessors can be reduced to three main issues. From a theological perspective, it is clear that the doctrine of unity of intellect threatens the notion of personal immortality. For if all humans share the same intellect, then upon physical death, all that remains of the person is an unindividualized intellect. Epistemologically, the doctrine is unable to account for how it is that two (or more) knowers can entertain contrary items of knowledge; or more stringently, how one person can be in error of an item that another person knows. And from a metaphysical perspective, the main problem is how to individuate this separate intellect when it is manifested in many individuals: for if it is individuated materially on the basis that individual bodies differ, then the substance is no longer incorporeal or separate. As Feldman has pointed out, in this theory an incorporeal substance either is a unique member of a species or is not a member of a species at all.[82]

Let us turn, then, to Gersonides' own position with respect to immortality. As we have seen, Gersonides agrees with Alexander that immortality consists in the intellectual perfection of the material intellect. However, he disagrees with Alexander over the precise nature of this intellectual attainment. For Alexander (according to Gersonides) had claimed that immortality is achieved when the intellect acquires knowledge of the Agent Intellect (hence the term "acquired intellect" is introduced). Immortality is thus understood by Alexander as a form of conjunction between the Agent and acquired intellects. "They [the followers of Alexander] maintain that the material intellect is capable of immortality and subsistence when it reaches that level of perfection where the objects of knowledge that it apprehends are themselves intellects, in particular the Agent Intellect... [material intellect] is immortal when it is united with the Agent Intellect."[83]

Gersonides rejects this notion of conjunction, however, and replaces it with a model of immortality according to which it is the content of knowledge of the acquired intellect that matters. When the content of the acquired intellect mirrors the rational ordering of the Agent Intellect, immortality is achieved. What is the content of this knowledge? The Agent Intellect must possess complete knowledge of the sublunary world; that is, it "contains a conception of the rational order obtaining in all individuals."[84] The anti-Platonic tenor of this position is emphasized when Gersonides describes in more detail what it is that the Agent Intellect knows. For according to Gersonides the knowledge of the Agent Intellect must be grounded in the domain of particulars.

Universality accrues to [this order] by virtue of its grounding in perceived particulars existing outside the mind... The definition is the very order that is in the mind of Agent Intellect according to which the genus is generated. This order is exhibited in some sense in each and every individual instance of that genus, as we have seen. It does not follow from this, however, that all these individuals are numerically one, as would be the case for those who believe in

---

[82] See Feldman's notes in Gersonides Wars vol. 1, 79.
[83] Gersonides Wars vol. 1, 1.8:170.   [84] Gersonides Wars vol. 1, 1.4:136.

[Platonic] universals. In this manner knowledge of accidental properties also is established, not just of essential properties...[85]

In this important passage, Gersonides suggests that his position avoids the epistemological difficulties apparent in a realist ontology. Inasmuch as the material intellect reflects the knowledge inherent in the Agent Intellect and inasmuch as this knowledge is grounded in particulars, it follows that humans can have knowledge of particulars; in this acquisition of knowledge lies immortality.

IV Immortality and Resurrection of the Body

We have seen that the majority of our thinkers adhere to some version of immortality of soul. But does immortality of soul include resurrection of the body, namely that the dead will be revived in their bodies and return to live on earth? We end this section with a brief discussion of physical resurrection, a doctrine that has thrived as a major component of Jewish eschatology: the idea that God can revive the dead appears already in biblical texts, and it is prescribed as an article of faith in the *Mishnah Sanhedrin* 10:1: "All of Israel has a portion in the world to come, as it is said (*Isaiah* 60:21) 'And Thy people are all righteous, at the End they shall inherit the land...' and the following have no portion in the world to come: one who says, 'There is no resurrection of the dead.'"

Saadiah Gaon provides an orthodox interpretation of the belief in resurrection. In Book 6 of *Doctrines and Beliefs*, Saadiah begins with a general "statement of faith" that the soul is created in the heart when the body is formed, lives with the body, separates from the body at death and is reconstituted with the body at resurrection. He summarizes and refutes six incorrect theories of soul, and then presents his own theory as the seventh, namely that the soul is a "created substance,"[86] the substance of which is "comparable in purity to that of the heavenly spheres... it attains luminosity as a result of the light which it receives from God."[87] Body and soul work together throughout life; after death, the body suffers corruption while the soul is stored in a celestial realm or treasury until the final resurrection when the two are reconstituted. In Books seven through nine, Saadiah focuses more specifically upon issues of resurrection, immortality and redemption.

Saadiah raises an interesting conundrum in chapter seven, which raises interesting questions of individuation and personal identity. Suppose, he writes, that a lion eats a person, the lion drowns and is eaten by a fish, the fish is then caught and eaten by an individual who is subsequently burned into ashes. "Whence would the Creator restore the first man? Would He do it from the lion or the fish or the second man or the fire or the ashes?"[88] In response, Saadiah distinguishes between total annihilation and disintegration of parts, and claims that the constituent parts of the original individual are "set aside, not being mixed with the elemental masses. Rather they

---

[85] Gersonides *Wars* vol. 1, 1.6:162–3.   [86] Saadiah *Beliefs* 6.3:241.
[87] Saadiah *Beliefs* 6.3:242.   [88] Saadiah *Beliefs* 7.7:278.

remain separate until the time of the resurrection."[89] And so resurrection in such an anomalous case is no more difficult than in any other.

Compare Saadiah's straightforward acceptance of physical resurrection with Maimonides' ambiguous response. As we have seen above, Maimonides repeatedly stated that immortality does not include the body: "In the world to come there is nothing corporeal, and no material substance; there are only souls of the righteous without bodies—like the ministering angels."[90] Further, no mention is made in the *Guide* about resurrection of a physical body. Attacked during his lifetime by rabbis who accused him of rejecting the (dogmatic) belief in physical resurrection of the body, Maimonides wrote the *Essay on Resurrection* in 1191 in an attempt to refute these charges. Since the controversy over Maimonides' views on resurrection came right when he was completing the *Guide*, he used this controversy as an opportunity to address the topic of miracle.[91] In this essay, Maimonides modifies his position on physical resurrection to suggest that souls are restored to their bodies after death, but only in the Messianic era, which precedes the period of the "world to come" (*olam ha-ba*). Maimonides explicitly connects the miracle of the resurrection of bodies with the creation of the world. Clearly, Maimonides' heart is not in proving that the doctrine of resurrection of the body is philosophically tenable. He presents it as a view outside the purview of rationality, as contrary to the natural order, and does not even try to offer rational arguments on its behalf.[92] Maimonides half-heartedly accedes to the masses, realizing how important the doctrine is to them theologically, but does not accept it himself.[93]

In response to Maimonides' half-hearted acquiescence, Ḥasdai Crescas returns to a more traditional view of resurrection. In chapter II.6 of *Light of the Lord*, he distinguishes four questions pertaining to resurrection of the body: whether the resurrection will be complete or partial; the time of the resurrection; whether persons

---

[89] Saadiah *Beliefs* 7.7:279.   [90] Maimonides *ER* 8.2:90a.

[91] Eran suggests that Maimonides might have been influenced by al-Ghazâlî's critique of Avicenna on this topic. In his *Incoherence of Philosophy* (*Tahâfut*), al-Ghazâlî accused the philosophers, with whom he included Avicenna, of denying that the body returns to the soul. Maimonides' counter-arguments echo fragments of this disputation between al-Ghazâlî and Avicenna. In fact, Maimonides disagrees with Avicenna on two counts: he denies corporeal pleasure in the world to come, and he denies individual survival of the soul, two doctrines espoused by Avicenna. See Eran 2001; al-Ghazâlî 1997.

[92] In this work, we will not enter into the complex issue of whether Maimonides ascribed to the doctrine of resurrection of the body. For further discussion of physical resurrection, see Rudavsky 2010; Ivry 2016.

[93] In Halkin and Hartman 1985, 246, Hartmann notes the irony involved in the fact that Maimonides, whose writings had deliberately neutralized the importance of the miraculous, was enjoined to compose a final work in ostensible support of the doctrine of miracles. Although explicitly written for the common person, this work is complex and reflects a deep ambivalence on Maimonides' part. One effect of this controversy over resurrection was to remind Maimonides of the importance of miracles in ordinary people's lives: miracles validate God's continuous interest in us, and God's miraculous intervention in the form of resurrecting our bodies serves as confirmation of God's concern for particulars, giving meaning not only to petitionary prayer, but to theories of providence as well. But let us not forget the vehemence with which Maimonides has attacked and rejected this anthropocentric view of God. From this perspective, the *Essay* reflects Maimonides' frustration with the masses, and his recognition of the pedagogical necessity to pander to their level. Remember, though, that Maimonides knows that philosophically inclined readers will not accept the creation of the world in time; presumably these same readers will understand that resurrection is rationally impossible, and will understand that resurrection of the body is an exoteric theory for the masses.

will die after their bodies are resurrected; and finally, whether the day of judgment will occur at the time of the resurrection. Crescas suggests that the resurrection will occur after the coming of the Messiah, leading him to claim that the righteous will live forever in their "refined" perfected bodies.

In contradistinction to the Aristotelian intellectualism reflected by both Maimonides and Gersonides, Crescas emphasizes a non-intellectual form of felicity. Crescas saw this emphasis upon intellectual contemplation of God as subversive to Judaism in part because it ignored the importance of performance of the commandments.[94] Crescas states his aim in *Light* II.6.1: "it will be demonstrated that the eternal happiness of the soul is consequent on the love and fear of God."[95] This demonstration rests on several propositions, including that the human soul is "a spiritual substance" and not an intellectual cognizing substance in itself, and that perfection of this spiritual soul brings about eternal felicity.[96] Arguing that the ultimate end of human existence requires perfections of the body, of the moral qualities, and perfection of "opinions," Crescas disagrees with both Maimonides and Gersonides about the content and importance of these latter. He first describes the view of those "that the intellect becomes constituted as a substance from what it apprehends of the intelligibles... accordingly eternal happiness consists of the apprehension of the acquired intelligibles... and each of those who attain happiness will rejoice and delight after death in that which he has apprehended."[97]

Crescas then rejects this Aristotelian/Maimonidean/Gersonidean claim that the ultimate human goal is intellectual perfection on several grounds, both theological and philosophical. Such opinions, he says, "destroy the Law and extract the roots of the Tradition," by denying theories of reward and punishment, rejecting the importance of the commandments, and denying theories of resurrection.[98] He first cites passages from traditional Jewish sources and then argues against the coherence of the intellectualist view on philosophical grounds. For example, the rabbis tell us that performance of the commandments offers eternal life; "the delight and misery of the souls [after death] shall be according to the number of merits and sins"; and that the practice of the commandments is important.[99] Crescas finds the doctrine unintelligible philosophically as well, offering a number of objections based on the ambiguity of the relation between the acquired intellect and the individual. He argues, for example that the acquired intellect is not the form of the individual, and that "the passing away of the incorporeal substance (sc. The acquired intellect) may surely be conceived without the passing away of the man."[100] For this and many other reasons, Crescas concludes that the doctrine of acquired intellect (in both its Maimonidean and Gersonidean permutations) is proved untenable: their followers "were seduced to follow them, and they did not perceive, nor did it enter their minds,

---

[94] For a comprehensive summary of Crescas' views on felicity, see Tirosh-Samuelson 2003; Tirosh-Samuelson 2009. See also Kent 1995 for discussion of the sea change in Christian ethics. She notes a similar move in Scholastic ethics as well.

[95] Crescas *Light* II.6.1 in Harvey 1998, 124.   [96] Crescas *Light* II.6.1 in Harvey 1998, 124.

[97] Crescas *Light* II.6.1 in Frank, Leaman, and Manekin 2000, 266.

[98] See Crescas *Light* II.6.1, in Frank, Leaman, and Manekin 2000.

[99] Crescas *Light* II.6.1, in Frank, Leaman, and Manekin 2000, 267.

[100] Crescas *Light* II.6.1, in Frank, Leaman, and Manekin 2000, 268.

how thereby they were razing the wall of the edifice of the Law and breaching its hedges, even as the theory itself is groundless!"[101]

After refuting the concept of an acquired intellect, Crescas then presents an alternative understanding of ultimate felicity based on observance of the law and commandments. Crescas denies that God is pure intellect, and replaces the intellectual depiction of God with passion, with joy and love. In contradistinction to Maimonides and especially Gersonides, Crescas emphasizes that joy and love are essential to God, and related to God's will.[102] Crescas portrays God not as an active knower, but as the active lover: "God's love expresses God's essence, goodness and benevolence...God's love not only sustains the world, it also functions as the perfection of natural things."[103] Crescas' redefinition of *imitatio Dei* in terms of love, rather than intellectual perfection, replaces the intellectualist view of felicity with a "non-intellectualist interpretation of human love that focuses on the willingness of the individual to be committed to God."[104] The eternal happiness of the soul, he avers, is not dependent upon holding the right opinions or upon actions, but rather the eternal happiness of soul is consequent upon the love and fear of God. It is "love for God...that leads to the eternal life of the individual soul...reflected not in the contemplation of intelligibles but in the actual performance of the commandments."[105] Seeing God as a "lover" reinforces the importance of the very act of loving for human beings: the notion of *imitatio Dei* in Crescas' thinking reflects the importance of *loving* God rather than *knowing* God. Crescas then tries to make the case that love and fear of God are the ultimate aim of philosophy as well, and so from this perspective, philosophers and the multitude stand on the same level: diligence in the satisfaction of the commandments, and not intellectual perfection, is what matters for ultimate felicity: "the greater the love between God and man, the greater and stronger will be the adhesion."[106]

By the mid-fourteenth century, Averroës' Middle Commentaries on Aristotle's *Organon* were translated into Hebrew, and as we noted in Chapter 1, the influence of scholastic logic permeated Jewish philosophy. The works of Jewish philosophers such as Narboni, Ibn Kaspi, and others working within this new intellectual climate contributed further to discussions of individuality. As we move into the latter part of the fifteenth century, the work of Judah Abravanel represents an excellent example of the fusion of Hebraic thought with the Latin west's revival of Greek philosophy (as exemplified by Ficino and others). Judah wrote his major dialogue *Dialoghi di Amore* with the interlocutors representing the epitome of Platonic lovers. In this work, he constructs an allegory between two Jewish courtiers, Philo and Sophia, in order to illustrate the importance of the philosophical love of God.[107] Philo has explained to Sophia the origins of love, which raises the more general question of when love was

---

[101] Crescas *Light* II.6.1, in Frank, Leaman, and Manekin 2000, 269. See Tirosh-Samuelson 2003, 383: "Crescas concludes that the doctrine of the acquired intellect is both philosophically unsound and religiously heretical."
[102] See Harvey's illuminating discussion in 1998, 100ff. Harvey notes (106) that Crescas is careful not to attribute passions per se to God.
[103] See Tirosh-Samuelson 2003, 385.   [104] See Tirosh-Samuelson 2003, 386.
[105] Tirosh-Samuelson 2003, 387.   [106] Crescas *Light* II.6.1, in Harvey 1998, 126.
[107] For details of Judah Abravanel's work, see Tirosh-Rothschild, 1997, 522ff.

born: was it produced from eternity or was it created in time? Philo immediately connects this question with the issue of the origin of the universe, which leads to a summary of the three regnant positions on the creation of the universe—that of Plato, that of Aristotle, and that of Moses. In the course of explaining why on the Aristotelian model the universe is eternal, Philo alludes to the view that time must likewise be eternal. Philo then attempts a reconciliation of Platonic theory with Mosaic law and mysticism, applying this reconciliation to the doctrine of love. The dialogue contains an elaborate description of the soul's ascent and union in an afterlife.[108]

The full extent of Abravanel's influence upon Spinoza remains an issue of contention.[109] We do know that Spinoza owned a copy of Abravanel's *Dialoghi di Amore* in his library, in a Spanish translation, and many of the themes in that work reappear in Spinoza. In his early work *Short Treatise*, Spinoza reiterates the general theme of *Dialoghi di Amore*, namely the intellectual love of God to which to aspire. This theme reappears in Book 5 of Spinoza's *Ethics* as well, and shares many features with Gersonides' theory of immortality. The final propositions of *Ethics* 5 can be reduced to three main doctrines: A part of the mind is eternal and survives decay of the body; Intuitive science (third kind of knowledge) yields blessedness; and blessedness consists in intellectual love of God. These three doctrines represent the culmination of several strands: the notion of the free human, the overcoming of the passions in order to achieve this notion of freedom, and the incorporation of knowledge as a criterion for freedom.[110] In *Ethics* 5:23, Spinoza states that "The human Mind cannot be absolutely destroyed with the Body, but something of it remains which is eternal."[111] Spinoza's demonstration of this proposition rests on *Ethics* 2:8c, namely that we do not attribute to the human mind any duration that can be defined by time except insofar as it expresses the actual existence of the body that is defined by duration and time. After the separation from or cessation of the body, however, duration no longer pertains to mind; because it is constituted by God's essence, mind will necessarily be eternal. Spinoza continues that "we feel and know by experience that we are eternal . . . this existence that it [our mind] has cannot be defined by time or explained through duration."[112]

I have argued elsewhere that in these passages, Spinoza comes closest to reflecting Gersonides' depiction of immortality in terms of knowledge of particulars: just as Gersonides argued above that the Agent Intellect represents the total intellectual cognitions acquired by an individual, so too Spinoza argues that the more singular things the mind understands, the more it understands God.[113] On the basis of this characterization, immortality, or eternity of mind, for Spinoza must be personal. Individuals are separate one from the other, and even after death, individuals retain their individuality with respect to one another and God. Of course, there is an

---

[108] For details, see the new translation of Abravanel's *Dialoghi di Amore* (Abravanel 2009).

[109] Wolfson, for example, has argued that "Leo Hebraeus' influence upon Spinoza has been unduly exaggerated" (Wolfson 1934, vol. 2, 277), and suggests that many of the supposed influential passages are not unique to Abravanel and can be traced to many other later medieval works.

[110] For extensive discussion of these themes, see Nadler 2001.   [111] Spinoza *Ethics* 5.23:607.

[112] Spinoza *Ethics* 5.23s:607-8.   [113] See Rudavsky 2000; Rudavsky 2001.

important difference between claiming that eternal minds differ from one another based on levels of knowledge achieved, and claiming that they contain individuating features that define their personal, individual nature. The first claim has to do with criteria of differentiation among minds, whereas the second has to do with criteria of individuation identifying minds within God. Both Gersonides and Spinoza want to claim that just because the knower becomes one with God or Active Intellect, it does not entail that the individuating features of the knower are dissolved into a general unity. And yet the threat of monopsychism underlies all of these thinkers. The implications of this threat unfold more fully when we turn now to moral and political theories.

9

Happiness, Virtue, and Political Society
Living the Good Life

I Introduction

In previous chapters, we have discussed topics that pertain directly to the tensions between a scientific world view and that of faith. Clearly, issues such as creation, cosmology, ontology, and natural science are rooted in the very structure of reality. The one topic we have not broached is that of practical morality. But have we now, with the introduction of ethical or practical behavior, moved to a topic that veers away from the challenges of science? Not at all. Even in the context of moral philosophy, Jewish philosophers discuss issues within the wider context of a rational scientific perspective. Hava Tirosh-Samuelson articulates clearly the point that the science of ethics concerns "many assumptions about the structure of the world, the nature of human beings, the purpose of human life... Therefore the discourse on virtue and happiness was inseparable from a host of metaphysical, cosmological, psychological, epistemological, political and theological theories."[1] Many of the themes and issues we have visited in previous chapters thus reappear in the context of how to live the good life.

Jewish philosophers incorporated material from Greek philosophy, from the rabbis, and from their intellectual contemporaries. Both Aristotelian and Neoplatonic systems of morality influenced their conception of virtue and happiness. The formative texts from Aristotle's *Nicomachean Ethics* promoted a view of happiness (*eudaimonia*) as a "human flourishing" or "psychic well-being." All human beings desire to be happy, Aristotle tells us, but we tend to confuse what we desire materially with what truly leads to happiness. The ultimate life of virtue is one that fulfills our function or *telos* as rational animals; *eudaimonia* thus results from living in accordance with reason.

In the *Nicomachean Ethics*, Aristotle provided an analysis of *eudaimonia* connected to his conception of good and virtue. Aristotle defined the good as the end for the sake of which every action is done, claiming that there are many ends, and many types of good actions. Aristotle argues that human happiness is predicated on the capacity to reason and is defined as life in accordance with the rational principle.

---

[1] Tirosh-Samuelson 2009, 707.

But scholars have noted a deep tension in Aristotle's works regarding the actualization of human happiness. On the one hand, happiness is actualized through moral action, and the happiest person is one who lives well in the moral and political sphere. On the other hand, in the final book of the *Ethics* (*NE* 10.7–8) Aristotle presents theoretical wisdom as the final end of human life. These two ways of life appear to be incommensurable: the contemplative life attaches little importance to the moral, and the morally virtuous individual places little or no importance on theoretical contemplation. Theoretical wisdom, Aristotle argues, is superior to all other activities since it perfects the noblest part of us, is self-sufficient, is done for its own sake, over a long period of time, and is the one activity that makes us like the gods.[2] Aristotle concludes that we should make ourselves immortal by cultivating that "which is divine in us."[3] But if immortality is predicated on intellectual knowledge, and if philosophers such as Maimonides and Gersonides have argued that many individuals are psycho-physically incapable of embarking on such a rigorous and philosophical course of study, does it follow that not all humans can achieve intellectual perfection: is the road the same, and open, to all? And is there only one road to ultimate felicity, or are there many routes?

Another set of issues pertains to the type of character training requisite to achieve ethical perfection. Both Aristotle and the early rabbis emphasized the importance of character development in the acquisition of a moral compass. Aristotle emphasizes the role played by habit, a habitual repetition of morally conducing actions, while the book of Proverbs emphasizes the development of character formation as part of moral education. But in Jewish texts, moral behavior was subsumed under the domain of divine law or *halakha*. On the one hand, the very notion of Jewish ethics can only be understood against the backdrop of the Mosaic commandments. *Halakha* covers a myriad of situations including rituals, sacred attitudes toward the Deity, and interpersonal relationships. These latter actions are commonly considered to comprise the moral domain.

But can there be ethical dictates independent of the commandments? The rabbis already worried whether there exists a domain of "right behavior" that pre-dates, or exists independently of divine commandment. Given the ubiquity of *halakha* (Jewish law) in practically every aspect of Jewish life, rabbis both modern and ancient have argued over whether *halakha* is all inclusive, or whether there exists an independent moral standard to which even *halakha* (and the giver of *halakha*, namely God) is beholden.[4] For if *halakha* is the only system providing what we might call "ethical" behavior, then what sense can we make of any natural law theory that imputes the foundation of *nomos* on something other than God? While there may be room for natural law in a theology not ultimately dependent upon divine

---

[2] Aristotle makes this point in several texts, including *NE* 6.7 1141a20–2; 10.7 1177a12–18.
[3] Aristotle *NE* 10.7 1177b31–4.
[4] Plato had already introduced this issue in his dialogue *The Euthyphro*, asking whether something is good because the gods love it, or whether the gods love it because it is pious. This Euthyphro-type conundrum has found contemporary currency in the words of the noted (and controversial) Israeli philosopher Aharon Lichtenstein, who claimed famously that there is no such thing as Jewish ethics, that there is no law, and that there is no room for any *nomos* beyond divine command. See Lichtenstein 1975.

command, we must consider the extent to which Jewish thinkers advocated a natural law theory.[5]

In this chapter, I briefly explore these moral issues against the backdrop of a scientific method of thinking about ethical behavior. We begin with specific moral codes developed by Jewish thinkers, focusing in particular upon the works of Ibn Gabirol, Baḥya ibn Paquda, Maimonides, and Crescas. Each of these thinkers manifests the tension described above, trying to accommodate biblical and rabbinic views of moral behavior with their philosophical peers. We then turn to the underpinnings of these laws, and whether we can locate a moral or ethical theory in medieval Jewish philosophy independent of *halakhah*. While I focus primarily upon the status of law and ethical theory in the works of Moses Maimonides, discussions of Saadiah Gaon, Baḥya ibn Paquda, and Joseph Albo enable us to situate Maimonides' discussions more fully.

Finally, we must discuss the extent to which human felicity can be achieved in this social and political environment. Melamed has argued that political philosophy in Judaism plays out against the political quality of revelation, which comprises divine law given through a prophet/lawgiver/political leader.[6] The prophet represents the ideal standard, as it were, of human perfection, combining both intellectual and practical virtues. For this reason, many of the issues surrounding the nature of divine law and of prophecy can be construed as political issues. Unlike Christian political thought, which distinguished between divine and natural law more sharply, for medieval Jews the two were intertwined: both medieval Jewish and Muslim political philosophies "were based upon a holistic perception of reality and human existence," and so for Jewish thinkers political issues arise in the context of *halakha*.[7] But not all our thinkers will agree on the necessary and sufficient conditions required to achieve prophecy, bringing us back full circle to the ultimate purpose of existence.

II Living the Good Life: Ibn Gabirol, Baḥya ibn Paquda, Maimonides, and Gersonides

While the commandments provide human beings with a general blueprint for how to conduct one's life, Jewish philosophers incorporated Aristotle's methods into their discussions. The practical syllogism, the doctrine of the mean, and Aristotle's intellectualism all played an important role in defining the domain of practical reason. For Aristotle, ethics is *not* an exact science and so unlike logic, it employs what Aristotle calls a "practical" as opposed to a "demonstrative" syllogism. In contradistinction to a demonstrative syllogism, which contains premises that are known to be true, practical syllogisms comprise a major premise that identifies some good to be achieved, and a minor premise that locates the good in some situational decision. Although we should expect a modicum of accuracy common to any study, ethics does not contain the sort of accuracy found in the demonstrative sciences. For Aristotle, our manner of investigation consists in beginning with the

---

[5] For a recent discussion of these issues, see Mittleman 2012.
[6] See Melamed 1997; 2009.   [7] Melamed 1997, 418. See also Kreisel 2001.

common views on virtue (*endoxa*) and then seeking out the "wise person's view." The wise and virtuous are the best judges of those areas in which they have knowledge and experience.[8]

Aristotle's virtue morality is couched in terms of his well-known doctrine of the mean, which represents an intermediate between excess and defect. Aristotle explains the intermediate as "that which is equidistant from each of the extremes, which is one and the same for all men," while at the sametime emphasizing that the intermediate is relative to the agent.[9] In other words, we must distinguish between the arithmetical mean, which represents a strict arithmetical proportion between two extremes, and the mean relative to us, which takes into account personal properties and situation. Thus, for example, the amount of training required by a marathon runner will be more than that required by a 10k runner, and the amount of food required by the former will be more than that required by the latter. Moral virtue, then, must aim at the mean: to feel fear, confidence, appetite, anger, pity, and the like "at the right times, with reference to the right objects, towards the right people, with the right motive, and in the right way, is what is both intermediate and best, and this is characteristic of virtue."[10]

Elements of the Aristotelian ethical theory appear in Jewish writings, as apparent in the works of Ibn Gabirol, Bahya, and Maimonides. Ibn Gabirol's major contribution to ethical literature is his work *Tikkun Middot ha-Nefesh* (*On the Improvement of the Moral Qualities*). Written in 1045 in Saragossa, this work is available in the original Arabic (*Aslah al Akhlâq-*), as well as in Judah ibn Tibbon's Hebrew translation, which has been reprinted in many versions. *Tikkun Middot ha-Nefesh* is primarily a treatise on practical morality, in which Ibn Gabirol develops a system of ethics dependent upon the rule of reason. Although his ideas are supported by biblical references, he also includes quotations from Greek philosophers and Arab poets. Like the Brethren of Purity, Ibn Gabirol "grounds moral training in human biology showing how human temperaments are rooted in human physiology, as understood by the medical ethics of Galen and Hippocrates."[11] Notably, he does not reference the Talmud and many of the standard elements of his work can be readily found within classical Jewish Neoplatonism. However, as Schlanger has pointed out, Ibn Gabirol does introduce an original element into his work, namely the connection between the moral and physiological makeup of the human.

Ibn Gabirol describes the qualities and defects of the soul, with particular emphasis upon the doctrine of the Aristotelian mean. The qualities of the soul, according to Ibn Gabirol, are made manifest through the five senses of sight, hearing, smell, taste, and touch. Each sense additionally governs four main moral qualities: sight corresponds to pride and humility, modesty and impudence; hearing to love and hate, mercy and cruelty; smell to anger and favoritism, jealousy and diligence; taste to joy and grief, confidence and remorse; and touch to generosity and parsimony, bravery and timidity.[12] Harvey notes that Ibn Gabirol's correlative pairs do not have an explicit precedent in philosophic literature, but rather seem to be drawn from Hebrew idioms.

---

[8] Aristotle *NE* I.3 1095a.   [9] Aristotle *NE* II.6 1106a.30.   [10] Aristotle *NE* II.6 1106b.20–2.
[11] Tirosh-Samuelson 2009, 726.
[12] See Ibn Gabirol 1901; W. Z. Harvey 2012, 88; Wise 1902.

"He must have presumed," writes Harvey, "that ancient Hebrew idioms reliably reflect human physiology and psychology and therefore may be used to construct a theory of moral qualities."[13]

Ibn Gabirol describes humans as representing the pinnacle of creation; inasmuch as the final purpose of human existence is perfection, they must overcome their passions and detach themselves from this base existence in order to attain felicity of the soul. The soul distinguishes humans from other living beings, and by developing his or her own soul, an individual can increase spiritual perfection. The body as well as the soul must participate in the person's aspirations toward felicity: "In the actions of the senses as well as in the moral actions, one must reside in the mean and not fall into excess or defect."[14] In effect, Ibn Gabirol has delineated a complete parallel between the microcosm as represented by the human being, and the macrocosm, which is the universe.

Bahya ibn Paquda's ethical system is more ambitious than that of Ibn Gabirol, and represents one of the first attempts to present ethical laws and duties espoused by Judaism in a coherent philosophical system. Like his Neoplatonic peers, Bahya emphasized that ultimate human happiness is dependent upon excellence of the intellect and can only be experienced in the afterlife. Well-being of the soul depends upon possessing an accurate knowledge of the structure of the world. Bahya emphasizes the importance of both science and logic to understand the workings of the created universe and its creator: a wise and discerning individual will "avail himself of the science of mathematics, the science of demonstration, and the science of logic."[15]

Bahya describes his motivation for compiling his ethical system in the introduction of the work. It was his impression that many Jews either paid little attention to the duties of Jewish law, or paid exclusive attention to duties performed by the body. He was underwhelmed by the supposed evidence that people were obeying and cultivating duties of the heart (or internal intentions), from which the work gets its title. Bahya's ethics is the first medieval Jewish work whose ideas evolved from Jewish thought. Unlike Ibn Gabirol, who refrained from quoting the Talmud and other rabbinic sources, Bahya referenced both biblical and rabbinical literatures.

In *Duties of the Heart*, Bahya distinguishes between two types of duties: duties of the heart and external duties. The former are purely rational and intellectual, while the latter are practical. The two types of duties are linked, as external duties (such as moving one's limbs or helping one's neighbor) are impossible without internal duties (consent of the mind in the former instance, and love or respect of one's neighbor in the second). In the introduction, Bahya characterizes the "inner duties of the heart" as connected to inward intentionality and expresses surprise that nobody had written about these duties, which he finds to be the "basis of all the commandments! If they were to be undermined, there would be no point to any of the duties of the limbs."[16] The ultimate purpose of these inner duties is to serve God. The ideal state, which Bahya terms "whole-heartedness," is reached when human beings achieve complete accord of the mind and body. When our outer and inner selves are in conflict, when

---

[13] W. Z. Harvey 2012, 88. [14] Schlanger 1968, 18. See Ibn Gabirol 1901.
[15] Bahya 2004, *Duties* Introduction, 59. [16] Bahya 2004, *Duties* Introduction, 11.

our actions are not matched by our intentions, "if the actions of our limbs are at odds with the convictions of our hearts," we cannot worship God whole-heartedly.[17] When "whole-heartedness" is impossible, then an unrealized intention is preferable to a correct deed completed without intention. In other words, inner spirituality is of greater importance than external behavior. *Duties of the Heart* is divided into ten chapters, representing the ten roots, or "gates" of the duties of the heart. These roots lead to a *wholehearted*, or what we might think of as a mindful, belief in God.

In *Duties of the Heart* III.10, Baḥya presents a list of twenty moral qualities, borrowed from those of Ibn Gabirol; unlike those pairs found in Ibn Gabirol, however, Baḥya's list is grouped into contrary pairs: 1) joy and grief; 2) fear and hope; 3) courage and timidity; 4) shame and brazenness; 5) anger and contentment; 6) mercy and ruthlessness; 7) pride and humility; 8) love and hate; 9) generosity and parsimony; 10) diligence and idleness.[18] He claims to have recorded the qualities as they occurred to him, and in no particular order. Each of the pairs is discussed in brief. Subsequent sections amplify these qualities in the context of the duties of the heart, and provide a way of achieving closeness to the Deity.

We turn now to Maimonides who, like his predecessors, focuses in his ethical work *Eight Chapters* primarily upon character traits. In *Eight Chapters*, he reserves the terms virtuous and vicious for character traits rather than for actions. Maimonides emphasizes the propaedeutic nature of moral virtues: "the improvements of moral habits is the same as the cure of the soul and its powers."[19] Note that the terms virtue and vice pertain not to human actions, but to characteristics in the human soul. While there is a connection between "inner" and "outer," and our outward behavior provides the best access we have to these inner characteristics, nevertheless the "outer" actions are themselves neither virtuous nor vicious.

Like Aristotle and al-Fârâbî, Maimonides distinguishes in *Eight Chapters* between two types of virtue: rational and moral. Rational virtues include wisdom and intelligence, which in turn comprise theoretical intellect, acquired intellect, and what he calls "brilliance and excellent comprehension" or intuition.[20] Moral virtues are found in the appetitive part of the soul, not the rational part, and include a number of characteristics: moderation, liberality, justice, gentleness, humility, contentment, and courage. This separation between intellectual and moral virtues raises a concern however about the epistemological status of ethical knowledge.[21] In the *Guide* Maimonides is very clear that only intellectual knowledge can lead to rational virtue, while imagination represents a lesser faculty of the soul and leads to social perfection.

The implications of this distinction between intellect and imagination are important when we turn to the justification of ethical claims in general. Maimonides argues that good and evil, as opposed to true and false, are not intellectual concepts, but rather are notions that arise as a result of the act of the imagination. More specifically, terms such as "good" (*tov*) and "bad" (*ra*) signify what Maimonides calls generally accepted opinions, things "generally accepted as known," and are not rooted in

---

[17] Baḥya 2004, *Duties* Introduction, 37.   [18] Baḥya 2004, *Duties* III.10.341–7.
[19] Maimonides *EC* I.61.   [20] Maimonides *EC* II.65.
[21] For discussion of this difficulty, see Twersky 1980, 453–9; Kellner 1990; Weiss 1991; Fox 1990, 93–151; Pines 1979, 95–157; Schatz 2005; Ivry 2016.

reality itself.[22] The relativism of ethical terms can be contrasted with the propositions of mathematics and physics, which we can know through the science of demonstration. Unaided reason (based on demonstration) can come to know objective concepts rooted in reality, but not subjective concepts such as "good" and "bad."

We have noted the importance of character development in determining the value of moral action. Maimonides, following Aristotle and al-Fârâbî, emphasizes the repetition of habitual actions for proper character formation. The very title of *Character Traits* (*Hilkhot Deot*) reinforces the importance of character development. The first four chapters set forth the morality of the wise individual who follows the middle way. Chapter five concerns the discipline of such a person and is concerned with actions rather than character traits, focusing on social interactions. Maimonides follows al-Fârâbî and claims that inculcation of virtues requires habitual repetition of "right actions": according to Maimonides, "a man shall habituate himself in these character traits until they are firmly established in him. Time after time, he shall perform actions in accordance with the character traits that are in the mean. He shall repeat them continually until performing them is easy for him and they are not burdensome and these character traits are firmly established in his soul."[23] Virtues are not innate; the most we can say is that individuals may have a natural proclivity toward particular virtues.

We come now to the heart of Maimonides' discussion of moral virtue, which incorporates Aristotle's doctrine of the mean. Maimonides reiterates Aristotle's theory, as mediated by al-Fârâbî, and presents the middle way, or life in accordance with the mean, as a way of achieving both personal serenity and communal well-being. Chapter four of *Eight Chapters* concerns the doctrine of the mean: "good actions are those balanced in the mean between two extremes, both of which are bad: one of them is an excess and the other a deficiency."[24] Virtues are defined as "states of the soul and settled dispositions in the mean between two bad states [of the soul], one of which is excessive and the other deficient."[25] Maimonides then gives a number of examples: moderation is the mean between lust and insensibility; liberality is the mean between miserliness and extravagance; humility is the mean between haughtiness and abasement; generosity is the mean between prodigality and stinginess. Maimonides says that these virtues can be firmly established in the soul by repeating the actions pertaining to a particular moral habit over a long period of time, resulting in our "becoming accustomed to them."[26]

But what about the fact that *halakha* mandates many actions that do not reflect the mean? How do we account, for example, for the dietary laws, many of which clearly do not reflect a doctrine of the mean? More generally, what correlation can we draw between acquisition of moral virtue and acquiescence to the commandments? Further, what do we do with Maimonides' characterization of the *ḥasid* or saint, whose extreme ascetic behavior reflects an apparent repudiation of the mean? Recognizing these difficulties, Maimonides adopts a less moderate position in the cases of humility and anger, advocating the saint to utter meekness "so as to leave not

---

[22] Maimonides *Guide* 1.2; II.33; 3.10.
[23] Maimonides *CT* I.7.30. For the main points in al-Fârâbî, see al-Fârâbî 1961; 2001.
[24] Maimonides *EC* IV.67.   [25] Ibid.   [26] Maimonides *EC* IV.68.

even a trace of pride in their soul."[27] In this regard, he appears to deviate markedly from Aristotle who in the *Nicomachean Ethics* presented both proper pride and appropriate anger as virtues to be achieved.[28]

Unlike these previous thinkers, Gersonides is not known for his ethical writings; as we have seen, most of his philosophical writings engage matters in the natural sciences. Why did Gersonides not include ethical precepts in the *Wars*? He explicitly states in *Wars* I. 130 (1:4) that there is nothing scientific about the domain of ethics. Nonetheless, ethical views do abound in Gersonides' biblical commentaries.[29] Focusing upon these commentaries, Alexander Green is concerned to distinguish between Maimonides' and Gersonides' ethical theories. We have seen that both Aristotle and Maimonides emphasize the doctrine of the mean as part of their ethical theory: on this model, virtues represent a balance between extremes. In *Eight Chapters*, Maimonides described many of the moral virtues as lying in the mean between excess. Green argues that like Maimonides, Gersonides focuses on the mean as the basis for ethics; but he adds two new virtue categories, virtues of self-preservation and virtues of altruism.[30] Self-preservation is reflected in the virtues of endeavor, diligence, and cunning, all of which aim at physical self-preservation. Gersonides' ethical theory is couched in the context of examples, or lessons, of the lives and actions of particular individuals, rather than in a scientific commentary.[31] Using biblical proof texts, he derives practical lessons (*to'alot*) meant to teach particular virtues; as Green notes, these practical lessons or *to'alot* are "practical maxims that enable one to achieve perfection."[32] In his *to'alot*, Gersonides includes "numerous strategies of personal advancement and methods of obtaining the necessities of life, often seemingly at the total disregard of, if not at the expense of, other human beings."[33] As noted in Chapter 5, Gersonides used the virtue of *haritzut*—the virtue of assiduous zeal and industry in actively pursuing one's goals—as a foil against the clutch of astral fate.

Gersonides thus introduces a new set of materialistic virtues that emphasize the importance of maximizing one's physical needs. The three virtues—endeavor, diligence, and cunning in crafting stratagems—are described at great length in his *to'alot*.[34] As Green and Horwitz point out, Gersonides attempts to reverse Maimonides' denigration of the physical body; he stresses the importance of physical preservation, especially in light of the whims of fate and fortune.[35] Take for example Abraham, who brought all his possessions with him from Canaan to Egypt. Gersonides extols Abraham, claiming that "A person must protect his possessions with as much diligence (*haritzut*) as possible."[36] In a similar vein, Gersonides explains Abraham's

---

[27] Maimonides Avot 4.4; 5:11. For a detailed discussion of these and other ethical traits, see Frank 1990.
[28] Aristotle *NE* IV. 3 1123b14.
[29] Horwitz notes that "ethics are consistently informed by his metaphysics." See Horwitz 1997, 289; Gersonides 1992 contains many of these passages. See also Green 2016, for a detailed discussion of Gersonides' ethics.
[30] Green 2016, 2. See also Horwitz 2006, who claims that Gersonidean ethics consists of more than the Maimonidean adoption of the mean between two extremes.
[31] Green 2016, 4.   [32] Green 2016, 6.   [33] Horwitz 2006, 34–5.
[34] Green 2016, 33.   [35] Green 2016, 34; see also Horwitz 1997.
[36] Gersonides *Commentary on Genesis, Ethical Lesson #6*, quoted in Green 2016, 42. Many of these ethical lessons can be found in Gersonides 1992.

actions when entering Egypt and passing off his wife Sara as his sister. Horwitz claims that in this case, following the lead of Maimonides in *Guide* 3:27, Gersonides "had to account for Abraham's pursuit of the prosaic but absolutely essential necessities of life," and did so by highlighting Abraham's need to perfect and preserve his body.[37]

As we shall see below, Gersonides' commentary on *Song of Songs* is imbued with an extended discussion of human felicity. Because of their inherent weakness and epistemological imperfections, most human beings are incapable of achieving felicity: "only very few individuals can acquire even a large measure of it."[38] For these masses, the Torah and its commandments function as the best guide to moral perfection. Although the ultimate purpose of the commandments is "being cleaved to God," most people are incapable of appreciating such an end, and so the Torah couches the end-goal as "that they who observe them will thereby achieve length of days, and many other fanciful felicities."[39]

III Politics and Law: Is there Room for Natural Law independent of Divine Law?

The exercise of trying to provide rational reasons for the commandments can be viewed as a scientific attempt to ground ethical precepts. The process dates back to rabbinic times, and continued throughout the medieval (into the modern) period. It is based on comments of earlier rabbinic sources, the most famous of which is the following: "'And My ordinances you shall practice' (*Leviticus* 18:4): These are matters written in the Torah which even if they had not been written there, reason would have required that they be written."[40] Clearly, the rabbis were suggesting that some commandments are "inherently" or "intuitively" grounded, and not totally dependent upon divine command. These laws, discussed in *Sanhedrin* 56–60 and *Melakhim* 8:10; 10:12, represent the minimal moral duties enjoined by the Bible upon all human beings.[41] One of the earliest articulations of what came to be known as the Noahide Laws is found in the *Tosefta*, a supplementary work to the Mishnah. The text states: "Concerning seven commandments were the sons of Noah admonished: [establishing courts of justice, idolatry, cursing the name [of God], illicit intercourse, bloodshed, thievery and consuming a limb from a living beast."[42] These commandments are derived ultimately from divine commands addressed to Adam and Noah, and are generally regarded by the rabbis as universally applicable. Do these Noahide laws present a natural law underpinning Jewish thought? The rabbis suggest in *Yoma* 67b that "they would have been made mandatory even had they not been revealed," thus implying a universally applicable, natural component to the law. Further, the fact that six of the laws were revealed to Adam suggests a universalistic thrust.[43]

---

[37] Horwitz 1997, 289–90.   [38] Gersonides 1998, *Song of Songs*, 6.   [39] Ibid.
[40] See for example the Talmudic passages in *Sifra Aharei-Mot*; B. *Yoma* 67b.
[41] See for example *Genesis Rabbah* 34; *Sanhedrin* 59b.
[42] Tractate *Avodah Zarah* 8:4, quoted in Van Zile 2017.
[43] *Genesis Rabbah* 16:6; 24:5.

Whether there exists a moral code independent of divine command is often couched in the context of natural law, but in Jewish philosophy the very process of defining a "natural law" independent of *halakha* is itself rife with problems. As Van Zile points out, natural law theorizes human morality as an autonomous function of human reason derived from nature, and thus separate from divine command: "Just as the Torah theoretically applied to all Jews with certain social and gender distinctions, Noahide law applied to all of humanity along with its own categorical distinctions typified by a Judeo-centric worldview."[44] Whether Noahide law can be identified with natural law is a contested question, and beyond the purview of our work.[45]

Albo's work *Book of Principles* is the only medieval Jewish work devoted at least in part to an investigation of the foundation or roots of all kinds of law. While he was one of the very few, if not only, Jewish philosophers to make use of the term "natural law," Albo's discussion, drawn primarily from Aquinas, is confused at best. Since Aquinas' theory is so well known, I shall not discuss it in detail except to point out that Aquinas' notion of natural law does incorporate divine command. In his canonical discussion of natural law in the *Summa Theologica*, Aquinas claims that natural law participates in the eternal law and as such reflects God's providential interaction with human beings: "we call such participation in the eternal law by rational creatures the natural law."[46] In addition to eternal and natural law, Aquinas recognizes both divine and human law: divine law represents the old and new covenants and circumscribes human action in general, while human law is essential for human survival in society. The precepts of natural law are analogous to those of scientific demonstration in that both sets of precepts are self-evident. The first precept of natural law, to do good and shun evil, is the basis for all subsequent precepts[47] and is the same for all human beings.[48]

Albo adapts portions of Aquinas' discussion and in the fifth chapter of the first part of the *Book of Principles*, Albo turns to the topic of natural law. He starts this chapter by noting that humans are political by nature, and that it is almost necessary for them to be part of a city,[49] but in order to preserve justice and eliminate wrongdoing, humans need what he terms a "natural law." This law is natural in the sense that it is something that humans need as part of their nature. Humans living in a group need a certain modicum of order allowing them to maintain justice; "this order the wise men call natural law, meaning by natural what is necessary for man by his nature, whether the order emanates from a wise man or a prophet."[50] Albo notes in II.31 that natural law is not sufficient for political society and must therefore be supplemented by a *nomos* or conventional law that enables political life to unfold. The prescriptions of natural law are indispensable for achieving the preservation of the species. Thus by the end of chapter five, the reader realizes that natural law must be supplemented by conventional law, and chapter six explains that divine law rules all other laws.

---

[44] Van Zile 2017, 3.
[45] For recent discussions, see for example Hayes 2015; Novak 1998; Mittleman 2012; Rudavsky 2012.
[46] Aquinas *Summa Theologica* vol. 2, 91.2.   [47] Aquinas *Summa Theologica* vol. 1, 94.2.
[48] Aquinas *Summa Theologica* vol. 1, 94.4.   [49] Albo 1946, vol. 1, I.5: 72.
[50] Albo 1946, vol. 1, Preface, 27.

In I.7, this notion of natural law is amplified. Albo asserts that there are three kinds of law—natural, conventional, and divine—and distinguishes them on the basis of both their establishment and intention: "there are three kinds of law, natural, positive or conventional, and divine. Natural law is the same among all peoples, at all times, and in all places. Positive or conventional is a law ordered by a wise man or men to suit the place and the time and the nature of the persons who are to be controlled by it...Divine law is one that is ordered by God through a prophet, like Adam or Noah, or like the custom or law which Abraham taught men,...or one that is ordered by God through a messenger whom He sends and through whom He gives a law, like the law of Moses."[51] Albo suggests that natural law is universal in that it applies equally to all humans, times, and places, the conventional law takes account of contingencies of place and time, and the divine law is ordered by God through a prophet or messenger (e.g., Adam, Noah, Moses, or Abraham). Albo's conventional law is thus analogous to Aquinas' human law. The reader is left with the impression that natural law serves as the foundation of the other kinds of law, each of which supplements and completes the natural law, but it is not clear from Albo's work what natural law actually is.

Apart from Albo's discussion, the term natural law does not appear in medieval Jewish texts. But the idea behind natural law is embedded in a number of related issues, including the nature of nature; the nature of reason itself; the relation between reason and revelation; the function of law; and the relation of law to human nature. While I take it as uncontroversial that ancient conceptions of natural law totally divorced from a providential divine lawgiver do not appear in Jewish texts, this does not mean that natural law theorizing is totally absent. Another way of making this point is to return to the Euthyphro conundrum with which we started, and ask whether any aspects of *halakha* are discoverable by reason alone, or whether they are completely dependent upon God's will. We have many ways of construing the role of law in Jewish thought, ranging from an explicit denial of any law independent of *halakha* to the implicit postulation of natural law theory in Maimonides and other authors.

As noted above, while Albo is the only Jewish philosopher to talk about "natural law" explicitly, other Jewish philosophers did broach the general topic surrounding the universality of the commandments in the context of trying to ascertain reasons for the commandments. This sense of an independent grounding for at least some of the commandments is articulated in a more systematic manner by Saadiah Gaon, who, as we mentioned in Chapter 2, was a strong opponent of Karaism. In Book II of *The Book of Beliefs and Opinions*, Saadiah distinguished between the rational commandments, which in theory are discoverable by means of reason, and the traditional laws, which comprise rituals and ceremonial laws (such as the dietary laws) that are not rooted in reason. Saadiah is the first Jewish philosopher to frame his discussion of ethical precepts in the context of their rational apprehension. In the introduction to the work, Saadiah distinguishes four sources of reliable knowledge: sensation, reason or *nous*, logical inference, and reliable tradition. Sense knowledge is based on empirical contingents and is posited as the basis for all other knowledge forms, which are rooted in this indubitable epistemic foundation. Reason represents the faculty of immediate, intuitive knowledge by means of which we apprehend self-evident axioms of reason. Reason, Saadiah tells us, emanates ultimately from God, resulting in an innatist theory according to which ideas are "implanted" in the mind. The word "implanted" connotes a source for knowledge that lies outside the realm of human consciousness. In chapter II.13, for example, Saadiah asks how is it possible to establish the concept of God in our minds if we have never seen God, and responds that "it is done in the same manner in which such notions arise in them as the approbation of the truth and the disapproval of lying, although these matters are not subject to the perception of any of our senses."[52] In a similar manner, we are able to "recognize" a violation of the law of non-contradiction, even though it is not based on the senses.

In contradistinction to reason, reliable tradition is not universal, but is common to "the community of monotheists." If, however, reason, with the help of this outside source, enables humans to determine both the self-evident axioms and necessary principles of thought, what becomes of tradition? In other words, why do we even bother with tradition if reason itself is sufficient to determine ethical (and other) precepts? Saadiah relegates to tradition two roles: first, tradition enables us to determine the particulars necessary for observing the more general rational precepts; and second, tradition also speeds up the rather tedious process of discovering these rational principles. Thus, while reason allows one a limited amount of epistemic authority, tradition with the aid of revelation enables us to achieve salvation. As Jospe points out, what is known in revelation is rational, and in principle is identical to the truth arrived at by rational investigation. Revelation permits us to access truth we could arrive at rationally after a long process.[53]

Based on these epistemological distinctions, the foundations for moral obligation are delineated primarily in Book three, while details on how to achieve the good life are to be found in Book ten. The classification of ethical precepts into rational and revelatory is straightforward: Rational commandments are those whose "approval" has been implanted in our minds.[54] In other words, humans have an intuitive grasp of the content of these commandments inasmuch as they determine right action. Saadiah further argues that the rational commandments are inherently related to the dictates of reason, and that they represent logical inferences from these dictates.[55] Revelatory commandments, which constitute the second general division of law, are not inherently dependent upon the above-mentioned rational dictates, but rather are imposed by God without regard to their inherent rationality. Hence, the approbation of these laws implies no more than simple submissiveness to God. As we shall see, however, Saadiah discerns a social utility for nearly all these laws. Thus, Saadiah will want to argue that although these laws are not grounded in reason, nevertheless they may too be justified by rational argument. Saadiah offers many examples (sanctifying certain times rather than others; the dietary laws, etc.) to explicate the overall social utility of the traditional laws.

---

[52] Saadiah Gaon *Beliefs* II.13:131.   [53] Jospe 2009, 59.
[54] See Saadiah Gaon *Beliefs* III.2:140.   [55] See Saadiah Gaon *Beliefs* II.5:106; III.1:139.

Working through Saadiah's examples, scholars have uniformly noted the tensions inherent in his presentation: on the one hand, Saadiah offers us rational justification that is based on intuition, whereas on the other hand, we have a faith-based system grounded in divine revelation.[56] Thus, for example, in book three, Saadiah evinces utilitarian arguments to substantiate the "innateness" of the rational command-ments, but these arguments are clearly incompatible with the spirit of rationality he has adduced earlier. Saadiah wants to argue that the approval of certain acts is implanted in our mind/reason, but at the same time, his examples all draw from utilitarian arguments. While I agree with critics who highlight the inherent tensions in Saadiah's discussion, I do think it is important to emphasize the overall spirit of Saadiah's attempt to uphold a distinction between the rational and revealed com-mandments based on the idea that the former have their own intrinsic rationality that, in his opinion, any rational person would recognize.[57] Seen in this light, Saadiah's system introduces a theory of rational obligation into the rubric of revela-tory commandments, thus incorporating an attempted synthesis, or at least an attempted reconciliation, between reason and revelation. Although I would not describe this attempt as a strict "natural law theory," we can nevertheless acknow-ledge Saadiah's sustained efforts to articulate the underlying idea that at least some of the commandments are objective, based on human nature, and accessible to human reasoning.

Maimonides' analysis of the commandments reflects Saadiah's distinction between rational and ritualistic commandments, but in contradistinction to Saadiah, Maimonides claims that all the commandments are rational: both the laws and the statutes have beneficial ends, the only difference being that the former are recogniz-able to all, whereas the latter possess ends that are only manifest to the wise. The laws correspond to Saadiah's rational commandments, while the statutes correspond (in general) to Saadiah's listing of ceremonial laws and rituals. For Maimonides, however, both laws and statutes have a basis in reason.

Aspects of a natural law sentiment can be found throughout Maimonides' work. Maimonides is clear that "governance of the Law is absolute and universal."[58] In Guide 3.25 Maimonides offers several proofs based on philosophical reasoning for the rationality of law. He argues that to attribute to God non-purposive and non-rational actions, namely laws that are the arbitrary result of God's will, would be blasphemous, for frivolous actions are the most demeaning. Furthermore, he argues that in order to command the respect of the nations of the world, Jewish law must be rational. In an interesting aside, Maimonides claims that were the law not rational, the peoples of the world would not look up to the Jews, and they would lose their standing among the moral peoples. Reflecting the Platonic dictum in the Euthyphro that the gods command pious acts because they are pious, Maimonides is suggesting that there exists a rational, autonomous basis to what is right: these actions have been commanded

---

[56] Altmann has argued that Saadiah's position represents a compromise between the Mu'tazilah who claimed that the rational commandments were commanded because of their inherent goodness, and the Ash'ariyyah who claimed that the traditional commandments are good because they were commanded. See Altmann 1944, 3–24.

[57] Rynhold 2009, 140.   [58] Maimonides Guide 3.34:534.

because they are intrinsically good and right. Theoretically (although such a person does not exist in actual fact), an individual ruled entirely by intellect, and not at all by his affections, would not entertain the notions of good and evil; such terms would be either meaningless or redundant.[59]

Turning specifically to the utility of commandments, Maimonides distinguishes between the generalities and the particulars of a commandment. While the generalities of the commandments were given for utilitarian reasons, the particular details may not have the same utilitarian value. While the overall purpose of the particulars is to purify the people,[60] Maimonides castigates those who try to find causes for every particular detail in the laws. Such individuals are stricken with "madness" and "are as far from truth as those who imagine that the generalities of a commandment are not designed with a view to some real utility."[61] In fact, Maimonides goes to great lengths to warn his reader that for some particulars, no cause can be found. Why, for example, did the Law prescribe the sacrifice of a ram rather than a lamb? No reason can be given, but one or other particular had to be chosen.

Maimonides argues further that the commandments serve to support social and political beliefs. In an extended passage, Maimonides offers a historical deconstruction of the law.[62] For example in the case of sacrifice, he traces the laws back to Moses' attempts to combat the Sabians, who were a polytheistic tribe steeped in magic and myth. According to Maimonides' deconstructive analysis, Moses knew that weaning the Israelites would be an arduous task, and so in order to wean the Israelites away from idolatry and sacrifice rituals gradually, the commandments regarding sacrifice were relaxed so as to require sacrifices only to God, the idea being that eventually sacrifices would be abandoned altogether.

But ought these rationally graspable and intelligible reasons for the commandments be divulged to the public? Maimonides clearly states that "all laws have causes and were given with a view to some utility."[63] This utility is applicable to both welfare of the soul (achieved by acquisition of true beliefs) and welfare of the body (achieved by practical and moral virtues). Might not the very process of uncovering the reasons for the commandments lead to a sort of philosophical anti-nomianism among the masses, if they were to understand both the causes and goals of particular commandments? Could not this understanding lead to the seductive conclusion that these prescribed actions are dispensable? If the goal of human existence (namely intellectual perfection) can be achieved in a way that does not require performance of the commandments, does that not render the commandments otiose? Maimonides offers no response to this challenge. Perhaps the best he can do is suggest that the laws function in much the same way as does Aristotle's virtuous individual: just as the virtuous individual provides the model for proper human behavior, so too has God

---

[59] Harvey draws the interesting parallel between Maimonides' discussion and that of Spinoza in the *Ethics*. According to Harvey, neither is fully a moral relativist, although both relegate the terms good and evil to the realm of the imaginative faculty. See Harvey 1981a, 151–72.

[60] See Maimonides *Guide* 3.26:508.   [61] Maimonides *Guide* 3.26:509.

[62] See Maimonides *Guide* 3.29:514–22; 3.32:525–31; 3.37:540–50; 3.45–6:575–92.

[63] Maimonides *Guide* 3.26:507.

provided us a model for proper behavior in the form of commandments. We shall return to this vexing problem below, in the context of prophecy.

IV Active Intellect, Prophecy, and the Political Dimension

With this last issue, we turn directly to the political demands and obligations placed upon the prophet. As noted above, the prophet exemplifies the pinnacle of spiritual and intellectual perfection available to humans. Occupying a central place in medieval thought, prophecy connects a number of issues in philosophical psychology, theory of knowledge, divine providence, the nature of Law, and political philosophy. In the Hebrew Bible, prophecy was presented as a major source of communication from God to the people Israel, the prophet functioning as the bearer of information. Think, for example, of Isaiah's admonitions to Israel, or Ezekiel's prophetic visions. Although we tend to think of prophetic statements as being about the future, this is not always the case. In some instances the prophets were clairvoyant and capable of predicting future events, as when Elijah predicted a drought (1 *Kings* 17:1), and Elisha predicted a seven-year famine (II *Kings* 2:3). More often, however, the prophet (*navi*) functioned as a moral and civic leader, presenting a model for human behavior and striving. In the Hebrew Bible, women could be prophets as well as men, as evidenced by Deborah the prophet. As the first prophet, Moses had direct access to the divine word and conveyed that word to the Israelites. (*Deuteronomy* 5:5; *Exodus* 19:19; *Deuteronomy* 18:15–19). But while the Bible is replete with stories about the prophets (Isaiah, Ezekiel, Amos, and others), very little explanation is offered as to how these particular individuals warranted their prophetic status: who they were, how they became prophets, how they differed from other individuals, and the relation between prophets and kings, is not discussed in Scripture. What we do know is that the prophet is chosen by God, often against his or her will, to convey God's word to the people of Israel.[64]

Elements of the biblical account, combined with philosophical ingredients drawn from Plato and Aristotle, were reflected in the medieval texts of Islamic and Jewish philosophers. Unlike Christian thinkers who were influenced by Aristotle's *Politics*, however, medieval Islamic and Jewish thinkers drew more heavily upon Plato's *Republic* and Aristotle's *Nicomachean Ethics*.[65] As we shall see below, Plato's "philosopher-king" could easily be identified with the prophet-lawgiver of the Abrahamic tradition. Both Jewish and Islamic thinkers grappled with the question of how the incorporeal, transcendent Deity can communicate with humans. Whether prophecy itself is a miraculous or supernatural event, one that depends upon the direct intervention of God, became the focus of debate among philosophers. Already in the work of Isaac Israeli, the prophet was presented as an individual who gains knowledge by means of both the imaginative and rational faculties. Saadiah is the first

---

[64] For a comprehensive study of prophecy in medieval Jewish thought, see Kreisel 2001; for a comprehensive summary of prophecy in Scripture, see Paul et al. 2007.

[65] See Melamed 1997; 2003; 2009 for the curious differences between these two transmission strands.

Jewish thinker to draw the connection explicitly between Plato's philosopher-king and the perfect individual. In *Emunot* he describes the thirteen types of human endeavor that the perfect individual must possess, and describes the perfect individual as having attributes of a king.[66]

In a similar vein, Halevi's *Kuzari* can be read as a reflection of Platonic themes, one in which the Khazar king aspires to be a philosopher-king, and hopes to learn how to achieve this role from the Ḥaver. As Melamed notes, Halevi's pious ruler is portrayed as being superior to the Platonic philosopher-king in that he seeks a perfection based on both human intellect and revelation.[67] In the *Kuzari*, Judah Halevi viewed prophecy as the ultimate perfection of the individual, resulting ultimately in a conjunction with the "divine matter" (*Amr Ilahi*). Drawing upon Saadiah's notion of the "created Glory," Halevi emphasized the epistemological ingredients necessary for prophecy, and placed importance upon both the rational and imaginative faculties. But how much is required of each faculty, and is the perfection of both faculties both necessary and sufficient for the acquisition of prophecy? This became a major issue in subsequent Jewish thought.

In addition to the role played by the Active Intellect, philosophers worried about the role of the imagination in knowledge acquisition. The process of knowledge acquisition begins with the senses, passes through the imagination, and as a result of interaction of the possible intellect with the Active Intellect, becomes intellectual. The role of the imagination in perception was depicted already by Aristotle in his *De Anima* III.3.429a. According to Aristotle, imagination cannot be a sense, but neither does it fit the general role of a faculty. Imagination is the result of a movement from sensation. Take for example the color red. At some time or other, I have seen the color red. This original experience carries with it a sensation. At a later time, I recreate for myself the color red; this second movement results from my imagination. This movement of the imagination serves as a source of error in human knowing. On this account, imagination is like a sense, but not actually a sense; it is a derived movement from sense.

This ambiguity on Aristotle's account allowed for great leeway among his medieval commentators. Islamic philosophers offered for the most part a naturalistic explanation of prophecy. They presented prophets as scientist-philosophers, well versed in the details of the natural universe. Avicenna for example held that the imagination not only receives movement from the senses, but in its most perfect state also receives movement from the intellect. Building upon Aristotle, al-Fârâbî's emphasis upon the importance of intellectual, rational reflection added a new dimension to the Scriptural view of prophecy, supplementing the supernatural view with a more naturalized conception. In al-Fârâbî's system, the prophet was presented as a combination of Imâm (priest) and philosopher-king, one who combined his religious and philosophical wisdom to rule the virtuous state. In his *Political Regime*, al-Fârâbî elevates Plato's philosopher-king to the individual who, having achieved perfect

---

[66] See Saadiah *Emunot* 10.12 and 10.17 for the characteristics of a king.
[67] See Melamed 1997, 424; also 2009, 776.

knowledge of the theoretical sciences, is able to attain to revelation. As a result of this attainment, he is able to establish an ideal law for society.[68]

Like al-Fârâbî, Maimonides contends that prophecy ranks as the highest human perfection. But unlike al-Fârâbî, Maimonides has no qualms about identifying the prophet as a recipient of revelation. As we shall see, Maimonides veers away from the Islamic Aristotelians on two counts: first, he claims that the prophet will not prophesy unless God wills it; this will is "eternal and unchanging."[69] This intervention on the part of God is "like all the miracles and takes the same course as they."[70] Second, Maimonides recognizes the importance of Moses, as a legislative prophet, as representative of a unique type of prophecy. Only Moses' prophecy resulted in a legislation that, according to Maimonides, remains non-abrogated.[71]

Maimonides approaches the issue of prophecy against the Islamic appropriation of Aristotle's doctrine of the imagination. In his halakhic works, Maimonides describes prophecy as dependent upon the perfection of a prophet's rational faculty. No mention is made of the imaginative faculty; nor are miracles mentioned to account for prophecy. In his outline of the basic principles of Judaism (*Perek Ḥelek*), he defines prophecy as follows:

One should know that among men are found certain people so gifted and perfected that they can receive pure intellectual form. Their human intellect clings to the Active Intellect, whither it is gloriously raised. These men are the prophets; this is what prophecy is.[72]

This definition emphasizes the importance of intellectual perfection, and includes no reference to a higher deity. For somebody not versed in Aristotelian philosophy, this definition would be practically unintelligible, as Maimonides himself acknowledges in the continuation to the sixth principle: "A full explanation of this root principle would require much more time."[73] Note that the reception of "pure intellectual form," and the clinging to the Active Intellect, are both presented as entirely natural phenomena and do not mention God's active role.

Turning to the *Guide*, prophecy is clearly highlighted as a major motif of the work. We have alluded several times to Maimonides' analogy in the introduction to the *Guide*, comparing prophetic parables to "apples of gold in settings of silver."

---

[68] Al-Fârâbî's text *The Political Regime* can be found in Lerner and Mahdi 1963; see also al-Fârâbî 2001. Al-Fârâbî distinguishes between prophecy and revelation, and in many texts, al-Fârâbî does not refer to the individual who receives revelation as a prophet. Several influential themes emerge in al-Fârâbî's account: first, he redefines the traditional religious concept of revelation in a way that makes it consistent with philosophy as the highest human pursuit. From the philosophical perspective, revelation is seen to be conditional upon an individual's having achieved intellectual perfection; on this description, no role is played by God in somebody's achieving this level. Further, al-Fârâbî does not dwell on the role of the prophet per se, preferring to focus on the characteristics of supreme ruler. This suggests that possibly al-Fârâbî (in line with Averroës) does not consider it necessary that a supreme ruler be accepted as a prophet. A third consideration has to do with the role played by the imaginative faculty in the process of revelation. Al-Fârâbî maintains that often the political ruler must use persuasion in order to convey correct ideas to the masses; persuasion is often best accomplished by appealing to the imagination of the masses, and presenting images in the form of religion. Often these images are even invented by the ruler. For further details, see Macy 1986.

[69] Maimonides *Guide* 1.10:36; 3.17:469.   [70] Maimonides *Guide* 2.32:361.

[71] Maimonides *Guide* 2.39.   [72] Maimonides *PH*, 419.   [73] Ibid.

In this extended analogy, Maimonides suggests that the prophet communicates on many levels to different people, and that gold nuggets of prophetic wisdom are often hidden amongst the external silver filigree. The exoteric meaning of prophetic statements contains wisdom useful to the masses, whereas their internal meaning "contains wisdom that is useful for beliefs concerned with the truth as it is."[74] In order to explain the manner in which prophets achieve their truths, Maimonides presents a hierarchy of truth, according to which only the prophet is able to experience prolonged flashes of lightning or truth. Unlike most individuals for whom "... sometimes truth flashes out to us so that we think it is day, and then matter and habit in their various forms conceal it so that we find ourselves again in an obscure night," the highest level of prophet is that individual for whom "the lightning flashes time and time again, so that he is always, as it were, in unceasing light. Thus night appears to him as day. That is the degree of the great one among the prophets..."[75] Prophecy on this model represents a form of intellectual illumination, one not achievable by the mass of humanity. Only the rare individual is privy to truth, and "is always... in unceasing light."

Maimonides turns in *Guide* 2.36 to a technical and philosophical account of prophecy that, couched in Aristotelian epistemology and psychology, focuses on the prophetic activity itself rather than the one who attains to prophecy. Maimonides defines prophecy as follows:

the true reality and quiddity of prophecy consists in its being an overflow from God ... through the intermediation of the Active Intellect, toward the rational faculty in the first place and thereafter toward the imaginative faculty. This is the highest degree of man and the ultimate term of perfection that can exist for his species; and this state is the ultimate term of perfection for the imaginative species.[76]

Against the backdrop of the Neoplatonized Aristotelian imagery of an overflow from a higher source to a lower one, Maimonides attributes the origin of prophecy ultimately to God. The overflow is then mediated by the Active Intellect first to the rational faculty, and from there to the imagination. On this account, God is seen as the remote agent, in contrast to the Active Intellect, which plays a more active role.

Both the physical and intellectual constitution of the prophet must be perfect: "the perfection of the bodily faculties ... is consequent upon the best possible temperament, the best possible size, and the purest possible matter, of the part of the body that is the substratum for the faculty in question."[77] Only such a perfectly constituted individual can attain to intellectual, imaginative, and moral perfection, by dissociating himself from all "bestial things," and by controlling emotion or passion.[78] In his quest for moral and intellectual perfection, the prophet epitomizes an ascetic lifestyle; eschewing all corporeal pleasures, he lives in solitude and avoids human interaction. When such an individual is overcome by emotions, or when his imagination is weak, he is unable to receive prophetic revelation.

---

[74] Maimonides *Guide* Intro: 12.   [75] Maimonides *Guide* Intro: 1:7–8.
[76] Maimonides *Guide* 2.36:369.   [77] Maimonides *Guide* 2.36:369.
[78] Maimonides *Guide* 2.36:371–2.

Maimonides distinguishes three types of people based on the power of their imaginative faculty: the philosopher, the prophet, and the statesman. The philosopher receives an influx from the Active Intellect through the rational faculty, resulting in knowledge of basic concepts, philosophical truths, and rational principles. The prophet receives this overflow first through the rational faculty, and then through the imaginative faculty, resulting not only in philosophical (theoretical) knowledge, but in political expertise as well. The statesman receives an overflow to the imaginative faculty alone, resulting in confused and vague images that offer only partial guidance.[79] Thus, the prophet represents the ideal knower, one who combines the best of both rational and imaginative knowledge. Note however, that the operative factor in prophecy is the Active Intellect and not the divine will.[80]

In Chapter 4, I argued that Maimonides does not rule out an eternal model of creation; similarly, I am arguing here in favor of a reading according to which prophecy has been naturalized in a way that minimizes God's direct intervention. This position does not deny the incorporation of anomalies into the natural order, but it does underscore a rationalist and naturalized understanding of both prophecy and miracle. This position also minimizes the role played by divine will, although it is important to note that according to Maimonides, God can choose to withhold prophecy from somebody who has satisfied all the other criteria.[81]

V Monarchy, Prophecy, and Politics in post-Maimonidean Thought

Post-Maimonidean thinkers grappled with Maimonides' model of the perfect philosopher-prophet, as Maimonides' successors disagreed over the nature of prophecy, the political role of the prophet, and the correlation of the prophet to monarchy. Can we make sense of monarchy within the context of the model of the philosopher-king? Nowhere in the Torah is kingship set forth as an imperative. Monarchy is presented as a hypothetical possibility, and as undesirable in principle. As Melamed notes, the wish on the part of the Israelites to set up a king is depicted as a desire to "be like other nations" and not as a good in itself. The hypothetical king is bound by the laws of the Torah and concern for the public good.[82] I Samuel 8 again reiterates the desire of the people of Israel to "be like other nations," and Samuel reluctantly provides the conditions under which kingship is acceptable. Medieval Jewish philosophers struggled with whether monarchy was a halakhic obligation or not: Maimonides claimed in Hilkhot Melakhim that it was, and many of his successors followed suit.[83] But Maimonides' conception of monarchy was rather narrow, inasmuch as he argued that the king owed allegiance to the prophet and priest; the powers of the king were thus quite limited in scope. As Melamed puts it, "in his [Maimonides'] halakhic writings, monarchy

---

[79] Maimonides *Guide* 2.37.
[80] See Kreisel 2001, for detailed examination of Maimonides' views on prophecy.
[81] Again, for a different picture of the role played by divine will, see Manekin 2008 and Ivry 2016, both of whom emphasize the importance of God's will in *withholding* prophecy to somebody otherwise deserving.
[82] Melamed 2003, 7. See, for example, *Deuteronomy* 17.
[83] See Melamed 2003, 9 for a discussion of the different sides to this debate.

appears as a halakhic norm, but its powers are greatly limited."[84] And Maimonides is careful not to draw a direct parallel between the king and the philosopher-prophet on the other.

Gersonides, even more than Maimonides, is committed to a naturalistic conception of prophecy. Turning to the relation between God and the world, Gersonides is able to analyze the details of this relation without violating the linguistic constraints he has established. Gersonides' first discussion of prophecy occurs in his supercommentary upon Averroës' *Epitome of Parva Naturalia*, a work that summarized Aristotle's treatise on divination.[85] In this work, Averroës links veridical dreams with divination and prophecy. He attempts to explain veridical dreams about the future in terms of the Active Intellect, as a way for an intellect that doesn't know sensible future contingents to have knowledge of the future. Gersonides accepts much of Averroës' approach: he agrees with Averroës that prophecy deals with knowledge of the future, and that the purpose of this knowledge is to lead people to felicity. He also agrees with Averroës (and Maimonides) that prophets require intellectual perfection.[86] Some of these themes are reinforced in *Wars* II.

We saw in Chapter 5 that according to Gersonides, God knows that certain states of affairs may or may not be actualized. But insofar as they are contingent states, he does not know which of the alternatives will be the case. For if God did know future contingents prior to their actualization, there could be no contingency in the world. In an attempt to explain how prophecies are possible in a system that denies the possibility of knowledge of future contingents, Gersonides will need to claim that the prophet does not receive knowledge of particular future events; rather his knowledge is of a general form, and he must instantiate this knowledge with particular facts. What distinguishes prophets from ordinary persons is that the former are more attuned to receive these universal messages and are in a position to apply them to particular circumstances. On this analysis, no essential distinction should be drawn between the philosopher and the prophet in terms of what they know. Feldman states clearly that the content of true philosophy is the same as the content of prophecy: "prophetic intuition turns out to be no more than a highly developed deductive faculty."[87]

In Book II of *Wars*, Gersonides turns to a discussion of dreams, divination, and prophecy. As in his supercommentary, the topic of veridical dreams sets the stage for prophecy. Veridical dreams, divination, and prophecy cannot come about by chance, but are "determined and ordered."[88] But how can chance events (in particular future contingents) be determined and ordered? What sort of information can the prophet transmit in reality? His analysis of prophetic statements occurs against the backdrop of his astrological determinism. Gersonides explains that the information transmitted by the prophet is of a general nature and does not pertain to the individual *qua* particular. The agent intellect serves as the repository for information communicated

---

[84] Melamed 2003, 47.

[85] Gersonides' text can be found in Altmann 1979–80. See Kreisel 2001, for a summary of this supercommentary.

[86] See Kreisel 2001, 341–4.   [87] Feldman in Gersonides *Wars* vol. 2, 18.

[88] Gersonides *Wars* vol. 2, II.1:28.

by the heavenly bodies. The patterns revealed in this communication between agent intellect and diviner (astrologer, prophet) are from the heavenly bodies, which themselves are endowed with intellects and so "apprehend the pattern that derives from them."[89] Each mover apprehends the order deriving from the heavenly body it moves, and not patterns that emanate from other heavenly bodies. As a result, the imaginative faculty receives the "pattern inherent in the intellects of the heavenly bodies from the influence deriving from them."[90] This influence derives from the position of the heavenly bodies "by the ascendant degree or the dominant planet [in a particular zodiacal position]".[91] The Agent Intellect cannot always impart the exact time, or the exact details of a predicted event. Furthermore, inasmuch as the heavenly bodies do not jointly cooperate with one another in this process, it is possible for the communication to be misconstrued. And of equal importance, the events may be circumvented: "our intellect and choice... have the power to move us contrary to that which is determined by the heavenly bodies."[92] In other words, as we noted in Chapter 6, human choice guided by reason can subvert astral patterns, and so contingency is retained.

We have mentioned above that the prophet and philosopher share certain characteristics, most notably their access to intellectual knowledge. The one exception is Moses, who differs from other prophets in two respects: first, in his reception of the emanation from the Active Intellect, only Moses' intellect (and not the imaginative faculty) was involved; and second, Moses, unlike the other prophets, was a law-giver.[93] Gersonides notes in *Wars* II.5 that one of the functions of prophecy is preservation of the species: "this type of communication is given him in order that he [can] avoid the evil that he [now] knows has been set for him or [he can] pursue the good that has been set for him."[94] The prophet functions as a disseminator of moral truths as well. In his commentary to *Song of Songs*, Gersonides claims that "what is understood by the multitudes from the words of the prophets guides one to moral perfection, and what is understood by the elite guides one to conceptual perfection."[95]

But Isaac Abravanel found the views of both Maimonides and Gersonides problematic. Let us first consider Isaac Abravanel's critique of Gersonides' theory of prophecy. As we noted in Chapter 7, Abravanel stresses the intention and will of the agent, namely God. That the one who wills is God and not the Agent Intellect is stated emphatically in his *Commentary on Job*: to think otherwise is a stumbling-block. Abravanel excoriates the philosophers, mentioning Gersonides by name, claiming that "this implied for them that prophecy was a natural matter, with the result that they denied the words of the prophet Isaiah... there is no escaping the fact that prophecy comes from Him (may He be blessed) by means of a particular, simple volition in miraculous fashion." Gersonides is named as one of those uttering such heresies: "The Ralbag's arguments are unsubstantial, for it is not the Agent Intellect that informs the prophet of the future. Rather it is God."[96]

[89] See Gersonides *Wars* vol. 2, II.6.   [90] Gersonides *Wars* vol. 2, II.6: 64.
[91] Gersonides *Wars* vol. 2, II.6: 64.   [92] Gersonides *Wars* vol. 2, II.2: 34.
[93] See Feldman's comments in Gersonides *Wars* vol. 2, 22.
[94] Gersonides *Wars* vol. 2, II.5: 48.   [95] Gersonides 1998, *Song of Songs*, 8.
[96] See Isaac Abravanel, *Commentary on Joshua*, in Frank, Leaman, and Manekin 2000, 274.

Further, Abravanel is one of the few late thinkers who rejected the monarchy model altogether, denying that the Bible commanded the Jews to establish a monarchy. Commenting on *Deuteronomy* 17:14–20, he first lays out the three duties of a king: waging war to save his people; to order the Laws; and to administer punishments. He then argues that the nation of Israel has no need of a king, because God has satisfied the first two of these duties, while the "great Court of Law," i.e., the Sanhedrin, metes out punishments. Abravanel concludes that "although it be admitted that a king is necessary for the [other] nations, that does not justify it for the Israelite nation."[97]

Abravanel continues his critique in his famous commentary on I *Samuel* 8:4–7. In that text, he presents what he calls "three speeches" in an attempt to explore the necessity of kings for other nations and for the nation of Israel. He first rejects what he understands to be Aristotle's model of kingship, and replaces it with a theological democracy in which "a people have many leaders who come together and unite and agree on a single plan, and that governance and judgment be according to their decision."[98] He then turns to whether a king is necessary for Israel, and argues that the proof texts in Scripture do not *command*, but only *permit* Israel to set up a king. He envisions such a ruler as being more of a prophet-king like Moses, one who does not occupy himself with temporal matters, but rather communes with God. Just as Jethro "guided Moses in the matter of the administration of justice, until he had taught him the way to appoint captains and how to govern the people," so too a prophet-king ruler relies upon an advisor.[99]

By the seventeenth century, the notion of prophecy, along with its correlation to political thought, had been dismantled. As Melamed notes, Spinoza takes Jewish political philosophy out of the medieval framework. We have already discussed (in Chapter 3) Spinoza's controversial views on how to read and evaluate statements in Scripture. Concerned to free philosophy and the study of nature from what he saw as the shackles of theology, his views regarding prophecy were embedded in his methodological concern with truth, and with scientific truth in particular. In the *Theological Political Treatise*, Spinoza postulates the incommensurability of religion and science: the authority of the prophets carries weight only in matters concerning morality and true virtue. In other matters, their beliefs are irrelevant. In this treatise, he presents the Torah as a humanly established law, contingent in nature. The role of the prophet is simply to share the ethical precepts contained in Scripture, and nothing more.

In short, truth for Spinoza is defined as residing in the domain of reason alone, and Spinoza concludes that Scripture cannot speak the truth. Scripture can give us moral claims, but we should be careful not to confuse moral claims, however salutary, with epistemic truths.[100] It is not just that Scripture does not, to paraphrase Galileo, tell us "how the heavens go," but that Scripture does not tell us how "anything at all goes." The purpose of Scripture is to teach obedience, not truth; because there are no epistemic claims to be found in Scripture, there can be no conflict between what

[97] Abravanel *Commentary* in Lerner and Mahdi 1963, 263.
[98] Abravanel *Commentary* in Lerner and Mahdi 1963, 265.
[99] Abravanel *Commentary* in Lerner and Mahdi 1963, 269.
[100] See Smith 1997, 66; Spinoza 2001.

Scripture exhorts and what we find to be the case in nature. For Spinoza, there is only one meaning to a scriptural text, and if that meaning is stupid or contravenes reason, then so much the worse for Scripture.

Spinoza thus concludes that the authority of the prophets carries weight only in matters concerning morality and true virtue. In other matters, their beliefs are irrelevant. Spinoza argues for a model according to which faith (theology) and reason (philosophy) occupy different realms: the domain of reason is truth and wisdom, while that of theology is piety and obedience. In chapter six of the *Treatise*, Spinoza reiterates that methods used in natural science must be applied to our understanding of Scripture. The Bible must be read and understood naturalistically, that is, in terms of the laws of physical causation. On Spinoza's model, Moses is no longer a divinely motivated prophet-king as envisioned by Maimonides and Abravanel, but a "shrewd Machiavellian politician who consciously exploited the mob's superstitions and their primitive fear of God to advance his own temporal political goals."[101]

VI On Human Felicity: The Meaning and Purpose of Life

Throughout this work, we have emphasized the tension between intellectual perfection on the one hand, and a more faith-based belief system on the other hand. Maimonides and Gersonides both claim that metaphysical knowledge alone leads to human immortality, and that immortality could only be achieved upon the completion of intellectual perfection, whereas Crescas and Halevi demur, emphasizing a more spiritually based perfection. But is it even possible for a human intellect, which itself is rooted in matter, to achieve knowledge of the Active Intellect? And how is knowledge of the Active Intellect correlated to knowledge of God? Furthermore, inasmuch as the rabbinic sages did not regard immortality as dependent upon intellectual perfection, how do our philosophers' views accord with those of the rabbis? What role, for example, does Torah study play in achieving ultimate human perfection?

In an attempt to deal with these issues, Maimonides provides in *Guide* 3.51 a famous parable of a king's palace.[102] Maimonides tells us that intellectual perfection is the only way to reach God, but this union can occur solely through the Active Intellect, exemplified by the king. Those lacking in intellectual perfection (the masses of humanity) never even enter the gates of the palace, let alone see the king. Maimonides describes the intellectual contemplation of God as a form of meditative stance, cautioning us not to contaminate inner worship with outer worldly matters. *Guide* 3.51 thus reinforces the view that very few individuals can actualize a purely intellectual self, one that has transcended a hylomorphic composite. Intellectual apprehension of God represents the truest form of worship. On the one hand, Maimonides tells us that love of God can only be achieved through intellectual and

---

[101] See Melamed 2009, 787.
[102] For details and differing interpretations of this famous parable, see Rudavsky 2010; Ivry 2016; Kellner 1990; Kellner 1991.

scientific pursuit: love of God "becomes valid only through the apprehension of the whole of Being as it is."[103] On what comes to be identified in later centuries as a Spinozistic model, it is the study of nature as a whole (the facts of the matter) that yields knowledge of the divine. On the other hand, Maimonides has argued that there are limits to what we can know demonstratively about God. The truest dimension of prayer consists in inner and outer silence, a silence that reflects the profound epistemological limits of human beings.

The very last chapter of the Guide presents yet another set of interpretative problems having to do with Maimonides' conception of happiness, and the relation between theoretical and moral ways of life. On the one hand, we find passages in the Guide that reflect Plato's exhortation in the famous parable of the cave: in this parable, the philosopher leaves the cave in search of knowledge and enlightenment, but has an obligation to return to the cave to educate and improve those who have remained prisoners.[104] In Guide 2.33, for example, Moses ascends the mountain to achieve union with God, but then descends back into society as a political and moral leader. But on the other hand, in Guide 3.51, Maimonides extols the intellectual life as one of "solitude and isolation," and suggests that the truly excellent person avoids human interaction and "does not meet anyone unless it is necessary."[105] Maimonides reflects statements in Aristotle and the Islamic philosophers, notably Ibn Bâjja, who upheld the theoretical, contemplative life as superior to the moral life.[106] We find a similar ambivalence in Maimonides' description of the four ways of achieving perfection; his description of these perfections is adapted from Ibn Bâjja's appropriation of Aristotle, and can be characterized as follows.[107] Material perfection comprises possession of material goods; bodily perfection comprises bodily health and strength; moral perfection comprises moral virtue and action; and rational or theoretical perfection consists in contemplation of divine matters.[108] Following Aristotle and Ibn Bâjja, Maimonides regards these four perfections as arranged hierarchically, from lowest (material) to highest (theoretical). Maimonides describes material possessions as "external" to the person, having no essential relation to the inner person: "all this is outside his self."[109]

Maimonides uses a quotation from Jeremiah (9:22–3) to support his defense of the intellectual virtues as the most perfect of the four. In fact, he follows this statement with another, claiming that the commandments do not compare with intellectual perfection: "all the actions prescribed by the Law—I refer to the various species of worship and also the moral habits that are useful to all people in their mutual dealings—that all this is not to be compared with this ultimate end, and does not equal it, being but preparations made for the sake of this end."[110] In this remarkable passage, Maimonides is suggesting that the purpose of the commandments has little

---

[103] Maimonides Guide 3.28.
[104] See Plato Republic Books 6–7, for Plato's famous description of the cave, and the philosopher's return to the cave.
[105] Maimonides Guide 3.51:621.
[106] See for example Aristotle NE 6.7 1141a 20–2; 10.8 1178b 33–5.
[107] For a detailed comparison of Maimonides and Ibn Bâjja, see Altmann 1972.
[108] Maimonides Guide 3.54:635.   [109] Maimonides Guide 3.54:634.
[110] Maimonides Guide 3.54:636.

to do with intellectual perfection, which is the true aim of human existence; the commandments only serve an instrumental purpose, enabling people to interact in a social situation. In *Guide* 3.54, Maimonides tells us that moral habits function only in a social context, and serve no deontological purpose in and of themselves, suggesting that one who has achieved intellectual perfection, and surpassed corporeality, has transcended the need for the commandments.[111]

Immediately following this passage from Jeremiah, Maimonides then adds what some scholars have described as a fifth perfection, which emphasizes the importance of imitating God's actions (*imitatio Dei*): that we should glory in the apprehension of God's attributes and actions, namely loving kindness, judgment, and righteousness.[112] Does this fifth perfection mark a radical break with the Aristotelian ideal, by reintroducing a practical component into the highest form of human existence; or does it represent a by-product of the fourth perfection, consisting in the pleasure one experiences as a result of contemplation; or does this fifth perfection reflect a reintroduction of Platonic themes in Maimonides, perhaps in line with al-Fârâbî and others? Each of these positions reflects a plausible interpretation of Maimonides' text.[113] We thus detect in Maimonides a tension between two world views: the Fârâbian representation of the Platonic model in which the intellectual ultimately fulfills his political obligations and returns to the community; and the model offered by Ibn Bâjja who, in his *Governance of the Solitary*, called upon the philosopher to withdraw from the community altogether and live a spiritual life in isolation.

No such tension exists in the mind of Gersonides, however, who repeatedly emphasizes the superiority of intellect in the attainment of ultimate felicity. As Horwitz points out, this theme is apparent in Gersonides' biblical commentaries: "a central role of Ralbag's biblical commentaries is the desire to help his readers attain eternal intellectual felicity through knowledge of the truth."[114] Immortality of intellect is impossible without attaining sufficient knowledge in this world. As we saw in Chapter 5, Gersonides' espousal of Elihu's viewpoint in the *Book of Job* reflected the importance of intellectual understanding. Nowhere is this emphasis seen more clearly than in Gersonides' commentary to *Song of Songs*. Ostensibly, the *Song of Songs* describes the love affair and desires of a shepherd for a maiden; generations of commentators saw in the work an allegory of the relation between God and Israel. Gersonides, however, provides a philosophical reading of the work that incorporates two sets of subsidiary dialogues, first between the human material intellect and the Active Intellect, and second between the faculties of the soul

---

[111] See Shatz 2005, for extended discussion of this point.

[112] Maimonides *Guide* 3.54:637.

[113] In an influential article, Shlomo Pines has argued that Maimonides' presentation in this passage represented a radical break with the Aristotelian ideal as laid down in the *Nicomachean Ethics*. Pines claims that in this final chapter, Maimonides does an about-face: because humans cannot have certain knowledge of metaphysics, it turns out that practical activity is the only perfection attainable. "The practical way of life, the *bios praktikos*," turns out to be superior to the theoretical. But others have argued that the practical activity is a consequence of intellectual life. Shatz has argued that "by achieving intellectual perfection, the perfect individual engages in a life *of imitatio Dei* with respect to the Deity's actions." See Shatz 2005, 186. According to Altmann, *imitatio Dei* is but the practical consequence of the intellectual love of God and is part and parcel of the ultimate perfection. See Altmann 1972, 24.

[114] See Horwitz 2006, 124.

and the material intellect. As summarized by Kellner, the main thrust of these two discussions relates to "the overwhelming desire of the material intellect to approach the Active Intellect and its attempts to enlist the [willing] aid of the other faculties of the soul in this quest."[115]

Gersonides spells out the import of these discussions in his introduction to the commentary. He first lays down the premise that "man's ultimate felicity resides in cognizing and knowing God to the extent that is possible for him."[116] Such knowledge is achieved through observation of the state of existing things in the natural universe, that is, through the beings that God has created and caused. Knowledge of God, therefore, is predicated on knowledge of the natural order. Following the Aristotelian theory of knowledge acquisition, Gersonides agrees that "all the intelligibles which we cognize are acquired," but no intelligible can be acquired without the Active Intellect.[117]

We have mentioned in Chapter 2 that Gersonides eschews esotericism, emphasizing ordinary, direct discourse. In this particular case, however, Gersonides claims that the purpose of Song of Songs is meant to guide only selected individuals to their felicity: "this book... guides the elite only to the way of achieving felicity, and thus its external meaning was not made useful to the masses."[118] In truth, however, Gersonides warns us that most ordinary mortals will not achieve this "stupendous felicity": "only very few individuals can acquire even a large measure of it."[119] Many obstacles stand in the way of most humans, including their hankering after their physical desires, as well as the misleading nature of imagination and opinion. Because it is so difficult to achieve felicity, the prophets have devoted much effort to guiding and helping ordinary mortals along.

Gersonides then unpacks the various levels of enlightenment that he finds in Song of Songs, moving from mathematics, to physics, astronomy, and finally metaphysics; In this way, Gersonides emphasizes the natural sciences, in particular physics, as a propaedeutic to metaphysics: "for Gersonides, learning truths about the physical universe also perfects us and brings us to immortality."[120] In fact, as Kellner points out, the study of physics is preferable to metaphysics, since the latter is both difficult, dangerous, and can lead one astray. Gersonides is clear that the science of physics builds upon moral knowledge derived from Scripture: "this science [Physics] is impossible for one who is not strongly settled on the true views from the perspective of Torah and speculation."[121] Gersonides then unpacks the various allegories and symbolic representations in the work, all of which point to the goal of ultimate felicity as the union with God via the Active Intellect. The theme of intellectual perfection is repeated in Wars as well. Book I of Wars is replete with descriptions of the attainment of intellectual perfection, and the felicity resulting from this knowledge after death.

---

[115] Kellner in Gersonides 1998, Song of Songs, xxi.
[116] Gersonides 1998, Song of Songs, 5.   [117] Ibid.
[118] Gersonides 1998, Song of Songs, 8; see Kellner 2010, 160.
[119] Gersonides 1998, Song of Songs, 6.   [120] Kellner 2010, 162.
[121] Gersonides 1998, Song of Songs, 11. See also the discussion in Chapter 3 of this work.

We end this chapter with Spinoza, who represents the culmination of Jewish philosophical thinking, incorporating pieces from Ibn Gabirol, Gersonides, and Abravanel. Spinoza's famous discussion of eternity of the mind, which is couched against the backdrop of what the human mind can know, is summed up in *Ethics* 5p23, "The human Mind cannot be absolutely destroyed with the Body, but something of it remains which is eternal."[122] Spinoza's demonstration of this proposition rests on *Ethics* 2p8c, namely, that we do not attribute to the human mind any duration that can be defined by time except insofar as it expresses the actual existence of the body that is defined by duration and time. After the separation from or cessation of the body, however, mind no longer pertains to duration; because it is constituted by God's essence, mind will necessarily be eternal. Spinoza continues that "we feel and know by experience that we are eternal...this existence that it [our mind] has cannot be defined by time or explained through duration."[123] It would appear, then, that when the body dies, we are left with the *idea* of extended essence, one that eschews personality, thus eliminating individual immortality. But how can Spinoza maintain on the one hand that we are eternal, and on the other hand that the eternal has no relation to time, knowing that as individuals we do exist in and through time? Only by recognizing the implications of Spinoza's thoroughgoing hylomorphic monism, and understanding its place in the long line of Jewish Neoplatonic hylomorphisms, can we fully understand Spinoza's views on individuation and eternality.

The final propositions of *Ethics* 5 can be reduced to three main doctrines:

9.1   A part of the mind is eternal and survives decay of the body.
9.2   Intuitive science (third kind of knowledge) yields blessedness.
9.3   Blessedness consists in intellectual love of God.

These doctrines represent the culmination of several strands: the notion of the free human, the overcoming of the passions in order to achieve this notion of freedom, and the incorporation of knowledge as a criterion for freedom. For Spinoza, the free individual functions as an ideal limiting condition for humans. The free person lives according to the dictates of reason alone (E4p67). Since s/he lives by reason, s/he has no fear, certainly not of death. Since good and evil are the result of inadequate ideas, the free person is not ruled by this conventional type of morality (E4p68). In the appendix to book four, Spinoza begins to extol the virtue of reason, and connects rational life with "blessedness." Blessedness is connected with rational perfection and intuitive knowledge of God. Hence the more we know (understand the cause of) a passion, the less we suffer from it. The main idea is that by understanding the causes of the emotions, we dissolve the power they have over

---

[122] Spinoza *Ethics* 5.23:607. Note that Spinoza does not use the term immortality to express the survival of part of the mind. The only time that the term "immortal" (*immortalis*) appears in the *Ethics* is in Vp41s: "There may be someone who, because he does not believe he can nourish his body with good food to eternity, should prefer to fill himself with poisons and other deadly things, or because he sees that the mind is not eternal or immortal...(*vel, quia videt Mentem non esse aeternam seu immortalem*)." Other discussions use the term eternal (*aeternam*) in talking about the continued existence of the soul.

[123] Spinoza *Ethics* 5.23sp607–8.

us; by having adequate knowledge (true knowledge, clear and distinct ideas), the passions become neutralized.

We can now move to the triad of doctrines in *Ethics* 5. On Spinoza's theory of individuation, part of what makes me who I am is that I am affected by other individuals; individuation on this model turns out to be relational, incorporating both material and formal elements. This identification with body remains embedded in the mind after the "death of the body." The crucial point is that for Spinoza there is a difference of degree, not of kind, between persons and other objects. To admit that the eternity of mind incorporates the idea of the body, as expressed in E2p7, and therefore that the corresponding body is eternal as well as the mind, simply reinforces Spinoza's rigorous monist ontology. This is precisely what the isomorphism of God/nature amounts to, and should not be regarded as an inconsistency in Spinoza's ontology. That Spinoza emphasizes the eternity of part of the mind, which incorporates the body *qua* idea of the mind, is undeniable in the sense that the mind has an idea of the "essence of body under the form of eternity."[124]

(9.2) and (9.3) suggest that eternity is tied to the third kind of knowledge, or intuition. This third level, which is constituted as knowledge of individuals, is different from the other two degrees (E5p36s). It is this level of knowledge that leads to intellectual love of God, or salvation. At this level, the individual achieves a level of intuitive union/knowledge, and is characterized by a "sort of repose" (E5p36s), or "peace of soul" (E5p62s) that results from recognizing the necessity inherent in himself, in God and in things. But this repose raises yet another worry, one that is aimed at the relation between God and mind. Spinoza has said in E1d8 that eternity pertains to God, alone inasmuch as God is the only entity in which essence is identical to existence; but in E5p23 he ascribes eternity to mind. If we are to make sense of the isomorphism between God and mind, then Spinoza's theory of eternity of mind must eschew individual immortality, on the grounds that in mind, essence is not identical to existence.

It is on this point that Spinoza comes closest to reflecting Gersonides' depiction of immortality in terms of knowledge of particulars. Just as Gersonides argued that the Agent Intellect represents the total intellectual cognitions acquired by an individual, so too Spinoza argues that the more singular things the mind understands, the more it understands God. On the basis of this characterization, what we call immortality of soul, characterized as eternity of mind, for Spinoza must be personal, but in a modified sense.

It might be argued that in an ontology that privileges identity of mind and body, a mind which is in any way "separated" from body cannot by definition be the "same" entity it was before the separation, and hence the eternal mind that unites with God in eternal blessedness cannot retain its personality in this union. But how can something that is finite and part of duration/time enter the domain of eternity? Spinoza's answer can only be that the eternity of substance, inasmuch as it comprises "everything that is," includes as well the realm of duration. The domain of "time in general" as opposed to particular instantiations of "space-time" is part of what we

---

[124] For a depiction of the three levels of knowledge, see Spinoza *Ethics* IIp40s2ff.

take to be eternity. That is precisely what Spinoza means when he states that "this something that pertains to the essence of the mind will necessarily be eternal."[125] Hence, by incorporating both temporality and the concomitant materiality expressed in a hylomorphic ontology, the individual retains its individuality while becoming one with God.

[125] Spinoza *Ethics* Vp23.

10

Concluding Comments

This volume has focused upon the relationship between "faith and reason" as articulated in the conflict between philosophical and scientific speculation on the one hand, and acceptance of Judaic beliefs on the other. Throughout this study we have witnessed medieval philosophers—Islamic, Christian and Jewish—wrestling with the project of reconciling "outside" sources and influences with their understanding of Scripture. Especially in the late medieval and early modern periods, religious belief was often threatened by the adoption of a scientific cosmology antithetical to religious thought, be it the cosmology of Plato, Aristotle, Ptolemy, or Copernicus. We envisioned three ways of thinking about this tension: conflict, independence, and integration, and we traced these models through the scope of medieval Jewish philosophy. Jewish philosophers were well aware of the dangers inherent with grappling with the threat of scientific paradigms, and often warned their readers (in the introductions to their works), either explicitly or implicitly, about the complexity of the issues. Maimonides' famous analogy of gold hidden in silver filigree served as a reminder to readers that on occasion, teachings based on science must be hidden from the general populace. On occasion, this wrestling resulted in a mode of discourse that obfuscated the full force of the compromise. Other times, as in the case of Spinoza, the wrestling resulted in expulsion from the Jewish community altogether. We noted that the methodology used, described regularly in the introductions to philosophical works, often emphasized the importance of hiding an esoteric, hidden level of discourse from the populace.

Chapter 4 described the tensions involved in describing and characterizing God. In his introduction to the *Guide*, Leo Strauss argues that "the teaching that positive attributes of God are impossible ... clearly contradicts the teaching of the law,"[1] while other scholars have tried to rescue Maimonides' theory.[2] All our thinkers agreed that God exists, and many of them provided proofs for God's existence. Some of these proofs were rooted in scientific paradigms drawn from natural philosophy. But with respect to actually applying predicates to God, apophatic theology would have us recognize that because humans cannot understand the ways, motives, or essence of

---

[1] In Pines 1963, xlviii–xlix.

[2] For a plethora of contemporary discussions, see Benor 1995; Manekin 2005; Seeskin 1991; Rudavsky 2010; Davies 2011, chapters 4 and 5; Halbertal 2015; Ivry 2016. Manekin suggests that ultimately we should understand Maimonides' theory as articulating God's inexplicability rather than God's unknowability: "God cannot be fully comprehended, despite the fact that we can (indeed, must) learn many things about Him" Manekin 2005, 35. Davies tries to reconceptualize Maimonides' negative predication in a way that permits of talking about God's perfections.

God, we cannot even begin to understand why God permits innocents to suffer, or error and sin to exist. But skeptical theism runs the risk of extending to moral knowledge as well. Erik Wielenberg notes: "skeptical theism is at odds with any religious tradition according to which there are certain claims that we can know to be true solely in virtue of the fact that God has told us that they are true."[3] Thus, skeptical theism about God's nature carries implications with respect to skepticism about divine assertions in general, and moral assertions in particular. How can we know whether any divine claims are true? If we are unable to distinguish lying from true divine claims, what sense can we attribute to the sacrifice of Isaac, a situation in which God intentionally creates in Abraham's mind the belief that Abraham is going to have to sacrifice Isaac, a belief that ultimately turns out to be false?

Chapters 5, 6, and 7 dealt in greater detail with the implications and tensions arising from Aristotelian and Ptolemaic cosmology and natural philosophy. Jewish philosophers clearly grappled with the tensions resulting from two traditions: on the one hand, a metaphysical system in which God was conceived as a unity, unchanging in essence, and all-knowing; and on the other hand, a tradition which claimed that God is intimately involved with a mutable world of possible entities. Does God's knowledge extend to this world of possibles? If not, then it might be claimed that God's knowledge is deficient—that is, that God's unawareness of the realm of the possible represents a deficiency in his nature. If God's knowledge does extend to the sublunar realm of possibility, then it might be argued that the possible must give way to the necessary—that is, that God's knowledge precludes the existence of the possible.

Compatibilists attempted to uphold both omniscience and the genuineness of the future. Saadiah and Halevi laid the groundwork for Maimonides' compatibilism. Maimonides himself upheld God's omniscience in the face of numerous objections, claiming that God knows both concrete and unactualized particulars. On the other hand, Ibn Daud and Gersonides both argued that foreknowledge coupled with infallibility precluded the contingency of the objects of God's knowledge. Unable to adopt a compatibilist solution, Ibn Daud and Gersonides therefore upheld a form of incompatibilism in an attempt to preserve the existence of contingency in the world. I have argued, however, that this analysis does not adequately account for the conditional nature of prophecies. For these and similar reasons, determinists such as Crescas attempted to salvage what remains of divine omniscience.

We then turned in Chapter 7 to the complex interrelationship between time, cosmology, and creation in medieval Jewish philosophy. Although early biblical and rabbinic works did not contain an ontology of time or place, the theological assumptions and constraints underlying these works reverberated throughout the medieval Jewish literature. Whereas in some cases these theological constraints were challenged, as reflected in the works of Maimonides and Gersonides, in other cases, these constraints were rejected altogether. I have depicted in this chapter those elements within biblical and rabbinic thought, as well as within Greek science and philosophy, that pertain to the themes of time and creation. Both the Jewish and

---

[3] Wielenberg 2010, 509.

Greek philosophical traditions have contributed important ingredients. From Scripture comes the unambiguous statement of a "Beginning." From the rabbis comes an understanding of the nuances inherent in interpreting the first instant of creation.

But how does one maintain a congruence between the cosmology expressed by the traditional Jewish sources and the "new science" represented by rival cosmologies— those of Aristotle, Ptolemy, and the Neoplatonists? Turning to a more careful examination of the natural order, we focused in Chapter 7 upon both the natural world that comprises the "sublunar" sphere (viz., the space between the earth and the moon) and the heavenly bodies that comprise the "superlunar" (above the moon). In a geocentric cosmology, the heavenly bodies occupied an important role in ancient and medieval cosmology, natural philosophy, metaphysics, medicine, and theology. Two rival cosmologies, those of Aristotle and of Ptolemy, competed for acceptance in the medieval world, and they affected related issues in natural philosophy as well as medieval views on astrology, as philosophers considered the causal efficacy of the heavenly bodies in the sublunar world.

The similarity of certain passages in Scripture to Plato's *Timaeus* is striking and did not go unnoticed by later Jewish thinkers. Later medieval Jewish philosophers were able to capitalize upon these similarities in order to emphasize the harmonization of Scripture and Greek philosophy. Both texts postulate the existence of a creator. Both impute to this creator the urge to create, the willful choosing to bring the universe into existence. Both recognize the importance of temporality in this creation process: the scriptural author(s) by focusing on the importance of the term "day *(yom)*" in the creation account, and Plato by introducing time as the ontological divide between the superlunar and sublunar spheres. And finally, both accounts allow for the *possibility* of creation occurring out of a "pre-existent matter," a chaotic, formless stuff upon which order is imposed.[4]

On the exoteric reading, much of Maimonides' effort was aimed at showing that the Scriptural view of creation is inconsistent with an Aristotelian theory. Gersonides was less willing ostensibly to compromise the temporal beginning of the universe, and so he creatively reinterpreted Aristotle's notion of the instant in such a way as to allow for a temporal beginning to creation out of a pre-existent matter. In contradistinction to Maimonides and Gersonides, both of whom adhere fairly closely to Aristotle's characterization of time as the measure of motion, Crescas and Albo deviated from this Aristotelian depiction of time in terms of motion.

We then turned to those events that, contravening the natural order, fall into the general category of miraculous events. Miracles provide the most pressing challenge, and we have seen both traditional and naturalistic explanations of the many miracles to be found in Scripture. How, in a cosmology ruled by law and order, can we account for miracles? Chapter 7 explored several attempts, ranging from Halevi's tacit acceptance of miracles to Maimonides' and Gersonides' naturalist account of miracles, and ending with Spinoza's rejection, in his *Tractatus*, of the very idea of miracle. Spelling out motifs already contained in embryo in his Jewish predecessors,

---

[4] For a discussion of additional similarities between *Genesis* and Plato's *Timaeus*, see Samuelson 1994, 194–7.

Spinoza maintained that Scripture provides only moral guidance and piety, not even moral truth, and certainly not scientific or mathematical truth. By pushing the views of Maimonides, Gersonides, and Ibn Ezra to their logical extreme, Spinoza thus destroyed the carefully constructed hermeneutic introduced by his Jewish predecessors.

Chapters 8 and 9 dealt broadly with philosophical anthropology—the psycho-physical composition of the human being and the implications of these theories upon moral theory and reward and punishment. In Chapter 8, we addressed the following issues: what is the soul, and how is it related to the body; if the soul is part of the body, does it perish along with the destruction of the body, or does a part of the soul survive; if part of the soul is immortal, can it acquire new knowledge after death; is the body resurrected in the world to come, or is salvation purely spiritual; if salvation is spiritual, are rewards and punishments in the world to come spiritual as well, or are they material? Concomitant with the issue of immortality is the connection obtaining between human intellect and the Active Intellect, as characterized by Avicenna and Averroës. Medieval philosophers took seriously the question of whether the soul retains its individuality upon separation from the body; in other words, whether immortality is personal or general. We thus examined problems of immortality, individuation, and individuality. Theories of soul inherited from the rabbinic corpus, Greek sources, and Islamic philosophy gave rise to varied conceptions of personal identity and immortality. Avicenna and Averroës helped to shape the Neoplatonic and Aristotelian dimensions of Jewish views of the soul, reflected in the works of Isaac Israeli, Halevi, and Ibn Gabirol. While Maimonides paved the way for future understanding of how immaterial substances could be individuated, not until Gersonides, however, were such issues discussed in their logical context. In his examination of the relation between universals and particulars, and in his insistence upon the primacy of individuals, Gersonides allowed for nominalist tendencies to take root in fourteenth-century Jewish thought. These roots flourished in the works of Spinoza.

The very doctrine of reward and punishment, embedded in a theory of human felicity, is predicated upon individual immortality of the soul. In Chapter 9, we returned to the ramifications of soul, in the context of the whole question of human social and political life. Our philosophers' responses to these interrelated issues reinforce themes we have seen discussed in Chapter 3, and reflect the attempt once again to reconcile Jewish beliefs with the views set forth by the ancient Greek philosophers.

Once again, Jewish philosophers incorporated material from Greek philosophy, from the rabbis, and from their intellectual peers. Both Aristotle and Neoplatonist thinkers influenced their conception of virtue and happiness. The formative texts from Aristotle's *Nicomachean Ethics* promoted a view of happiness (or *eudaimonia*) as a "human flourishing" or "psychic well-being." All human beings desire to be happy, Aristotle tells us, but we tend to confuse what we desire materially with what truly leads to happiness. The ultimate life of virtue is one that fulfills our function or telos as rational animals; *Eudaimonia* thus results from living in accordance with reason. In book ten of the *Ethics*, Aristotle adds to this conception the notion that ultimate happiness for the truly rational individual can be achieved by "imitating" or emulating that which is divine in us.

Yet another question pertained to the psycho-physical determinist strains we have located in various works. If immortality is predicated on intellectual knowledge, and philosophers such as Maimonides and Gersonides have argued that many individuals are psycho-physically incapable of embarking on such a rigorous and philosophical course of study, does it follow that not all humans can achieve intellectual perfection: is the road the same, and open, to all? And is there only one road to ultimate felicity, or are there many routes? On the one hand, the very notion of Jewish ethics can only be understood against the backdrop of the Mosaic commandments and law, reinforcing the political dimension of our discussion. The 613 commandments articulated in the Pentateuch cover a myriad of situations: they include rituals, sacred attitudes toward the Deity, and inter-personal relationships. These latter actions are commonly considered to comprise the moral domain. Nonetheless, we do find mention of an independent standard for morality rooted in reason, leading us to wonder about the extent to which Jewish thinkers advocated a natural law theory.

Let us close this work by emphasizing the importance of both intellectual and moral perfection in the overall Neoplatonic scheme of emanation. We have noted several times that Neoplatonic ontology places matter at one end of the hierarchy, God at the other, and the human soul as engaged on a quest away from the material world and back to God. We have seen that in Plotinus, matter is identified with the principle of evil, non-being, and lack of existence, residing as it does at the lowest pole of the emanation hierarchy. Ibn Gabirol introduced a new element into Neoplatonic thinking by suggesting that matter is a principle of generality that occurs on all levels: even incorporeal substances have matter as their base. Distinguishing between corporeal and spiritual matter, he argues that matter as such is incorporeal and must unite with the form of materiality. Although the doctrine of emanation, with its insistence upon the debasement of matter, is a basic ingredient in the majority of Neoplatonic texts, it is tempered by the biblical insistence upon creation *ex nihilo*. Our authors have all grappled with the underlying ontological question: "How can the many be generated from the One?" and have offered a variety of responses. According to Ibn Gabirol, for example, creation is dynamic and occurs outside of time. In his emanation scheme, the emphasis is upon the relation of form to matter, rather than on just a "flow" from the deity.

This human soul represents within itself all levels of created existence: functioning as a microcosmic prism, it incorporates elements of matter, form, intellect, and will. The soul is engaged in a perennial journey back to its source, the success of which is wholly dependent upon its moral character. We have seen how our thinkers parse "moral character" in many ways, some of which emphasize intellectual perfection, and others emphasize actions. Maimonides describes the state of perfection of one who has achieved the fullness of philosophical study encouraged in the *Guide*. Reflecting the Neoplatonic motif that corporeal bodies hinder immaterial perfection, he emphasizes the separation from corporeality as a necessary condition for spiritual perfection. It is important to note that a young person is never capable of achieving this level of perfection. The instant of ultimate perfection is manifested by the divesting of corporeality, a state that is not possible for a youth still subject to passions. In fact, Maimonides tells us that only three individuals have ever reached this level. Ultimate perfection, which can only be achieved at the instant of death, is consummated with a kiss: "Because of this the Sages have indicated with reference to the deaths of Moses, Aaron and Miriam that the three of them died by a kiss... And they said of Miriam in the same way: She also died by a kiss. But with regard to her it is not said, by the mouth of the Lord; because she was a woman, the use of the figurative expression was not suitable with regard to her. Their purpose was to indicate that the three of them died in the pleasure of this apprehension due to the intensity of passionate love."[5]

In a similar vein, the fate of the soul has been eloquently described by the anonymous author of *Ibn Ḥasdai's Neoplatonist*, who contrasts the fates of the rational and sinful soul respectively. The sinful soul, which has not cleansed itself from the defilements of this world, deserves its exile:

It remains sad and despondent... hungering and thirsting to find a way so as to go home to its country and return to its native place. It resembles a man who travelled away from his house, brothers, children and wife, relatives and family, and stayed abroad for a long time. When finally he was on his way back and approached his country and the goal of his desires... and was filled with the strongest desire to reach his home and rest in his house—obstacles were put in his way and the gates were shut and he was prevented from passing through. He called, but it was of no avail... He wandered about perplexed to find a refuge, weeping bitterly and sorrowfully bewailing the great good which he has lost and the evil which had befallen him.[6]

The rational soul, on the other hand, acts according to truth, purifies itself from the corporeal defilement of the material world, and thus receives its just reward:

If the rational soul is righteous... it is then worthy of receiving its reward and goes to the world of intellect and reaches the light which is created from the Power, its pure brilliance and unmixed splendor and perfect wisdom, from where it had been derived; it is then delighted by its understanding and knowledge. This delight is not one of eating, drinking and other bodily delights, but the joy of the soul in what it sees and hears, a delight which has nothing in common with other delights except the name.[7]

This reward, in the world of medieval Jewish philosophy, represents the ultimate aim of human existence.

---

[5] Maimonides *Guide* 3.51:627–8. For the importance of including Miriam among those who have achieved union with God, see Rudavsky 2010; Kellner 1998.

[6] Stern 1961, 120.   [7] Stern 1961, 119.

Bibliography

Primary Sources

Abraham ibn Daud (1986), *The Exalted Faith (Emunah Ramah)*, Norbert Samuelson (trans.) and Gershon Weiss (ed.) (Associated University Presses: London).

Abraham ibn Ezra (1939), *Reshit Hokhma (The Beginning of Wisdom)*, Raphael Levy and Francisco Cantera (ed. and trans.) (Baltimore: Johns Hopkins Press).

Abraham ibn Ezra (1977), *Perushe ha-Torah le-rabbenu Avraham ibn Ezra 1: bereshit*, A. Weiser (ed.) (Jerusalem: Mossad ha-rav Kook).

Abraham ibn Ezra (1985), *Sefer Yesod Mora ve-Yesod Torah*, in *Yalqut Abraham ibn Ezra* (New York and Tel Aviv: Israel Matz Hebrew Classics Ltd.).

Abraham ibn Ezra (1988), (1988–2001), *Commentary of the Torah*, Norman Strickman and Arthur M. Silver (trans. and annotated) (New York: Menorah).

Abraham ibn Ezra (1995), *The Secret of the Torah: A Translation of Abraham ibn Ezra's Sefer Yesod Mora Ve-Sod Ha-Torah*, Norman Strickman (trans. and annotated) (Northvale, NJ: Jason Aronson, Inc.).

Al-Fârâbî (1961), *Fusûl al-Madanî: Aphorisms of the Statesman*, D. M. Dunlop (ed. and trans.) (Cambridge: Cambridge University Press).

Al-Fârâbî (2001), *Alfarabi: The Political Writings; Selected Aphorisms and Other Texts*, Charles E. Butterworth (trans. and ed.) (Ithaca and London: Cornell University).

Al-Ghazâlî (1997), *The Incoherence of the Philosophers*, Michael E. Marmura (ed. and trans.) (Provo, UT: Brigham Young University).

Albo, Joseph (1946), *Sefer 'Iqqarim (Book of Principles)*, I. Husik (trans.) (Philadelphia: Jewish Publication Society).

Aquinas, Thomas (1964), *Summa Theologica* (London: Blackfriars).

Aristotle (1984), *The Collected Work of Aristotle*, Jonathan Barnes (ed.) (Princeton, NJ: Princeton University Press).

Averroes (1969), *Tahâfut al-Tahâfut (The Incoherence of Philosophy)*, Simon van den Bergh (trans.) (London: Luzac and Co.).

Bacon, Roger (1928), *Opus Maius*, R. B. Burke (trans.) (Philadelphia: University of Pennsylvania Press; repr. New York: Russell, 1962).

Bahya ibn Pakuda (2004), *The Book of Direction to the Duties of the Heart*, Menahem Mansoor (trans.) (Oxford: The Littman Library of Jewish Civilization).

Boethius (1957), *The Consolation of Philosophy*, James J. Buchanan (ed.) (New York: Frederick Ungar).

Crescas, Hasdai (1866a), *The Light of the Lord (Sefer Or Adonai or Or Ha-Shem)*, Shlomo Fisher (ed.) (Jerusalem, *Editio princeps*: Ferrara, 1555).

Crescas, Hasdai (1929), *'Or Adonai* [selections], in H. A. Wolfson, *Crescas' Critique of Aristotle* (Cambridge, MA: Harvard University Press).

Crescas, Hasdai (1970), *'Or Adonai*, E. Schweid (intro. and ed. note) (Jerusalem: Makor).

Crescas, Hasdai (1973), *'Or Adonai* [selections], in Warren Zev Harvey, "Hasdai Crescas' Critique of the Acquired Intellect," PhD Thesis, Columbia University.

Delmedigo, Joseph, *Sefer Elim* (Amsterdam, 1629; repr. Odessa: M. Grinshpan Publ., 1864–7).

Galen (1996), *On the Elements According to Hippocrates*, Phillip de Lacy (ed. and trans.) (Berlin: Academie Verlag).

Gersonides (1329), *Sefer Milhamot Ha-Shem (The Wars of the Lord)* (Riva di Trento, 1560; Leipzig, 1866; Berlin, 1923).

Gersonides (1946), *The Commentary of Levi ben Gerson on the Book of Job*, Abraham L. Lassen (trans.) (New York: Bloch).

Gersonides (1984; 1987; 1999), *The Wars of the Lord*, 3 vols., Seymour Feldman (trans.) (Philadelphia: Jewish Publication Society of America).

Gersonides (1992), *Perush al ha-Torah* (*Commentary on the Pentateuch*), vol. 1, Baruch Brenner and Eli Fraiman (eds.) (Maale Adumim: Maaliot).

Gersonides (1998), *Commentary on Song of Songs. Levi ben Gershom* (*Gersonides*), Menachem Kellner (trans.) (New Haven: Yale University Press).

Goldstein, Bernard R. (1975), "The Astronomical Tables of Rabbi Levi ben Gerson," *Transactions of the Connecticut Academy of Arts and Sciences*, vol. 45 (Hamden, CT: Shoestring Press).

Halevi, Judah (1964), *Book of Kuzari*, Hartwig Hirschfeld (ed.) (New York: Pardes Publishing House).

Ibn Gabirol (1901), *Tikkun Middot ha-Nefesh* (*The Improvement of Moral Qualities*), Stephen S. Wise (trans.) (New York: Columbia University Press).

Ibn Gabirol (1926), *Sefer Mekor Hayyim*, Jacob Blaustein (trans. into Hebrew) (Tel Aviv: Mossad Ha-Rav Kook).

Ibn Gabirol (1961), *The Kingly Crown*, Bernard Lewis (trans.) (London: Valentine, Mitchell).

Isaac Abravanel (1988), *Mif'a lot Elohim*, B. Genut-Dror (ed.) (Jerusalem: Reuben Mass), selection contained in Frank, Leaman, and Manekin (2000).

Isaac Israeli (1958), "Book of Spirit and Soul," in *Isaac Israeli: A Neoplatonic philosopher of the early tenth century* (Oxford: Clarendon Press; repr. 2009 (Chicago: University of Chicago Press), 106–17).

Isaac Israeli (1958), "Sefer Yesodot," in *Isaac Israeli: A Neoplatonic philosopher of the early tenth century* (Oxford: Clarendon Press).

Judah Abravanel (2009), *Dialogues of Love*, Damian Bacich and Rossella Pescatori (trans.) (Toronto: University of Toronto Press).

Kaplan, Aryeh (1997), *Sefer Yetzirah: The Book of Creation* (York Beach Maine: Samuel Weiser).

Maimonides, Moses (1926), "Letter on Astrology," in "The Correspondence between the Rabbis of Southern France and Maimonides about Astrology," Alexander Marx (trans.), *Hebrew Union College Annual*, 3, 311–58.

Maimonides, Moses (1962), *Mishneh Torah: Book of Knowledge*, Moses Hyamson (trans.) (Jerusalem: Boys Town Publishers).

Maimonides, Moses (1963), *Guide of the Perplexed* [Arabic: *Dalâlat al-hâirîn*; Hebrew: *Moreh Nevukhim*], 2 vols., Shlomo Pines (trans.) (Chicago: University of Chicago Press, 2002); Hebrew trans., Michael Schwartz, 2 vols. (Ramat Aviv: Tel Aviv University Press).

Maimonides, Moses (1966), "Maimonides' Arabic Treatise on Logic," *Proceedings of the American Academy of Jewish Research*, 34: 155–60 [English]; 34: 1–42 [Arabic].

Maimonides, Moses (1968), *Treatise on the Art of Logic*, Israel Efros (trans. and ed.), *Proceedings of the American Academy of Jewish Research*, 8: 1–65 [English sect.]; 8: 1–136 [Hebrew sect.].

Maimonides, Moses (1970–1), *Medical Aphorisms of Moses Maimonides*, Fred Rosner and Suessman Muntner (ed. and trans.) (New York: Yeshiva University Press).

Maimonides, Moses (1972a), *Commentary on the Mishnah. Introduction to Helek: Sanhedrin, Chapter Ten*, in Isadore Twersky (ed.), *A Maimonides Reader* (New York: Behrman House), 387–400.

Maimonides, Moses (1972b), "Kings and Wars," in Isadore Twersky (ed.), *A Maimonides Reader* (New York: Behrman House), 215–27.

Maimonides, Moses (1975a), *Eight Chapters* [introduction to commentary on *Mishnah Avot*], in Raymond L. Weiss with Charles Butterworth (eds. and trans.), *Ethical Writings of Maimonides* (New York: Dover Press), 60–104.

Maimonides, Moses (1975b), *Laws Concerning Character Traits*, in Raymond L. Weiss with Charles Butterworth (eds. and trans.), *Ethical Writings of Maimonides* (New York: Dover), 27–58.

Maimonides, Moses (1985a), "Epistle to Yemen," in Abraham Halkin and David Hartmann (eds. and trans.), *Crisis and Leadership: Epistles of Maimonides* (Philadelphia: Jewish Publication Society), 91–131.

Maimonides, Moses (1985b), *Essay on Resurrection*, in Abraham Halkin and David Hartmann (eds. and trans.), *Crisis and Leadership: Epistles of Maimonides* (Philadelphia: Jewish Publication Society), 209–33.

Maimonides, Moses (2000), *Letter on Astrology*, in Isadore Twersky (ed.), *A Maimonides Reader* (New York: Behrman House), 463–73.

Philo (1960a), *Allegorical Interpretation of Genesis* (*Legum Allegoria*), vol., 1, F. H. Colson and G. H. Whitaker (trans.) (Cambridge, MA: Harvard University Press).

Philo (1960b), *On the Account of the World's Creation* (*De Opificio Mundi*), vol. 1, F. H. Colson and G. H. Whitaker (trans.) (Cambridge, MA: Harvard University Press).

Philo (1960c), *On the Eternity of the World* (*De Aeternitate Mundi*), vol. 9, F. H. Colson and G. H. Whitaker (trans.) (Cambridge, MA: Harvard University Press).

Philo (1960d), *On the Unchangeableness of God* (*Quod Deus Immutabilis Sit*), vol. 3, F. H. Colson and G. H. Whitaker (trans.) (Cambridge, MA: Harvard University Press).

Philo (2001), *On the Creation of the Cosmos according to Moses*, David T. Runia (trans. and commentary) (Leiden: E. J. Brill).

Philoponus, John (1987). *Philoponus: Against Aristotle on the Eternity of the World*, Christian Wildberg (trans.) (Ithaca, NY: Cornell University Press).

Plotinus (1966), *The Enneads*, H. A. Armstrong (trans. and notes) (Cambridge, MA: Harvard University Press).

Ptolemy (1940), *Tetrabiblos*, F. E. Robbins (ed. and trans.) (Cambridge, MA: Harvard University Press).

Ptolemy (1984), *Almagest*, G. J. Toomer (trans. and annotated) (London: Duckworth).

Saadiah Gaon (1948), *The Book of Beliefs and Opinions*, Samuel Rosenblatt (ed.) (New Haven: Yale University Press).

Saadiah Gaon (1972a), *The Book of Doctrines and Beliefs* (abridged translation), in Hans Lewy, Alexander Altmann, and Isaac Heinemann (eds.), *Three Jewish Philosophers* (New York: Athenaeum).

Saadiah Gaon (1972b), *Commentary: Sefer Yetzirah 'im Perush Rabbenu Sa'adia ben Yosef Fayyumi* (*Ga'on*), Arabic text edited with Hebrew translation by Yosef Kafih (Jerusalem).

Saadiah Gaon (1988), *The Book of Theodicy: Translation and Commentary on the Book of Job*, Lenn Goodman (trans.) (New Haven: Yale University Press).

Spinoza, Benedict (1985), "Ethics," in Edwin Curley (ed. and trans.), *Collected Works of Spinoza* (Princeton, NJ: Princeton University Press).

Spinoza, Benedict (2001), *Theological-Political Treatise*, 2nd edition, Samuel Shirley (trans.) (Indianapolis: Hackett).

Secondary Sources

Ackerman, Ari (2009), "Miracles," in Steven Nadler and T. M. Rudavsky (eds.), *The Cambridge History of Jewish Philosophy: From Antiquity through the Seventeenth Century* (Cambridge: Cambridge University Press), 362–87.

Adamson, Peter (2016), *Philosophy in the Islamic World* (Oxford: Oxford University Press).

Adamson, Peter and Richard C. Taylor (eds.) (2005), *The Cambridge Companion to Arabic Philosophy* (Cambridge: Cambridge University Press).

Adler, Jacob (2008), "J. S. Delmedigo as Teacher of Spinoza: The case of Noncomplex Propositions," *Studia Spinozana*, 177–83.

Aertsen, Jan A., Kent Emery Jr., and Andreas Speer (eds.) (2001), *After the Condemnation of 1277. Philosophy and Theology at the University of Paris in the Last Quarter of the Thirteenth Century. Studies and Texts* (Berlin: Walter de Gruyter).

Altmann, Alexander (1944), "Saadya's Conception of the Law," *Bulletin of the John Rylands Library*, 28: 3–24.

Altmann, Alexander (1965), "Ibn-Bajja on Ultimate Felicity," in S. Lieberman (ed.), *H. A. Wolfson Jubilee Volume* (Jerusalem: American Academy for Jewish Research), 47–87.

Altmann, Alexander (1971), "Astrology," *Encyclopaedia Judaica*, 3: 787–95.

Altmann, Alexander (1972), "Maimonides' Four Perfections," *Israel Oriental Studies*, 2: 15–24.

Altmann, Alexander (1974), "The Religion of the Thinkers: Free Will and Predestination in Saadia, Bahya, and Maimonides," in S. D. Goitein (ed.), *Religion in a Religious Age* (Cambridge, MA: AJS Press), 25–52.

Altmann, Alexander (1979–80), "Gersonides' Commentary on Averroës *Epitome of Parva Naturalia* II.3," *Proceedings of the American Academy for Jewish Research Jubilee*, 66–7: 1–31.

Altmann, Alexander and Daniel J. Lasker (2007), "Israeli, Isaac ben Solomon," in Michael Berenbaum and Fred Skolnik (eds.), *Encyclopaedia Judaica*, 2nd edition, vol. 10 (Detroit: Macmillan Reference USA), 751–3.

Altmann, Alexander and Samuel M. Stern (1958a), *Isaac Israeli: A Neoplatonic philosopher of the early tenth century* (Oxford: Clarendon Press).

Altmann, Alexander and Samuel M. Stern (1958b), "Sefer Yesodot," in Isaac Israeli (ed.), *Isaac Israeli: A Neoplatonic philosopher of the early tenth century* (Oxford: Clarendon Press).

Barbour, Ian (1997), *Religion and Science: Historical and Contemporary Issues* (San Francisco: Harper Books).

Barker, Peter (1991), "Stoic Contributions to Early Modern Science," in Margaret J. Osler (ed.), *Atoms, Pneuma, and Tranquility* (Cambridge: Cambridge University Press), 137–54.

Barr, J. (1962), *Biblical Words for Time* (Naperville, Ill: Alec R. Allenson).

Barzilay, I. (1974), *Yoseph Shlomo Delmedigo (Yashar of Candia): His Life, Works, and Times* (Leiden: Brill).

Ben-Shammai, Haggai (1997), "Kalâm in Medieval Jewish Philosophy," in Daniel H. Frank and Oliver Leaman (eds.), *History of Jewish Philosophy* (London: Routledge), 115–48.

Benor, Ehud (1995), *Worship of the Heart: A Study in Maimonides' Philosophy of Religion* (Albany: State University of New York Press).

Berman, Lawrence (1974), "Maimonides, the Disciple of Alfarabi," *Israel Oriental Studies*, 4: 154–78.

Black, Deborah (2007), "Psychology: Soul and Intellect," in Peter Adamson and Richard C. Taylor (eds.), *The Cambridge Companion to Arabic Philosophy* (Cambridge: Cambridge University Press), 308–26.

Blumberg, Z. (1970), "Ha-Rambam al Musag al-Tajwiz beshittatam shel ha-mutakalimun," *Tarbiz*, 39: 268–76.

Blumenthal, H. J. (1981), "Plotinus in Later Platonism," in H. J. Blumenthal and R. A. Markus (eds.), *Neoplatonism and Early Christian Thought: Essays in Honour of A. H. Armstrong* (London: Variorum Publications), 212–22.

Brooke, John H. (1991), *Science and Religion: Some Historical Perspectives* (Cambridge: Cambridge University Press).

Brown, Jeremy (2013), *New Heavens and New Earth: The Jewish Reception of Copernican Thought* (New York: Oxford University Press).

Brunner, Fernand (1997), *Métaphysique d'Ibn Gabirol et de la tradition platonicienne* (Aldershot: Ashgate).

Cantor, Geoffrey and Chris Kenny (2001), "Barbour's Fourfold Way: Problems with his Taxonomy of Science-Religion Relationships," *Zygon*, 36 (4): 765–82.

Carmy, Shalom and David Shatz (1997), "The Bible as a Source for Philosophical Reflection," in Daniel H. Frank and Oliver Leaman (eds.), *History of Jewish Philosophy* (London: Routledge), 13–37.

Curley, Edwin (1994), "Notes on a Neglected Masterpiece: Spinoza and the Science of Hermeneutics," in Graeme Hunter (ed.), *Spinoza: The Enduring Questions* (Toronto: University of Toronto Press), 65–99.

Dales, Richard C. (1990), *Medieval Discussions of the Eternity of the World* (Leiden: E. J. Brill).

Davidson, Herbert A. (1979), "Maimonides' Secret Position on Creation," in I. Twersky (ed.), *Studies in Medieval Jewish History and Literature* (Cambridge, MA: Harvard University Press), 16–40.

Davidson, Herbert A. (1987), *Proofs for Eternity, Creation, and the Existence of God in Medieval Islamic and Jewish Philosophy* (New York: Oxford University Press).

Davidson, Herbert A. (1992–3), "Maimonides on Metaphysical Knowledge," *Maimonidean Studies*, 3: 49–103.

Davidson, Herbert A. (2005), *Moses Maimonides: The Man and his Works* (Oxford and New York: Oxford University Press).

Davies, Daniel (2011), *Method and Metaphysics in Maimonides' Guide for the Perplexed* (Oxford: Oxford University Press).

Dhanani, Alnoor (1994), *The Physical Theory of Kalam: Atoms, Space and Void in Basrian Mu'tazili Cosmology* (Leiden: E. J. Brill).

Dillon, John (1992), "Solomon Ibn Gabirol's Doctrine of Intelligible Matter," in Lenn Evan Goodman (ed.), *Neoplatonism in Jewish Thought* (Albany: State University of New York Press), 43–59.

Draper, J. W. (1874), *History of the Conflict between Religion and Science* (New York: Appleton Press).

Drews, Wolfram (2004), "Medieval Controversies about Maimonidean Teachings," in Görge K. Hasselhoff (ed.), *Dicit Rabbi Moyses. Studien zum Bild von Moses Maimonides im lateinischen Western vom 13. bis zum 15. Jahrhundert* (Würzburg: Königshausen und Neumann), 113–35.

Duhem, Pierre (1913–59), *Le Système du monde* (Paris: A. Hermann Press).

Duhem, Pierre (1985), *Medieval Cosmology*, Roger Ariew (trans.) (Chicago: University of Chicago Press).

Efros, Israel (1917), *The Problem of Space in Jewish Medieval Philosophy* (New York: Columbia University Press).

Ehrlich, Dror (2016), "Joseph Albo," in *The Stanford Encyclopedia of Philosophy* (Winter 2016 Edition), Edward N. Zalta (ed.), stanford.edu/archives/win2016/entries/albo-joseph/ (last accessed February 12, 2018).

Eisen, Robert (1995), *Gersonides on Providence, Covenant, and the Jewish People* (Albany: State University of New York Press).

Eisen, Robert (2004), *The Book of Job in Medieval Jewish Philosophy* (Oxford: Oxford University Press).

Eisenmann, Esti and Shalom Sadik (2015), "Criticism of Aristotelian science in fourteenth-century Jewish Thought," *Journal of Jewish Studies*, 66 (1): 116–37.

El-Bizri, Nader (2007), "Some Phenomenological and Classical Corollaries on Time," in A.-T. Tymieniecka (ed.), *Timing and Temporality in Islamic Philosophy and Phenomenology of Life* (Dordrecht: Springer), 137–55.

Emery, Kent (2001), "Introduction," in Jan A. Aertsen, Kent Emery Jr., and Andreas Speer (eds.), *After the Condemnation of 1277. Philosophy and Theology at the University of Paris in the Last Quarter of the Thirteenth Century. Studies and Texts* (Berlin: Walter de Gruyter), 3–19.

Eran, Amira (2001), "Al-Ghazali and Maimonides on the World to Come and Spiritual Pleasures," *Jewish Studies Quarterly*, 8 (2): 137–66.

Eran, Amira (2008), "Intuition and Inspiration – The Causes of Jewish Thinkers' Objections to Avicenna's Intellectual Prophecy (Hads)," *Jewish Studies Quarterly*, 14 (1): 39–71.

Feldhay, Rivka (1998), "The Use and Abuse of Mathematical Entities: Galileo and the Jesuits Revisited," in Peter Machamer (ed.), *The Cambridge Companion to Galileo* (Cambridge: Cambridge University Press), 80–145.

Feldhay, Rivka (1995), *Galileo and the Church: Political Inquisition or Critical Dialogue* (Cambridge: Cambridge University Press).

Feldman, Seymour (1967), "Gersonides' Proofs for the Creation of the Universe," *Proceedings of the American Academy for Jewish Research*, 35: 113–37.

Feldman, Seymour (1975), "Platonic Themes in Gersonides' Cosmology," in Saul Lieberman (ed.), *Salo Whitmayer Baron Jubilee Volume on the Occasion of his Eightieth Birthday* (Jerusalem: American Academy for Jewish Research), 383–405.

Feldman, Seymour (1980), "The Theory of Eternal Creation in Hasdai Crescas and Some of his Predecessors," *Viator*, 11: 289–320.

Feldman, Seymour (1982), "Crescas' Theological Determinism," *Da'at*, 9: 2–28.

Feldman, Seymour (1984), "A Debate Concerning Determinism in Late Medieval Jewish Philosophy," *Proceedings of the American Academy for Jewish Research*, 51: 15–54.

Feldman, Seymour (1992), "Platonic Themes in Gersonides' Doctrine of the Active Intellect," in Lenn Evan Goodman (ed.), *Neoplatonism and Jewish Thought* (Albany: State University of New York Press), 255–77.

Feldman, Seymour (2003), *Philosophy in a Time of Crisis: Don Isaac Abravanel: Defender of the Faith* (London: Routledge).

Feldman, Seymour (2009), "Divine Omnipotence, Omniscience, and Human Freedom," in T. M. Rudavsky and S. Nadler (eds.), *The Cambridge History of Jewish Philosophy: From Antiquity through the Seventeenth Century* (Cambridge: Cambridge University Press), 659–706.

Feldman, Seymour (2010), *Judaism within the Limits of Reason* (Oxford: Littman Library of Jewish Civilization).

Fenton, Paul (1976), "Gleanings from Moses Ibn Ezra's Maqalat al-Hadiqa," *Sefarad*, 36: 285–98.

Fenton, Paul (1986), "The Arabic and Hebrew Versions of the *Theology of Aristotle*," in J. Kraye (ed.), *Pseudo-Aristotle in the Middle Ages: The "Theology of Aristotle" and Other Texts* (London: Warburg Institute), 241–64.

Fenton, Paul (1992), "Shem Tov ibn Falaquera and the Theology of Aristotle," *Da'at*, 29: 27–39.

Fontaine, Resianne (2000), "Judah ben Solomon ha-Cohen's Midrash ha-Hokhmah: Its Sources and Use of Sources," in Steven Harvey (ed.), *The Medieval Hebrew Encyclopedias of Science and Philosophy* (Dordrecht: Kluwer Academic Publishers), 191–210.

Fontaine, T. A. M. (1990), *In Defense of Judaism: Abraham Ibn Daud* (Assen, Netherlands: Van Gorcum Press).

Fox, Marvin (1990), "Maimonides and Aquinas on Natural Law," *Interpreting Maimonides: Studies in Methodology, Metaphysics, and Moral Philosophy* (Chicago: University of Chicago Press), 124–51.

Fox, Marvin and Yehoshua M. Grintz (2007), "God," in *Encyclopaedia Judaica*, 2nd edition, 7:658–64.

Fraenkel, Carlos (2009), "God's Existence and Attributes," in Steven Nadler and T. M. Rudavsky (eds.), *The Cambridge History of Jewish Philosophy: From Antiquity through the Seventeenth Century* (Cambridge: Cambridge University Press), 561–98.

Frank, Daniel H. (1990), "Anger as a Vice: A Maimonidean Critique of Aristotle's Ethics," *History of Philosophy Quarterly*, 7: 269–81.

Frank, Daniel H. and Oliver Leaman (eds.) (2003), *The Cambridge Companion to Medieval Jewish Philosophy* (Cambridge: Cambridge University Press).

Frank, Daniel H., Oliver Leaman and Charles H. Manekin (eds.) (2000), *The Jewish Philosophy Reader* (London: Routledge).

Frank, Richard (1992), "The Science of Kalam," *Arabic Sciences and Philosophy*, 2: 7–37.

Freudenthal, J. (1899), *Die Lebensgeschichte Spinozas in Quellenschriften, Urkunden und Nichtamtlichen Nachrichten* (Leipzig: Verlag Von Veit).

Freudenthal, J. (1904), *Spinoza. Sein Leben und Seine Lehre* (Stuttgart: Fr. Frommanns Verlag).

Freudenthal, Gad (ed.) (1992), *Studies on Gersonides: A Fourteenth-century Jewish philosopher-scientist* (Leiden: E. J. Brill).

Freudenthal, Gad (1996), "Stoic Physics in the Writings of R. Saadia Ga'On Al-Fayyumi and its Aftermath in Medieval Jewish Mysticism," *Arabic Sciences and Philosophy*, 6: 113–36.

Freudenthal, Gad (2000), "Providence, Astrology and Celestial Influences on the Sublunar World in Shem-Tov Ibn Falaquera's De'ot Ha-Filosofim," in Steven Harvey (ed.), *The Medieval Hebrew Encyclopedias of Science and Philosophy* (Dordrecht: Kluwer Academic Publishers), 335–70.

Freudenthal, Gad (2005a), *Science in the Medieval Hebrew and Arabic Traditions* (Aldershot: Ashgate).

Freudenthal, Gad (2005b), "Maimonides' Philosophy of Science," in Kenneth Seeskin (ed.), *The Cambridge Companion to Maimonides* (Cambridge: Cambridge University Press), 134–66.

Freudenthal, Gad (2009), "Cosmology: The Heavenly Bodies," in Steven Nadler and T. M. Rudavsky (eds.), *The Cambridge History of Jewish Philosophy: From Antiquity through the Seventeenth Century* (Cambridge: Cambridge University Press), 302–61.

Funkenstein, Amos (1986), *Theology and the Scientific Imagination from the Middle Ages to the Seventeenth Century* (Princeton, NJ: Princeton University Press).

Furley, David J. (1967), *Two Studies in the Greek Atomists: Study I. Indivisible Magnitudes* (Princeton, NJ: Princeton University Press).

Galileo, Galilei (1989), "Galileo's Letter to the Grand Duchess Christina," in Maurice A. Finocchiaro (ed.), *The Galileo Affair: A Documentary History* (Berkeley: University of California Press), 87–118.

Gaukroger, Stephen (2006), *The Emergence of a Scientific Culture: Science and the Shaping of Modernity, 1210–1685* (Oxford: Clarendon Press).

Gellman, J. (1989), "Freedom and Determinism in Maimonides' Philosophy," in E. L. Ormsby (ed.), *Moses Maimonides and His Time* (Washington, DC: Catholic University of America Press), 139–50.

Gerson, Lloyd (1983), *Graceful Reason: Essays in Ancient and Medieval Philosophy Presented to Joseph Owens* (Toronto: Pontifical Institute).

Gerson, Lloyd (1994), *Plotinus* (London & New York: Routledge).

Glasner, Ruth (1996), "The Early Stages in the Evolution of *Gersonides' The Wars of the Lord*," *Jewish Quarterly Review*, 87: 1–46.

Glasner, Ruth (2015), *Gersonides: A Portrait of a Fourteenth-Century Philosopher-Scientist* (Oxford: Oxford University Press).

Goldstein, Bernard R. (1974), *The Astronomical Tables of Levi ben Gerson* (New Haven: Connecticut Academy of Arts and Sciences).

Goldstein, Bernard R. (1980), "The Status of Models in Ancient and Medieval Astronomy," *Centaurus*, 24: 132–47.

Goldstein, Bernard R. (1985a), *The Astronomy of Levi ben Gerson 1288–1344: A Critical Edition of Chapters 1–20* (New York: Springer Verlag).

Goldstein, Bernard R. (1985b), *Theory and Observation in Ancient and Medieval Astronomy* (London: Variorum Reprints).

Goldstein, Bernard R. (1996), "Astronomy and Astrology in the Works of Abraham Ibn Ezra," *Arabic Sciences and Philosophy*, 6: 9–21.

Goldstein, Bernard R. and David Pingree (1990), "Levi ben Gerson's Prognostication for the Conjunction of 1345," *Transactions of the American Philosophical Society*, 80: 1–60.

Grant, Edward (1982), "The Effect of the Condemnation of 1277," in Anthony Kenny, Norman Kretzmann, and Jan Pinborg (eds.), *The Cambridge History of Later Medieval Philosophy* (Cambridge: Cambridge University Press), 537–40.

Grant, Edward (1987), "Eccentrics and Epicycles in Medieval Cosmology," in Edward Grant and John E. Murdoch (eds.), *Mathematics and Its Applications to Science and Natural Philosophy in the Middle Ages* (Cambridge: Cambridge University Press), 189–213.

Grant, Edward (1997), *Physical Science in the Middle Ages* (Cambridge: Cambridge University Press).

Green, Alexander (2016), *The Virtue Ethics of Levi Gersonides* (London: Palgrave Macmillan).

Guttmann, Julius (1964), *Philosophies of Judaism*, David Silverman (trans.) (New York: Holt, Rinehart and Winston).

Hackett, Jeremiah (1997), "Roger Bacon on Astronomy-Astrology: The Sources of the Scientia Experimentalis," in Jeremiah Hackett (ed.), *Roger Bacon and the Sciences: Commemorative Essays* (Leiden and New York: E. J. Brill), 195–8.

Halbertal, Moshe (2015), *Maimonides: Life and Thought* (Princeton, NJ: Princeton University Press).

Halkin, Abraham S. and David Hartman (1985), *Crisis and Leadership: Epistles of Maimonides* (Philadelphia: The Jewish Publication Society of America).

Harris, Jay (ed.) (2007), *Maimonides after 800 Years: Essays on Maimonides and His Influence* (Cambridge, MA: Harvard University Press).

Harris, R. B. (1992), "Preface," in L. E. Goodman (ed.), *Neoplatonism and Jewish Thought* (Albany: State University of New York Press).

Harvey, Steven (2000a), *The Medieval Hebrew Encyclopedias of Science and Philosophy* (Dordrecht: Kluwer Academic Publishers).

Harvey, Steven (2000b), "Shem-Tov Ibn Falaquera's De'ot ha-Filosofim: Its sources and use of sources," in Steven Harvey (ed.), *The Medieval Hebrew Encyclopedias of Science and Philosophy* (Dordrecht: Kluwer Academic Publishers), 211–37.

Harvey, Warren Z. (1981a), "Albo's Discussion of Time," *Jewish Quarterly Review*, 71: 210–38.

Harvey, Warren Z. (1981b), "The Term 'Hitdabbekut' in Crescas' Definition of Time," *Jewish Quarterly Review*, 71: 44–7.

Harvey, Warren Z. (1981c), "A Third Approach to Maimonides' Cosmogony-Prophetology Puzzle," *Harvard Theological Review*, 74 (3): 287–301.

Harvey, Warren Z. (1998), *Physics and Metaphysics in Hasdai Crescas* (Amsterdam: J.C. Gieben).

Harvey, Warren Z. (2007), "Crescas," in *Encyclopaedia Judaica*, 2nd edition, 5: 284–8.

Harvey, Warren Z. (2010), *Rabbi Hasdai Crescas [Hebrew]* (Jerusalem: Zalman Shazar Edition).

Harvey, Warren Z. (2012), "Ethical Theories Among Medieval Jewish Philosophers," in Elliot N. Dorff and Jonathan K. Crane (eds.), *The Oxford Handbook of Jewish Ethics and Morality* (Oxford: Oxford University Press), 84–98.

Hasselhoff, Görge K. (2002), "Maimonides in the Latin Middle Ages: an Introductory Survey," *Jewish Studies Quarterly*, 9: 1–20.

Hayes, Christine (2015), *What's Divine about Divine Law? Early Perspectives* (Princeton, NJ: Princeton University Press).

Hayoun, Maurice Ruben (1989), *La Philosophie et la théologie de Moise de Narbonne* (Tübingen: J. C. B. Mohr).

Heller-Wilensky, Sara R. (1956), *Yitzhak Arama and his Philosophy* [Hebrew] (Jerusalem: Bialik Institute).

Higgins, Anne (1989), "Medieval Notions of Time," *Journal of Medieval and Renaissance Studies*, 19: 227–50.

Horwitz, David (1997), "Ha-Haritzut Emet: Ralbag's View of a Central Pragmatic/Ethical Characteristic of Abraham," in Yaakov Elman and Jeffrey S. Gurock (eds), *Hazon Nahum: Studies in Jewish Law, Thought and History Presented to Dr. Norman Lamm on the Occasion of His Seventieth Birthday* (New York: Yeshiva University Press), 265–309.

Horwitz, David (2006), *Gersonides' Ethics: The To 'a lot be-Middot in Ralbag's Biblical Commentaries*, PhD Diss., Yeshiva University.

Husik, Isaac (1916), "Studies in Gersonides," *Jewish Quarterly Review*, 553–94.

Husik, Isaac (1946), *A History of Medieval Jewish Philosophy* (Philadelphia: Jewish Publication Society).

Hyman, Arthur (1987), "Maimonides on Creation and Emanation," in J. F. Wippel (ed.), *Studies in Medieval Philosophy* (Washington, DC: Catholic University of America Press), 45–61.

Hyman, Arthur (1997), "Aspects of the Medieval Jewish and Islamic Discussions of Free Choice," in C. Manekin and M. Kellner (eds.), *Freedom and Responsibility: General and Jewish Perspectives* (Baltimore: University Press of Maryland), 133–52.

Israel, Jonathan (1985), *European Jewry in the Age of Mercantilism 1550-1750* (Oxford: Oxford University Press).

Ivry, Alfred (1974), *Al-Kindi's Metaphysics* (Albany, NY: SUNY Press).

Ivry, Alfred (1986), "Islamic and Greek Influences on Maimonides' Philosophy," in Shlomo Pines and Yirmiyahu Yovel (eds.), *Maimonides and Philosophy* (Dordrecht: Martinus Nijhoff Publishers), 139–56.

Ivry, Alfred (2007), "Intellect," *Encyclopaedia Judaica*, 2nd edition, 9: 809–10.

Ivry, Alfred (2016), *Maimonides' Guide of the Perplexed: A Philosophical Guide* (Chicago: University of Chicago Press).

Jenni, E. (1962), "Time," in *The Interpreter's Dictionary of the Bible*, vol. IV (New York: Abingdon), 642–9.

Jospe, Raphael (1988), *Torah and Sophia: The Life and Thought of Shem Tov Ibn Falaquera* (Cincinnati: HUC Press).

Jospe, Raphael (1990), "Early Philosophical Commentaries on the *Sefer Yezirah*: Some Comments," *Revue des Études Juives*, CXLIX (Oct/Nov, 4): 369–415.

Jospe, Raphael (2009), *Jewish Philosophy in the Middle Ages* (Boston: Academic Studies Press).

Kaplan, Aryeh (1997), *Sefer Yetzirah: The Book of Creation* (Boston, MA and York Beach, ME: Samuel Weiser).

Kaplan, Lawrence (1977), "Maimonides on the Miraculous Element in Prophecy," *Harvard Theological Review*, 70: 233–56.

Kasher, Hannah (1998), "Biblical Miracles and the Universality of Natural Law: Maimonides' Three Methods of Harmonization," *Journal of Jewish Thought and Philosophy*, 8: 25–52.

Katz, Steven T. (1992), "Utterance and Ineffability in Jewish Philosophy," in Lenn E. Goodman (ed.), *Neoplatonism and Jewish Thought* (Albany, NY: SUNY Press), 279–98.

Kaufman, David (1962), "The Pseudo-Empedocles as a Source of Salomon Ibn Gabirol," in D. Kaufman (ed.), *Mehqarim be-sifrut ha'ivrit shel yemei ha-binayim* (Jerusalem: Mossad Ha-Rav Kook), 78–165.

Kaye, Lynn (2018), *Time in the Babylonian Talmud: Natural and Imagined Times in Jewish Law and Narrative* (Cambridge; New York: Cambridge University Press).

Kellner, Menachem (1986), *Dogma in Medieval Jewish Thought: From Maimonides to Abravanel* (Oxford: Oxford University Press).

Kellner, Menachem (1990), *Maimonides on Human Perfection* (Atlanta: Scholars Press).

Kellner, Menachem (1991), *Maimonides on Judaism and the Jewish People* (Albany: State University of New York Press).

Kellner, Menachem (1998), "Philosophical Misogyny in Medieval Jewish Thought: Gersonides vs. Maimonides," in Aviezer Ravitzky (ed.), *Y. Sermonetta Memorial Volume* (Jerusalem: Magnes Press), 113–28.

Kellner, Menachem (2010), *Torah in the Observatory: Gersonides, Maimonides, Song of Songs* (Boston: Academic Studies Press).

Kellner, Menachem (2013), "Gersonides' To'aliyyot: Sixteenth-Century Italy Versus Nineteenth-Century Poland," in Bentsi Cohen (ed.), *As a Perennial Spring: A Festschrift Honoring Rabbi Dr. Norman Lamm* (New York: Downhill Publ.), 281–304.

Kenny, Anthony (1979), *God and the Philosophers* (Oxford: Clarendon Press).

Kent, Bonnie (1995), *Virtues of the Will: Transformation of Ethics in the Late Thirteenth Century* (Washington, DC: The Catholic University of America).

Klein-Braslavy, Sara (1975), "The Existence of Time and the First Days of Creation in Medieval Jewish Philosophy [Hebrew]," *Tarbiz*, 45: 107–27.

Klein-Braslavy, Sara (1986), *Maimonides' Interpretation of the Adam Stories in Genesis* [Hebrew] (Jerusalem: R. Mas Publ.).

Klein-Braslavy, Sara (1987), *Maimonides' Interpretation of the Story of Creation* (Jerusalem: Israel Society for Biblical Research).

Klein-Braslavy, Sara (1988), "Maimonides' Interpretations of Jacob's Dream of the Ladder [Hebrew]," *Sefer Bar-Ilan*, 22–3: 329–49.

Klein-Braslavy, Sara (1989), "Determinism, Possibility, Choice and Foreknowledge in Ralbag," *Da'at*, 22: 4–53.

Kogan, Barry S. (1985), "Some Reflections on the Problem of Future Contingency in Alfarabi, Avicenna and Averroes," in Rudavsky 1985, 95–104.

Kraemer, Joel L. (1989), "Maimonides on Aristotle and Scientific Method," in E. L. Ormsby (ed.), *Moses Maimonides and His Time* (Washington, DC: The Catholic University of America Press), 53–88.

Kraemer, Joel L. (2005), "Moses Maimonides: An Intellectual Portrait," in Kenneth Seeskin (ed.), *The Cambridge Companion to Maimonides* (Cambridge: Cambridge University Press), 10–57.

Kraemer, Joel L. (2008), *Maimonides: The Life and World of one of Civilization's Greatest Minds* (New York: Doubleday Press).

Kreisel, Howard (1984), "Miracles in Medieval Jewish Philosophy," *Jewish Quarterly Review*, 75: 99–133.

Kreisel, Howard (2001), *Prophecy: The History of an Idea in Medieval Jewish Philosophy* (Dordrecht: Kluwer Academic Publishers).

Krinis, Ehud (2013), "The Arabic Background of the *Kuzari*," *Journal of Jewish Thought and Philosophy*, 21: 1–56.

Lamm, Norman (1990), *Torah u-Madda: The Encounter of Religious Learning and Worldly Knowledge in the Jewish Tradition* (Northvale, NJ: Jason Aronson, Inc.).

Langermann, Y. Tzvi (1993), "Some Astrological Themes in the Thought of Abraham ibn Ezra," in Isadore Twersky and Jay M. Harris (eds.), *Rabbi Abraham ibn Ezra: Studies in the Writings of a Twelfth-Century Polymath* (Cambridge, MA; London: Harvard University Press), 28–85.

Langermann, Y. Tzvi (1999), *The Jews and the Sciences in the Middle Ages* (Aldershot: Ashgate; Variorum Collected Studies Series).

Langermann, Y. Tzvi (2004), "Maimonides and Miracles: The Growth of a (Dis)belief," *Jewish History*, 18: 147–72.

Langermann, Y. Tzvi (2008), "My Truest Perplexities," *Aleph*, 8: 301–17.

Langermann, Y. Tzvi (2009), "Islamic Atomism and the Galenic Tradition," *History of Science*, xlvii: 277–95.

Leaman, Oliver (1995), *Evil and Suffering in Jewish Philosophy* (Cambridge: Cambridge University Press).

Leftow, Brian (2010), "Arguments for God's Existence," in Robert Pasnau and Christina Van Dyke (eds.), *The Cambridge History of Medieval Philosophy*, vol. 2 (Cambridge: Cambridge University Press), 735–48.

LeGoff, Jacques (1982), *Time, Work and Culture in the Middle Age*, Arthur Goldhammer (trans.) (Chicago: University of Chicago Press).

Lemay, Richard (1987), "The True Place of Astrology in Medieval Science and Philosophy: Towards a Definition," in Patrick Curry (ed.), *Astrology, Science and Society: Historical Essays* (Woodbridge: The Boydell Press), 57–74.

Lerner, Ralph (1968), "Maimonides' Letter on Astrology," *History of Religions*, 8 (2): 143–58.

Lerner, Ralph and Muhsin Mahdi (eds.) (1963), *Medieval Political Philosophy* (New York: Collier-Macmillan Limited).

Levine, Hillel (1983), "Paradise not Surrendered: Jewish Reactions to Copernicus and the Growth of Modern Science," in R. S. Cohen and M. W. Wartofsky (eds.), *Epistemology, Methodology and the Social Sciences* (Dordrecht: D. Reidel), 203–25.

Levy, Ze'ev (1987), *Between Yafeth and Shem: On the Relationship between Jewish and General Philosophy* (New York: Peter Lang).

Levy, Ze'ev (1989), *Baruch or Benedict: On Some Jewish Aspects of Spinoza's Philosophy* (New York: Peter Lang).

Lichtenstein, Aharon (1975), "Does Jewish Tradition Recognize an Ethic Independent of Halakha?," in Marvin Fox (ed.), *Modern Jewish Ethics: Theory and Practice* (Columbus: Ohio State University Press), 62–88.

Lieberman, Saul (1963), "How Much Greek in Jewish Palestine," in A. Altmann (ed.), *Biblical and Other Studies* (Cambridge, MA: Harvard University Press).

Lloyd, G. E. R. (1970), *Early Greek Science: Thales to Aristotle* (New York: W. W. Norton).

Lloyd, G. E. R. (1973), *Greek Science after Aristotle* (New York: W. W. Norton).

Lloyd, G. E. R. (1976), "Views on time in Greek Thought," in L. Gardet, A. J. Gurevich et al. (eds.), *Cultures and Time* (Paris: The Unesco Press), 117–49.

Loewe, Raphael (1979), "Ibn Gabirol's Treatment of Sources in the *Keter Malkhuth*," in S. Stein and R. Loewe (eds.), *Studies in Jewish Religious and Intellectual History Presented to Alexander Altmann* (Cambridge, MA: Harvard University Press), 183–94.

Macy, Jeffrey (1986), "Prophecy in al-Farabi and Maimonides," in Shlomo Pines and Yirmiyahu Yovel (eds.), *Maimonides and Philosophy: Papers Presented at the Sixth Jerusalem Philosophical Encounter, May 1985* (Dordrecht: Martinus Nijhoff Publishers), 185–201.

Mandonnet, P. (1908), *Siger de Brabant: Textes inédits* (Louvain: Institut Supérieur de Philosophie de l'Université).

Manekin, Charles H. (ed. and trans.) (1992), *The Logic of Gersonides: A Translation of the Sefer ha-Heqqesh ha-Yashar* (Dordrecht: D. Reidel).

Manekin, Charles H. (1997a), "Freedom within Reason? Gersonides on Human Choice," in Charles Manekin and Menachem Kellner (eds.), *Freedom and Moral Responsibility* (Bethesda: University Press of Maryland), 165–204.

Manekin, Charles H. (1997b), "Hebrew Philosophy in the Fourteenth and Fifteenth Centuries: An overview," in Daniel H. Frank and Oliver Leaman (eds.), *Routledge History of World Philosophies: History of Jewish Philosophy*, vol. 2 (London: Routledge), 350–78.

Manekin, Charles H. (2005), *On Maimonides* (Belmont, CA: Thomson Wadsworth).

Manekin, Charles H. (2007), *Medieval Jewish Philosophical Writings* (Cambridge: Cambridge University Press).

Manekin, Charles H. (2008), "Divine Will in Maimonides' Later Writings," in Arthur Hyman and Alfred Ivry (eds.), *Maimonidean Studies* (New York: Ktav Publishing House Inc.), 189–222.

Manekin, Charles H. (2011), "Logic in Medieval Jewish Culture," in Gad Freudenthal (ed.), *Science in Medieval Jewish Cultures* (Cambridge: Cambridge University Press), 113–36.

Marenbon, John (1987), *Later Medieval Philosophy: (1150–1350): An Introduction* (London: Routledge & Kegan Paul).

Marx, Alexander (1926), "The Correspondence between the Rabbis of Southern France and Maimonides about Astrology," *Hebrew Union College Annual*, 3: 311–58.

Marx, Alexander (1934–5), "Texts by and About Maimonides. The Unpublished Translation of Maimonides' Letter to Ibn Tibbon," *Jewish Quarterly Review*, 25: 374–81.

McGinn, Bernard (1992), "Ibn Gabirol: The Sage among the Schoolmen," in Lenn Evan Goodman (ed.), *Neoplatonism and Jewish Thought* (Albany: State University of New York Press), 77–109.

McGinnis, Jon (2010), *Avicenna* (Oxford: Oxford University Press).

McKirahan, Richard D. (1994), *Philosophy before Socrates* (Indianapolis: Hackett).

McMullin, Ernan (1978), "The Conception of Science in Galileo's Work," in Robert E. Butts and Joseph C. Pitt (eds.), *New Perspectives on Galileo* (Dordrecht: D. Reidel), 209–58.

McMullin, Ernan (2005), "Galileo's Theological Venture," in E. McMullin (ed.), *The Church and Galileo: Studies in Science and the Humanities from the Reilly Center for Science, Technology, and Values* (Notre Dame, IN: University of Notre Dame Press), 88–116.

McTaggart, J. M. E. (1978), "The Nature of Existence," in Richard Gale (ed.), *The Philosophy of Time: A Collection of Essays* (Atlantic Highlands, NJ: Humanities Press).

Melamed, Abraham (1997), "Medieval and Renaissance Jewish Political Philosophy," in D. Frank and O. Leaman (eds.), *History of Jewish Philosophy* (London: Routledge).

Melamed, Abraham (2003), *The Philosopher-King in Medieval and Renaissance Jewish Political Thought* (Albany: State University of New York Press).

Melamed, Abraham (2009), "Politics and the State," in S. Nadler and T. M. Rudavsky (eds.), *The Cambridge History of Jewish Philosophy* (Cambridge: Cambridge University Press), 768–89.

Mittleman, Alan (2012), *A Short History of Jewish Ethics: Conduct and Character in the Context of Covenant* (West Sussex: Wiley-Blackwell).

Morgan, Michael L. and Peter E. Gordon (2007), *The Cambridge Companion to Modern Jewish Philosophy* (Cambridge: Cambridge University Press).

Murdoch, John (1991), "Pierre Duhem and the History of Late Medieval Science and Philosophy in the Latin West," in *Gli Studi di Filosofia Medievale Fra Otto e Novecento* (Rome: Edizioni di Storia e Letteratura), 253–302.

Nadler, Steven (1999), *Spinoza: A Life* (Cambridge: Cambridge University Press).

Nadler, Steven (2001), *Spinoza's Heresy: Immortality and the Jewish Mind* (Oxford: Oxford University Press).

Nadler, Steven (2009), "Theodicy and Providence," in Steven Nadler and T. M. Rudavsky (eds.), *The Cambridge History of Jewish Philosophy: From Antiquity through the Seventeenth Century* (Cambridge: Cambridge University Press), 619–58.

Nadler, Steven and T. M. Rudavsky (eds.) (2009), *The Cambridge History of Jewish Philosophy: From Antiquity through the Seventeenth Century* (Cambridge: Cambridge University Press).

Neher, Andre (1976), "The View of Time and History in Jewish Culture," in L. Gardet and A. J. Gurevich et al. (eds.), *Cultures and Time* (Paris: The Unesco Press), 149–68.

Neusner, Jacob (1985), *Genesis Rabbah: The Judaic Commentary to the Book of Genesis*, vol. 1 (Chico, CA: Scholars Press).

Neusner, Jacob (1991), *Judaism as philosophy: the method and message of the Mishnah* (Columbia, SC: University of South Carolina Press).

Normore, Calvin (1982), "Future Contingents," in A. Kenny, N. Kretzmann, and J. Pinborg (eds.), *The Cambridge History of Later Medieval Philosophy* (Cambridge: Cambridge University Press), 358–82.

Normore, Calvin (1985), "Divine Omniscience, Omnipotence and Future Contingents: An Overview," in T. M. Rudavsky (ed.), *Divine Omniscience and Omnipotence in Medieval Philosophy* (Dordrecht: D. Reidel).

North, John D. (1987), "Medieval Concepts of Celestial Influence: A Survey," in Patrick Curry (ed.), *Astrology, Science and Society: Historical Essays* (Woodbridge, Suffolk: The Boydell Press), 5–18.

North, John D. (1989), *Stars, Minds and Fate – Essays in Ancient and Medieval Cosmology* (London and Ronceverte: Bloomsbury, Continuum Press).

Novak, David (1997), "The Talmud as a Source for Philosophical Reflection," in Daniel H. Frank and Oliver Leaman (eds.), *History of Jewish Philosophy* (London: Routledge), 62–82.

Novak, David (1998), *Natural Law in Judaism* (Cambridge: Cambridge University Press).

O'Rourke, Fran (1992), *Pseudo-Dionysius and the Metaphysics of Aristotle* (Leiden/New York: Brill).

Paul, Shalom, S. Sperling, Louis Rabinowitz, Ralph Lerner, Howard Kreisel, and Walt Wurzburger (2007), "Prophets and Prophecy," in Michael Berenbaum and Fred Skolnik (eds.), *Encyclopaedia Judaica*, 2nd edition, vol. 16 (Detroit: Macmillan Reference USA), 566–86.

Pederson, Olaf (1978), "Astronomy," in David Lindberg (ed.), *Science in the Middle Ages* (Chicago and London: University of Chicago Press), 303–37.

Pessin, Sarah (2007), "The Influence of Islamic Thought on Maimonides," in *The Stanford Encyclopedia of Philosophy* (Spring 2016 Edition), Edward N. Zalta (ed.), URL = https://plato.stanford.edu/archives/spr2016/entries/maimonides-islamic/ (last accessed February 20, 2018).

Pessin, Sarah (2013), *Ibn Gabirol's Theology of Desire: Matter and Method in Jewish Medieval Neoplatonism* (Cambridge: Cambridge University Press).

Pines, Shlomo (1963), "Translator's Introduction: The Philosophic Sources of *The Guide of the Perplexed*," in Maimonides (ed.), *The Guide of the Perplexed* (Chicago: University of Chicago Press), lvii–cxxxiv.

Pines, Shlomo (1977), "Scholasticism after Thomas Aquinas and the Teachings of Hasdai Crescas and his Predecessors," in Warren Zev Harvey and Moshe Idel (eds.), *Proceedings of the Israel Academy of Sciences and Humanities 1.10*; reprinted in *The Collected Works of Shlomo Pines: Studies in the History of Jewish Thought*, vol. 5 (Jerusalem: The Magnes Press), 1–101.

Pines, Shlomo (1979), "The Limits of Human Knowledge According to Al-Farabi, Ibn Bajja and Maimonides," *Studies in Medieval Jewish History and Literature*, 1: 82–109.

Pines, Shlomo (1989), "Points of Similarity between the Exposition of the Doctrine of the Sefirot in the Sefer Yetzirah and a Text of the Pseudo-Clementine Homilies: The Implications of this Resemblance," *Proceedings of the Israel Academy of Sciences and Humanities*, 7.3: 63–142.

Pines, Shlomo (1997), *Studies in Islamic Atomism*, Michael Schwarz (trans.) (Jerusalem: The Magnes Press).

Popkin, Richard H. (1986), "Some New Light on the Roots of Spinoza's Science of Bible Study," in Marjorie Grene and Nancy Maull (eds.), *Spinoza and the Sciences* (Dordrecht: D. Reidel), 171–90.

Popkin, Richard H. (1987), *Isaac La Peyrere (1596–1676): His Life, Work and Influence* (Leiden: E. J. Brill).

Popkin, Richard H. (1996), "Spinoza and Bible Scholarship," in Don Garrett (ed.), *The Cambridge Companion to Spinoza* (Cambridge: Cambridge University Press), 383–407.

Ravitzky, Aviezer (1981), "Samuel Ibn Tibbon and the Esoteric Character of *The Guide of the Perplexed*," *Association for Jewish Studies Review*, 6: 87–123.

Ravitzky, Aviezer (1981–2), "Hitpatkhut Hashkafato shel R'Hasdai Crescas bi-She'elat Hofesh ha-Ratzon," *Tarbiz*, 51: 445–70.

Ravitzky, Aviezer (1988), *Derashat ha-Pesah le-Rab Hasdai Crescas u-Mehqarim be-Mishnato ha-Pilosofit* (Jerusalem: Israel Academy of Sciences and Humanities).

Robbins, Ellen (1997), "Time Telling in Ritual and Myth," *Journal of Jewish Thought and Philosophy*, 6: 71–88.

Robinson, James T. (2009), "Soul and Intellect," in S. Nadler and T. M. Rudavsky (eds.), *The Cambridge History of Jewish Philosophy: From Antiquity through the Seventeenth Century* (Cambridge: Cambridge University Press).

Rosenberg, Shalom (1978), "Necessary and Possible in Medieval Logic [Hebrew]," *Iyyun*, 28: 103–55.

Rosenthal, Franz (1970), *Knowledge Triumphant* (Leiden: E. J. Brill).

Rubenstein, Jeffrey L. (1997), "Mythic Time and the Festival Cycle," *Journal of Jewish Thought and Philosophy*, 6: 157–83.

Rubio, Mercedes (2006), *Aquinas and Maimonides on the Possibility of the Knowledge of God* (Dordrecht: Springer).

Rudavsky, T. M. (1982), "Individuals and the Doctrine of Individuation in Gersonides," *The New Scholasticism*, 51: 30–50.

Rudavsky, T. M. (1983), "Divine Omniscience and Future Contingents in Gersonides," *Journal of the History of Philosophy*, 21: 513–36.

Rudavsky, T. M. (1993), "The Jewish Tradition: Maimonides, Gersonides and Bedersi," in J. J. Gracia (ed.), *Individuation in Late Scholasticism and the Counter-Reformation* (Albany: State University of New York Press), 69–96.

Rudavsky, T. M. (1997), "Medieval Jewish Neoplatonism," in Daniel H. Frank and Oliver Leaman (eds.), *History of Jewish Philosophy* (London: Routledge), 149–87.

Rudavsky, T. M. (2000), *Time Matters: Time, Creation and Cosmology in Medieval Jewish Philosophy* (Albany: State University of New York Press).

Rudavsky, T. M. (2001), "Galileo and Spinoza: Heroes, Heretics and Hermeneutics," *Journal of the History of Ideas*, 64 (4): 611–31.

Rudavsky, T. M. (2009), "Time, Space and Infinity," in S. Nadler and T. M. Rudavsky (eds.), *The Cambridge History of Jewish Philosophy: From Antiquity through the Seventeenth Century* (Cambridge: Cambridge University Press), 388–433.

Rudavsky, T. M. (2010), *Maimonides* (London: Wiley-Blackwell).

Rudavsky, T. M. (2012), "Natural Law Morality in Jewish Philosophy," in Jon Jacobs (ed.), *Reason, Religion and Natural Law: From Plato to Spinoza* (Oxford: Oxford University Press).

Rudavsky, T. M. and Nathaniel Rudavsky-Brody (2012), "The Necessity of Sailing: Of Gods' Fate and the Sea," in Patrick Goold (ed.), *Sailing: Philosophy for Everyone: Catching the Drift of Why We Sail* (Chichester: Wiley-Blackwell), 164–75.

Ruderman, David (1995), *Jewish Thought and Scientific Discovery in Early Modern Europe* (New Haven: Yale University Press).

Runia, David (1986), *Philo of Alexandria and the Timaeus of Plato* (Leiden: E. J. Brill).

Rynhold, Daniel (2009), *An Introduction to Medieval Jewish Philosophy* (London: I. B. Taurus Publishers).

Sabra, A. I. (2006), "Kalam Atomism as an Alternative Philosophy to Hellenizing Falsafa," in James E. Montgomery (ed.), *Arabic theology, Arabic philosophy, from the many to the one: Essays in celebration of Richard M. Frank* (Leuven, Paris, and Dudley, MA: Peeters Publ.), 191–272.

Samuelson, Norbert (1972), "Gersonides' Account of God's Knowledge of Particulars," *Journal of the History of Philosophy*, 10: 399–416.

Samuelson, Norbert M. (1997), "Medieval Jewish Aristotelianism: An introduction," in Daniel H. Frank and Oliver Leaman (eds.), *History of Jewish Philosophy* (London: Routledge), 228–44.

Samuelson, Norbert M. (2003), *Jewish Philosophy: A Historical Introduction* (London: Routledge).

Samuelson, Norbert M. (2009), "Reasoning and Demonstration," in S. Nadler and T. M. Rudavsky (eds.), *The Cambridge History of Jewish Philosophy: From Antiquity through the Seventeenth Century* (Cambridge: Cambridge University Press), 188–229.

Saperstein, Marc (1996), *Jewish Preaching, 1200–1800: An Anthology* (New Haven: Yale University Press).

Scheindlin, Raymond (2016), *Vultures in a Cage: Poems by Solomon Ibn Gabirol* (New York: Archipelago Books).

Schlanger, Jacques (1968), *La Philosophie de Salomon ibn Gabirol: Étude d'un néoplatonisme* (Leiden: E. J. Brill).

Scholem, Gershom (1995), *Major Trends in Jewish Mysticism* (New York: Schocken).

Scholem, Gershom (2007), "Yeẓirah, Sefer," in Michael Berenbaum and Fred Skolnik (eds.), *Encyclopaedia Judaica*, 2nd edition, vol. 21 (Detroit: Macmillan Reference USA), 328–31.

Schwarz, Michael (1991; 1992–3), "Who Were Maimonides' Mutakallimun? Some Remarks on *Guide of the Perplexed, Part I, Chapter 73*," in Arthur Hyman (ed.), *Maimonides Studies*, vols. 2 and 3 (New York: Yeshivah University Press), 159–209.

Schweid, Eliezer (1970), "Dibre Mabo," in Hasdai Crescas, *Light of the Lord* (Jerusalem: Makor).

Schweid, Eliezer (2007), "Miracles," in Michael Berenbaum and Fred Skolnik (eds.), *Encyclopaedia Judaica*, 2nd edition, vol. 14 (Detroit: Macmillan Reference USA, 2007), 305–10.

Seeskin, Kenneth (1991), *Maimonides: A Guide for Today's Perplexed* (New Jersey: Behrman House).

Sela, Shlomo (2000), "Encyclopedic Aspects of Abraham Ibn Ezra's Scientific Corpus," in S. Harvey (ed.), *The Medieval Hebrew Encyclopedia of Science and Philosophy* (Dordrecht: Kluwer Academic Publishers), 154–70.

Sela, Shlomo (2001), "Abraham Ibn Ezra's Scientific Corpus: Basic Constituents and General Characterization," *Arabic Sciences and Philosophy*, 11: 91–149.

Sela, Shlomo (2003), *Abraham Ibn Ezra and the Rise of Medieval Hebrew Science* (Leiden and Boston: E. J. Brill).

Sela, Shlomo (2004), "Queries on Astrology Sent from Southern France to Maimonides: Critical Edition of the Hebrew Text, Translation, and Commentary," *Aleph*, 4: 89–190.

Sells, Michael A. (1994), *Mystical Languages of Unsaying* (Chicago: University of Chicago Press).

Sharf, Alexander (1976), *The Universe of Shabbetai Donnolo* (New York: KTAV Publishing House Inc.).

Shatz, David (2005), "Maimonides' Moral Theory," in Kenneth Seeskin (ed.), *The Cambridge Companion to Maimonides* (Cambridge: Cambridge University Press), 167–93.

Singer, Charles (1978), "Science and Judaism," in Louis Finkelstein (ed.), *The Jews: Their Role in Civilization* (New York: Schocken), 216–65.

Sirat, Colette (1969), *Les théories des visions surnaturelles dans la pensée juive dumoyen-âge* (Leiden: E. J. Brill).

Sirat, Colette (1990), *A History of Jewish Philosophy in the Middle Ages* (Cambridge: Cambridge University Press).

Sleigh, Robert, Jr., Vere Chappell, and Michael Della Rocca (1998), "Determinism and Human Freedom," in Daniel Garber and Michael Ayers (eds.), *The Cambridge History of Seventeenth Century Philosophy* (Cambridge: Cambridge University Press).

Smith, Steven B. (1997), *Spinoza, Liberalism, and the Question of Jewish Identity* (New Haven: Yale University Press).

Sorabji, Richard (1983), *Time, Creation and the Continuum* (Ithaca, NY: Cornell University Press).

Stampfer, Shaul (2013), "Did the Khazars Convert to Judaism," *Jewish Social Studies*, 19: 3, 1–72.

Staub, Jacob (1982), *The Creation of the World According to Gersonides* (Chico, CA: Scholars Press).

Steensgaard, P. (1993), "Time in Judaism," in Anindita Niyogis Balslev and J. N. Mohanty (eds.), *Religion and Time* (Leiden: E. J. Brill), 63–108.

Stern, Josef (1997), "The Fall and Rise of Myth in Ritual: Maimonides versus Nahmanides on the Huqqim, Astrology, and the War against Idolatry," *Journal of Jewish Thought and Philosophy*, 6: 185–263.

Stern, Josef (2001), "Maimonides' Demonstrations: Principles and Practice," *Medieval Philosophy and Theology*, 10: 47–84.

Stern, Josef (2013), *The Matter and Form of Maimonides' Guide* (Cambridge, MA: Harvard University Press).

Stern, S. M. (1961), "Ibn Hasdai's Neoplatonist – A Neoplatonic Treatise and His Influence on Isaac Israeli and the Longer Version of the Theology of Aristotle," *Oriens*, 13–14: 58–120.

Stern, Sacha (1996), "Fictitious Calendars: Early Rabbinic Notions of Time, Astronomy, and Reality," *Jewish Quarterly Review*, 88: 103–29.

Stern, Sacha (2003), *Time and Process in Ancient Judaism* (Oxford, and Portland, OR: Oxford University Press).

Strauss, Leo (1952), *Persecution and the Art of Writing* (Chicago: University of Chicago Press).

Strauss, Leo (1963), "How to Begin to Study The Guide of the Perplexed," in Shlomo Pines (ed.), *Moses Maimonides: The Guide of the Perplexed* (Chicago: University of Chicago Press).

Stump, Eleanore (1997), "Saadiah Gaon on the Problem of Evil," *Faith and Philosophy*, 14 (4): 523–49.

Sweeney, Leo (1983), "Are Plotinus and Albertus Magnus Neoplatonists?," in Lloyd P. Gerson (ed.), *Graceful Reason: Essays in Ancient and Medieval Philosophy Presented to Joseph Owens, CSSR* (Toronto: Pontifical Institute for Medieval Studies), 177–202.

Tahiri, Hassan (2008), "The Birth of Scientific Controversies. The Dynamics of the Arabic Tradition and its Impact on the Development of Science: Ibn al-Haytham's Challenge of Ptolemy's *Almagest*," in S. Rahman et al. (eds.), *The Unity of Science in the Arabic Tradition* (New York: Springer), 183–225.

Talmage, Frank Ephraim (1999), *Apples of Gold in Settings of Silver: Studies in Medieval Jewish Exegesis and Polemics*, Barry Dov Walfish (ed.) (Toronto: Pontifical Institute of Medieval Studies).

Tanenbaum, Adena (2002), *The Contemplative Soul: Hebrew Poetry and Philosophical Theory in Medieval Spain* (Leiden: E. J. Brill).

Taylor, R. C. (1992), "A Critical Analysis of the Structure of the *Kalam fi mahd al-Khair* (*Liber de Causis*)," in Parviz Morewedge (ed.), *Neoplatonism and Islamic Thought* (*Studies in Neoplatonism: Ancient and Modern*), 5 (Albany, NY: SUNY Press), 11–31.

Thijssen, J. M. M. H. (1998), *Censure and Heresy at the University of Paris 1200–1400* (Philadelphia: University of Pennsylvania Press).

Thorndike, Lynne (1955), "The True Place of Astrology in the History of Science," *Isis*, 46: 273–8.

Tirosh-Rothschild, Hava (1991), *Between Worlds: The Life and Thought of Rabbi David Ben Judah Messer Leon* (Albany, NY: SUNY Press).

Tirosh-Rothschild, Hava (1997), "Jewish Philosophy on the Eve of Modernity," in Daniel H. Frank and Oliver Leaman (eds.), *Routledge History of World Philosophies: History of Jewish Philosophy* (London: Routledge), 499–573.

Tirosh-Samuelson, Hava (2003), *Happiness in Premodern Judaism: Virtue, Knowledge, and Well Being* (Cincinnati: Hebrew Union College).

Tirosh-Samuelson, Hava (2009), "Virtue and Happiness," in S. Nadler and T. M. Rudavsky (eds.), *The Cambridge History of Jewish Philosophy: From Antiquity through the Seventeenth Century* (Cambridge: Cambridge University Press), 707–67.

Tirosh-Samuelson, Hava (2011), "Kabbalah and Science in the Middle Ages: Preliminary Remarks," in Gad Freudenthal (ed.), *Science in Medieval Jewish Cultures* (Cambridge: Cambridge University Press), 454–75.

Touati, Charles (1973), *La pensée philosophique et theologique de Gersonide* (Paris: Les Editions de Minuit).

Touati, Charles (1974), "Hasday Crescas et ses paradoxes sur la Liberté," in *Mélanges d'histoire des Religions offerts à Charles-Henry Puech* (Paris: Presses Universitaires de France), 573–8.

Travaglia, Pinella (1999), *Magic, Causality and Intentionality: The doctrine of rays in al-Kindî* (Sismel: Edizioni del Galluzzo).

Twersky, Isadore (ed.) (1972), *A Maimonides Reader* (New York: Behrman House).

Twersky, Isadore (1980), *Introduction to the Code of Maimonides* (*Mishneh Torah*) (New Haven: Yale University Press).

Urbach, Ephraim E. (1975), *The Sages: Their concepts and beliefs*, Israel Abrahams (trans.) (Jerusalem: Magnes Press).

Vajda, Georges (1957), *L'Amour de Dieu dans la théologie juive du moyen âge* (Paris: Librairie Philosophique, Vrin).

Vajda, Georges (1960), *Isaac Albalag* (Paris: Vrin).

Van Zile, Matthew (2017), "The Sons of Noah and the Sons of Abraham: The Origins of Noahide Law," *Journal for the Study of Judaism*, 48: 1–32.

Vermij, Rienk (2002), *The Calvinist Copernicans: The Reception of the New Astronomy in the Dutch Republic* (Amsterdam: Koninklijke Nederlandse Akademie van Wetenschappen).

Weiss, Raymond L. (1991), *Maimonides' Ethics: The Encounter of Philosophic and Religious Morality* (Chicago: University of Chicago Press).

Weiss, Roslyn (2007), "Natural Order or Divine Will: Maimonides on Cosmogony and Prophecy," *Journal of Jewish Thought and Philosophy*, 15 (1): 1–25.

Weiss, Shira (2017), *Joseph Albo on Free Choice* (New York: Oxford University Press).

White, Mitchell J. (1992), *The Continuous and the Discrete: Ancient Physical Theories from a Contemporary Perspective* (Oxford: Clarendon Press).

Whitrow, G. J. (1988), *Time in History* (New York: Oxford University Press).

Wielenberg, Erik J. (2010), "Sceptical theism and divine lies," *Religious Studies*, 46: 509–23.

Winston, David (1997), "Hellenistic Jewish Philosophy," in Daniel H. Frank and Oliver Leaman (eds.), *History of Jewish Philosophy* (London: Routledge), 38–61.

Wise, Stephen (1902), "Introduction," *The Improvement of the Moral Qualities: An Ethical Treatise of the Eleventh Century by Solomon Ibn Gabirol* (New York: Columbia University Press), 1–28.

Wolfson, Elliot R. (1994), *Through a Speculum That Shines* (Princeton, NJ: Princeton University Press).

Wolfson, H. A. (1929), *Crescas' Critique of Aristotle* (Cambridge, MA: Harvard University Press).

Wolfson, H. A. (1934), *The Philosophy of Spinoza*, 2 vols. (Cambridge, MA: Harvard University Press).

Wolfson, H. A (1959), "The Meaning of Ex Nihilo in Isaac Israeli," *Jewish Quarterly Review*, 50: 1–12.

Wolfson, H. A. (1976), *The Philosophy of the Kalam* (Cambridge, MA: Harvard University Press).

Wolfson, Harry A. (1947), *Philo: The Foundations of Religious Philosophy in Judaism*, 2 vols. (Cambridge, MA: Harvard University Press).

Wolfson, Harry A. (1977), "Maimonides on Negative Attributes," in Harry A. Wolfson (ed.), *Studies in the History of Philosophy and Religion*, vol. 2 (Cambridge, MA: Harvard University Press), 195–230.

Yarden, Dov (1973), *Shirei ha-Qodesh le-Rabbi Shelomo ibn Gabirol*, 2 vols. (Jerusalem: Dov Yarden Publ.).

Yerushalmi, Yosef (1982), *Zakhor: Jewish History and Jewish Memory* (Seattle: University of Washington Press).

Zonta, Mauro (2000), "The Relationship of European Jewish Philosophy to Islamic and Christian Philosophies in the Late Middle Ages," *Jewish Studies Quarterly*, 7 (2): 127–40.

Zonta, Mauro (2007), "Influence of Arabic and Islamic Philosophy on Judaic Thought," in *The Stanford Encyclopedia of Philosophy* (Winter 2016 Edition), Edward N. Zalta (ed.), URL = <https://plato.stanford.edu/archives/win2016/entries/arabic-islamic-judaic/> (last accessed February 20, 2018).

Index